Gap. Bk. Stores
Dallas, Texas

Jacob Q. Gurley
1972

The Acts of the Apostles

THE ACTS
OF THE APOSTLES

By

G CAMPBELL MORGAN, D. D.

Fleming H. Revell Company

To my four Sons,

PERCIVAL CAMPBELL MORGAN
KINGSLEY JOHN MORGAN
FRANK CROSSLEY MORGAN
HOWARD MOODY MORGAN

Who are also my brethren in The Ministry
of the Word,

I DEDICATE THIS BOOK;

Praying that to the end, their work may be
in the Apostolic Succession of freedom in the
bonds of the Gospel, so wonderfully re-
vealed in this inspired story of Beginnings

FOREWORD

I DON'T want to write a preface. Yet perhaps it is necessary. At any rate I have the example of the Writer of the Book we call The Acts of the Apostles to encourage me. He revealed his subject: The Word; gave the sources of his information; Eyewitnesses and Ministers; described his method; Accurate tracing of the course of all things, Writing them in order; and declared the purpose; that of giving Certainty to Theophilos—a catechumen.

My book is concerned with the one which is a sequel to the book thus introduced, and it is an attempt to help the plain man, and the teacher, in its study. I do not attempt to deal with what generally comes under the heading of " Introduction." From the start I assume the Lucan authorship, and the authenticity of the history. The work of Sir William Ramsay and Harnack has settled that problem for me. I recognize also that the book is by no means a full history of the period it covers, but that it is rather a selection of incidents revealing the lines and tendencies, the principle and passion, of that first generation of Christianity in the world. In this is at once its charm and its value. Each new page flames with some surprise, and one is held in suspense to the end—and then left to dream dreams of all that has not been recorded—and of all that followed after. Nevertheless every story reveals principles and laws, operating with undeviating regularity, and contributing the secrets of the amazing spread of that which had seemed threatened with extinction at Golgotha—but which rose into power on the Resurrection morning, and began a propagation of sweeping victory at Pentecost.

[5]

FOREWORD

My work is that of Exposition based on Exegesis. It is really intended as a handbook to the reader who desires a true apprehension of the spiritual force and method of these first years of Christianity at work in human history. My own work on the story has impressed me with the glorious regularity of the irregular in the work of the Church by the Holy Spirit. It is a powerful argument against the stereotyped in Christian organization and method; and consequently a plea for room for the operation of that Spirit, who like the wind—Bloweth where He listeth.

It may be that I have advanced things which enter into the realm of ancient controversies—or which raise new questions. If this is so, it has not been intentional —nor with desire. Whenever the reader is conscious of anything of this kind, let appeal be made from me to Luke, and so to the mind of the Lord. I have desired only to make plain what is written, and that in order to enable all who are also called to the great fellowship and service of witness, to understand its power as here revealed. In an hour unhappily rife with strife, and happily alive with opportunity, and characterized by earnest desire to be true to Christ, my hope is that in a return to a study of the beginnings there may be something of value.

G. C. M.

Athens, Ga.

The Acts of the Apostles

Acts 1 : 1–5

THE book which we call the Acts of the Apostles may be said to complete the Pentateuch of New Testament history. Four of these books present the Person of our Lord; while the fifth gives the first page of the history of the Church; that is, the story of the first activities of Christ, in power, in the history of the race.

The story of these first things in the life of the Church has a fascination from which there is no escape. However it may be read, it interests. But to see its true character, before beginning to deal with it in detail, we need to recognize the nature of the book as a whole, and its place in the New Testament revelation.

The book opens with a reference to one of the earlier books, in the words,—" The former treatise." The Lucan authorship of the Acts of the Apostles needs no argument. We take that as fully established, both by the long-continued opinion of the Church, and by the conclusions of the most recent scholarship. Consequently we may take it for granted that this reference, at the commencement of the book, is to the Gospel which bears Luke's name.

In order that the value of this may be gained, we will read the prologue to Luke's Gospel:

" Forasmuch as many have taken in hand to draw up a narrative concerning those matters which have been fulfilled among us, even as they delivered them unto us, who from the beginning were eye-witnesses and ministers of the Word, it seemed good to me also, having

[7]

THE ACTS OF THE APOSTLES

traced the course of all things accurately from the first, to write unto thee in order, most excellent Theophilus, that thou mightest know the certainty concerning the things wherein thou wast instructed."

We then take up the book of the Acts of the Apostles and read, " The former treatise I made, O Theophilus." The continuity is apparent on the surface. We have the same writer, Luke; the same reader, Theophilus; the same subject, Jesus.

Yet perhaps the whole of that does not appear immediately. One is inclined to say; the writer is the same; the reader is the same; but is the subject the same?

First let us recognize that the title of the book is an unfortunate one. To one taking up the book for the first time, that title, " The Acts of the Apostles," would seem to suggest that in the book we should find a chronicle of all the doings of all the apostles. We know that this is not so. As a matter of fact the Greek title of the manuscript is "Acts of Apostles." That is more indefinite, suggesting only that it records some acts of some apostles, which comes far nearer the truth. Some of the apostles are never named beyond their inclusion in the list given before the account of the Pentecostal effusion. Further, not all the acts of any one apostle are recorded. The book as history is merely a fragment, and in some senses a disappointing fragment; but the incompleteness of the story is part of the method of the Spirit. When we come to its last sentences, we inevitably put it down, feeling that there are a hundred questions we want to ask. The last picture we have in the book is that of Paul in his own hired house in Rome, receiving all that came to him; teaching them the things concerning Jesus; and preaching to them the Kingdom of God. Before he went to Rome he wrote to the Romans that he hoped to go on by them unto Spain, for his eyes were ever fixed on regions beyond. We should like to know if he ever did pass on to

Spain; yes, and more, whether the feet of the intrepid apostle ever actually stood on the soil of Britain. These things the book does not tell us. It is an unfinished fragment.

Nevertheless in the imperfect nature of the book there is a perfect system. It is the story of the first movements of the Christian fact in the world; revealing principles, indicating methods, showing failure; and all in order that there might be at least one page of inspired Church history, which, men reading, might know the true meaning and mission of the Church in the history of the world.

But this fact that the book is the first page of Church history is not a final or perfect definition of its value. To discover what its supreme value is, we must come back once more to the initial phrase, in which we shall find the key which unlocks the book:—" The former treatise I made, O Theophilus, concerning all that Jesus *began* both to do and to teach." Observe carefully that word *began.* If the writer had written: " All that Jesus *did* and *taught,*" the suggestion would have been entirely different. That would have suggested a conception of the mission of the Lord in the world, which was not that of the writer of this treatise; it would also have suggested a conception of the purpose of this treatise, which was not that of its writer.

The words, " the former treatise," as we have seen, take us back to the Gospel so full of exquisite beauty in its artistic setting forth of the matchless glory of the Person of Jesus Christ; the Gospel which pays little attention to chronology, but groups events so as to present the perfect Man, perfected through processes, and perfecting others by the mystery of His work. With that Gospel in our minds, we take up the new treatise by the same writer, and find that it is linked to this Gospel.

What then is the Gospel of Luke? It is the story of the birth and being; of the childhood and confirmation;

[9]

of the attesting and anointing of Jesus. It gives the account of the processes of teaching, and temptation, and transfiguration through which He passed. It records His descent to the valley; His going to the Cross; His resurrection; and His ascension. This surely is the story of all Jesus did and taught. No; according to Luke: it is the story of all He *began* to do and to teach.

The same writer now commences a second treatise, and the inference of this method of introduction is, that he is about to write the story of the continuity of the doings and teachings of the same Person.

When we gather in worship to-day, we do not do so in memory of a dead leader; but in the real presence of a living Lord. We do not merely think of One Who did and taught, in the dim distance of times of which we know very little. We are not following One of Whom we have read in the records. That is not the truth concerning Christianity. We gather about the living Christ, Whose touch has still its ancient power; the thrill of communion with Whom by the Spirit is the flame that inspires us to new endeavour; the inspiration of Whose love within our heart, draws us to sacrificial service for men. The former treatise was concerning all that Jesus *began* to do and to teach; and the new treatise is concerning the things He *continues* to do and to teach. It is not final. It is concerned with the things that Christ is still doing and teaching; and in the Apocalypse, the last Unveiling, we come to dreams and revelations, to signs and symbols and mysteries revealing the things He is yet to do.

We have seen the Christ in Matthew, Mark, Luke, and John; as King and Servant; as Man and God; the face of the lion, and of the ox, of the man, and of the eagle; to borrow the ancient mystic symbolism of the East.

We see Him in the Acts proceeding to kingly empire by the royal race of men and women, who look upon their girding as His bond-slaves as being a greater honour than any crowns that can be placed upon their brows. We see Him in the Acts proceeding through processes, toward the making of men and women conformed to the image of His manhood, and made partakers of the Divine nature.

But the story is not completed. The last picture is that of an Apostle in prison, while others have been slain, and others persecuted. The victory is not won; and we thank God therefore for the fact that there is another book; and in it the story of a great Throne, and in the midst of the Throne a Lamb as it had been slain, and round about the Throne four living creatures with the faces of the lion, and the ox, and the man, and the eagle; which story foretells His ultimate victory.

When we come to the study of this book, therefore, we must understand that it is not a merely mechanical story of the journeyings of Paul, or of the doings of Peter. It is intended to reveal to us the processes through which Christ proceeds in new power, consequent upon the things He began to do and teach, toward the ultimate and final victory, which we see symbolized in the mystic language of Revelation.

There is a soliloquy of Jesus contained in the Gospel of Luke, and in no other (Luke 12: 49, 50). In the midst of our Lord's teaching of the crowd He seems suddenly to have paused, and in these two verses we have what must be described as a soliloquy.

" I came to cast fire upon the earth; and what do I desire if it is already kindled? But I have a baptism to be baptized with; and how am I straitened till it be accomplished." Mark the strange word here, the arresting word, " How am I *straitened* till it be accomplished." This is Christ's own word; it is something He said of Himself, in the midst of His strenuous life and ministry; I am constrained; I am imprisoned; I cannot yet do My mightiest work. What was His mightiest work? " I came to cast fire upon the earth." So His herald had

[11]

THE ACTS OF THE APOSTLES

declared. John's voice had rung out over the mountains and plains, saying: "I indeed baptize you in water unto repentance, but He that cometh after me is mightier than I, Whose shoes I am not worthy to bear: He shall baptize you in the Holy Spirit and in fire." Christ uttered the same thought when He said, "I came to cast fire." That was the purpose of His coming, but He said: I cannot cast it yet; I am straitened; I have a baptism to be baptized with; and I cannot realize the fulfilment of My mission save by the way of that baptism—the baptism of My Passion and My Cross. That is the whole story of the Gospel.

We come now to the Acts of the Apostles, and we find the same Christ, but no longer straitened. The baptism is accomplished, the whelming is over. He has passed into the infinite morning, and the larger life, and He is about to scatter the fire. He could not cast that fire until His passion was accomplished. On that side of the Cross He was straitened; but on this side He is no longer straitened.

Let us try and express this in the terms of the experience of the disciples.

Jesus said to His disciples, "It is expedient"—and reverently let us change His word for the moment—"It is *better* for you that I go away;" better that My hands should not rest upon your head again, John; better that you should not be able to lay your head upon this bosom of Mine, and feel the beating of My heart; for if I go not away, the Comforter, the Paraclete, will not come.

The better thing, then, is the presence of the Christ, by the Spirit, in the heart and life of the disciples. Supposing, for the sake of argument, that He had stayed in the world, living an eternal life on the human level merely, and in physical presence. How we should have been straitened! If He were in Judæa He could not be in England. If He were in London, and had gathered with His people in one place, He could not be in another.

THE ACTS OF THE APOSTLES

[Acts 1 : 1-5]

But now, in the great cathedral; in the church; in the chapel; in the Salvation Army citadel; in the cottage; with the two or three gathered together, everywhere is the Christ.

He came again and was not straitened, was not limited. The geographical limitations were ended, and the spiritual presence began. Paul, that man who saw so clearly into the heart of the Christian fact, wrote—and we now begin to understand the meaning of his exulting writing— "Wherefore we henceforth know no man after the flesh; even though we have known Christ after the flesh, yet now we know Him so no more." In this book of the Acts then, we see Christ with all human sympathy, and Divine power, everywhere present by the Spirit, beginning to live and work, not in Judæa only, but also in Samaria, and to the uttermost part of the earth. He is seen, being completed in His Body, the Church; and His Church is seen, becoming the instrument through which the Spirit of His life moves forward in salvation, and to empire.

We might, therefore, call this book which we are studying, not the Acts of the Apostles, but "The book of the continued doing and teaching of the living Christ by the Holy Spirit through His Body which is the Church."

The study of the Acts of the Apostles will have a two-fold effect upon us;—it will fill us with hope; it will fill us with shame. We shall see in it, how the Body of the Christ was indeed the instrument of His victory. Yet we shall see Him straitened in the imperfection of the Body which is His Church.

Before this risen glorified One passed out of human sight, to return in spiritual power at Pentecost, He stood in the midst of a group of disciples, and He said to them: Ye shall be My witnesses;—My evidences, My credentials, My arguments;—in Jerusalem, in Judæa, in Samaria, and to the uttermost part of the earth.

Yet now, nearly two thousand years after, we have

[13]

not reached the uttermost part of the earth. We need cast no reflection on past centuries; but if we catch the vision of this Christ, and feel the tenderness of His yearning heart, and are brought by the study of this book under the compulsion of His great demand, before the generation passes, the whole earth will have heard the witness.

There is failure all through this book, but there is yet gracious victory here also. As we read it, we shall find a revelation of purpose and power; and we shall find the indication of the perils that confront us as the members of His Body.

Acts 1: 6–26

This paragraph serves as a link between the things of the "former treatise of Luke," and those of his new story. Here we have our last glimpse of the disciples before Pentecost; and our last vision of Jesus—to use Paul's descriptive phrase, "after the flesh"—present among His disciples in bodily form. Surely the artistic hand of Luke is evident in the placing of this paragraph here.

Here we see the Lord, and the apostles; and yet a larger group, consisting of "the women, and Mary the mother of Jesus, and His brethren"; gathered together. As we look at this group we recognize that the picture is intimately related to all that we have seen in the Gospel story. This is the same Jesus, Whose birth was there recorded, Whose ministry was chronicled, Whose crucifixion was described, Whose resurrection was declared, and Who was finally revealed as One ascended to God. He is spoken of as "Jesus," as the "Lord Jesus." It is the old word, the old title; the name by which He had been called in the days of His life at Nazareth, the title by which His disciples had addressed Him in the days of His public ministry. The Person is very familiar;

[14]

coming from the olden days. This is equally true of the men and women round about Him. We seem to know them all.

All this is to emphasize the statement, that this paragraph constitutes a page between the preface and the main story of the book. Moreover we shall never again meet Christ through all the story as we meet Him here. We shall never in this book see Him again in the same visible and material relationship to these men. He will be absent. No more the walk between Jerusalem and Jericho. No more the laying of the hand upon the children brought to Him. No more the actual looking of the human eye, into the eye of some decrepit soul needing help. No more the human tone of the voice in answer to which disease flees. We shall never meet Him thus again. Henceforth know we not Christ " after the flesh."

But we shall see these men again; and yet, all the way through the book, they will be changed, and different; not in the visible externals; but absolutely changed in the hidden facts of the life. A new light will shine through the same eyes. A new tone will come into the same voices. A new atmosphere will be generated by the same presences. Peter will be the same man, and yet absolutely changed. All the old impulsiveness will be present, and all the enthusiasm and the fire and the fervour that made him fit companion of the sons of thunder, Boanerges. But there will be something else. The change will not be that which denies the natural, but the change that baptizes it with the supernatural, until it becomes its fitting and magnificent instrument.

The picture of Jesus and His disciples given to us in this paragraph, serves to reveal, first, the results of the things He began to do and to teach; and, secondly, the need for that coming of the Paraclete, which was immediately to follow. As we look at the picture we are first amazed at the wonderful results of the things Jesus began to do and to teach, as manifested in these men; but

[15]

THE ACTS OF THE APOSTLES

we are supremely impressed with the truth of what the Lord Himself said to them in the paschal discourses just preceding His Cross, " It is expedient for you that I go away."

We will divide our present study into two parts; dealing first, with the last glimpse of the disciples before Pentecost; and secondly, with the last vision of Jesus after the flesh.

I.) In considering the last glimpse of the disciples before Pentecost, let us carefully notice the two things already indicated; first, the wonderful results of the things He began to do and to teach; and secondly, the necessity revealed for the coming of the Paraclete.

We begin then with the results of the things Jesus began to do and to teach.

We have first, the story of their gathering about Him, of His final commission, and of His departure. Then we have the story of their going back, after His departure, to Jerusalem; of their being of one accord in one place, steadfastly given to prayer. Finally we have the story of Peter's address concerning the vacancy in the apostolate created by the death of Judas, and of how they proceeded to fill the vacancy by the election of Matthias.

In the first of these things their wonderful confidence in Him is revealed; their confidence in each other is revealed in the second; and their confidence in the Scriptures of truth is revealed in the third. All these were the direct result of their having been the disciples of Jesus during the three years of His public ministry. They were the issue of the things He had said to them in many a patient discourse by the way, and in many a long and lonely walk; of the things He had wrought miraculously among the sons of men; of the mystery of the Cross and of the wonder of the Resurrection.

We are impressed supremely with their confidence in Him. They asked Him: " Lord, dost Thou at this time

restore the kingdom to Israel?" Let us forget for a
moment the mistake they made; forget the narrowness of
their outlook; and mark their quiet confidence in Him,
as revealed in their assumptions.

They assumed His Lordship, addressing Him as Lord.
They assumed His ability to bring the ancient economy
and purpose of God to a final consummation. They were
Hebrews. They had grown up in the great hope of the
Hebrew people. For long years, perchance through all
the early years of their lives, it had been a very faint
hope; but as they had walked with Him, and talked with
Him along the way—and especially in those final discourses after resurrection, when, as Luke has told us, He
opened to them the Scriptures, and gave them to understand the meaning of their own nationality and economy
—they had come to see the larger vision; the kingdom
restored to Israel; God's ancient purpose fulfilled. They
believed He was able to do this. But a little while ago
they had questioned His ability, when at Cæsarea Philippi
they said in effect: That be far from Thee, Lord; if Thou
dost take Thy way to the Cross, Thou wilt be defeated;
and disaster will overtake Thee rather than victory!
Two of them on the way to Emmaus had said, "We
hoped that it was He Who should redeem Israel." "We
hoped"—the past tense; for hope had been extinguished,
and their confidence had failed.

But now all this was changed, and here they stood
about Him, having perfect confidence in His ability to
fulfil their highest and truest hope—the restoration of
the kingdom to Israel; to establish the will of God, to
consummate the purposes of the Most High.

We are next impressed by their confidence in each
other. When they were come together into the one
place, Luke tells us, they were of one mind. Notice the
grouping of the apostles here. It would be unsafe to
build a doctrine upon this, or to overemphasize its value,
but it is interesting to see that the moment we get into

THE ACTS OF THE APOSTLES

the Acts of the Apostles, the grouping of these men is changed.

Peter and John. That is new. It always used to be Peter and James and John. Now, " Peter and John and James and Andrew "; that is the first group. There were only three in the olden days, and we speak of them as the men of special privilege, taken to special places of vision. Perhaps, after all, Peter, James, and John needed more especial care because of the weakness of their boanergic temperament. When Luke groups them in the Acts he brings Andrew in, the man who never seems to have occupied a place of privilege, of whom we know nothing at all, save that he called Peter. Now Luke puts him in with the first three, and thus associates the ordinary and outside man with those more notable.

Then again, Peter and John were never agreed in the Gospel story. They never understood each other. Peter was the practical man, John was the poet. Peter was always doing, John was always dreaming. When you get to the last chapter of John, John is still troubling Peter, so that he says to the Lord: " Lord, and what shall this man do? " In the new grouping, they have gone into partnership; the doer and the dreamer; the practical man and the poet. Then James and Andrew, the courteous and the curious. Next Philip and Thomas. Philip the reserved man, who believed everything, and was willing to be on the edge of the crowd and bring strangers to Jesus. Thomas, the sceptic, who demanded proof, or he would believe nothing. Then Bartholomew and Matthew; Nathanael, the guileless worshipper; and Matthew the publican, the astute tax-gatherer. Then three, " James the son of Alphæus, and Simon the Zealot, and Judas the son of James." No one knows anything about the first two, and Judas is only known as one who asked a question in the upper room (John 14 : 22).

Is not all this at least suggestive? Does it not seem to say to us that the Cross and the Resurrection brought

[18]

men into an affinity that cancelled all merely temperamental discords?

"And certain women, and Mary the mother of Jesus." That is the last glimpse of the highly favoured Virgin Mother. "And His brethren." They were never with Him in the days of His flesh, but they are gathered now in the one accord. Confidence in each other is the basis of a new fellowship.

And once again, observe their confidence in the Scriptures. Peter now commenced to interpret the present by the Scriptures of the past. He made quotation from two of the great Psalms (79 and 109) and distinctly, and without any hesitation, said that David wrote these things by the Holy Spirit concerning Judas. If we read Psalm 79 or 109, without the illumination of this interpretation, we should never dream that there was a reference in them to Judas, or that there was a reference in them to the Messiah. The great Messianic psalms are indeed Messianic psalms; but the writers did not understand the full richness of their Messianic values. David was referring to one of his own enemies; but Peter deliberately and quietly quotes the old and familiar passage, and says that finally it had reference to Judas and to Jesus. One of the last things that Luke tells us in his Gospel story is of how Jesus walked and talked with the disciples, and opened to them all the Scriptures, beginning from Moses; of how He spoke to this selfsame group just before leaving them, and taught them that it behoved Him to suffer, that all things written in the Scriptures should be fulfilled; naming the three great divisions, Moses, and the prophets, and the psalms. Peter was a Hebrew brought up on the very Scriptures which he was quoting, familiar with their letter, undoubtedly; but now he read them with a new understanding. He had seen a new light in them.

Thus we see gathered about Jesus a group of men with perfect confidence in their Lord; with joyful confidence

[19]

THE ACTS OF THE APOSTLES

in each other; with an absolute confidence in the value of the Scriptures of the Old Testament. These things all resulted from the things He began to do and to teach.

But now let us briefly notice the incompleteness manifested, which necessitated the coming of the Paraclete.

The first fact observable is that of their ignorance of Christ's purpose. "Dost Thou at this time restore the kingdom to Israel?" Christ rebuked, not their conception that the kingdom is to be restored to Israel —for that He never rebuked—but their desire to know when it would take place. "It is not for you to know times or seasons, which the Father hath set within His own authority." A popular interpretation of this is that Christ said to them: "There is to be no restoration of the kingdom to Israel." Christ did not say so. What He did say was: It is not for you to know the times or seasons. You have other work to do. "Ye shall receive power when the Holy Spirit is come upon you: and ye shall be My witnesses."

These men did not understand that. They loved Him, they were loyal to Him, they loved each other, they loved their own Scriptures, they had come to a new appreciation of them; but they were not ready for their work, because they had not seen what it would be. They had no conception of this new spiritual mission to which they were called. They did not understand the method by which God was about to work toward the ultimate consummation. They had heard Him, had seen Him, had come to love Him, and believe in Him; but they were absolutely ignorant of the next step in the programme of God; and they never did understand it until Pentecost, and the consequent interpretation by the Spirit of all the things that Jesus had said.

In the next place notice their consequent inability to execute His commission. He had said to them that they were to be witnesses. But here they were in the upper room; of one accord; steadfast in prayer; happy in their

mutual comradeships; constant in their loyalty; but quite
unable to witness. They could do nothing to bear testimony to Him until after Pentecost.

And again—this is a debated point in interpretation—
but my own conviction is that we have a revelation of
their inefficiency for organization; that the election of
Matthias was wrong. Their idea of what was necessary
as a witness to the resurrection was wrong. They said
that a witness must have been with them from the baptism of John. They thought a witness must be one who
had seen Jesus prior to His ascension. As a matter of
fact the most powerful incentive to witness was the seeing of Christ after resurrection, as when He arrested
Saul of Tarsus on his way to Damascus. So their principle of selection was wrong. Their method of selection
was also wrong. The method of casting lots was no
longer necessary. Thus we have the wrong appointment
of Matthias. He was a good man, but the wrong man
for this position, and he passed out of sight; and when
presently we come to the final glory of the city of God,
we see twelve foundation stones, and twelve apostles'
names, and I am not prepared to omit Paul from the
twelve, believing that he was God's man for the filling
of the gap.

These men were perfectly sincere, proceeding on the
lines of revealed truth, but they were ignorant of God's
next method; unable to bear their witness; unable to
organize themselves for the doing of the work; and
consequently needing the coming of the Paraclete.

II. In conclusion, let us look at this last vision of
Jesus " after the flesh." His last teaching was a correction; a promise; and a commission. He corrected them.
He did not deny their hope that the kingdom should be
restored to Israel. He only rebuked their curiosity, and
in that last word He taught His disciples and His Church
that they have nothing to do with the times and the
seasons of Israel; nothing to do with dates and days

[21]

THE ACTS OF THE APOSTLES

and calendars and predictions. What, then, are they to
do? First they are to recognize that for the doing of
that to which He calls them, they need power: " Ye shall
receive power after that the Holy Spirit is come upon
you." Then follows the commission. He gathered the
whole earth into His declaration of purpose. Beginning
in Jerusalem, passing out through Judæa and Samaria,
and at last reaching the uttermost part of the earth, they
were to be witnesses.

The last doing of Jesus after the flesh was that of
vanishing. The last act was that of disappearing. As
they looked upon Him, He was received up, and so He
vanished out of their sight. He did not go away; He
went out of sight as to bodily presence. We are perfectly
correct in using the word *up*—He was received up—
that is, on to the higher level of life; the life that is
higher than the merely material, and manifest, and local-
ized, and limited. The man Jesus vanished from sight,
but the Christ did not depart. He had said, " Lo, I am
with you always, even unto the end of the age."

The body in which He began to do and to teach passed
out of their sight. It did not cease to be, but for their
sakes it vanished to make way for the body in which
He would continue to do and to teach, which is His
Church, " the fulness of Him that filleth all in all." The
days of limited service were over, the days of unlimited
service were about to begin. The body of earthly service
passed out of sight, and the new body was there, not
having come to birth and might, but waiting for the
Pentecostal effusion.

The Man of Nazareth is still a man in God's universe.
The terms up or down, far or near, we shall have to
cancel when presently we drop this robe of flesh, and
pass into the light and into the glory; but the Man of
Nazareth will forever be the central point of manifestation, as He was in the world. The Christ of God, the
Son of God, the Saviour, Who wrought out into visibility,

through His body, the infinite facts of the Divine Being
and of human redemption, was still near to His disciples,
but they must be trained to faith, and not to sight.
Therefore He vanished. The last vision is that of the
vanishing, but not that of departing, not of going away.

One other word. We see these men looking, gazing
toward heaven. The cloud had enwrapped Him, and He
had gone, and yet they were gazing. Then there stood
by them two men. We nearly always say angels, but the
Bible says " Men." Perhaps they were Moses and Elijah,
the men who appeared on the mount of transfiguration.
Two men stood by them. They had lost one Man, the
One was gone, but two were there. These two said, " Ye
men of Galilee, why stand ye looking into heaven? This
Jesus shall so come in like manner." The form that you
have loved to look upon will yet be seen of your eyes.
For to-day, He is out of sight; but He is not away from
you.

He had passed out of sight, but He knew how their
hearts would break; He knew how difficult it would be
to realize Him when He was gone; and so He sent them
a message out of the unseen. Two other men bore that
message. What a startling thing it was! One Man had
gone, but there were two. So they knew that the One
was not lost. In a moment the two were also gone!
What had the disciples learned? That they knew nothing
about that which was around them, save that at any
moment the One might appear again.

We do not understand it, but the fragrance of it is all
about us, and whereas we worship the mystic, and the
eternal, and the unseen Christ, we still work in comradeship with the Man of Nazareth.

" Warm, sweet, tender, even yet
A present help is He;
And faith has still its Olivet,
And love its Galilee."

[23]

[Acts 2: 1–4]

Acts 2: 1–4

This paragraph contains the story of the formation of the Christian Church. It is so familiar that probably all could recite it. Therefore we need do no more than glance at its details by way of introduction, and then pass to the consideration of some of the spiritual significances of this wonderful event.

The time was the day of Pentecost, fifty days after Passover. The persons assembled, described as " they," were those named in the previous chapter—the eleven apostles, also Matthias, certain women, the virgin mother, and the brothers of Jesus. The actual place of their assembly is not named. Undoubtedly it was in the Temple. (Compare Luke 24: 52, 53; Acts 1: 14; Acts 2: 1; Acts 2: 46.)[1] Upon this company of units, united by a common love for, and loyalty to, the departed Jesus, there came the mystic mystery of the baptism of the Spirit. Two symbols were given—one appealing to hearing, and the other to seeing. The symbol of sound— " a rushing mighty wind "; the symbol of sight— " tongues . . . of fire," a plurality and a unity, the tongues were many; but the fire was One.

These were but symbols, of no value save as signs for the moment. It is necessary to observe that fact, because there is always a hunger in the carnal heart for signs. These signs were material; to-day we do not need them; they were needed at the commencement.

That which is of supreme importance is the experience described in the words: " They were all filled with the Holy Spirit." The Spirit was unseen and unheard. The wind was but Christ's chosen symbol of that Spirit, and was not the Spirit; they did not hear the coming of the Spirit; they heard the sound as of the " rushing mighty wind "; and thus, the symbol which their Lord had used when He said to Nicodemus, " The wind bloweth where

[1] See Philip Mauro's conclusive booklet, " Where did the Holy Spirit descend at Pentecost? "

it will, and thou hearest the voice thereof, but knowest not whence it cometh, and whither it goeth: so is every one that is born of the Spirit," would remind them of His teaching, and emphasize the presence of the Spirit. The Spirit is not fire, and did not come in the fire they saw. That was the symbol granted; but never granted since, because unnecessary. The abiding fact was that of the Spirit filling these waiting souls.

Then a new day dawned in human history, a new departure was initiated in the economy of God. Taking the Bible as the history of God's dealings with men, there had never been anything like this before, though everything had looked toward it, waited for it, and hoped for it.

When Peter preached his first great sermon in the power of the Pentecostal effusion, he interpreted its meaning by citing the ancient prophecy of Joel. Through all the Old Testament Scripture; in the types, and shadows, and whisperings; in the gleams of light, the songs of hope, and the visions of coming things; this is the event toward which men were looking. When Peter began to interpret the things in the midst of which he and the disciples found themselves, he said, " This is that which hath been spoken through the prophet." Up to this time there had been expectation, without realization.

Not that the Spirit had been wholly absent from human affairs. The restoration of creation came by the ministry of the Spirit, brooding upon chaos, and producing cosmos. The Spirit is referred to over and over again in the study of the Old Testament, as clothing men with Himself; clothing Himself with men; coming in power upon individuals for the doing of mighty deeds; coming with sweet gentleness in the inspiration of art, in order that men might work cunningly in gold and silver and other things for the temple of God.

But such a day as this had never dawned. This was the beginning of a new departure in the economy of God;

THE ACTS OF THE APOSTLES

not a new departure rendered necessary by the failure
of the past, but a new departure rendered necessary by
the accomplishments of the past. Everything in the
economy of God had been preparatory to this. This
never could have been until this hour. But the hour had
come; everything was accomplished; all the preparatory
work was over, and there broke upon human history a
new dawning; there began a new economy in the enterprises of God.

In order to an understanding of all that is to follow
in the book of the Acts of the Apostles, and in order to
an understanding of all our own life and service, it is
necessary for us to consider two matters; first, the new
facts following Pentecost; and, secondly, the limitations
of the Pentecostal age.

We will tabulate the new facts following Pentecost,
and consider them under three headings; the new facts
as to the Christ; the new facts as to the Church; the
new facts as to the world.

In order to recognize the new facts as to the Christ,
we must remind ourselves of the things prior to Pentecost concerning Him. These we may very briefly summarize as the facts of the Incarnation, and the Decease.
We use that word " decease " as it is used in the Gospel
stories. One would much prefer to use our form of the
Greek word, *the Exodus.*

The Incarnation ;—the fact of His coming, the mystery
of His birth, His being, and His presence in human
history;—was an accomplished fact before Pentecost.
So also was the Exodus, which included the Cross, the
Resurrection, and the Ascension.

In the Gospel of John, our Lord Himself is reported
as expressing the whole fact of His mission in these
words, " I came out from the Father, and am come into
the world: again, I leave the world, and go unto the
Father." " I came out from the Father and am come
into the world "; that is Incarnation. " Again I leave

the world and go unto the Father "; that is a simple statement, thrilling with meaning, including in itself the mystery of His Cross, the victory of His Resurrection, and
the glory of His Ascension; or briefly the Exodus. These
things were all accomplished before Pentecost. The
value of Incarnation is that of revelation; the value of
the Exodus is that of redemption. He came to reveal;
He came to redeem. He revealed by the Incarnation.
He redeemed by the Exodus.

The Incarnation was revelation. Let us take another
word instead of revelation—exhibition. We associate
the word with spectacular displays. Then let us take yet
another word. It is a word which is coming into use for
the same purpose, borrowed from the French—exposition.

What then is an exhibition? It is the gathering together in one place, the focussing, of certain things from
the far distances, in order that men may see and understand. What is an exposition? It is expository work, a
method of revealing, a method of showing, a method by
which men are brought face to face with things they
would not otherwise understand. Perhaps the best illustration is found by going back to the first Exhibition
of 1851, where the purpose, primarily, was not commercial as it now is; but that of the revelation of truths
concerning other peoples, in order to produce unity of
heart in the world.

Before Pentecost there was Exposition. Jesus was
Himself the great Expositor; the Exhibition of God to
men; also of heaven, of truth, and of all spiritual verities.
That is not to say that the world had seen, or that the
disciples had seen. One would be prepared to say they
had neither seen nor understood. But there was the
Exhibition, the Exposition, the Revelation in Christ, of
all essential truth.

We have seen exhibitions, and have never seen them.
We have passed by the grounds, and have said to our

[Acts 2: 1-4]

friends: I saw the exhibition. But we never entered it. Or we have entered the gates, and have spent a few brief hours there; but we never saw it; we saw parts of it.

God gave an Exposition of Himself in human history by the way of the Incarnation, and men did not see it. This was before Pentecost.

So also with the Exodus—the going out, the return to the Father by the Cross, by the Resurrection, by the Ascension. These things were all accomplished before Pentecost. Thus before Pentecost the Christ had revealed and redeemed.

The new things which came with Pentecost were those of the administration of redemption in the actual lives of men; and the multiplication of the revelation through the lives in which redemption was administered.

On the day of Pentecost, Christ by the coming of His Holy Spirit, was able to make over to trusting souls the actual value of His Cross, so that when the Spirit filled them, they were crucified with Him, because He Himself in them administered the value of His Cross. In that moment He was able to make over to them the virtue of His Resurrection, so that they began to live a life they could not live until the Spirit thus came to administer the power of His Resurrection. In that moment He won in them the victory of His Ascension, so that they began to love—to use Paul's radiant phrase—"the things above."

Thus Christ found by the coming of the Spirit the new and enlarged opportunity for which He had prepared by His own advent. This takes us back again to the opening phrase of the book, "The former treatise I made . . . concerning all that Jesus began both to do and to teach." Now, by the Spirit, Christ, the Revealer and Redeemer, came to administer redemption in the actual experience of human souls, and so to multiply the revelation by the souls transformed into His own likeness.

At this point, questions naturally arise. Were not

these men born again before Pentecost? Was not Abraham born again? Were not the men of the old economy born again? The answer to that enquiry is, Abraham, and Isaac, and Jacob, and the Prophets, and the men of the old economy, were brought into true relationship with God upon the basis of their faith in Him. Their faith in Him received a reward, because of His faith in Himself, and in the coming of the Christ. These men in their essential spiritual life were renewed, were born again, if you will. There is no objection to the word itself. That they received divine life there can be no doubt.

But here upon the day of Pentecost, that which happened was not merely the renewal of the life of these men; it was the imparting to them of a new germ of life, a new principle of life, something they had never had before, that Abraham never had; there was given to them the life of the Christ, the Incarnate One; so that there came to these men that which made them one with Him and with each other, and constituted their membership in the Church of the first-born.

Thus our first consideration merges into the second, and we may now speak of the new facts as to the Church. It is well that we remind ourselves that the word Church is in some senses an unfortunate one. The word Church is not true translation. It is a useful word, and one would not suggest that it be altered. But let us remember what it really means. This word Church which has passed into common speech, is a word, the root meaning of which is simply *the Lord's*. The Greek word *Ecclesia* means an assembly. The word Church is a beautiful word applied to the Assembly, but it is not translation, it has not caught the meaning of the word of which it is supposed to be a translation. The word so translated is used in three relationships in the New Testament. We read of " The assembly in the wilderness," which is translated, " The Church in the wilderness." We read

[Acts 2: 1-4]

of " The assembly of God," which is translated, " The Church of God," and we read once of " The Assembly " in a heathen town, which is so translated.

The word assembly in every instance refers to a select and gathered-out company, having certain qualifications, and being committed to certain work. The men who constituted the town assembly in a Greek city were all free men. To them was committed the welfare of others. They constituted a governing body, consisting of free men. That was the Greek use of the word.

The Hebrew use of the word had reference to the Hebrew nation as the peculiar people of God. Christ thus took hold of a word in common use when He said " My Ecclesia." The Hebrew understood it; it meant one thing to him. The Greek understood it; it meant another thing to him. Gather the principles out of the Hebrew and Greek uses of the word, and combine them, and we find exactly what Christ meant when He said—My Assembly. He referred to His called-out ones, who, fulfilling certain qualifications, are committed to certain work. In that sense the Christian Assembly did not exist prior to Pentecost. Pentecost created the Assembly.

Now let us glance at the previous conditions as we see them in the story of the Passover Feast (Luke 22: 1-34), because there we see the same men as we now see at the Pentecostal Feast.

They were disciples; that is they were loyal to Him as Master and Teacher. They were comrades; that is they were willing to stand by Him as far as they were able, as He Himself said, through all the process of His trial. They were servants; that is they were willing to run on His errands and deliver His message. All these things were they, before Pentecost.

Then what was new as the result of the coming of the Spirit? Comprehensively, by that whelming of the Spirit, these men, disciples, friends, servants—outside the actuality of His life though loving and loyal—were made

[30]

actually, though mystically, one with Him in the very fact of His own life. They were made sharers of the life of the Christ. They had never been that before. They were sentimentally one with Him, and that word is not used in an objectionable sense. They were emotionally one with Him, agreeing with His ideals, consecrating themselves to Him, yet separate from Him, as all men had been separate from all teachers, and are still, except in this one case. Buddha, rare and wonderful soul, was never able to communicate his actual life to his disciples. Confucius, great and remarkable ethical teacher, was never able to communicate dynamic to the men who learned his ethic. Neither has any other teacher been able to do this in the history of the world. Prior to Pentecost the disciples were disciples, standing away, yet very near—I would not undervalue the nearness of those days—but they were not one with Him.

When the Spirit came, His actual life passed into their lives, and from that moment they were able to say what Paul himself expressed so graphically in the familiar language of the Galatian letter, "I have been crucified with Christ; and it is no longer I that live, but Christ liveth in me: and that life which I now live in the flesh I live in faith, the faith which is in the Son of God, Who loved me, and gave Himself up for me."

What did it do for them? Did it change the old relationships? By no means; it fulfilled them. They were still disciples, but they had a new vision. Not a new vision coming upon them from the outside, but a new vision coming from the actual shining in them of His life, so that they began to see as He sees. That is the mystery, the marvel, and the majesty, of Christianity. It is when I see something, not which Christ interprets to me as from without;—many men see from without, and are reverent;—but when through these poor dim eyes of mine the light of His own vision illuminates all that is without. then I know what Pentecost means. In half

[Acts 2: 1–4]

an hour after Pentecost they knew more about Jesus Christ than they had ever known before. Peter, the impetuous man to the end—for the Spirit never alters a man's natural temperament—became the Apostle who proclaimed the Cross in Jerusalem, and gloried in it, because Christ looked through his eyes, and spoke with his tongue. That is the great mystery.

Did these men cease to be the friends of Jesus? Surely not. They were still His comrades, not comrades standing by His side merely, but comrades by identity of life. He was in them. He suffered, and their suffering was His suffering. He rejoiced, and their rejoicing was His joy. He fought, and their fighting was His fighting. That was the great change.

Were they no longer His servants? Surely His servants, but no longer sent from Him, but the very instruments of His own going. Their hands became His hands to touch men tenderly; their feet, His feet to run on swift errands of God's love; their eyes His eyes, to flame with His tenderness; themselves part of Himself.

This is mysticism. Christianity is mysticism. But if it be mysticism, it is fact. It is not scientific, it is not honest, to deny the mysticism, until you can otherwise account for the fact. Take the men, the fact of themselves, the changed outlook, the changed behaviour, the moral regeneration, the moral passion, the uplifting fervour, and account for it in any other way.

As to the world. In the past there had been, as John beautifully puts it, the unapprehended Light—the Light never extinguished, always shining somewhere, and in measure in every man. In the Incarnation, the Light had come into the world. But now after Pentecost there was a new conviction for the world. " He, when He is come, will convict the world in respect of sin, and of righteousness and of judgment." The Spirit of truth came to create the Assembly; and the world's conviction of sin, of righteousness, and of judgment, is to be ac-

[32]

complished by the Spirit, through the Church. Thus there came to the world this new conviction. The quality of the conviction was new; the weight of the conviction was new; the result of the conviction was new.

There came also a new constraint by the Church; the constraint of His love shed abroad in the heart of the Assembly, and ultimately in the hearts of men outside, luring them; the constraint of the Church's light shining in the dark places, revealing sin, and indicating the way to holiness; the constraint of the Church's life poured out in sacrifice. The Church has won Christ's victories by sacrifice, and in no other way. It is never until she is wounded that she wins. It is by weariness and death and suffering that she has coöperation with Christ. Wherever, in the distant places of the Mission field, in slum or suburb, the body of the Christ suffers, the life of the Christ is communicated to the world. By this way of Pentecost there came the dawning of a new day for the world; a day of new conviction and constraint.

What then are the limits of the Pentecostal age? First of all as to Christ Himself. His resources are limitless. While He was still in the world He said, " How am I straitened." He can say so no longer. In Himself there is the ultimate and final and perfect revelation, and to borrow that exquisite phrase of the Old Testament, there is also " plenteous redemption." His resources are limitless for the doing of His work.

But Christ is limited in His Body which is the Church. If the Assembly in those early days had been absolutely perfect in its loyalty, He was still limited. He cannot win the ultimate victory but through the perfecting of His Body. He was limited, therefore, through all those ages in His Body, the Church, for which in some senses no blame is to be attached to her, nor to any; it is part of a Divine process.

In other senses, great blame is to be attached to her. He cannot reach China save through her. He cannot

THE ACTS OF THE APOSTLES

[Acts 2: 1-4]

accomplish the purpose of His Word in Africa save through His Body. It is an appalling truth, a mystery one cannot pretend to understand, but it is God's method. Not by angels can He preach the reconciling Word, but through His Body, the Church; and the whole process of God to final victory is halted, in some respects necessarily, and properly, and rightly; in many respects unnecessarily, improperly and wrongly through His Body, the Church.

That thought naturally merges into the next—the limitations of the Pentecostal age as to the Church. Here again, we must begin as we began before—the Church's resources are limitless. But the Church is limited, first, in the necessity for growth. The Church is not even until this age a perfect instrument, because she has not grown to the measure of the stature of her fulness in Christ. That is a proper limitation. In the hurried fretfulness of our brief life we would fain hurry these things; but in calmer moments, when we rise into the consciousness of the eternity of God, we know that it is vulgarity that hurries, and so does poor work. The processes of God are necessarily slow to human thinking; but they move with absolute certainty to the ultimate goal.

The Church is limited in the Pentecostal age when she grieves the Holy Spirit, when she quenches the Spirit. These are two significant words, " Grieve "—having to do with the matter of the Church's life; " Quench "—having to do with the matter of the Church's service. How often has the Church grieved the Spirit, quenched the Spirit, and so limited herself! This is the appalling thing, the thing that brings heartbreak!

As to the world, what shall we say concerning limitation? Again we begin where we have begun in each case —the world has limitless resources in Christ. There is nothing the world needs that is not found in Him. Everything needed, of social well-being, and political emancipation; everything that makes for the uplifting of the race, is in Christ. Limitless resources are in the world's Redeemer.

But the world is limited in the Church's failure. That is not the world's fault. If there be blood-guiltiness, it is upon the Church.

But finally the world is limited in its own resistance. That is the third word in the Bible marking the forms in which the work of the Spirit may be hindered. " Resist," is a word not spoken to the Church, but to those outside. Men can resist.

There has been no lessening of the resources. It is such a commonplace thing to say, and we all agree; but does the Church really believe it? Have we not some kind of subconscious heresy in our minds that Pentecost is passed, and that Pentecostal power has weakened in the process of the centuries? It is not so. The resources are as limitless now as they were in the dawning of that great day. The question for our hearts should be: Is Christ limited in us? If only by the necessity of our feebleness and our growth, we need have no anxiety, because God's processes always seem slow. But if He is limited because we grieve or quench the Spirit, then it is necessary that judgment should begin at the House of God. We must repent, renounce, return.

We need waste no time in talking about a revival in the world until there is a revival in the Church. It is when, within this mystic Assembly of the Christ, He is unlimited, allowed full sway by the indwelling Spirit, that the light will flame upon the darkness without, and the great victory will come.

Is the world limited in us? If so, it is because the Christ is limited in us. " They were all filled with the Holy Spirit." Are we? And if not, why not? Let us leave the questions, as such, for our individual heart-searching.

Acts 2: 5–13

With this paragraph begins the story of the Church witnessing. In obedience to her Lord's command she began in Jerusalem. The story of this witness in Jerusalem is that of the first things; and this lends charm and value to the study. We have in sequence: the first impression produced in Jerusalem; the first message delivered in the power of the Pentecostal effusion; the first opposition raised to the infant Church; the first attempt to realize the communism of the Christian Church; the first fearful and fiery discipline by which the Church was made pure; the first outbreak of persecution against the Church; the first Church organization in the setting apart of the deacons; and the first Christian martyr.

As we study these, we shall discover the lines of Church life, and Church service, according to the will of the Spirit of God, Who came to interpret the things of Christ, and realize them, in the Church, and through the Church in the world.

Our present study is concerned with the first impressions produced by the witnessing Church. Let us follow two lines of consideration. First, the impressive facts; and secondly, the impressions made. The supreme matter in this study is not that of the facts, but that of the impressions. We have often been in danger, in reading this story of the Pentecostal effusion, of laying an undue emphasis upon the manifestations, to the forgetfulness of the impressions made.

I. Let us first notice the impressive facts.

Of these the first-named is that of " a sound as of the rushing of a mighty wind." Concerning this, Luke says: " Now there were dwelling at Jerusalem Jews, devout men, from every nation under heaven. And when this sound was heard, the multitude came together."

There is no question whatever that this is a far more helpful translation than that which reads, " when this was noised abroad." To read it thus would seem to

suggest that the multitude was gathered together when
they heard about these people speaking with tongues; but
that certainly is not the meaning of this statement. The
Greek word here translated _sound_ is never used for a
rumour or a report. It is always used of some sound
that arrests attention. The reference here undoubtedly
is to the rushing mighty wind, which was heard throughout the whole city of Jerusalem. It was a startling sound,
as of a hurricane.

Luke describes it as coming " from heaven." It was
a descending hurricane, settling upon, and centring at,
one place, the Temple where these men were assembled.
Jerusalem heard it. It was this sound of a mighty rushing wind, marvellous, mysterious, that brought the multitude together. That was the first impressive fact; something outside the ordinary, something supernatural.

But a still more impressive fact of that day to Jerusalem was that of the crowd of disciples. Jerusalem
saw and heard a company of about one hundred and
twenty men and women all " speaking "—probably all
singing, or chanting—" the mighty works of God." This
was the common subject of the ancient psalmody of the
Hebrew people. This was the subject of Peter and this
gathered company of men and women. But that did not
arrest attention. That would not have startled any Jewish multitude. It was not the singing, it was not the
things of which they sang, but it was that they, the
gathered Parthians, and Medes, and Elamites, and the
dwellers in Mesopotamia, heard with absolute distinctness and accuracy all they were singing, in their own
tongue. In many tongues and dialects, with perfect distinctness, this chanting, this ecstatic utterance of the
newly baptized company of disciples, broke upon the
astonished and listening ear of that assembled multitude.
" They were all filled with the Holy Spirit, and began
to speak with other tongues, as the Spirit gave them
utterance."

THE ACTS OF THE APOSTLES

[Acts 2 : 5–13]

All the references in Acts, Corinthians, and Ephesians, show that the exercise of tongues consisted of ecstatic utterance. These people were not preaching, they were praising; they were not indulging in set discourse, they were pouring out the rapture that filled their souls. In the filling of the Spirit there had come to them a new vision of their Lord; and a new consciousness of His life throbbing through their lives. They realized that all the hopes and aspirations of the past were being fulfilled. They knew that the river of God had come by the way of the altar, and that they were in the full flood tide of its healing and life-giving waters. They were praising God for His mighty works.

Did they know they were speaking in other tongues? One cannot be at all sure that they did. Were they familiar with the tongues in which they were speaking? Probably not. They praised with a new inspiration, they poured out their songs, and lo, Parthians, Medes, and Elamites, sojourners from Rome, people from Mesopotamia, men of all dialects, listened; and they heard the songs in their own language, with perfect accuracy and distinctness. The Resurrection was the first note, in their singing, as it came to be the first note in apostolic preaching. One could almost wish that one could have listened to that first chanting of the Church, in which the singers set forth the mighty works of God.

II. We may now consider the impressions made upon Jerusalem. " They were all amazed, and were perplexed, saying one to another, What meaneth this? But others mocking said, They are filled with new wine." In that one statement we have a record of the first impression made by the Church in Jerusalem. It was a threefold impression. First, amazement; secondly, perplexity; thirdly, criticism.

What was this amazement? It was mental arrest; not yet illumination. They did not know the meaning of what they heard and saw; but they wondered. Out of

[38]

wonder worship is born. Where wonder ceases worship
ceases. Wonder is not worship, but it is the first movement toward worship. For the moment, Jerusalem was
compelled to turn from other interests, to attend to this
matter. It was only a beginning, but it was a beginning.
For a brief hour or two at least, men left the schools, and
the disputations, and the quarrellings, forgot their differences, and united in common amazement in the presence of something in their midst for which they could
not account. The amazement was mental arrest, a compulsion laid upon the men of a city, to turn from all other
matters, in wonder.

As they observed, and as they listened, they were not
only amazed, they were perplexed. If amazement is
mental arrest, perplexity is mental defeat; not yet illumination. The amazement meant that they did not
know. The perplexity meant that they knew they did
not know. There is no moment more hopeful to an intellectual soul than that in which it comes to the point
of known ignorance. That is the opportunity for discovery.

Men amazed, arrested, compelled to drop other matters to look and listen; men finding that when they look
they cannot see everything, that when they hear they
have missed some note, and are in the presence of a
mystery they cannot fathom; are driven to enquire. That
is an advance upon amazement.

Perplexity was followed by criticism. Criticism is
mental activity. These men, amazed, perplexed, were
compelled to come to some conclusion. They first stated
the problem to be discussed: " What meaneth this? "
Some of them arrived at a conclusion: " They are filled
with new wine," which meant that they were drunk.
They were much nearer the mark than appears at first
sight. They had first been arrested, compelled to turn
from other things to consider. They then were perplexed,
defeated; they could not understand. Then the mind

had become active. What is this? Look and listen.
Look at the glory in the eyes. Listen to the abandonment
in the voice. Mark the pulsating passion of these people. To some of them there could be but one explanation. They were drunk!

They were nearer the truth than they knew, but they
were exactly as far from it as hell is from heaven. What
they said was a fair conclusion. Carefully observe
Peter's answer: " These are not drunken, as ye suppose "
—that is, in the way you think. Compare this with
Paul's injunction in Ephesians 5 : 18. The one is a false
and destructive method of attempting to realize life in
its fulness. The other is the true and effective method.

What is the relation of this story to the era in the midst
of which we are living?

First of all we must remember that these signs of the
day of Pentecost were initial, and produced no final result. The gift of tongues exercised in the midst of the
multitudes, to the astonishment of the multitude, and
probably to the astonishment of the disciples also, brought
nothing to a conclusion. It did not produce conviction,
either of sin, or concerning Christ. It needed prophecy
to complete it. It created the opportunity for prophecy.
Directly it had produced the impressions referred to,
of amazement, and perplexity, and criticism, Peter
prophesied. Mark the relationship between tongues and
prophecy, and see the perfect harmony of this revelation
with what Paul taught, when he said, " I had rather speak
five words with my understanding, that I might instruct
others also, than ten thousand words in a tongue."
Prophecy is the final method for bringing conviction, and
accomplishing the will of God.

All this was initial; and it was incomplete. It was
necessary as a sign, to arrest the attention of Jerusalem.
With the development of the spiritual fact, the necessity
for signs passed away. In this connection it is well to
remember Christ's attitude toward signs. Men have al-

ways sought them. Evil and adulterous generations are forever saying, Show us a sign; and the Christ is forevermore saying, There shall be no sign given unto you. The sign is the occasional thing, the thing better done without. Christ said to His own disciples, " Believe Me." That was His great appeal. " Or else," He continued— if you cannot do that, if that is too large a thing, and too high a thing, and too noble a thing at first—" believe Me for the very works' sake." The signs were evidences, made necessary in order to arrest attention, but they never produced conviction. That comes through prophesying in the power of the Spirit. At the beginning there must be the mighty sound out of heaven; this arresting thunder of a great wind; these strange and wonderful and yet distinct ecstatic utterances in all tongues; but these can accomplish nothing beyond arousing attention. They were Divine, directly and positively; but they were transient, never repeated because never needed.

What then are the abiding values of this story? The Spirit-filled Church always presents to the world supernatural phenomena, producing amazement, perplexity, criticism. These phenomena vary according to the needs of the time. In the book of the Acts of the Apostles they changed immediately. We shall find as we go through the book, that wherever the messengers of Christ came—the Spirit-filled witnesses—something happened, something that startled men, something that produced exactly the same results as were produced at first by the Pentecostal tongues. Presently it was a lame man healed. Again it was the shaking of a prison, and the releasing of Apostles. Presently it was the privileges of the new fellowship—men desired to join the new fellowship who had not submitted to the one Lord. Again it was the death of a man. Stephen was bruised and battered, and made bloody with stones. Look at his face! There shone the light that never was on land or sea. It was supernatural dying. There was one fine, scholarly, clean, sin-

[41]

cere, young Pharisee saw that face, and never lost its effect. He was amazed, he was perplexed, he was critical; and then he was converted. Presently it was the apostolic work in Samaria, and Simon Magus wanting to buy a partnership with Peter and John. Again it was Paul's conversion, and its effect upon Festus, upon Felix, upon Agrippa.

Amazement, perplexity, criticism; these were the effects produced by the tongues. God has many methods of producing these effects; but the real value of the method which startles, is always that of the effect it produces, and of the opportunity it creates for prophesying.

If these impressions are not produced, it is because the Church is not Spirit-filled. Is the Church of God amazing the city, perplexing the city, making the city criticize? The trouble too often is that the world is not at all amazed, not at all perplexed, not at all critical; because there is nothing to amaze, to perplex, to criticize. The work of the Church is to be Spirit-filled, and amaze the city, and perplex the city, and make the city listen. Are we doing it? Thank God yes, sometimes!

With much truth it may be added that there is only one criticism that is worth anything; the criticism of the world that is of value is that criticism in which it says that the Church is drunk! Has any one ever charged you with being drunk with your Christianity? O God, how seldom men have thought us drunk. We lack the flashing eye, and the pulsating song, and the tremendous enthusiasm of an overwhelming conviction. That is what the city needs to produce the amazement, the perplexity, and the criticism which create the opportunity for prophesying.

Our responsibility is not that of endeavouring to reproduce past phenomena. One need not be at all anxious to hear men talking in other tongues, who have been too lazy to learn them. There is a whole philosophy in that passing remark. The Church had not had time to learn the languages then, and so spiritual equipment was provided to meet the need of the mixed multitudes. A minister in New York once said in my hearing that New York presented a grave problem because all nations and languages are found there. But surely that is a Pentecostal opportunity. We have not the gift of tongues, but we have time to learn the languages. God never makes up by miraculous intervention what man lacks through laziness.

The Church's responsibility is that her members be so Spirit-filled that the Spirit may be able to produce the new phenomena required to startle this age. The Church has been far more anxious about emperors, and states, and wealth, and theologies, and organizations, than about the Spirit. It is the Church Spirit-filled which makes the city amazed, perplexed, critical. That is the Church's opportunity for preaching. What is the use of Peter preaching when the world is not amazed? The psychic moment for preaching comes when the city is amazed, perplexed and critical, as the result of the living testimony of the Spirit-filled Church. Then upon the astonished ear of the amazed people the Word will fall as thunder and as benediction, and results will be produced. Our responsibility then is only that of seeing to it that we are filled with the Spirit.

Acts 2 : 14–47

In this paragraph we have the account of the first Pentecostal message, and of the results following its delivery. The passage is full of importance; both in its revelation of the true method and subject matter of preaching; and in the picture it presents of the things that follow such preaching. In our present study we take a general survey of the whole; considering the message as to its method and its matter; and glancing at the results, both immediate and continuous; postponing the actual things said in the power of the outpoured Spirit

[43]

[Acts 2: 14-47]

to this amazed, perplexed, and critical audience gathered together in Jerusalem.

I. Let us first of all notice the method of this discourse, in which so far as principles are concerned, we have a revelation of what preaching ought to be.

We will notice first, the matters which may be described as physical; secondly, the mental; finally and supremely, the spiritual.

The first of these need not detain us long. They are all contained in the statement: " Peter, standing up with the eleven, lifted up his voice, and spake forth unto them."

That is a perfect and final lesson in elocution for every man called to preach. " Standing up with the eleven." This in itself was a new method. It was not the method of the Rabbis. Jesus had significantly said to His disciples, before leaving them, that they were not to be called Rabbi. They were no longer to be teachers merely, they were to be heralds. Teachers sat; heralds stood.

It is quite unnecessary to make any comment upon the next phrase—" He lifted up his voice." If three thousand are to hear, it is no use speaking for thirty to hear. The voice must reach the listener who is furthest away.

The next phrase is equally important. " He spake forth." The Greek word means that he enunciated clearly; there was a correct articulation, so that every man in the crowd could understand. This particular word occurs on two other occasions. The first is in the second chapter when it is said that they spake with other tongues " as the Spirit gave them *utterance.*" The other case is when Paul, standing before Agrippa pleading his cause, replied to the interruption of Festus by saying, " I am not mad, most excellent Festus, but *speak forth* words of truth and soberness." In each case the idea is that of clear enunciation. Thus the first Christian preacher stood up as a herald; lifted up his voice so that the whole multitude might hear; and articulated with perfect distinctness.

Finally, and by no means of least importance is the declaration that he " spake forth *unto them.*"

Preaching too often to-day is preaching *before* people, rather than preaching *to* them; and there is all the difference in the world between the two methods.

It is not very long ago that in a ministerial conference I heard a minister say that years ago the work of the Christian preacher was that of a combat, in which he wrestled with souls, and compelled them to obedience; and he lamented that the days had passed. He was right in his regret, if he was right in his conclusion that such days had passed. That is the work of the Christian preacher; even though he have ability to instruct intellectually; even though he be able to move emotionally; if his preaching end with the intellect, or with the emotion, then his preaching is a disastrous failure.

We pass now to consider the mental method of this preaching. Notice in the first place that Peter recognized their right to enquire. This will be made perfectly clear by observing a simple word and its place in this narrative. I refer to the word *this.* " Be *this* known unto you " (verse 14). *"This* is that which hath been spoken through the prophet Joel " (verse 16). " He hath poured forth *this"* (verse 33).

The assembled crowd when they became critical said, " What meaneth *this?* " In their use of the word " *this,*" was included all they saw and heard; the things that amazed and perplexed them; the sound of the wind; the strange, and to them, grotesque vision of a company of people hilarious, ecstatic, praising, singing; and then that strange and compelling wonder, that as these people sang or praised, all those gathered about them, understood them in their own tongues, Parthians and Medes, and Elamites, and so on.

Now said the crowd, " What meaneth *this?* "

THE ACTS OF THE APOSTLES

[Acts 2: 14-47]

When Peter commenced his address he said, " Ye men of Judæa, and all ye that dwell at Jerusalem, be *this* known unto you"; by which he meant, I am about to explain *this;* I am about to answer your enquiry. He then contradicted their foolish attempt to answer their own question. Some of them had said: " These men are filled with new wine." Peter answered, " These are not drunken as ye suppose, seeing it is but the third hour of the day." The third hour of the day was the hour of sacrifice, and men neither ate nor drank until that hour. Having replied to this false suggestion, he proceeded to explain that which had perplexed them: " *This* is that which hath been spoken by the prophet Joel." In these words he related the things seen, to the ancient predictions.

He then traced the history of Jesus of Nazareth, ending with the declaration, " He hath poured forth *this*."

The whole message proceeded upon the assumption of the right of the multitude to ask an explanation. " What meaneth this?" was an honest and proper question. " These men are filled with new wine," was a blundering attempt to get at the truth. Peter was not angry with them. He was neither angry with them for their mistake, nor for their attempt to discover. He said, " Be *this* known unto you." Listen, I will explain; *this* is not so strange as you think; " *this* is that which hath been spoken through the prophet Joel," your own prophet; and moreover Jesus of Nazareth Whom you all know, " He hath shed forth *this*." The first note of the mental mood of the Christian preacher must be that of his recognition of the right of men to enquire, and a willingness on his part to answer their enquiry.

But again, the apostle made his appeal to the things they knew. This we have already seen, but it is of special importance, and so we return to it. He began his explanation of the things they did not know, by taking them back to the things with which they were familiar.

THE ACTS OF THE APOSTLES

This is that of which your own prophet wrote. This is
the outcome of the life and death and resurrection of
the Man Jesus, Whom you know.

This is the true art of preaching, whether it be in
London, or Bombay; whether it be in the heart of Africa,
or in the midst of the wealthiest civilization, matters
nothing. At Athens, quote your Greek poets; make the
barbarians at Lycaonia put Jupiter and Mercury into
contrast with Jehovah. Begin with the things men know.

The Christian preacher must always recognize that
there is a light that lighteth every man that cometh into
the world; that God has never left humanity utterly without witness. Therefore the true preacher and the true
missionary begin with the things known, and show their
relationship to the Christ.

Observe in the next place, that there was in this address an orderly statement of truth. We will only refer
to it, now, for we shall examine it more carefully in
future studies. Beginning with the words, "Jesus of
Nazareth," the whole truth concerning Christ was declared in orderly sequence.

The final fact to be noticed in the mental method of
the sermon is that the ultimate proclamation was that of
the Lordship of Christ. "Let all the house of Israel,
therefore know assuredly, that God hath made Him
both Lord and Christ, this Jesus Whom ye crucified."

Such was the mental method of the sermon—recognizing their right to enquire; appealing to the things they
knew; making an orderly statement of truth; and,
finally, appealing by the proclamation of the Lordship of
Christ.

The spiritual method is of supreme importance, yet it
perhaps needs the least exposition because it is so patent.
We observe, first, Peter's ready obedience to the Spirit.
Christ had said to him, and to the rest, not above two
weeks before, "When the Holy Spirit is come upon you
. . . ye shall be My witnesses." The Spirit came, and

THE ACTS OF THE APOSTLES

immediately the spiritual method of preaching was that of quick and ready and direct obedience to the Spirit, seizing the opportunity created by the amazement, perplexity, and criticism of the crowd, and declaring His message.

But notice also, the conviction of this preacher. It was the conviction of clear vision, resulting from the illumination of the Spirit. Not once in all the course of that first sermon do we find such phrases as: *In all probability;* or *It is reasonable to suppose.* There is not a nebulous statement in this message from beginning to end. It is positive, convinced, courteous declaration.

The courage of the preacher is equally patent. The crowds were amazed, perplexed, critical; but all the rulers were opposed to the Nazarene heresy, and he began by naming Nazareth. Peter now confronted the great mass of the people gathered from Judæa and from far and near, and he said boldly: " Jesus of Nazareth, a man approved of God unto you . . . God hath made Him both Lord and Christ, this Jesus Whom ye crucified." It was the courage of spiritual conviction, resulting from the illumination of the Holy Spirit.

The mental orderliness of statement, to which we have referred, was the result of spiritual illumination. To every man who heard, a double witness was borne; the witness of the man, and the witness of the constraining Spirit of God. When the Sadducean opposition began, the rulers said to him: How dare you preach when we have forbidden? Carefully notice his answer, " We must obey God rather than men. . . . We are witnesses of these things; and so is the Holy Spirit."

The last spiritual note is that of victory. This was manifested finally in the multitude who believed; but its first manifestation was in the preacher. The Spirit of God, Who had come with the sound and symbol of the wind and the fire, turned this cringing, fearful man of seven weeks ago, into a prophet, an apostle, an evangelist of the new age, and made him victorious in the delivery of his first message.

II.   Lastly let us briefly notice the matter of the sermon.   Peter commenced with the Old Testament Scriptures; and there is evident a fine sense of fitness in his selection of the passage from Joel; Joel who was either the earliest or the latest of the prophets, and whose message concerning the Spirit is more clear than any other of the ancient prophecies.   This is the message Peter chose.   Of that message he quoted part which was fulfilled immediately; part which is being fulfilled now; and part which is yet to be fulfilled.   The day of the Lord has not come, and the signs of its coming are not yet. He quoted all the prophecy, because he knew that with the descent of the Spirit consequent upon the exaltation of the Christ, the movement had commenced, though it would take millenniums to work itself out to finality.

He then proceeded to declare the things of Christ.   We will only name them.

The fact of Jesus: " Jesus a man."

The perfection of His manhood, and the work of His ministry: " approved of God unto you, by mighty works and wonders and signs."

The Death of Jesus: " Him being delivered up by the determinate counsel and foreknowledge of God, ye by the hand of lawless men did crucify and slay."

The Resurrection of Jesus: " It was not possible that He should be holden of it."

His exaltation and reception of the Spirit: He is exalted, He is glorified, He has received from the Father the gift of the Spirit.

His activity: " He hath poured forth *this*."

The results were immediate and continuous.   The immediate were those of conviction and enquiry; instruction and exhortation; obedience and addition.   Men said, " What shall we do? " Peter answered them immediately, and led them forward.

[49]

[Acts 2 : 16-21]

The continuous results were those of the new ordinances; the new fellowship; the new experience; and the growth; to all of which we shall return.

From this general survey we can only gather broad applications. As to the Christian message, we learn that it is wholly a proclamation of what God has to say to men. The Word written—Joel's prophecy; the Word living—Jesus of Nazareth; but always what God has to say to men. The business of the Christian preacher is to tell men what God has to say to them. The business of the preacher is not to speculate, or to attempt to evolve from the appearances of the hour some underlying truth. He is to come to the age saying to it, " Thus saith Jehovah."

This address reveals the further fact that the preacher deals with the spiritual, and produces spiritual results. He does not begin at the circumference of things, but at the centre. But he affects the uttermost circumference, by beginning at the centre. He says to individual men, Crown the Christ Who is at the right hand of God; and then from that central point readjust all your life, correct everything.

Finally we learn from this study that the Christian messenger must know by experience, or he cannot preach; that he must be filled with the Spirit if there are to be any results from his preaching; and that he must be wise, for " he that winneth souls is wise."

Acts 2: 16-21

The brief and incomplete statement, " *This is that,*" constitutes a key to this passage, in which we have the first movement in Peter's answer to the enquiry of the amazed, perplexed, and critical multitude—" What meaneth this? " Recognizing their right to enquire, and taking advantage of the opportunity which that enquiry afforded him, the apostle first took them back to the prophetic writings with which they were familiar, and reminded them that in these prophecies these things were foretold—" This is that which hath been spoken through the prophet Joel."

The similarity between the manifestations predicted, and those being witnessed, was marked; and so Peter was able to remind them of the predicted cause—" I will pour forth of My Spirit upon all flesh "; and thus to claim that, as explaining what was passing around them, rather than the filling of new wine, as some of them had suggested. " What meaneth this? " said they; and some of them mocking made a guess: These men are drunken—" filled with new wine."

This relation between the Pentecostal effusion and the ancient prophecy is of interest to us also. Taking the brief phrase, " This is that " as text, these are our divisions: first, " That "; secondly, " This." We will look back to the ancient prophecy; and then we will observe the fulfilment of it in its first manifestation, and in its suggestiveness as to the age of the Spirit.

I. In considering this prophecy which Peter quoted upon the day of Pentecost we will first take a broad survey of the whole book, considering the context as well as the text.

It is difficult to place the prophecy of Joel with historic accuracy, but we may say with practical certainty that he was either the earliest, or nearly the last of the prophets. He makes no reference to Cyrus, to the Assyrians, or to the Chaldeans. He but mentions Tyre, Zidon, and Philistia. He makes no reference throughout the whole of his message to idolatry, or to corruption. He refers throughout the whole of the prophecy to the Temple services as being maintained. He is quite silent as to kings or princes, but constantly refers to leaders and to priests. He has none of the scorn for sacrifice which marks the writings of other prophets; on the contrary he mourns that through the locust plague there are no offerings to bring to the Temple. A number of

passages found in the prophecy of Joel are also found in
other books; which suggests that he quoted from them,
or they from him. It is agreed that the prophecy could
not have been uttered during the period covered by the
prophets from Amos to Zechariah. It must have been
earlier or later. This particular reference to the work
of the Spirit, which is so peculiarly clear, concise, definite,
positive; was either one of the earliest or one of the
latest, and was in itself inclusive. Ezekiel said much
concerning the work of the Spirit of God under different figures; Isaiah made clear reference to the coming of the Spirit; but in all the ancient writings there is
no passage quite as precise, as definite, as positive, as
this paragraph which Peter selected for quotation upon
the day of Pentecost. Either it was the earliest utterance of prophecy, concerning the dispensation of the
Spirit, which served as inspiration to those which followed; or else it was the last, gathering up into clear
statement all the things that had been said.

But now, what is the burden of the whole prophecy
of Joel? Joel was first of all impressed by a plague of
locusts, which had swept over the country, devastating
everything. The men of the time were conscious of the
calamity, but were not connecting it with their relationship to the throne of God. Just as to-day some plague,
some catastrophe, some war, will occupy the thought of
men, they will be deeply interested in it; but will fail to
climb the heights, and interpret the events of the hour
in their relation to the throne of God.

This however is precisely what Joel did. His prophecy
was based upon the actual locust plague. He first called
the people to contemplation. He made his appeal to the
old men; he made his appeal to memory; he made his
appeal to the drunkards; he made his appeal to the young.
He called all to contemplation, and then declared that this
visitation of the locust plague was an activity of the day
of the Lord, that God was proceeding in judgment against

them on account of their sin. He next called them to
humiliation, as well as to contemplation.

When he had observed the things in the midst of which
he lived, and interpreted their meaning to his age; he
predicted another judgment, and used the past as illustrating that which was imminent, employing the locusts
as symbolic of the armies coming upon them in battle
and judgment.

In both these connections he indicated the Divine judgment, and announced the Divine grace. He told the
people that if they would repent and humble themselves
before God, He would spare them. So far, the prophecy
seems to be of little interest to us. But now, the prophet
said, "And it shall come to pass afterward." Verse
twenty-eight of chapter two in our Bible, is verse one of
chapter three in the Hebrew Bible. Those who rear-
ranged these chapter divisions thought they knew better
than the Hebrews. They did not. Our arrangement at
least seems to suggest that what now followed was to
take place immediately. As a matter of fact the word
"afterward" shows that the prophet now climbed a
little higher, and looked into the distances, and from
that moment to the end, was uttering a prophecy of
things that he saw far away. As he thus looked far
ahead he saw a movement remarkable, strange, different
from anything that had been seen in the history of his
own people: "I will pour out My Spirit upon all flesh."

The prophet had risen above his own times, above the
immediate future, and he saw, what he described in the
words, "I will pour out My Spirit upon all flesh; and
your sons and your daughters shall prophesy; your old
men shall dream dreams, your young men shall see visions, and also upon the servants and upon the handmaids
in those days, will I pour out My Spirit."

In these words every prejudice of the Hebrew was
attacked. The Spirit was not to be poured upon the
Hebrew nation only, but "upon all flesh." The right to

[53]

prophesy was not to be the peculiar privilege of priests, or Levites, or men, but "your sons and your daughters shall prophesy." It was not to be the peculiar privilege of sons and daughters, but servants and handmaids were to be among the prophets. There was to be an effusion of the Spirit of God upon all the race. There was to be an outpouring of the Spirit of God that should give men and women the power of prophesying. There was to be a bestowment of the Spirit of God, that should sweep out caste, and give slaves the high honour of proclaiming the spiritual mysteries.

What more did he see? "And I will show wonders in the heavens, and in the earth, blood, and fire, and pillars of smoke. The sun shall be turned into darkness, and the moon into blood, before the great and terrible day of Jehovah cometh. And it shall come to pass, that whosoever shall call on the name of Jehovah shall be delivered; for in Mount Zion and in Jerusalem there shall be those that escape, as Jehovah hath said, and among the remnant those whom Jehovah doth call. For, behold, in those days, and in that time, when I shall bring again the captivity of Judah and Jerusalem, I will gather all nations."

Now the prophet saw far beyond the Pentecostal effusion. He was still looking on, and in his vision, century merged into century, and age lay beyond age, in strange and wonderful perspective. Looking to the final things, he saw that God will bring again the captivity of Judah and Jerusalem; will gather Israel from its scattered position o'er all the world, and will bring it back to the place of privilege and power and responsibility. This, God has never done yet. That prophecy is not fulfilled.

To summarize. Joel stood in local circumstances, and saw the locust plague as an act of God; and so interpreted it to his age. He then rose to a higher height of vision, and saw that the outcome of their sin must be a new judgment, and declared that it was coming. He then climbed still higher, and saw the age of the Spirit poured upon all flesh; the age when sons and daughters and bondservants and bondmaidens prophesy; the age when the old men dream dreams, and young men see visions. Then he said, before the day of the Lord come, there shall be signs on the earth and in the heavens, blood, and fire, and pillars of smoke; and during that day of signs, whoever calls on the name of the Lord shall be delivered.

In Joel's prophecy then we have a description of the whole dispensation of the Spirit; its commencement—" I will pour out My Spirit upon all flesh;" its characteristics—" Your sons and your daughters shall prophesy, your old men shall dream dreams, your young men shall see visions, and also upon the servants and upon the handmaids in those days will I pour out My Spirit "; its consummation—before the great day of the Lord come—" I will shew wonders in the heavens."

Thus, according to this prophecy, the dispensation of the Spirit is not measured. There is no time given. It opens with the pouring out of the Spirit upon all flesh. Its characteristics are those of prophecy and vision. It will end with supernatural signs.

When on the Day of Pentecost, the multitudes amazed, perplexed, critical, enquired, " What meaneth *this?* " Peter answered, " *This* is that which hath been spoken by the prophet Joel."

According to this ancient prophecy, upon which the apostle of the new economy set his seal, what do we mean when we speak of the Day of Pentecost? The Day of Pentecost historically, was the day upon which the Spirit was poured upon all flesh. The day of Pentecost dispensationally, is that whole period following, during which the true characteristics are those of prophecy, and of dreams and visions. The Day of Pentecost finally, is that period when, before the final acts begin, supernatural signs will indicate the end of the period, and the approach of God's new and last method with the world.

THE ACTS OF THE APOSTLES
[Acts 2: 16–21]

Where then are we placed now? The dawn has passed away. The day is proceeding. The darkness has not yet come. Dawn: "I will pour forth of My Spirit upon all flesh." Day: "Your sons and your daughters shall prophesy, and your young men shall see visions, and your old men shall dream dreams, yea, and on My servants and on My handmaidens in those days will I pour forth of My Spirit; and they shall prophesy." Darkness: "The great and notable day . . . the sun turned into darkness, and the moon into blood." That has not yet come.

This prophetic teaching should make us cease speaking of the day of Pentecost as though it were passed. This is the day of Pentecost. The dawn has passed, but who regrets the dawn when the sun has climbed to the heavens? Sometimes we think that it is westering; that the shadows are already about us. It would seem that we are approaching the end of this dispensation of grace; but there is no sorrow in our heart, there is no regret. We do not believe that this dispensation is the last activity of God for the world. Our hope is also in the movements that lie beyond it; in the fact that He will gather Judah to Jerusalem, and Israel to Himself, and in other ways proceed to the accomplishment of His purpose. The whole subject is not for consideration now, but what it is important to remember is that this very age in which we live and serve, is part of God's plan, but not the whole of it. It is an integral part of the whole. God has never been trying experiments with humanity. He has been moving surely, certainly on, and this age in which we live and serve is part of a larger whole. We need not sigh for the dawn; we thank God for it, and the story of its breaking always fascinates us. We need not waste time looking for the ending of the age; for ere it come there will be supernatural signs that herald its approach.

In concluding this study, let us glance at the characteristics of this day of the Spirit. It is the Day of the Spirit *poured forth*. The Spirit has been associated with all human history. We begin our Bible with the Spirit: " In the beginning God created the heavens and the earth. And the earth was waste and void; and darkness was upon the face of the deep; and the Spirit of God moved upon the face of the waters." All the way through we find the Spirit—clothing Himself with a man, clothing a man with Himself, inspiring men to be cunning workers in gold and silver for the making of the Tabernacle. In all the past the Spirit is discovered, coming, departing; visiting, retiring. As, over the original chaos He brooded for the production of the new cosmos, so over the processional chaos, He was ever brooding, until there came the Word made flesh, conceived in the womb of the virgin by the Holy Spirit. The day of Pentecost was not the day when the Spirit of God began. It was the day in which the Spirit was " poured forth." It was the day of a definite and specific beginning. The Spirit of God was to be no longer a Visitor, dwelling with lonely men and individual souls, but poured out in all fulness.

But again, the Spirit was " poured forth upon all flesh." Take the Old Testament, and observe the recurrence of the phrase " all flesh." It is sometimes used—once in Daniel, and notably in other of the prophetic writings— in reference to all animal life from the lowest to the highest; but where it is used evidently of human beings, it always refers to all human beings. The phrase " all flesh " is never used in the Old Testament of one nation, not even of the Hebrew nation. It is never used in any smaller application than to the whole of humanity. The Spirit was poured upon all flesh. That is, there is a sense in which on the day of Pentecost the Spirit of God came into relationship with the whole of humanity. Concerning the Christ, through Whom the Spirit was poured upon all flesh, it is written: " In the beginning was the Word, and the Word was with God, and the Word was

[57]

THE ACTS OF THE APOSTLES

God. . . . And the Word became flesh." Now that
is not merely a description of the individuality of the
Man of Nazareth; it is the generic term, showing that
He came into contact with the whole race. When He
became flesh, He took not on Him the nature of angels;
He laid hold upon human nature. When He became
flesh, He became a member, not merely of the Hebrew
race, but of the human race. Presently, when His work
as representative of the race was accomplished, and He
had ascended on high, the Spirit was poured upon that
whole race into union with which He had come, when
He was made flesh.

The Spirit is upon all flesh for clearly defined purposes.
He is on all flesh to convict of sin, of righteousness, of
judgment. He is in the human race as the power that
hinders evil, and He will hinder until He be taken out of
the way.

The characteristics of the Day of the outpoured Spirit
are those of visions, dreams, and prophesying.

What is a vision? Something seen by a watcher.
What is a dream? Something seen by a sleeper. Visions
are for the young men, who should be watching. Dreams
are for the old men, who should be resting.

The New Testament prophet is a witness in speech,
and the prophets are to be men and women, bond and
free. This Spirit came to scorch and burn and destroy
the false divisions which existed; He came to recognize
humanity, irrespective of caste or sex; sons and daughters, bondslaves and bondmaidens.

What are the things we need to fear supremely? First,
silence. If we cannot speak—not necessarily to a crowd
—for our Master, wherever the opportunity is given, then
we should be afraid. The Spirit was poured out to give
us power to prophesy. Let us be very afraid of silence.

We need also to fear if there is an absence of visions
and dreams. If we have no dreams and no visions, why
not? It is because we are not responsive to the Spirit.

THE ACTS OF THE APOSTLES

If we do not do this, it is not merely that we fail. We limit God; for the marvellous and matchless mystery of the Pentecostal age is this—that while the Spirit is on all flesh, He waits for a partner, and the partner must be a man, a woman, a child. God bring us into fellowship that we may give His message and hasten the Kingdom.

Acts 2:22-36

The more carefully this first message delivered in the power of the outpoured Spirit is pondered, the more wonderful does it appear. We have considered the first section, summarized in the words, "This is that." We may now proceed to the study of the second section summarized in the words, "He hath poured forth this." In this section there are three things of preëminent importance.

Peter first traced the process which culminated in Pentecost, beginning with the words, "Jesus of Nazareth"; and ending with the words, "He hath poured forth this."

In reading the section we notice how much of it, in some senses, is in parenthesis. At verse twenty-five, with the words, "For David saith concerning Him," we are conscious of the fact that Peter departed for the time being, from the main line of his statement, as he quoted from the Psalms, and proceeded to make application of what he quoted. At verse thirty-two he practically repeated what he had already said in verse twenty-four, "Whom God raised up," in the words, "This Jesus did God raise up." The whole of that paragraph then (verses twenty-five to thirty-two) is in parentheses. I do not suggest that it is unimportant, but rather supremely important, showing that the apostle was dealing with what we may speak of as the pivotal fact in the mission of Jesus. This, indeed, is the second thing of value in this part of the discourse.

Then finally, having traced the process that culminated

[59]

THE ACTS OF THE APOSTLES

in Pentecost, and having parenthetically taken time to deal with the pivotal fact of the Resurrection, he made the Pentecostal proclamation, Jesus is Lord, and Christ.

Our present meditation is concerned with the process which culminated in the outpouring of the Spirit on the day of Pentecost. The apostle distinctly indicated seven stages in the process.

He began by naming the Person, perfectly familiar in this way at least, to the crowds that were round about him: " Jesus of Nazareth."

He next said that this Man, Jesus of Nazareth, had been demonstrated as a perfect Man in their midst;—" a Man approved of God unto you by mighty works and wonders and signs, which God did by Him in the midst of you, even as ye yourselves know."

He then referred to the death of this Person in terms full of significance: " Him, being delivered up by the determinate counsel and foreknowledge of God, ye by the hand of lawless men did crucify and slay."

He then declared that this selfsame Person was raised from the dead: " Whom God raised up, having loosed the pangs of death; because it was not possible that He should be holden of it."

He then affirmed that the Person so raised from the dead was exalted: " Being therefore by the right hand of God exalted."

He then announced that the Person so exalted had received in some peculiar and special manner the fulfilment of the ancient promise of Jehovah: " Having received of the Father the promise of the Holy Spirit."

He finally declared that this selfsame Person poured forth the Spirit: " He hath poured forth this, which ye see and hear."

To more briefly summarize the stages: The apostle spoke of the Person; His demonstrated perfection; His death; His resurrection; His exaltation; His reception of the Spirit; His bestowal of the Spirit.

Of these, the central fact is that of resurrection. Three precede it: The being and Person of Jesus of Nazareth; His perfection; His death by the way of the Cross. Three follow it: His exaltation to the right hand of power; His reception of the Spirit; His pouring forth of that Spirit upon the waiting disciples. Thus, at the heart of the mission of Jesus is the fact of the Resurrection.

Now let us consider these seven stages. We will attempt to do so by dealing with each of the sentences.

Peter commenced by the use of a phrase which was familiar to the men who listened, " Jesus of Nazareth." He thus designated the Person, upon Whom he would fix attention. In doing so he appealed to the knowledge of his hearers. The fame of Jesus had spread far and wide. Very many had seen Him. Multitudes of those who had never seen Him had yet heard of Him. He had become widely known by this peculiar designation, " Jesus of Nazareth." So far as our records reveal, Philip first made use of it. When speaking to Nathanael he said, " We have found Him, of Whom Moses in the Law, and the Prophets wrote, Jesus of Nazareth, the Son of Joseph." This designation arrested the attention and aroused the criticism of Nathanael who said, " Can any good thing come out of Nazareth? " Presently a demon-possessed man looked into the face of Jesus and said, " What have we to do with Thee, Thou Jesus of Nazareth? " Later on in His ministry, as He entered Jerusalem, on what we speak of as the triumphal occasion, the multitudes said, " Who is this? " The Galilean crowd in triumph answered, " This is the prophet Jesus, from Nazareth of Galilee." When, on the dark betrayal night, the soldiers came to arrest Him, He said to them, " Whom seek ye? " and they replied, " Jesus of Nazareth." When Peter was warming himself at the fire built in the outer court, a servant maid looked at him, and said, " Thou also wast with the Nazarene Jesus."

THE ACTS OF THE APOSTLES

[Acts 2: 22-36]

Pilate the Roman Procurator commanded to be written, and affixed to the cross, this designation of the Crucified —"Jesus of Nazareth, the King of the Jews." At the Resurrection, the angel said to the waiting and weeping women: "Ye seek Jesus the Nazarene, Who hath been crucified." Two men were walking to Emmaus when a stranger joined them, and asked them why they looked so sad; and they said to Him, "Dost Thou alone sojourn in Jerusalem and not know the things that are come to pass in these days?" "What things?" said He. "They said unto Him, The things concerning Jesus of Nazareth, Who was a prophet mighty in deed and word before God and all the people." These instances are only given to emphasize what seems of importance here, the fact namely, that He was known as Jesus of Nazareth.

Peter took hold of that peculiar designation, which would appeal to his hearers, because they were perfectly familiar with it, and in view of the things he was about to declare, commenced by reference to the actual Personality with which these men were familiar, either by sight or hearing—"Jesus of Nazareth." He thus reminded them of the fact of His humanity.

The effusion of the Spirit upon human life, with all that has followed, is related to the humanity of Jesus Christ, to the absolute fact of His presence in the world, as a Man of our manhood, a member of the human race. In that first descriptive phrase then, we immediately feel ourselves close to Him, and there can be no question that it was the intention of Peter to emphasize that relationship.

This designation of the Person was immediately followed by the words: "A Man approved of God unto you by mighty works, and wonders, and signs, which God did by Him in the midst of you, even as ye yourselves know." We must very carefully note the plain, first meaning of this statement. The apostle did not by these words intend to declare that the Man of Nazareth was pleasing to God.

We are a little apt to read the word *"approved"* as though it meant that. Let us change the word, and instead of "A Man *approved* of God unto you," let us read, "A Man *demonstrated* of God unto you."

Peter's declaration was that the Man of Nazareth was proved to them by mighty works, and wonders and signs. The question that arises is, what was proved by these things? In order to answer that, we must give careful attention to the whole statement. Let us begin with the method of the demonstration, or proof. It was that of mighty works, and wonders, and signs. The first word, "powers," or "mighty works," indicates the exercise of a power. The next word, "wonders," indicates the effect produced by the power upon the mind of other people. The last word, "signs," indicates the value of the power and of the wonder it produced.

Peter declared that these were works of God; that they were things which "God did by Him in the midst of you." If for a moment the statement seems as though it were robbing Jesus of some dignity, let us remember what He Himself said, "I do nothing of Myself; I work the works of Him that sent Me." The works which became wonders, and were signs, were wrought by God, but they were wrought by God through Him. This Man of Nazareth was the Instrument through Whom God wrought. The Man of Nazareth was a fitting and perfect instrument of God; was a Being absolutely at the disposal of God, through Whom God could exercise His powers, produce His wonders, give His signs. What then did this prove concerning Him? It was not the demonstration of Deity; it was rather the demonstration of His perfect realization of the Divine ideal in His human life, so that He was an instrument absolutely fitted to the use of God, one through Whom God could work. That is the difference between Jesus and ourselves, on the level of humanity. We are men; so was He. We are imperfect; He was perfect. God cannot

THE ACTS OF THE APOSTLES

through us do all His work. Jesus was so absolutely perfect as an instrument, that through Him God could work in such a way as to produce wonder in the minds of sinning men, and to give signs to them of the things He would have them know. This second movement of the apostle's interpretation of the process that led to Pentecost reveals Jesus as a perfect Man, and a sinless Man.

Then the apostle passed to the next step in the process. Still emphasizing the identity of the Person by the introductory pronoun he said: "*Him,* being delivered up by the determinate counsel and foreknowledge of God, ye by the hand of lawless men did crucify and slay." In that statement we find the whole mystery of the Cross. In it the apostle recognized the Divine side, and the human side in that Cross. We are nineteen centuries away from it. The men who listened to him were not more than seven or eight weeks away from it. They remembered it; that rough, cruel, bloody, Roman gibbet. They knew what crucifixion meant. When he referred to it he did not begin with the brutality of it; he did not begin with the dastardliness of it; he began from the heights and from the infinite distances: "Him being delivered up by the determinate counsel and foreknowledge of God." That is the aspect of the Cross to which man clings in the hour when he knows himself a sinner. We are not saved by the murder of a Man. We are saved by the death of the One Who was delivered up by the determinate counsel and foreknowledge of God. It was a murder; a vile murder; but it was more, infinitely more. It was something that took place "by the determinate counsel and foreknowledge of God." The Greek word translated "determinate" here, is the word from which we derive our word "horizon." The phrase "determinate counsel," suggests the plan of God, that which was within the boundaries of His purpose. The death of Jesus, said Peter in effect upon the day of Pentecost, was not an accident, not something brought about by men. It was the working out, in human history, and into visibility, of an eternal purpose and plan and power.

But there was a human side to it, and Peter brought all the guilty face to face with the Cross. Carefully notice his recognition of the two human agencies; "*ye*" and "*lawless men.*" The "ye" referred to the men of Israel whom he was addressing; the "lawless men," that is men without law, referred to Gentiles, the procurator, and the soldiers. All were involved, the Israelites, and the Gentiles. So the human element is seen. When that Cross was lifted, and that One was nailed to it; men under the law, violated law; men without law, seared their consciences. On the human side His death was caused by sin, dastardly, grievous, final; beyond which there is no sin. Jesus of Nazareth, the Man demonstrated perfect, sinless, was delivered by the counsel of God, and executed by the crime of men.

Peter immediately continued, and again insisted upon the identity of the Person by the first word of his statement: "*Whom* God raised up." That was the central fact. We will not pause there now, but leaving the statement in its simple sublimity, will return in our next study to its exposition by the Psalms which the apostle quoted. It is of special importance at this point however that we emphasize the identity of the Person. It is the same Person from beginning to end: Jesus of Nazareth; a Man demonstrated; Him delivered; Whom God raised. If the identity be denied here, then there is no meaning in this message, and the whole superstructure of Christianity has been erected upon an imaginary foundation, indeed upon a lie, which is absurd.

The next stage in the process the apostle described in the words: "Being therefore by the right hand of God exalted." This was a reference to the Ascension.

A glance to verse thirty-four will give us the interpretation of the word "exalted." There we have a quotation from David: "The Lord said unto my Lord, sit thou on my right hand." This is one of the occasions in which it would be a good thing to retain the Hebrew form—"Jehovah saith to Adonai." If we turn to the Psalm (one hundred and ten) we see the meaning of the statement. That this Psalm is Messianic, all Hebrew commentators and Christian interpreters are agreed. In it we see the Messiah crowned and enthroned; and so winning His ultimate victories. That is the meaning here of the declaration that God exalted Him. Jesus of Nazareth, demonstrated perfect, crucified, raised, was exalted to the place of power and authority, to the centre of the universe of God; and His exaltation was in order to His final victory—"Till I make Thine enemies Thy footstool."

The next phrase of the apostle, in language which is full of mystery, reveals to us what took place at that centre of the universe. Here all earthly language fails. We speak of location and place, and we must do so in order to follow the process, and yet it is difficult to follow. Peter declared that being thus exalted, as David had foretold, to the right hand of power, to wait until His enemies are the footstool of His feet, "He received of the Father the promise of the Holy Spirit." This expression "the promise of the Holy Spirit" takes our minds back to the things which our Lord Himself had said before He left them: "Behold I send forth the promise of My Father upon you." What, then, was the promise of the Father? Let us glance back at the ancient writings. God had said by Isaiah—"I will pour out My Spirit." He had said by Joel—"And it shall come to pass afterward, that I will pour My Spirit upon all flesh." He had said by Jesus Himself—"I will inquire of the Father and He shall give you another Comforter." Now, said Peter, this Man of Nazareth, perfect, crucified, raised, exalted, received the promise of the Father; that is, He received the Spirit for all flesh; the Spirit for the

[Acts 2: 22-36]
new age. Thus Peter described poetically and yet actually, the fact that, when there came into that centre of
the universe the crucified and risen Man of Nazareth,
God fulfilled the ancient promise and gave Him, not for
Himself, but as a deposit for all flesh, the fulness of the
Spirit; " He received the promise of the Father."

One can never read this without attempting to witness
the august and glorious event, without in imagination
observing the coming of the Man of Nazareth to the high
and exalted place of His glory. He was the first Man
to enter into the perfect light of heaven, in the right of
His own holiness. Heaven had never before received
such a Man. Abel had passed home by faith and prophetic sacrifice; and all the long line of the spirits of the
just men made perfect were there upon the basis of the
mercy of God. But on that Ascension Day there came
into heaven a Man Who asked no mercy. Pure, spotless,
victorious, He came into the light of heaven, and caused
no shadow there.

But, as we look at Him, we wonder, and we say: How
is it that the perfect is wounded? What mean these
wound-prints in hands, and feet, and side? Tell me ye
angel spirits! There is but one answer, and it is the
answer that comes welling up out of our ransomed
nature; " He loved me, and gave Himself for me." To
the wounded Man, Who had won the victory for the lost
race, God gave the Spirit, and gave it Him for the race,
which He had redeemed.

Then Peter ended his story of the great procession,
and declared its consummation. Here again the identity
of the Person is emphasized by the first word: " *He* hath
poured forth this." Do not think of a vapourized presence, a lost individuality—" He hath poured forth this."
All the vision, and the ecstasy, the light and the power,
which had astonished Jerusalem, had come through
Jesus of Nazareth.

Finally observe that the great argument of Peter's

declaration is, that the whole mission of Jesus was of God. God demonstrated His perfection; God delivered Him to death; God raised Him from the dead; God exalted Him to the throne; God gave Him the Spirit. Thus the statement is a revelation of the victory of grace over sin. Men acted to a certain point. They watched Jesus and listened to Him. Then they crucified Him. In that they had done the worst thing. In that act, sin finally expressed itself. Grace operated all through. It gave Jesus to human life. It delivered Him to death. Then it continued, when sin had ended. God raised Him, He exalted Him, He gave Him the Spirit. Sin and grace are seen in dire conflict in the Cross. The victory is with grace, not with sin.

> The very spear that pierced His side,
> Drew forth the blood to save.

By that poured-out Spirit, the declaration is uttered to all the ages of the triumph of the grace of God.

Acts 2: 24-32

This paragraph is an exposition, in the apostolic preaching, of the central fact concerning Jesus of Nazareth, that, namely, of His Resurrection. The statement concerning the resurrection stands at the centre of the whole movement of this discourse. Three facts precede it;—the manhood, the perfection, and the death of Jesus; three facts follow it;—His exaltation, His reception of the Spirit, His bestowal of the Spirit upon the assembled disciples. The former three culminated in the resurrection. The latter three resulted from the resurrection.

Let us first notice briefly, but carefully, the structure of this particular paragraph. It consists of three parts; —a declaration; an affirmation; and an explanation. The declaration;—" God raised Him "; the affirmation; —" It was not possible that He should be holden of it "; the explanation is found in the Psalm quotations.

The declaration is simple and explicit. The affirmation which follows it is bold and defiant. In reading it the emphasis should be placed on the pronouns: " It was not possible that *He* should be holden of *it."* The *He* refers to that one Person, Jesus of Nazareth, demonstrated perfect, crucified by the determinate counsel and foreknowledge of God. Of Him the apostle said: " It was not possible that *He* should be holden of *it."* The simple meaning of that affirmation is that God was bound to raise Him in the very nature of the case.

This affirmation he then explained by quoting one of the Psalms:

" For David saith concerning Him,
    I beheld the Lord always before My face;
    For He is on My right hand, that I should not be
        moved;
    Therefore My heart was glad, and My tongue rejoiced;
    Moreover My flesh also shall dwell in hope;
    Because Thou wilt not leave My soul unto Hades,
    Neither wilt Thou give Thy Holy One to see corruption.
    Thou madest known unto Me the ways of life;
    Thou shalt make Me full of gladness with Thy countenance."

Then followed the defence of his use of the Psalm. It was quite within the bounds of possibility that somebody listening to him might have said, What right have you to make use of that language as applicable to Christ? Peter therefore declared that all that was suggested by the Psalm was not fulfilled in the experience of David, for " he both died and was buried, and his tomb is with us unto this day." Peter interpreted the Psalm as prophesying the Resurrection; he understood that the writer of it was referring to some one who should pass into death, triumph over it, and emerge from it. David did no such thing; he died and was buried, and his sepulchre was with them unto that day. He declared—and let us carefully remember that he was speaking under the inspiration of the new baptism of the Spirit which he had received—that when David wrote that, he wrote as a prophet more than as a Psalmist: "Knowing that God had sworn with an oath to him, that of the fruit of his loins he would set one upon his throne; he foreseeing this, spake of the resurrection of the Messiah."

The affirmation—"It was not possible that He should be holden of it"—was both bold and defiant. The boldness was born of the confidence that God cannot violate eternal principles. The defiance was born of the assurance that death had been conquered in the resurrection of Jesus.

The explanation was a radiant revelation of the evidence for resurrection, as contained in the necessity of the case. We often defend the truth of the resurrection by historical evidence, and there is ample proof along that line, for if the testimony of these men is not to be accepted, then there is no testimony upon which we can depend concerning anything in the history of mankind. Peter's evidence here, however, was not that he had seen the risen Christ, although he came back to that when presently he said, "Whereof we are witnesses." The line of his argument here is that if the things he had already declared concerning Jesus were true, then the resurrection was absolutely necessary, or else God was violating eternal principles. If this Jesus of Nazareth was indeed demonstrated by the works, wonders, and signs, perfectly sinless; then, though He died, death could not hold Him. It is as though Peter had said: An understanding of *Him* and an understanding of *it*, will demonstrate the fact that there could be no final relationship between *Him* and *it;* that His passing into " it " was a necessary, and a voluntary act, but that, even though He passed into " it," it could not fasten upon Him, and hold Him. It held David. David foresaw a victory;

David sang a song of great confidence; David was filled with hope; nevertheless he died, and was buried, and his sepulchre is with us unto this day; but this Jesus was other than David; other than any other man; and it was impossible that *He* should be holden of *it*. Peter's reason for this affirmation is revealed in the quotation which he made from the Psalm. Let us then first of all examine the quotation itself. There are three parts to it.

There is first a description of life:

" I beheld the Lord always before My face;
    For He is on My right hand, that I should not be
        moved:
    Therefore My heart was glad, and My tongue re-
        joiced."

Immediately following it, is a description of death, in which an attitude toward death is assumed that can be postulated of no human being, except this One:

" Moreover My flesh shall also encamp in hope;
    Because Thou wilt not leave My soul unto Hades,
    Neither wilt Thou give Thy Holy One to see corrup-
        tion."

Then, after life and after death, is a description of the resurrection:

" Thou madest known unto Me the ways of life;
    Thou shalt make Me full of gladness with Thy counte-
        nance."

Cause and effect are set in relation to each other in this Psalm quotation. Let us trace the effect to the cause. We begin with the effect, which was that of resurrection. That resurrection resulted from the peculiar nature of death. The way of life was made open to One Who, laying down flesh in hope, was certain that His soul could not be left in Hades, nor His flesh see corruption.

[Acts 2: 24–32]

The peculiar nature of that death, which issued in resurrection, resulted from the peculiarity of life, the life which could say:

"I beheld the Lord always before My face;
  For He is on My right hand, that I should not be moved.
  Therefore My heart was glad, and My tongue rejoiced."

Let us take the same line of thought, tracing it in the other direction, and observing the sequence. The life described was such that in death encamped in hope; such death made resurrection necessary in order to the maintenance of eternal order.

Let us now confine ourselves to the reasons for the resurrection, as here set forth. In the words of the Psalm describing the life and death, there is revealed a threefold victory over sin; first the victory over the possibility of originating evil,—"I beheld the Lord always before My face"; secondly, the victory over evil as suggested from without,—"For He is on My right hand that I should not be moved"; and finally, the victory over evil as responsibility assumed:

"Therefore My heart was glad, and My tongue rejoiced:
  Moreover My flesh also shall encamp in hope;
  Because Thou wilt not leave My soul unto Hades;
  Neither wilt Thou give Thy Holy One to see corruption."

Victory over the possibility of originating evil is claimed in the words, "I beheld the Lord always before my face." Whenever we think of this Man of Nazareth we must remember His unique and lonely personality. He was very God and very man. Therefore He was other than either, because He was both. Other than man, because God as well as man. Other than God, be-

{ 72 }

cause man as well as God. So that when this Man of Nazareth, very man and very God, came into our human life, there came into the universe of God a new Being, a new creation. In His coming the first movement was that He took the form of a servant. In that great word in the Philippian letter, in which Paul was describing that descent from heights that we cannot see, to depths that we know experimentally, he declared that He, being in the form of God, thought it not a prize to be snatched at, this equality with God, but emptied Himself and took upon Him the form of a servant. That statement is followed by the words, " Being made in the likeness of men." The first fact then that we have to consider when we see this new Being in the universe of God, is that He was a Servant, on the plane of angel relationship, though not of angel nature. " He took not on Him the nature of angels," but He stood on their plane of relationship to God. It was a descent from sovereignty to subjectivity. This is a mystery that cannot be fully explained; it transcends all human experience, but we dwell upon it in order that we may see the meaning of this first phase of victory.

As we look upon this Man of Nazareth Who is very God and very Man, standing in relation to the eternal God as Servant, we see at once that a new possibility is created of the origination of evil. Jude declared of the angels that fell, that " they kept not their own principality, but left their proper habitation." There is a difference between the sin of angels and that of Adam. Man did not originate evil by his own volition; he responded to temptation from without. The mystery of evil in the universe is older than the history of man. The story of the fall of the angels is that they kept not their habitation. That is not an account of punishment; it is an account of sin. When Isaiah sang the song of the fall of the king of Babylon, he interpreted the mystery of evil. Lucifer, son of the morning, left his

own orbit when he said, " I will ascend into heaven.
. . . I will be like the Most High." Then he left his
proper habitation, so losing his principality, and falling.
That, so far as we know from revelation, was the origination of evil.

When the Son of God came into a new sphere of existence, for the purpose of carrying out the eternal coun-
sels of God, an opportunity was created for a new origination of evil. For the servants of God a habitation is
ordained by God; and the law of maintaining their habitation, of moving in their orbit, is that of always keeping
Him before their face as King. In the case of Lucifer
and those angels who followed him there came a moment
when they chose to exercise their will outside of relationship to the command of God. In that moment there was
a beginning of evil, not by suggestion as from without,
but by the action of the will in independence, instead of
in dependence, upon God.

That conception of the possibility of choosing evil, not
in answer to allurement from without, but by original
action, is involved in this word: " I beheld the Lord
always before My face." It is as though this One had
said: I never indulged in independent or self-caused
action; I never left My proper habitation; and so I have
reserved My principality. I took upon Me the form of
a Servant, and having taken the form of a Servant, I
never rebelled against the service, or chose My own
method of life—" I beheld the Lord always before My
face." By the very mystery and uniqueness of His
Being, this Person might have been a centre from which
evil should originate and spread out in ever-increasing
circles; but He says: " I beheld the Lord always before
My face "; I kept My first habitation; I held My original
principality; I never broke from My allegiance to the God
Whose Servant I became in the mystery of My being.
That is the story of the Being Who passed into death.
He was One Who could say, " I beheld the Lord always

[74]

before My face "; One Who did not originate evil. That was the first phase of His victory over evil.

Let us pass to the next declaration: " For He is on My right hand, that I should not be moved." The difference is apparent. The first declaration may thus be expressed, " *I have not moved.*" The second declaration may thus be expressed, "*I have not been moved.*" I have not moved by My own volition, choosing to act as apart from Divine movement; and I have not allowed any outside attack to overcome that allegiance. This brings us to the consideration of the position of Jesus in the world, to the fact of His Manhood. He came into a world where the force of evil was already in existence, and active. He stood through all the years of His human life between two arguments, the argument of right, and the argument of wrong, just where we stand; He stood between two forces, the force that forevermore was drawing Him towards the Throne, and that which was drawing Him from the Throne. Between these two arguments, these two forces, He, in common with all humanity, was called upon to choose. Angels fell by their own volition and choice. Man fell because standing between these two arguments, he listened and yielded to the one of rebellion. Jesus stood in both places. With regard to the first He said, " I set the Lord always before My face." With regard to the second He said, " Because He is on My right hand, that I should not be moved. Therefore My heart was glad, and My tongue rejoiced "; which means, being expressed in other language: I found the way of pure happiness, because I recognized His nearness to Me, and made Him My defence against all the assaults of the evil one. He gained His victory over the temptations that assailed Him from without, by constant coöperation with the God Who was at His right hand. As the Servant of God, on the angelic plane of relationship, He set the Lord before Him, and never left His habitation. As the Man on the human plane of relationship, He recognized God on His right hand, and availing Himself of His strength, was never moved by the forces that were against Him. Thus He gained a victory over the possibility of originating evil; and over evil as suggested from without. Thus a double victory over sin was gained in the life of this Man.

We now come to the third phase of His victory, that gained through the mystery of His death. If we could but free our minds from matters with which we are familiar in this story of Jesus, we should never read of His death without being startled. Here was One Who, as Servant, had not left His habitation: Who, as Man, had won His victory of purity and holiness by coöperation with God; in Whom therefore there was no reason for death. We see Him passing to death. But now carefully observe His attitude toward death. Out of the midst of this life of victory, this double victory over evil in life, He looked at death, and He said: " My flesh shall rest in hope." He looked to that which lay beyond death, and He said, " Thou wilt not leave My soul unto Hades, neither wilt Thou give Thy Holy One to see corruption." As a Servant He had won victory on the first plane; He had not originated evil. As man He had won victory on the second plane; He had overcome evil in its assaults from without. He now said: I am going into death, but death cannot hold Me. Death is the wage of sin. Death is that which has resulted from the fact of rebellion against God. I am going into it, but it cannot hold Me;

" Thou wilt not leave My soul unto Hades,
Neither wilt Thou give Thy Holy One to see corrup·
    tion."

This was His claim to victory over evil, as responsibility assumed. Why passed He into death, this Man of perfect life? The explanation can only be gathered from all the teaching of the New Testament. It is hinted at in this very discourse when the apostle said: " Him being delivered up by the determinate counsel and foreknowledge of God." The meaning of it had been suggested by our Lord Himself ere He departed, when He said: "No man taketh My life away from Me, but I lay it down of Myself. I have power to lay it down, and I have power to take it again." The reason why He laid it down is declared in the selfsame discourse, in these words, "I am the Good Shepherd; the Good Shepherd layeth down His life for the sheep." The meaning of that death is declared by all the writers of the New Testament. "Who His own self bare our sins in His body upon the tree." "God commendeth His own love toward us, in that, while we were yet sinners, Christ died for us." This Man of perfect victory went down to death because He had assumed the responsibility of sin not His own. "Behold the Lamb of God, that taketh away the sin of the world."

It is sometimes said that it is difficult to understand how one Person could take such responsibility. There is no difficulty if we remember Who the Person was Who took the responsibility. It must not be forgotten that He was more than man or servant; Who in the midst of His Manhood's days could say, "I and My Father are One"; "I do nothing of Myself, but the things of the Father"; "My Father worketh and I work." This is the One Who went down to death, and so into the grave.

Did He never rise? Was the stone never rolled away? Did He never come back, the Man of Nazareth? Then of all men we are the most miserable. Then is our preaching vain, and our faith is vain also. But more is involved. If the story of the perfect life be true, God has violated eternal principles in allowing death to hold One in Whom there was no place for death. That is what Peter meant when he said: "It was not possible that *He* should be holden of *it*." God raised Him up; and the raising was proof finally of victory, over the possibility of orginating evil, over evil as suggested, and

[Acts 2: 34-36]

over evil as responsibility assumed. " It was impossible that He should be holden of it." We accept that dictum; we accept the witness of the actual fact of the Resurrection; and so we know that He Who took the responsibility of human guilt has been able to accomplish His purpose; He has turned His vision into victory, and His victory into virtue.

We never stood on the angel plane, and so never could have originated evil as could they; but we have stood as men upon the human plane, and we have listened to the voice of the tempter, and we have yielded; our record is spoilt, we have failed, we are broken. But this Man Who never failed, took the awful, and the mysterious and incomprehensible responsibility of our failure, and went down into death, and sang as He went: " My flesh shall rest in hope." From death He emerged, His soul delivered from Hades, His flesh never having seen corruption, and by that resurrection we know that the value of His dying is at our disposal. If Christ won this threefold victory, death could not hold Him. If Christ rose, He did so because He had won. Therefore the central verity of the Christian faith, and the central note of Christian preaching is the Resurrection. This explains the meaning of the Cross; and must issue in the exaltation and the coming of the King.

Acts 2: 34-36

We come now to the final words of the apostolic discourse; words to which all the rest have led up; words which constitute the Pentecostal proclamation.

Peter had commenced by saying, " Be this known unto you." He had continued by explaining that all they saw was in fulfilment of their ancient prophecies: " This is that which hath been spoken by the prophet Joel "; and that all had come to pass as the result of the ministry of Jesus.

He now passed from explanation to application. He

had completed his argument, and was seeking a verdict. His last words were: " Let all the house of Israel therefore know assuredly, that God hath made Him both Lord and Christ, this Jesus Whom ye crucified." This proclamation was preceded by an arresting illustration:

" For David ascended not into the heavens: but he saith himself,

> The Lord said unto my Lord, Sit Thou on my right hand,
> Till I make Thine enemies the footstool of Thy feet."

In our examination of this final movement in the apostolic discourse we will take first the proclamation, and then return to the illustration.

The last note of the proclamation took the men who were listening back to the apostle's first reference to the Person. He had commenced on the level of their knowledge, and in the region of their contempt, with the words: " Jesus of Nazareth." Then he had led them on to statements concerning Christ which had challenged their belief, and which had probably raised many questions in their minds. With stately argument, and scriptural demonstration, he had proceeded from point to point;—A Man approved of God; a Man crucified, not by accident nor by blunder, but by the determinate counsel of high heaven; a Man raised from among the dead in spite of all their Sadducean unbelief; a Man lifted high and placed at the right hand of God in glory; a Man receiving there in mystic manner the gift long promised to the nation, of the outpoured Spirit; a Man pouring out this gift. As they had followed and wondered, perhaps they had lost sight of the Man of Nazareth, and forgot the villainy of their own crucifixion of Him, in the strange things that were being said to them. So the apostle finally brought them back face to face with the same Person, in the words, " This Jesus Whom ye crucified."

This is a matter of great importance, as it serves to emphasize the identity of the Person. If these men were inclined to think that perhaps the apostle's conception of Jesus was changing, and that as he ascended the heights and saw the light of the heavenly, he was forgetful himself of the Person to Whom he had been attached; they found that he brought them back again very definitely to that same Person; " This Jesus Whom ye crucified."

The proclamation, by claiming that this Jesus had been made by God, both Lord and Christ, emphasized the central doctrine of the Resurrection. The One at the right hand of power, the One elevated by God to Lordship, and manifested as the anointed Christ, fulfilling all the promises and purposes of the past; this One is the actual One Who was crucified, and therefore must be the One Who had been raised.

The actual proclamation was that " God hath made Him both Lord and Christ." A natural reading of this word of the apostle makes it plain that he intended to declare that in the fact of resurrection, and in the fact of ascension, and in all those mysteries which are so difficult to speak of in the language of time and sense, God did definitely put Him in the place indicated by the twofold designation, " Lord and Christ." The word " *made* " here, is a very common one, but it is a word that is always indicative of a single act; it indicates a crisis; it indicates the fact that now, the process being ended, the consummation had been reached. " God hath *made* Him."

The intention of the apostle's declaration was not that of signifying the perpetual Lordship of Christ, though that also was included. There is a sense in which through all the years of public ministry He was God's anointed One, speaking the word of authority; both Lord and Christ. Here, however, the apostle indicated the fact that at a crisis, definitely, positively, God did by one act, make Him both Lord and Christ. In the eternal counsel and purpose of God, the Son of God was the Saviour before sin was committed, for the Lamb was slain in that eternal counsel from the foundation of the world. But now this fact had become part of human history, as well as part of a divine purpose.

This was, and is *the* Pentecostal proclamation. God hath made him *Lord.* The word Lord indicates His personal supremacy. He hath made Him *Christ.* The word Christ indicates His relative supremacy.

God hath made Him Lord; that is, hath vindicated His Lordship; hath declared in the sight of heaven, and earth, and hell, the fact that He is Lord by an inherent superiority. That fact was ratified by God in His resurrection, and in His ascension. When one speaks of the inherent supremacy of Jesus Christ, one refers to the fact that He is Lord,—whether we will or not,—by virtue of what He is. Jesus of Nazareth is Lord. He is *facile princeps* among the sons of men, incomparable in ideals and realizations, in ethical purposes, in moral achievement, in grace, and grandeur, and beauty of character. Whether we submit to Him or not, is another matter. Whether we choose to have other lords reigning over us, is not now the question.

There is none other to compare with Him. No other ideal has broken upon the imagination of man that comes into comparison with the supernal and superlative loveliness and light of the strange picture that the four Gospels give us of the man called Jesus of Nazareth.

This Lordship God has recognized and ratified. He has lifted out of the human race this Man Who is of it, and He has put Him in the place of Lordship. In His humanity Jesus fulfilled, not merely the hope and aspiration of humanity, but the will and intention of Deity. " Let us make man in our own image " was the ancient and eternal counsel. Behold this Man in Jesus. God hath made Him Lord.

But, thank God, there is another word. He hath made Him Lord *and* Christ. We must interpret the word

[81]

THE ACTS OF THE APOSTLES

Christ by the Old Testament. We must go back to its ritual and its ceremony, to its hopes, its aspirations, its increasing light, to its sob, and its sigh, and its singing, if we would know what the word Christ means. When we know it all, we do not fully know what Christ means. We need the New Testament also to tell us what Christ means. For first values we need the Old Testament. The word itself emerges in a very dark day in Israel's history. In the day of the Judges, when chaos was everywhere, one woman in answer to faith was given a child, Samuel; and she sang a song. It was her own song. Probably Hannah did not know the value of her song in its wider application, but it was an interpretation of the Divine method in that dark age. That song ended with the words " His anointed "; and the Septuagint, the Greek version of the Scriptures, translates it " His Christ." There the great idea first appears. According to that song the Christ was the King Who was to come. We move on through the history to those days of clearer vision, the days of the prophets, and we find that the Anointed was seen as anointed to loose the captive, to open the prison door, to bind up the broken-hearted, to preach the acceptable year of our Lord, and the day of vengeance of our God. There we see the Anointed supreme in a great and glorious sovereignty; but we also see the Anointed bowed and broken beneath a weight of sorrows, and we hear the Seer sing of Him, " He was wounded for our transgressions, He was bruised for our iniquities; the chastisement of our peace was upon Him." Now said Peter, He hath made Him—this Jesus—the Anointed. He it is Who has fulfilled the hope, realized the aspiration, provided the Atonement, made possible the restoration.

This final declaration of Peter must be interpreted by all his previous argument. We must go over those seven movements again if we would understand the ultimate meaning of His Lordship and Messiahship. Who is this

that God makes Lord and Christ? Jesus of Nazareth;
a Man approved of God; delivered to death; raised from
the dead; ascended to the right hand; Receiver of the
fulness of the Holy Spirit; Communicator of that fulness to the waiting souls on earth. All these things are
necessary, for an interpretation of the royalty of Jesus,
and of the virtues and values of His saviourhood.

Let us take those seven matters once again, and refer
to them in other terms, attempting to deduce from the
historic facts their moral and spiritual values. He hath
made *Him* Lord and Christ; crowned humanity, is at the
centre of the universe; vindicated holiness, holds the
sceptre; sacrifice, as the principle of deliverance, is upon
the Throne; ultimate victory, as demonstrated by resurrection is there, and all the fight is the skirmishing
of administration;—spiritually Armageddon is already
fought and won; it is not open to debate as to whether
God or the devil is going to win; the victory is won;—
He received the promise of the Father, and so established
fellowship between God and humanity.

Yes, but more; He, pouring forth this gift upon frail
and fainting men and women, their paralyzed lives were
remade.

So the moral and spiritual values of the Lordship of
Christ are these—A crowned humanity, holiness, sacrifice, victory, fellowship, and power. " Let all the house
of Israel therefore know assuredly, that God hath made
Him both Lord and Christ."

Now let us turn back to Peter's illustration. Speaking
to these men, familiar with the ancient Scriptures, he
said, " David ascended not into the heavens." That
takes us back to what he had already said concerning
David when arguing for Resurrection—" Brethren, I
may say unto you freely of the patriarch David, that he
both died and was buried, and his tomb is with us unto
this day." Exactly the same thought is now expressed
with regard to ascension and to crowning.

[83]

[Acts 2:34-36]

In this statement we have a clear revelation of what Peter meant by ascension. If ascension was merely the passing of the spirit out from material limitation into the larger life that lay beyond, then David did ascend into the heavens. But if ascension meant the coming out of death of the body of the person that passed into it, and the passing of that same body into the heavens, then David did not ascend, for, as the apostle says, " His tomb is with us unto this day." Peter now made a quotation from the Psalms, and said it was from a Psalm which David wrote. In our Bibles it is Psalm 110. One wonders whether Peter would ever have quoted that Psalm in this connection if he had not heard Jesus Him-self do so (Matt. 22:44).

Reference to this Psalm will show that it is peculiarly a Psalm of the Messiah. It falls into two parts. In the first four verses the Messiah-King is presented in His relation to Jehovah. In the last verses the same King is presented in His own might, and in the ultimate victory of His judgment. In the first four verses the Psalmist sang of the King; Who is seen in relation to Jehovah, appointed and strengthened by Jehovah, surrounded by His people; and the King is Priest;

> " Thou art a priest forever,
> After the order of Melchizedek."

In the closing part of the Psalm this selfsame King is seen in His might and victory, proceeding through judgment to the ultimate establishment of His Kingdom. This is the Psalm that Peter quoted in exposition or illustration of the claim he made for Jesus of Nazareth. All that the Psalmist saw in dim and distant vision from some mountain height, and expressed in song, is fulfilled in the Christ. The Christ is the One appointed and strengthened by Jehovah. The Christ is the One Who gathers His people around Him, the people that become willing in the day of His power, the people who are as

dew issuing from the womb of the morning, in freshness
and beauty, and strength. That is the vision Peter had
in mind as he declared that Jesus of Nazareth, the Person Whom they crucified, was thus appointed of God.

But let us turn to our Lord's quotation of this selfsame
passage, as it is found in the Gospel of Matthew.

" Now while the Pharisees were gathered together,
Jesus asked them a question, saying, What think ye of the
Christ? Whose Son is He? They say unto Him, The
Son of David. He saith unto them, How then doth
David in the Spirit call Him Lord, saying,

> The Lord said unto My Lord,
> Sit Thou on My right hand,
> Till I put Thine enemies underneath Thy feet?

If David then calleth Him Lord, How is He His Son?
And no one was able to answer Him a word."

Let us observe the relation of that question of Christ
to what had gone before. His enemies had asked Him
three questions; and He asked one. Every one they
asked, He answered; the one He asked, they could not
answer. Their first was a political question. It was
asked by a coalition of Pharisees and Herodians. It was
concerned with the paying of tribute. The second question was a theological one. It was asked by Sadducees,
and had to do with resurrection in which they did not
believe. The last was an ethical question. It was asked
by a lawyer, a sincere man, and yet for the moment in all
probability a tool and mouthpiece of the rest, as to which
was the greatest commandment.

Jesus answered particularly and in detail every one of
them. To the question about tribute, He said: " Render
therefore unto Cæsar the things that are Cæsar's; and
unto God the things that are God's "; to the question
about resurrection, " In the resurrection they neither
marry nor are given in marriage. . . . God is not the
God of the dead, but of the living; " to the question about

[85]

THE ACTS OF THE APOSTLES

law, "Thou shalt love the Lord thy God with all thy heart, and with all thy soul, and with all thy mind, thou shalt love thy neighbour as thyself." He then explained how He had been able to answer, by drawing attention to Himself, and setting up the claims of an absolute supremacy in every department. "The Lord said unto My Lord." Whose son is that? David's. Then how does David call his Son his Lord? They gave Him no answer. We know the answer. David's Son is David's Lord, because David's Son, of David's nature, is also of other nature than David's nature.

Interpreting the quotation then by Christ's own use of it, the Lordship of Jesus is that of His final authority in matters political, theological, ethical. He is still the supreme authority in all national and international matters. He is moreover Lord in an everlasting dominion, dealing with the whole life, that which lies beyond the present, finally cancelling death in His Lordship. He is Lord to-day, ruling this life, giving us the laws of conduct for time, and earthly conditions. Death has become a mere transition, for we are in His empire now, and shall forever be.

The quotation shows that the appointment is also to restful dominion.

"The Lord said unto My Lord, Sit Thou on My right hand." The right hand is the place of power and the place of peace. There is no panic in the nature of God, and there is no need for it in those who know Him.

But observe finally that the appointment has its limits: "Till I make Thine enemies the footstool of Thy feet." Not *while* I make Thine enemies the footstool of Thy feet. That is not the word; it is not that God has put Him there as Lord and Christ while He carries on a process of getting His Kingdom ready for Him. God has not yet begun to make His foes the footstool of His feet. The doing of that lies beyond the present age.

To quote another passage: "He shall not cry, nor lift

up His voice, nor cause it to be heard in the street. A bruised reed will He not break, and a dimly burning wick will He not quench; *He will bring forth justice in truth."* When He sends forth judgment to victory He will break the bruised reed and quench the smoking flax, and will win His last victory over finally rebellious hearts by the processes of judgment.

That day has not come. When is it coming? We know not. God has given us no calendar. We do not ask to know. Our comfort is that He sits at the right hand now, the Lord and the Christ.

That is the Pentecostal message; that is the all-inclusive witness of the Spirit to-day; and therefore it is the all-inclusive witness of the Church; that alone for which the Church can claim Pentecostal power. Our business—may God grant that it may be more than our business, our passion it ought to be,—to make Him Lord and Christ, Whom God hath made Lord and Christ, in our own lives, in our homes, in our cities, in the wide wide world.

Acts 2: 37-47

In the Hebrew Economy Pentecost was described as the " Feast of harvest, the first fruits of thy labours." The spiritual suggestiveness of the feast was fulfilled in the Christian dispensation on this occasion.

We have followed the course of Peter's sermon. Now we consider the results of the preaching of that sermon. The story is contained in these verses. The immediate results are chronicled in the first five (37–41); and the continuous results in the remainder of the paragraph (vv. 42–47).

The immediate results were: First, conviction and enquiry; secondly, instruction and exhortation; and finally, obedience, and the addition of those who received the Spirit.

When they heard the message of the apostle they were

[Acts 2: 37-47]

pricked in their heart, and said: "Brethren, what shall we do?" This enquiry immediately followed Peter's final proclamation concerning the Lordship of Jesus. In making that proclamation he did so in such a manner as to urge upon these people the sin of the death of Jesus—"God hath made Him both Lord and Christ, this Jesus Whom ye crucified." Two thoughts were thus borne in upon the mind of the people that listened;—first, the fact of the Lordship of Jesus; and secondly, the fact of their sin in the light of that Lordship. Conviction of these two things produced the immediate enquiry, "Brethren, what shall we do?"

The preaching which is to produce conviction in the minds of men concerning their need must be that which presents the Lordship of Christ. It was the fact of the absolute supremacy of Jesus, that produced in the minds of these men the sense of their own sin. We are often being told that men to-day lack the sense of sin that characterized the thinking and conviction of our fathers. That is probably true. One of the greatest difficulties of the hour is that men are not conscious of sin. Among the reasons for this may be the fact that we have too often brought men to the Mosaic Law, and too little to the pure majesty and lonely splendour of the Lordship of Christ. There are men to-day who never tremble though they recite the Decalogue with great regularity; but we have yet to meet the man who can be brought face to face with the Lord Jesus Christ as He is presented to us in these Gospel stories, who can stand in the presence of His inherent Lordship, and of that Lordship which He won by the process of His work of redemption, without coming to the conviction of sin. If we are to measure our life by the standards of any law, including the Hebrew law, we may know little of trembling; but when we stand in the presence of this Lord—first in the presence of the light, the holiness, and the splendour of His character; and then in the presence of that ineffable mystery of His Passion, in which Love has wrought itself out into visibility—then we shall place our hand upon our lip and cry Unclean! It was when Peter traced the story of this Man of Nazareth, crowned Lord of all, God's eternal Type, as well as God's perfect Redeemer, that these men cried out in the consciousness of their own sin.

This conviction was produced by the double witness, that of a man, and that of the Holy Spirit. To attempt to produce this conviction by the preaching of Christ in one's own strength, would be to utterly fail. And it is also true that the Spirit is dependent upon the witness of man. Where these two are united in witness, then these results follow.

Then followed the apostle's instruction and exhortation. His instruction as to sin was expressed in the words: "Repent ye, and be baptized every one of you in the name of the Lord Jesus Christ, unto the remission of your sins." His instruction as to the Lordship of Christ, in the words: "And ye shall receive the gift of the Holy Spirit." There must be on the part of those who raise this enquiry, a turning from sin, and faith, which is symbolized by baptism; but there must also be the reception of the Spirit, in order that they may know the Lordship of Christ and obey that Lordship. His encouragement was expressed in words which declared that the ancient promise was made to them, and to their children, and to all such as God should call. Moreover he warned them to save themselves from the untoward generation.

Now observe carefully what is written about that which followed immediately: "They that received his word were baptized; and there were added . . . about three thousand souls." The use of that word "added" here, is an interesting and valuable one to observe. The old Version read that they "were added to the Church." The phrase "to the Church" has been omitted, and the italized words "Unto them" substituted. As an actual

[89]

THE ACTS OF THE APOSTLES
fact neither phrase is in the text. Presently, it is again written, "The Lord added to them," and here also the words "to them" are not to be found in the text. The statements respectively are, "There were added, . . . three thousand souls"; and, again, "The Lord added . . . those that were being saved." In each case the real intention is that of showing the growth of the Church. The word translated "added" literally means to *place forward;* that is, the placing of certain things next to things already in existence, for the increase of that which is already in existence. Secondarily, these people were added to the one hundred and twenty, added to the company of the disciples; but primarily, they were added to the Lord. In that hour when the Holy Spirit fell upon the hundred and twenty, the hundred and twenty were added to the Lord, made members of His Body, His flesh and His bones; in the deep and mystic sense of the New Testament teaching, they began to share the common life of the Christ of God. Here also on this day of Pentecost these people convinced, obedient, were added to the Lord, and in their addition they gained all the values of His death, and the virtues of His life. In their addition to Him, He gained the enlarged instrument through which to proclaim His message, and to do His work in the world.

So the first results of the Pentecostal sermon are seen. Conviction and enquiry produced not by the eloquence of the preacher, not by his logical argument, but by his declaration of truth concerning Jesus in the power of the Spirit; and by the Spirit's demonstration of the truth declared, in the mind and heart of those who listened.

Conviction and enquiry were immediately followed by instruction and exhortation on the part of the apostle and the other apostles who were with him. Obedience, by turning to Christ as Lord, and repentance in the presence of sin, was followed by the reception of the Spirit, and the adding of these souls to the Lord. So the Church

THE ACTS OF THE APOSTLES

grew, the instrument through which our Master was able to deliver His message, and carry on His work.

Now let us glance at the continuous results. There were unquestionably untabulated results of that first sermon in the power of Pentecost. There were gathered together at the Feast devout men from every nation under heaven. In that company of three thousand, who heard, and were convinced, who enquired, and obeyed, who received the Spirit, and were added to the Lord, were people from the whole known and civilized world. As they returned to their lands and homes, they went as members of the mystic body of Christ, sharing His life. In the places to which they went, Christ found His opportunity through them.

There are two instances at least in the Acts of the Apostles that reveal the truth of this. The most conspicuous perhaps is that of the Church in Rome. Paul wrote his letter to the saints in Rome. Desiring to see them, and being prevented, he sent them a letter. Whence came the Church there? We have no story of the visit of an apostle. " Sojourners from Rome " heard that Pentecostal sermon. " Sojourners from Rome " became obedient to the message, and went back, and so in all likelihood the infant Church was founded. When Saul of Tarsus was stricken by the roadside it was to the Church in Damascus that he was going. Believers were gathered together in that city. Whence came they? We have no account of an apostolic visitation. Most probably as a result of this first sermon, men had gone back to Damascus, and so the Church had been formed. How far the results went no man can ever tell. The sermon was preached in the power of the Spirit concerning Christ. Immediate results followed, but all the results of such preaching can never be tabulated. The scattered people, going here, there, and everywhere, carried the evangel, carried more than the evangel,—they carried the power of the Christ-life by the Spirit.

THE ACTS OF THE APOSTLES

But there were other clearly manifest results. The picture of the new society, the Christian Church, is full of interest. Notice its ordinances. " They continued stedfastly in the apostles' teaching, and fellowship, in the breaking of bread and the prayers." These are four ordinances of Christian fellowship. Baptism is not an ordinance of Christian fellowship; it is the ordinance that indicates the entrance upon fellowship. The four ordinances to be constantly observed in Christian fellowship are: the apostles' teaching, the fellowship, the breaking of bread, and the prayers. These are not the ordinances of Christian service, but of Christian fellowship. Service lies beyond them. They form the method of equipment for service, and are the ordinances for conserving the life of the members of the Church. With the subject of the apostles' teaching we need not tarry now. Suffice it to say it is preserved for us in the New Testament. The ordinance of fellowship, we have too much neglected. Are we not tempted to read these two words " teaching " and " fellowship " together, as though they indicated but one fact? Or are we not inclined to think of fellowship as merely the sentimental oneness of people, who were listening to apostolic doctrine? But that surely is not the meaning of the word here. The use of the word fellowship here indicates certain definite habits of the Saints in their assembling together. I believe that one of the secrets of the success of the Methodist Church has been its Class Meeting. In that meeting they have had at any rate something of the realization of Christian fellowship. Dr. Dale of Birmingham once said to me, " If I could graft the Methodist Class Meeting on to our Congregational Church life, I would do it to-morrow, and make attendance upon it obligatory." It has become very difficult for Christian people to talk of the things of Christ to each other. They meet together in ordinary life, and they talk of everything except the deepest things of their spiritual life; and that not because

THE ACTS OF THE APOSTLES

they have not deep experience, not because they are unfamiliar with the things of God and His Kingdom, but because they have never learned how to help each other in mutual converse concerning them. Those early Christians talked together of the things of their spiritual life, and there is no surer way to conserve and strengthen Christian life than that of such fellowship. The Old Testament has a gracious illustration of it in its last book. In those days of formalism against which Malachi thundered: " Then they that feared Jehovah spake one with another." That was not a Prayer meeting, that was a fellowship meeting.

Then there was the breaking of the bread; that is, the gathering together as members of one family, around the one table, in obedience to the Lord's command, to take the emblems of bread and the fruit of the vine, in memory of Him, and in proclamation of His death upon the Cross.

Finally there was the ordinance of " prayers," that is of systematic, definite, positive praying, not as individuals only, but in connection with one another.

The effect produced by this company of people who continued steadfastly in the apostles' teaching, in fellowship, in the breaking of bread, and in the prayers, was that " fear came upon every soul." The outside multitudes were conscious of fear in the presence of this strange new society existing in the midst of their life.

The fellowship in spiritual things had its outcome in other fellowship;—the fellowship of goods, fellowship in worship—they continued in the temple worshipping; fellowship in home life—from house to house they passed in social inter-relationship, eating " with gladness and singleness of heart." They did all this, " praising God " —and mark this well—" having favour with all the people." The persecution of the early Christians never originated with the people, but always with the rulers, the priests.

[Acts 2: 37–47]

"Having favour with all the people." If we fail there, if the Church is not in that attitude now, what are we to do? Are we to leave the Church and criticize it? A thousand times No! Rather let us face the fact of our failure, repent, do the first works, realize the Christian fellowship, and so begin to win back the favour we have lost. Have we lost favour with the people? To-day it is being admitted on every hand that the Church, as such, has ceased to have favour with the masses of the people. If so, why is it? Fundamentally she has failed to realize her own corporate life and to reveal the life of the Christ of God. She has turned to other lords and other masters, and has adopted other methods than the methods of the Christ Himself.

The Church of Christ—take a local Chuch as indicating the great and ideal application—a local Church, so at the disposal of the Spirit as that the Spirit through the Church can flash and flame upon the outside world, so as to amaze, perplex, and raise an enquiry; a local Church, one within its own borders in fellowship with Christ, and testifying to Christ is invariably a Church in favour with the people. Not that we should seek the patronage of the multitude, but that we are so to reveal Christ as to be centres of attraction to the multitude. The moment we depart from Him, we lose the crowd. The Church of Christ, where the Christ Himself is the supreme revelation made,—not only through the individual lives of its members, but in its corporate capacity,—where the compassion of Christ and the life of Christ are manifest in the mutual inter-relationship of the souls forming the Christian Church, is the Church to which the weary and woebegone will turn. That is the truly influential Church. How we have degraded that word influential. We call a Church influential now because of the kind of people that attend it, because of the money which it raises for philanthropic objects. There was a Church in the olden days that said: "I am rich, and have gotten riches, and have need of nothing," and the Master walking amid the golden candlesticks said: "Thou . . . knowest not that thou art the wretched one and miserable and poor and blind and naked." So He would say to-day to many Churches which we describe as influential. The influential Church is the company of loyal souls who "continue steadfastly in the apostles' teaching and fellowship, and in the breaking of bread and the prayers," who eat their meat with gladness and singleness of heart, who manifest in their individual lives and corporate capacity the strength, the beauty, the glory, the compassion of the Christ. Wherever there is such a Church you will find the Church that has favour with the people.

The lessons of this study for the worker, and especially for those in the ministry are patent. First, preach for a verdict. That is what Peter did. Secondly, when you have preached, take time to gather your results. Thirdly, having gathered them, set them in order.

Finally let us remember for our encouragement that all the results of our teaching and preaching, if we are at the disposal of the Spirit of God, can never be tabulated. If we can tabulate the results of preaching, then the preaching is a comparative failure. But it is not so with any man who will but bring himself, with his ignorance or knowledge, with his weakness or strength, with his halting or eloquence, to the Spirit of God, for the declaration of this evangel. Rome will feel its power, Damascus will feel the effect of it. The far distant places of the world will be the places where the last ripples of the water touch the shore, and he will never know till the Day break. Cast thy bread upon the waters, for after many days thou shalt find it.

Acts 3: 1-10

We have dealt with the first impression produced by the Church, and have considered the first sermon preached in the light and power of the Holy Spirit. We now commence the section dealing with the first opposition (3-4: 31). The cause of this opposition was that of a miracle wrought, the preaching of the resurrection which resulted, and the consequent hatred of the Sadducees, who were rationalists in religion. The effect of the opposition was that Peter bore a new testimony, the priests indulged in a new threatening, and the Church received a new filling of power.

Our present meditation is concerned with the miracle. This is the first miracle recorded in the book of the Acts of the Apostles. As time passed on there was a gradual decrease in physical miracles, and a corresponding increase in spiritual wonders. Our Lord never set any great value upon the physical miracles He wrought, as arguments or credentials, either for His Divinity or His mission. He distinctly said to His own disciples, "Believe Me . . . or else believe Me for the very works' sake." His supreme evidence was Himself. His supreme argument was Himself. But in the midst of that unbelieving and superstitious and materialistic age, it was necessary that there should be material manifestations of power to arrest the attention. In proportion as the Church emerged into all her spiritual glory, she ceased to see the material miracles which were necessary in the earthly ministry of Christ. They were rendered unnecessary in view of the wider and more spacious work of spiritual testimony and power. In that fact is revealed the meaning of Christ's word to His disciples, "Greater works than these shall ye do; because I go unto the Father." By that word He did not mean that they would work more wonderful miracles in the material realm, for they did not do so. He meant rather that the miracle wrought in the material is never so marvellous as the miracle wrought in the spiritual realm. When He passed to the Father they were to work greater works—the wonders in the spiritual realm.

Yet the story of this miracle is very interesting, and there is no doubt that it is recorded here because it is necessary to the elucidation of what followed. The preaching which stirred up opposition was the result of this miracle. The opposition which resulted in further preaching and greater boldness, grew immediately out of this miracle. We will pass over the story three times; first to notice the simple facts; secondly, to notice the supreme facts; and finally, to suggest the symbolized facts.

The simple facts may be dismissed briefly. This is the story of a lame man healed. Luke declares that this man was a cripple from birth. That in itself is suggestive. Observe carefully the particular words made use of in the story of his healing: " Immediately his *feet* and his *ankle-bones received strength.* And *leaping up,* he stood, and began to walk." Perhaps only medical men can fully appreciate the meaning of these words; they are the peculiar, technical words of a medical man. The word translated *feet,* is only used by Luke, and occurs nowhere else. It indicates his discrimination between different parts of the human foot. This particular word refers to the base, or heel. The phrase *ankle-bones* is again a medical phrase, to be found nowhere else. The word " leaping up " describes the coming suddenly into socket of something that was out of place, the articulation of a joint. This then is a very careful medical description of what happened in connection with this man.

This then is the simple story. A man crippled, not as the result of accident, not as the result of sin in his own life, but from birth, suffering from congenital disease, was suddenly made to stand, to walk; in the exuberance of a new-found strength he suddenly leapt within the precincts of the Temple.

How was this wrought? At the word of Peter and John. How great was the gap between the second and third chapters of this book we cannot tell. Chapter two

THE ACTS OF THE APOSTLES

ends with the statement of the fact that the Lord added to the company of believers, by adding to Himself, day by day, those that were being saved. That statement ended the chapter of enthusiasm, the chapter of ecstasy, the chapter of a flaming vision, the chapter of song and praise and proclamation, and of crowds swept into relationship with Jesus Christ. Chapter three begins with the statement that two men, Peter and John, were going to the Temple. They were " going up . . . at the hour of prayer, being the ninth hour." There were three hours in the day, separate hours, at which people gathered to the Temple, and the evening hour was the hour of sacrifice, the ninth hour. The hour of prayer was half an hour after the sacrifice had been offered. In it the incense offering was ascending and men prayed. Peter and John went to the Temple, not at the hour of sacrifice, but at the hour of prayer which followed sacrifice. As we look at these two men, going up to the Temple, no tongue of fire was resting upon their heads; there was nothing to attract attention; they were walking in the commonplace; the ecstasy of the day of Pentecost had passed. They were two men who, in the earlier years of their life, had known each other, and had been friends; who yet had probably been perpetual irritants to each other. Peter was the practical man. John was the poet. Peter was a doer of deeds. John was a dreamer of dreams. The whole fact of their difference flames out in the last picture we have of them before the day of Pentecost. Peter, standing on the shores of the lake, after Jesus had restored him, said, " Lord, and what shall this man do? " It was the question of his perplexity about John. Peter's prescription for all trouble was doing. He had little patience with dreaming. Yet mark the sacred and beautiful significance of the fact that beyond the Cross and Resurrection, and after Pentecost, Peter the doer and John the dreamer went into close fellowship. They had found

[98]

that they were not antagonistic but complementary to
each other. At the word of Peter, spoken in the comradeship of the silence of the dreamer, this man, lame
from birth, walked, leapt, and praised God.

The word was spoken in the name of Jesus Christ of
Nazareth; but it was spoken by a man who was in possession of all that the name indicated. " Silver and gold
have I none; but what I *have,* that give I thee. In the
name of Jesus Christ of Nazareth, walk." This was no
apology. Peter meant rather to boast in his Lord. True
he had neither silver nor gold, but he had something far
better, and in the name of Jesus of Nazareth he pronounced his commanding and powerful word.

The simple facts then are that a cripple whose life was
maintained by the alms of those who passed to the Temple—a man who, had he lived in this day, would have
been designated a professional beggar—was suddenly
lifted, and set upon his feet, and made into an ardent
worshipper in the spiritual realm, by the word of two
men who used the name of Jesus.

Let us then consider the supreme facts revealed. The
first grows entirely out of our clear vision of the simple
facts already referred to. The supreme fact is that of
the continuity of the activity of the Christ. He was still
at work, and doing exactly what He had done in the days
of His flesh. We cannot read this story of the healing
of the man, a cripple from birth, without being reminded
of the story of the life of our Lord, Who when passing
through the Bethesda porches, found a man who for
thirty and eight years had been in the grip of an infirmity,
and healed him. The healing of that man in the Bethesda
porches, humanly speaking, cost Jesus His life. When
He had healed him He told him to carry his bed, and the
rulers criticized him for carrying his bed on the Sabbath
day. When they found Jesus they charged Him with
Sabbath breaking. Jesus answered them, " My Father
worketh even until now, and I work." In effect He said

to these men who charged Him with breaking Sabbath;
I have no Sabbath, for God has no Sabbath, in the presence of human suffering! I have worked on the Sabbath Day to give this man the chance of Sabbath, such as he has never had! "For this cause *therefore* the Jews sought the more to kill Him, because He not only brake the Sabbath, but also called God His own Father, making Himself equal with God"; and they never ceased their hatred; and their planning and plotting never ended until they had killed Him. Humanly speaking the healing of that man cost Him His life. Divinely speaking also it cost Him His life. He had healed that sinning man by the right of atonement, not then made visible to human sight, but existing in the nature of God, to be wrought out into visibility by the very Cross, which resulted from what He had done. Now said Peter, "In the name of Jesus Christ of Nazareth, walk!" In the name of the One Who wrought with God to set right human limitation by dealing with human sin. So, as we see this man responding, we see the Christ continuing His work.

But if in this miracle we see the continuity of the activity of the Christ, we see also the commencement of activity through His Body, which is the Church. Peter and John were no longer isolated disciples. They were "members of His body, of His flesh, and of His bones," to use the mystic language of the New Testament writer. Peter and John were living members of the living Christ, and therefore the instruments of His will and of His power. Christ healed through these two men. Peter fastened his eyes upon this man. Peter spoke directly to this man. "Silver and gold have I none; but what I have, that give I thee." Then he took him by the hand, and the Greek word signifies a seizing by the hand, a grip that lifted. There is not the slightest evidence in the story of any faith on the part of the man. Nearly all the commentators say that he must have exercised his faith in order to be healed, but it is not stated in the story. His healing was a direct act of the Christ, through these men. Peter looked, and through the eyes of Peter there flashed the love of the Christ. Then Peter spoke, and it was the very language of Jesus. He also was a Man of poverty so far as this world's goods were concerned, and now through two members of His Body He was able to say, " Silver and gold have I none; but what I have, that give I thee." Through that touch, that lifting with a strong hand, Christ was making contact with human need, through the members of His Body.

The third supreme fact then was that of the communication of life, in order to the correction of disability. What was the need so far as the man was concerned? Leaping instead of lameness; giving praise instead of asking alms. This communication of life, equal to the accomplishment of both the wonders, was wrought by the living Christ, through the members of His Body.

We turn now to the last line of our consideration. Here as always, the miracle has a spiritual significance. He Who in the days of His flesh said, " I am the Truth," by that declaration suggested the unification of all life in His own Person. Jesus never divided as we do, between the sacred and the secular; and the very laws by which He operated in the physical realm, were those by which He wrought in the spiritual. There was not a miracle He wrought but has its spiritual significance as well as its material demonstration; and what is true of the Master was true here also. The day of Pentecost as a day, as an event, as an initiation, was over. The tongues of fire had passed out of sight. The sound of the mighty rushing wind was no more. The ecstatic, enthusiastic songs were silenced. This is the first picture of the Church as she is to be, as the result of the tongue of fire and the mighty rushing wind, and the enthusiasm. Pentecost as a flaming fire was never intended to be the continuous and normal condition of the Christian Church. The conditions after Pentecost are symbolized in these chapters

THE ACTS OF THE APOSTLES

of the Acts of the Apostles. The normal for the Church of God is in the commonplaces, and among the cripples. The places of inspiration and vision are given, in order that we may translate them into virtue and victory, as we go to the world in its need.

What then are the symbolized facts? First that the Church's opportunity is lame humanity, lame from its birth. It is waste of time to discuss how humanity came to be lame; it is lame, and that is the trouble. The Church's opportunity is not to build schools and erect forums where we shall discuss how men were born lame. The disciples of old came to Jesus with a question, a wonderfully tempting metaphysical and psychological question, " Rabbi, who sinned, this man, or his parents, that he should be born blind?" He dismissed their question: " Neither did this man sin, nor his parents; but that the works of God should be made manifest in him we must work the works of Him that sent Me." Lame humanity is the Church's opportunity. This is indeed a pathetic story and picture; lame humanity at the Beautiful Gate, but outside! There at the gate, with all the mountains' far-flung splendours encircling the city; there, where the steps went up to the Temple, he lay; but outside. That is humanity's position, in the midst of beauty, but not of it; in the realm of things lovely and of good report, but excluded. That is the position of humanity everywhere; it sighs and sobs and is in agony at the Beautiful Gate; but it cannot get in. There is the Church's opportunity.

What was this man doing? He was not seeking for strength to walk, but for alms. Alms are the means by which men live, in spite of disability, and without work. That is what humanity is doing everywhere. Work is never the result of sin. The result of sin is that man is trying to live on alms without work! Men are asking alms everywhere; they are paupers, at the Beautiful Gate; and that is the Church's opportunity.

[Acts 3: 1–10]

Secondly the Church's gift is here revealed. "Silver and gold have I none; but what I have, that give I thee." What hast thou then, O Peter, to give to humanity, lame at the Beautiful Gate, excluded, begging? That which cancels disability, that which communicates ability; and ultimately, that which creates worship. First that which cancels disability. Said Peter to this man, I have nothing to give you that will help you to maintain your life while you are a cripple; but I have something to cure the crippled condition; and make you able to earn your own living. That is Christianity. Christianity has not come into the presence of the world's wounds and woes and agony to give out doles in order to help it to bear its limitation. Christianity comes to give men life, and put them on their feet, and so enable them to do without alms. Christianity faces a man with a gift that cancels his disability. Christianity takes hold of a man whose ankles are out of joint, and makes them articulate. That man knew more about ankles than any man in Jerusalem, for he had lain on the steps, and had seen all the people coming up to the Temple for years. A man may know much about ankles, and never know how to walk. Christianity does not come to teach a man philosophy. It comes to give him life, to give him that which cancels his disability, and to communicate ability, and so to create worship.

If that is the Church's gift, then what is the Church's method? She must speak and work in the name of Jesus Christ of Nazareth, the risen Christ. We are on the other side of the story of the Cross and the Resurrection. This word was spoken in His name; but it was spoken by a man who shared His very nature. If we go to lame humanity at the Beautiful Gate in our own name, or in any other name, we may even give them some alms that will help them to bear their disability, but we shall never set them on their feet. It is in His name that the Church must go.

[103]

Again, Peter and John went in coöperation. " Look on us," said they, as they steadfastly looked at him. Moreover there was contact. Peter took him by the hand and lifted him. " He took him by the right hand, and raised him up." That is the final thing in the Church's method. We must come to the man that lies at the Beautiful Gate begging alms, outside; and take him by the hand. There must be personal, immediate, direct contact. The Church standing afar off, and singing a song which she hopes will reach the dweller in the valley does but mock the need of the dweller in the valley. The Church that comes down to the side of the wounded, weary, woebegone world, and holds out the right hand, and lifts, is the Church through which the Christ is doing His own work, through which the Christ will win His ultimate victory.

Acts 3: 11–26

This paragraph contains the story of how Peter explained to the crowds the meaning of the things that had happened. The scene is peculiarly Hebrew. The place was the Temple, in Solomon's porch. The people were almost undoubtedly permanent residents in Jerusalem, a different crowd from that which had surrounded the apostles on the day of Pentecost. Pentecost was a Jewish feast, and men gathered in the city from all parts. That feast was now over, the multitudes had departed to their own homes; and the company of people who ran into Solomon's porch, gazing with wonder at the healed man, was undoubtedly a company almost exclusively of Hebrews, that is of Israelites.

This address of Peter was peculiarly Hebrew. He referred to God as " The God of Abraham, and of Isaac, and of Jacob "; he declared that " God foreshewed by the mouth of all the prophets "; and toward the end of the address he spoke of the covenant which God made with " Your father Abraham."

The references to Jesus were almost all borrowed from

THE ACTS OF THE APOSTLES

Old Testament Scripture: " The Servant of God " (not
as rendered in the Authorized Version, " the Son," but as
it is accurately translated throughout this passage in the
Revision, " The Servant of God ") ; a word which took
them naturally back to the great prophecy of Isaiah:
" The Holy and the Righteous One," being two descriptions of the Old Testament, each of them having Messianic value; and finally " the Christ " which was but the
Greek form of the Hebrew word Messiah, indicating the
great hope of the people.

The terms in which he spoke of the hopes which Jesus
had created were equally suggestive. " That your sins
may be blotted out," was an immediate quotation from
the great psalm of penitence; " seasons of refreshing
from the presence of the Lord," gathered up and expressed the perpetual note of hopefulness that had sung
itself out in the psalms and prophecies of the ancient
covenant; and when he spoke of the teaching, he referred
to the fulfilment in the Person of Jesus, of the promise
of Moses, that another prophet should be raised up.

The opening and closing words of the address indicate
the fact that the message was peculiarly one to the
Israelitish nation. He said, " Ye men of Israel, why
marvel ye at this man." The apostle meant to say that
men, not of Israel, might have marvelled with greater
show of reason. When we come to the close of the
address, notice very carefully these words, " Unto you
first God having raised up His Servant." The thought
most evidently is that he had been expressing himself
throughout the whole of this explanation of the miracle,
peculiarly and directly to the men of Israel.

It is necessary to emphasize this in order that we may
understand this message. Whatever spiritual principles
are taught, the first application was to the men of Israel.
Let us first consider in broad outline the message to
Israel, and secondly the teaching for ourselves, which
may be deduced therefrom.

[Acts 3: 11–26]

This message from the apostle to Israel falls into three parts. Beginning at the eleventh verse we have the account of the running of the people into Solomon's porch, and the taking hold of Peter and John by this man. It is a graphic picture. It seems as though the healed man was loath to let these men go, who had been the instruments of his healing and blessing. As he laid hold of them, and the people gathered together, Peter seized the opportunity for the correction of the attitude of the people who had gathered together: " Ye men of Israel, why marvel ye at this man? or why fasten ye your eyes on us, as though by our own power or godliness we had made him to walk? " He thus asked them two questions which constituted almost a rebuke, and certainly a correction of their attitude. Then immediately, having rebuked their misapprehension of what they had seen, he began his explanation. His instruction begins at the thirteenth verse and ends with the sixteenth. " The God of Abraham, and of Isaac, and of Jacob "—commencing upon ground that was perfectly familiar to these people, taking them back to the central fact of their religion—he stated two historical facts leading up, so far as they were concerned, to the healing of that man who stood in the midst of them.

Then notice the new note at verse seventeen. " And now, brethren, I know that in ignorance ye did it, as did also your rulers. But the things which God foreshewed by the mouth of all the prophets, that His Christ should suffer, He thus fulfilled." From that verse to the end of the paragraph we have the apostolic appeal. First the correction of the wrong outlook of the house of Israel in the presence of the miracle; then instruction of the men of Israel concerning the real significance of the miracle and its relation to eternal things; and finally the appeal, based upon correction and instruction, to the house of Israel to repent, and to turn back again to God. Such were the main divisions of the address.

His correction consisted of two questions. The first
was, " Why marvel ye at this man? " Now, why should
they not marvel at this man? Was there not a reason
and a cause for marvelling? Here was a man who had
been for forty years incompetent, lame from birth, seeking alms at the Beautiful Gate, a familiar figure to the
crowds of Jerusalem; now he was on his feet, and instead of asking alms from men, he was giving praise to
God. It was a great and wonderful transformation, why
should they not marvel? When the apostle said " Why
marvel ye? " he was preparing the way for something
which was to follow. His choice of words was not careless: " Ye men of Israel"; . . . " The God of
Abraham, of Isaac, and Jacob." If he had only said,
" the God of Abraham," Ishmaelites might have claimed
inclusion in that description. If he had said, " The God
of Abraham and Isaac," Edomites might have come
within that description. He narrowed down the company to whom he spoke when he said, " The God of
Abraham, and Isaac, and Jacob." Jacob became Israel,
and he spoke to them as men of Israel, men who stood
in fleshly and covenant relationship to Jacob, and to him
as Israel, the man ruled by God. He thus reminded them
of their past history. They were men of the covenant,
of the Scriptures, and of the prophets. Therefore he
said, " Ye men of Israel, why marvel *ye?* " You, men
of such history, of such a heritage; you, men with the
records of miracles stretching back through all the centuries; you, men who have seen in these last days so
much of the manifestation of God's power in setting disability right,—" Why marvel *ye* at this man? "

Then followed the second question: " Or why fasten
ye your eyes on us, as though by our own power or godliness we had made him to walk? " Their wonder in the
presence of the miracle was due to their forgetfulness
of their past history, and to the fact that they were out
of fellowship therewith; and the explanation which they

[Acts 3: 11–26]

offered in their own mind as they gazed upon Peter and John, was a false explanation unworthy of that history. He charged the men of Israel with being false to their own history in wondering in the presence of the miracle they had just seen; and he charged them with being unable to interpret the secret of what they had seen. They had never understood or been true to the historical facts, in which they made their boast, or else they would have seen that the ultimate, logical result of all the things they believed, and in the fellowship of which they had lived, was represented in the man at the Beautiful Gate who was healed.

Then immediately he turned to explanation. As he began to explain he went back: " The God of Abraham, and of Isaac, and of Jacob, the God of our fathers." He then made a startling declaration in the ears of those who were listening. One commentator says that the miracle of the speech of Peter is a far more wonderful one than the miracle wrought in the healing of the man who lay at the Beautiful Gate. Notice the daring of Peter, and remember the fear that characterized him before Pentecost. See him now, standing in the temple in Solomon's porch, with the crowds, residents of Jerusalem, about him. He declared " The God of Abraham, and of Isaac, and of Jacob, the God of our fathers, hath glorified His Servant Jesus." A parenthesis commences here, with the words, " Whom ye delivered up " and runs on to the end of the fifteenth verse. The immediate connection of declaration is found by taking the first part of verse thirteen and linking it with verse sixteen. " The God of Abraham, and of Isaac, and of Jacob, the God of our fathers hath glorified His Servant Jesus . . . and by faith in His name hath His name made this man strong, whom ye behold and know: yea, the faith which is through Him hath given him this perfect soundness in the presence of you all." Thus in effect he said: The God of Abraham, the God of your history, the God of your nationality, " the God of our fathers hath glorified His Servant Jesus," hath lifted, exalted Him, to power. The resurrection was not mentioned, but it was implied.

These men were men of Israel, with all the prejudice and the pride of men of Israel; they had looked in amazement at the healed man, feeling that what they saw was a part of this new movement of power, which they thought was outside the covenant, and therefore contrary to the purpose of God. Peter declared that they were blind and foolish, in that they did not see that this thing was part of the operation of their own God, the God Who created their nation, Who was at the centre of all their history.

In stating all this, Peter borrowed the great word of Isaiah " His Servant." That word " Servant " may not appeal to us as it did to a Hebrew. The great prophecy of Isaiah is the prophecy of the Servant of God. We need not now discuss the question as to whether the Servant of God as seen by Isaiah was the ideal nation, or a Person. Both things are surely true. Isaiah saw the nation as a Servant; but he also saw the true principle and purpose realized in a Person in the dim and distant future. The title Servant of God was to the Hebrew a word expressing a hope, a word reminding him forevermore of the ancient prophecies. We must get back into the atmosphere of Solomon's porch, and of these Hebrews thronging Peter, before we begin to apprehend how startling was the thing he said. " The God of Abraham, and of Isaac, and of Jacob, the God of our fathers, hath glorified His Servant." These men would catch the prophetic allusion, and be ready to ask, Who is the Servant of God? Before the enquiry could be put, Peter answered in uttering that word " Jesus." He thus claimed the fulfilment in Christ of all Messianic hope and prediction, declaring that God had glorified Him. These men might well say, and doubtless would say Glorified Him! We saw Him die, He was crucified.

[109]

THE ACTS OF THE APOSTLES

Now return to the parenthesis: " Whom ye delivered up and denied before the face of Pilate, when he had determined to release Him." That was the historic truth. They had denied Him, and delivered Him up, and that in spite of a Gentile attempt to set Him free. Thus he was fastening the guilt upon Israel. Mark the carefulness of his word, " But ye denied the Holy and Righteous One, and asked for a murderer to be granted unto you, and killed the Prince of Life." Here is a case when one wishes that a word might be translated differently. " Prince " is not wholly wrong; but the Greek word is the word that occurs in the Hebrew letter, when the writer speaks of the *Author* and Finisher of faith. We might translate here " The *Author* of Life." Yet *Author* hardly conveys the thought. Very literally, the word means a file-leader, one who takes precedence, one who goes first. This was a hint of what he was about to declare more fully, a hint of resurrection. Let us attempt to keep in mind the background they had of a crucified Man on the green hill, of a malefactor on Golgotha. He said to them, You killed the Holy and Righteous One; you chose the murderer, and flung out the File-Leader in the procession of life, its Author, its Prince. God replied to what you did by raising Him from the dead, and making us witnesses of that resurrection. All that is in parenthesis, but we now see it, in relation to the whole.

Then Peter said: " By faith in His name," the name of Jesus Whom ye saw die, Whose death you brought about, Whom God raised from the dead, and Who is glorified and demonstrated the Servant of God, the long-looked for Messiah; " by faith in His name," this man has been healed. They had marvelled because they had become blind to the goings of their own God, because they were out of harmony with the processes and procedure of the God of Abraham and of Isaac and of Jacob; and consequently they had failed to be able to explain the mystery of the healed man. So that in this instructive

[110]

part of the address, Peter took that man, and showed that his healing was the natural outcome of the economy in the midst of which they lived.

The rest of the address was of the nature of appeal. "And now, brethren, I know that in ignorance ye did it, as did also your rulers." Notice the tenderness of this. One is almost inclined to say, has he not weakened his argument? Would it not have been better if he had refrained from anything like this admission? Does he not seem to take away from the guilt that he has been charging upon them? I think the answer to such enquiries is to be found in the word of Peter, "I *know* that in ignorance ye did it." It does not express his opinion of the situation; it is rather his declaration of the fact that he accepted the truth of what Jesus had said, when in the very hour of His dying, He prayed, "Father, forgive them, for they know not what they do." I know, said Peter, "that in ignorance ye did it, as also did your rulers." Nevertheless he charged them with the guilt, and showed them it was by their will, and their decision on the human side, that this Man Jesus was murdered. "But the things which God foreshewed by the mouth of all the prophets, that His Christ should suffer, He thus fulfilled." In these words, over against the blunder, the calamity, the tragedy of the ignorant murder of Jesus, he set that infinite purpose of grace which triumphed over their sin, and fulfilled the very purposes of God as declared in the past, in the death and resurrection of Jesus.

Immediately, he made his definite appeal: "Repent ye therefore, and turn again." Into that "therefore" we must read everything that was meant. Why should they repent and turn again? The things that follow declare the issues of repentance, but the things preceding declare the reason for repentance on the part of the house of Israel. These reasons were: that Jesus was the Servant of God; that through Jesus, God had been carrying on

[111]

and carrying out His purposes; that when they procured
the death of Jesus, forcing Pilate to condemn Him, they
blundered, and were guilty of refusing the Holy and
Righteous One; and that in spite of their blindness and
sin and ignorance and blundering, God raised Him and
fulfilled His purpose, the purpose of grace and the purpose of life. " Therefore," because of their sin, and of
His grace; because in the putting away of Jesus they fell
out of the line of their own progressive national history,
and because by the raising of Jesus, God made possible
the putting away of the very sin which they committed
in His murder, " therefore " they were to " repent . . .
and turn again." He thus called these people back from
ignorance into light; and so back from all the sins that
had grown out of ignorance, into the true line of conduct.

Peter having called these people to repentance, promised certain results. " Repent . . . and turn again;
that your sins may be blotted out, that so there may
come seasons of refreshing from the presence of the
Lord, and that He may send the Christ Who hath been
appointed for you, even Jesus; Whom the heavens must
receive until the times of restoration of all things."
There can be no explanation of this save by remembering
that he was talking to the house of Israel. To make it
applicable to all the world, is to miss its real meaning.
When he began to speak of the issues of repentance and
turning again, the application was narrowed to the house
of Israel. The first phase, " That your sins may be
blotted out," may have a general application. But let
us follow on. What was to be the result of blotting out
of sin? " That so there may come seasons of refreshing
from the presence of the Lord." What was to be the
issue of these seasons of refreshing from the Lord?
" That He may send the Christ Who hath been appointed
for you "—the house of Israel—" even Jesus; Whom
the heavens must receive until the times of restoration of
all things." If we take these words as applicable to the

house of Israel, at once the sequence is seen. The restoration of all things is intimately associated with the coming of Christ to the house of Israel, the Messiah for them, and to them; and His coming to them waits for the repentance and turning to Him of the house of Israel. Or, to take it in the other order, when the house of Israel repents and turns to Jehovah, then the sins of the house of Israel will be blotted out; and then there will come to the house of Israel seasons of refreshing from the presence of the Lord; then there will come through the house of Israel the restoration of all things, and that in connection with the advent of Messiah. We speak of it as a second advent, but it will be the first advent in which He will be received by His own people. If I am asked if I believe that what Peter expected will be so, without any hesitation, I say Yes. I do not think Israel is a lost and abandoned nation. I believe that Israel is to be found and gathered together. It is because I so believe, that I cannot accept any theory that robs Israel of its present living identity, and merges it in some other nation. Israel will yet repent and turn to Him, and He will blot out their sins. Until this time there has been no repentance of Israel; but there will be a day of repentance, and a day of turning to Him.

What, for us, is the teaching of this address, delivered so distinctly and particularly to the house of Israel? It seems to me there are three lessons as to the economy of God. First, that His ancient purposes are unchanged; secondly, that the restoration of all things waits the Advent of Jesus; and thirdly, that this will be the time of the recovery of Israel.

But what are the spiritual principles that I learn as I read this address? In that part of the address which I have described as corrective, two spiritual principles are involved; first, that wonder in the presence of the supernatural demonstrates infidelity; and secondly, that infidelity creates false explanations. The man who is attempting to get rid of the supernatural from his Bible and from his religion does not believe in God. He may have some idea of God as of a moral force, but the God of the Bible cannot be believed in by a man who wonders, and is startled in the presence of, and attempts to account for supernatural manifestations along other lines. Wonder in the presence of the supernatural always demonstrates infidelity. Granted the truth of the first verse in the Bible, and there is no difficulty with the miracles. "In the beginning God created the heavens and the earth." This is the supreme miracle, and it is no miracle when God is postulated. It was the simple activity of His power. The supernatural is that which is a little higher than man can see, a little profounder than he can understand.

In the instructive part of this address moreover, there are spiritual principles. The patent one is that of the unutterable sin and foolishness of rejecting Jesus. The triumph of God even over such sin and folly, is seen in His raising Him from the dead, and thus making Him the Saviour of man.

Finally, the appeal emphasizes the fact that the children of privilege have responsibilities; and upon their fulfilment of such responsibilities depends the continuity and the enlargement of privilege.

If Israel be to-day a people scattered and peeled over the face of the world, the reason for the scattering and peeling for long and weary years, in which she is cast away from service, is that she became self-centred, and lived wholly alone, and forgot the surrounding nations she ought to have blessed.

Therein is a message for the Church. If our privileges are high and holy, our responsibilities are correspondingly great. As we forget our responsibilities, so surely the privileges themselves become grave-clothes that hinder and bury, rather than inspirations that drive and elp.

THE ACTS OF THE APOSTLES

Acts 4: 1-22

The story of this paragraph still gathers around the healed man. We first saw the wonder wrought in the Name. Then we heard Peter's explanation to the men of Israel delivered in Solomon's porch. We now come to a smaller company, in some ways a more remarkable one, in many ways a very interesting one. Suddenly, while teaching the people in Solomon's porch, Peter and John were arrested, and kept in ward for a night. Immediately outside Solomon's portico was to be found the Basilica in which the Sanhedrim assembled, and that means that it was outside the Beautiful Gate of the Temple. Outside that Beautiful Gate the lame man had been found. Having been healed, he had laid hold upon Peter and John, his mouth filled with thanksgiving; and the people seeing this, had gathered together in the porch, where Peter had specifically and directly spoken to the men of Israel. Now his speech was interrupted and hindered. This was the first open opposition to the apostolic message in the new activity of Christianity. Let us examine the court; watch the proceedings; and consider the lessons of permanent value.

Whereas the word is not used, it is perfectly evident that the court before which Peter and John were arraigned was that of the Sanhedrim, for its composition, as described by Luke in the opening words of this chapter, can leave us in no doubt on the matter. The apostles were arrested by "the priests and the captain of the Temple." The phrase is an interesting one, indicating the fact that at that time the Hebrew people still had the right of life and death in the matter of offences committed in the Temple. They were entirely under Roman rule, they had been forbidden to pass the death penalty for any civil offence, but Rome still permitted them to visit with death any who violated the sanctity of the Temple. The captain of the Temple was the head of that body of religious police, whose business it was to watch

[115]

the Temple courts, and see that there was no violation of their sanctity. "The priests and the captain of the Temple and the Sadducees came upon them." Thus the cause of the arrest was that the priests had reported to the captain, inspired by their own Sadducean conviction.

Then in verse five, we are told—and here we have an exact description of the Sanhedrim—"It came to pass on the morrow, that their rulers, and elders, and scribes, were gathered together in Jerusalem." That was the constitution of the ancient Sanhedrim; the rulers, that is, the priests and the officials; the elders, the heads of the chief families in Israel; the scribes, the interpreters of the law and teachers of the people. The Sanhedrim consisted of seventy-one members, twenty-three forming a quorum, before which such cases as those already referred to, of the violation of the sanctity of the temple courts, might be brought. It was, so far as it went, a legal assembly.

Standing in remarkable contrast to the method these men adopted with Christ, is the method they now adopted with His apostles. They waited till the morning. This was according to their own law, which in the case of Christ they did not observe. Certain names are given: Annas the high priest, deposed by the Romans, but still held in honour by Israel; Caiaphas, appointed by Roman rule; and two evidently notable persons, John, and Alexander. Notice the significant phrase, "As many as were of the kindred of the high priest." The aristocratic religion of the hour was Sadducean; the democratic was Pharisaic. All the wealthy people in Jerusalem belonged to the Sadducees.

This then was a remarkable gathering of the Sanhedrim, properly constituted; together with the wealthy Sadducean rulers of society, and of religious thinking in Jerusalem. It was a very remarkable assembly. Here is a picture waiting for some artist to paint. The tribunal, in all the glory of robing and the dignity of the men, would be seated in a semicircle, with the president in the centre; and probably gathered round, as was the custom of the time, the law students, listening to every case, and so becoming acquainted with the processes of law.

But let us notice quite carefully, and principally, the mental attitude of that court. We have already noticed that these men were Sadducees. It is evident that the Sanhedrim was packed that morning of set purpose with Sadducees. The high priest was a Sadducee; his friends and kindred were specially named as present. Notable men were also there, and we see in the first word de- clared, that the inspiration of the arrest was Sadducean.

Now who were the Sadducees? There are three things to be borne in mind concerning them, one of which is of supreme interest to us. Sadducees denied the super- natural; they affirmed the freedom of human will; and, the oral traditions, repeated by Pharisees, taught by Pharisees, insisted upon by Pharisees, they held in con- tempt. The principal matter which we need to remem- ber, is that they were rationalists in religion. They were religious undoubtedly, for they believed in God, and in the Mosaic law, but they denied every story of the miraculous. To take the description of them that is found in another verse in this book, they believed neither in angels, spirits, nor resurrection. They were the men who had turned the Hebrew economy into an ethical system. Their belief in God was not the belief of the Pharisees. Resurrection they denied; the existence of angels they laughed at; and the idea of spirit they had abandoned. This was the mental attitude of the San hedrim that morning when Peter and John were ar- raigned before them. The inspiration of opposition to Christianity had now changed from Pharisaism to Sad- duceeism. In the life of Christ the opposition was chiefly Pharisaic. Very little is said about the opposition of the Sadducees in His life. They are sometimes seen in coali-

THE ACTS OF THE APOSTLES

tion with the Pharisees, but the deadly opposition that ended in the death of Jesus was Pharisaic. In the Acts the Pharisees are hardly seen at all. As a matter of fact they are seen rather friendly to Christianity. Twice a Pharisee lifted his voice in defence of some Christian evangelist later on, and the whole opposition to Christianity that is revealed in the Acts of the Apostles has a new inspiration. It came from a different centre. This is in itself a revelation of the impression made at the time as to the central truth of the Christian propaganda. The whole idea was spiritual, and therefore in conflict necessarily with that which was severely material. The whole impression made upon Jerusalem and upon those who listened and watched these men was that of their absolute confidence in the supreme reality of unseen things. They believed in angels. Presently they will affirm that an angel opened the prison door and liberated them. The whole burden of their claim was that they were working in coöperation with the Holy Spirit of God. The one central note of all their proclamation was the declaration that Jesus had been raised from the dead and was alive. The angels are not patent to common vision; the Spirit breatheth where He listeth, and men cannot watch the processes of His coming and going; Jesus had passed out of mortal sight; but these men believed in the absolute and final reality of the things unseen, and they were asserting them.

It was inevitable that there should be conflict between the Sadducees and these men. Either Sadduceeism must end, or Christianity must be stamped out. Observe carefully Luke's declaration, that they were " sore troubled because they taught the people, and proclaimed in Jesus the resurrection from the dead." It was not merely that they declared Jesus Himself was risen from the dead, but in preaching that, they preached the Resurrection. Such was the court, and such the mental mood of the judges.

Let us now look at those who were placed in the centre
of that court, Peter and John. We have already noticed
the close comradeship existing between these two men;
Peter the practical and John the poet; John the dreamer,
and Peter the doer. These were the men arraigned before the assembly, the speaker and the thinker.

But there was a third man there: "And seeing the
man which was healed standing with them." We do not
know whether he had been locked up for the night; if
not, in all probability he had waited until morning, until
these men who had given him what none other had, were
released. Now he stood with them.

Carefully observe Peter and John, and observe that
which cannot be seen with the eyes of sense. They were
"filled with the Holy Spirit." That means that they had
clear vision, absolute certainty, strong passion, and unflinching courage. As we first look upon this scene, and
see the dignity surrounding these men, notice the cold
analytical acumen of Sadducean philosophy confronting
them, we wonder how these two fisherfolk will fare. But
we need have no fear; for they were filled with the Holy
Ghost, and they stood in the midst of that assembly, with
unflinching courage.

What impression did they make upon the council?
Let us run a little ahead of the story, for the impression
is not described until after the process of the examination; but it is well that we should notice it here. The
impression that they made was, "that they had been
with Jesus." Men filled with the Spirit always make
that impression. That is the impression which the filling
of the Spirit creates. If a man shall tell me he has received specific gifts at some specific hour which he describes, and the impression he makes upon me is antagonistic to the mind of Jesus, I know that he is not filled
with the Spirit. The word "ignorant" used to describe
these men is a little unfortunate; "plebeian" would better
convey the idea. They were unlearned and plebeian men,

that is men of the common class. But they had boldness
of speech, and boldness does not merely mean braveness,
but clarity, clearness of statement. On another occasion
when Jesus was talking in the metropolitan centre of the
learning of His time, they said, "How knoweth this
Man letters, having never learned?" This puzzle was
repeated in the case of Peter and John. "They took
knowledge of them, that they had been with Jesus."
Notice the mistake they made. This was the result of
their own philosophy. They spoke of the men as having
been with Jesus, in a past tense. What was the truth?
Christ was in the men, and speaking through the men;
and the similarity which they detected was not that lingering from contact with a lost teacher, but that created
by the presence of the living Christ.

Now let us watch the proceedings. There are four
things to observe in the challenge made to these men.
The court first enquired, "By what power, or in what
Name, have ye done this?" One can imagine that the
accused might have said, What do you mean by "*this*"?
They did not do so, for the meaning was patent. There
was the healed man; and when they said "this" they
tacitly admitted that they were in the presence of a fact
for which they could not account. In their very question
there was a recognition of something done. We must
begin there. The Sadducees could not escape from it.
Every one knew the man who had been for forty years
and more in that condition, a cripple at the Beautiful
Gate, asking alms. He was now standing in the circle of
the Sanhedrim, with a light on his face, and gladness in
his heart, near to the two men who had healed him.
They admitted the patent fact from which they could not
escape. The question was how it had been done. This
was an attempt to divert the thinking from the supreme
and final evidence, into a metaphysical disquisition. This
is a favourite method of the enemies of Christianity.

We now come to the enquiry itself: "By what power,"

that is, what force did you employ to set this man upon his feet? or, " In what Name." This was a very technical question. It was a refusal to entertain the view presented in Solomon's porch. There Peter had declared distinctly that in the Name of Jesus of Nazareth the man had been healed. They swept that aside. They did not entertain it for a moment. Then they asked, " By what power or in what Name have ye done this? " There is a great deal of light on this story in the book of Deuteronomy. In the thirteenth chapter, there are instructions carefully given to the rulers of the people concerning possible manifestations in their history. Let us read one or two words. " If there arise in the midst of thee a prophet, or a dreamer of dreams "—and a perfect description of the two men who stood before the Sanhedrim is then given—" and he give thee a sign or a wonder, and the sign or the wonder come to pass," and if that sign actually wrought is intended to lead you from Jehovah to other gods, you are not to hearken, and this man is to be punished with death. In the fourteenth verse we read: " Then shalt thou enquire, and make search, and ask diligently; and, behold, if it be truth, and the thing certain, that such abomination is wrought in the midst of thee " then—there was to be punishment. The Sanhedrim was obeying this ancient instruction to their people. Here were two men, a prophet and a dreamer of dreams, standing side by side. They had definitely and positively wrought a sign; and, according to the ancient instruction, the rulers of the people were to search and enquire diligently. The death penalty was to be passed upon men attempting to lead men from Jehovah to some other god. Thus is revealed the subtlety of their question and their method.

There was a marked method in Peter's answer. It exactly replied to all contained in the challenge. First the challenge was a recognition of something done. Peter drew attention to that in his reply. " If we this day are examined concerning a good deed done to an impotent man." Notice in this, the inferential revelation of the unworthiness of their opposition. You are examining us for a good deed done to an impotent man. Again, they had asked for the power and the Name. Peter gave the exact information, but in the other order. He began with the Name, and then declared the power: " Jesus Christ of Nazareth, Whom ye crucified." Peter did not intend that there should be any mistake. Not *the Messiah*, not *Jesus* merely; but with deliberateness, carefulness, he fastened their attention upon the One Whose Name they fain would make forgotten forever. Jesus, the Messiah, of Nazareth Whom ye crucified. That was the Name. But what was the power? He immediately went on, " Whom God raised from the dead, in Him doth this man stand here before you whole." This is the Name, the Name in which you charged us not to speak; this is the power, the raising of that One Whom you declared did not rise, because there is no resurrection. Thus Peter insisted upon the declaration made in Solomon's porch, which they had declined to receive.

But notice very particularly how Peter finished. That Deuteronomic instruction said that if there should be an actual sign wrought, tending to lead men from Jehovah, the men working the sign must die. He, said Peter, " is the Stone which was set at nought of you the builders, which was made the head of the corner. And in none other is there salvation; for neither is there any other Name under heaven, that is given among men, wherein we must be saved." By that quotation from Psalm 118 he denied that he was leading men away from Jehovah; and claimed that he was acting in harmony with the foretelling of their ancient Scriptures, which was the burden of the message he had delivered in the porch of Solomon.

Then followed the conference. The prisoners were excluded; and we see the measure of the intelligence of the Sanhedrim. First we note their discovery of the relation of Peter and John to Jesus, and the certainty of the miracle, and their decision not to attempt to deny it. We see also the measure of their ignorance in their decision to threaten these men. Imagine any court threatening a man who is filled with the Holy Spirit. But of course there was no Holy Spirit according to their philosophy, and therefore that was the proper thing to do. If one man be threatened by a Tribunal, composed of the forces of culture, there is little hope of him; but if that man be filled with the Holy Spirit, he will challenge the whole company, and the victory will be with him.

When they charged these men to be silent, Peter flung back their judgment on them, and set over against their threatening the one eternal principle of right. " Whether it be right," that is the question. Waive your technicalities and have done with your casuistry. Is it right? If it be right, threatening is of no avail.

This story of the first opposition reveals for all time the nature of opposition to Christianity; and also the real secrets of the Church's power. Opposition to Christianity is always based on Sadduceeism, is always rooted in rationalism, is always the outcome of materialistic philosophy. James when describing the wisdom of the world, the wisdom of men, putting it into contrast with the wisdom that comes from heaven does so in biting, burning words. He speaks of the "wisdom of the world" as being " earthly, sensual, devilish "; it is earthly in its outlook; sensual in its desire; devilish in its choices. The intellect in looking out, sees only the earth; the emotion desiring, is wholly sensual; the will choosing is under the dominion of devils. It is the rationalistic conception of life that is angry with Christianity, most subtle of all foes, and most to be dreaded. Mrs. Besant lecturing for the Secular Society in the old days bitterly attacked Christianity. Mrs. Besant, theosophist, never attacked Christianity. I am not defending her position,

but it is interesting to remember that a spiritual conception does not attack Christianity. It is the material ideal,
the ideal that says in the wilderness, Bread out of stones
is all you need; the ideal that says in the midst of the
life of to-day, Let us eat and drink for to-morrow we die;
that is the force against Christianity; and it is always
Sadducean.

This story teaches also that opposition to Christianity
is always opposition to actual good being done in the
world. The whole work of Christ is that of healing,
helping, saving. The hour has come surely when the
Church must decline to allow responsibility to rest upon
Christ for her ofttime blunders, and misrepresentations
of His purpose. The business of the Church in the
world is not the discussion of theories, is not that of
indulging in speculations, or formulating philosophies; it
is that of seeking and saving that which is lost. It is out
to find men lying at the Beautiful Gate, excluded from
worship, and to put them on their feet, and make them
worshippers.

Finally opposition to Christ is always opposition in
spite of conclusive evidence. There is the healed man,
Oh ye men of the Sanhedrim, confronting you! In God's
name, why waste time accounting for him, why not let
this thing go on? The healed man has been multiplied
in all the centuries. The healed man is in all the world
to-day. The healed man is here, healed mentally,
spiritually, physically, in proportion as he is true to
the great spiritual truths to which he has submitted
himself.

Then, on the other side, the story reveals the Church's
secret of power. The reality of the spiritual is demonstrated by results produced in the visible and material.
The Church has no argument unless she has a healed
man, and the Church that is not healing men, remaking
them, has no argument for her Christianity; " Seeing the
man which was healed standing with them, they could say

nothing against it." The unassailable and final answer of
Christianity to detraction is the healed man.

The basis of courage is spiritual and such courage is
vindicated by such results. Vindicated? I take the
word back. Courage is created by such results. Are we
a little afraid to-day in the presence of the materialism of
the age? No man with his eyes open will deny that the
age is material. Is the Church afraid of it? Are we
halting, speculating, and attempting to recast things so
as to meet the materialistic age? If so the reason is that
there is a dearth of healed men. I would like always to
preach as Peter and John did that day, with the healed
man by my side; men who have been healed and remade,
men upon whose faces there is the light that never was
on sea or land; these are the men that make the preacher
courageous. If we are to face the materialism of the
age with purpose and courage, we must have these evidences.

Finally, opposition on the part of the material to the
spiritual eventuates in the destruction of the material.
Dr. John Hall, for so many years the minister of Fifth
Avenue Presbyterian Church, New York, once illustrated
that in this way. He said: "A serpent fastens upon a
steel file and attempts to gnaw it through; it is at first
gratified at the evidences of apparent success; but presently blood is there, and the serpent finds that the file has
been destroying its tooth rather than its tooth the file."

If Christianity is becoming materialized, God have
mercy on us and the world. It must be the Christianity
of men and women filled with the Holy Spirit, knowing
the power of the One Name, and bringing men to deliverance through it, which alone can be victorious.

Acts 4: 23-31

In this paragraph we come to the last scene in the story
of the opposition resulting from the healing of the man
at the Beautiful Gate. Here we find ourselves in entirely

THE ACTS OF THE APOSTLES

new surroundings, in striking contrast to those of the previous study. This paragraph opens with the declaration "And being let go, they came to their own company"; and we can imagine the different atmosphere into which Peter and John, and in all likelihood the lame man, now passed. "Their own company" was most probably the apostolic band and the whole Church. We last saw them standing in the midst of the Sanhedrim and the Sadducean atmosphere. Now we see them in the midst of their own company, and the spiritual atmosphere.

In considering the story of how the Sanhedrim dealt with these men, we noticed that the opposition was based upon the Sadducean conception of life, which was entirely materialistic. They had stood in the hostile and critical atmosphere of that Sadducean philosophy, defending their position by reaffirming the truth of the resurrection of Jesus. We now see them in an entirely new atmosphere. "Being let go, they came to their own company," a company of those who in all probability during the hours of their imprisonment had been in prayer for them, perhaps with a great deal of fear in their hearts. To this company of believers, and in this atmosphere of spirituality, Peter and John told their story. It was a story of opposition, intellectual and active. The rulers of the people had now taken definite action, in this first arrest and arraignment of the apostles, and this first charge to them not to speak in the name of Jesus. The dealing of the Sanhedrim with the apostles had for the moment been characterized by mildness; but they had left no doubt in the minds of the apostles that they were in active and definite hostility to the preaching of the resurrection; and so this company of the apostolic band, gathered together and listening to Peter and John were conscious of growing hostility without, indicative of danger. The One in Whose name they were gathered and Whose evangel they were proclaiming had been crucified. They had come to see the larger meanings of that crucifixion—and that they had done so, is evident in the prayer we have now to consider. Nevertheless, they saw what that fact of crucifixion meant on the human plane. Jesus had been crucified because of His testimony to the spiritual, in an age characterized by material thinking. Because of His affirmation of the supremacy of the spiritual, His persistent calling of men back from dust to Deity, men had at last attempted to silence His voice by crucifying Him. Their message was that of His Resurrection, which was that of His victory. They knew the issue of this kind of preaching. They knew that the hostility that was stirred against them was determined and definite and daring; that as it had stopped at nothing in order to silence the voice of the supreme Teacher, so now it would stand at nothing in order to silence the voices of those who were repeating what He had said, with the added argument and force of their declaration of His resurrection.

The last statement of the paragraph reveals the ultimate effect of this opposition of the Sadducees upon the apostolic band. "They spake the word of God with boldness." They continued to do, what two of their number had done at the Beautiful Gate, in Solomon's porch, and before the Sanhedrim. At the Beautiful Gate Peter had said to the lame man, "Silver and gold have I none; but what I have, that give I thee." Taking him by the hand in the name of the risen Christ he had commanded him to rise, and straightway he had stood upon his feet. In Solomon's porch Peter had rebuked the rationalism of the men of Israel, showing that if they were true to their own history they would not be surprised at the wonder wrought. Before the Sanhedrim, without any hesitation, or apology, they had declared the selfsame truths. When the chief priests and the Sadducees "beheld the boldness of Peter and John, and had perceived that they were unlearned and ignorant men, they marvelled; and they took knowledge of them, that

[127]

they had been with Jesus." The threatening which followed was not that of the vulgar mob, but that of the cultured elders; it was not that of a crowd swept by passion, but that of quiet, calculating, subtle foes. They threatened them and let them go. The apostles had come back to their own company and all were perfectly conscious of this hostility, which was in the air, and now was beginning to manifest itself. They saw definitely what it meant in the future; but the effect produced was that " They spake the word of God with boldness."

We shall attempt to discover the secrets of this boldness. There is nothing more interesting in this part of the book, or indeed throughout the whole apostolic story than its continuity. The word " boldness " suggests clear and daring statement; a clear enunciation of certain truths, so that there could be no mistaking of the meaning; and an almost blunt and defiant enunciation, that arrested attention, and compelled men to listen. This note of boldness runs through all the apostolic teaching. There is an utter absence of apology; or of hesitation. Prophets and apostles forevermore faced men and said: These things are so, Thus saith the Lord. This first manifestation arrests our attention, and we enquire the secrets of it.

Broadly stated, the boldness of this apostolic band resulted from prayer offered and answered. That tells the whole story of this paragraph. These men prayed, and the answer came. These men heard the story that Peter and John had to tell, and then one of them undoubtedly speaking the mind of the rest,—for they were of one mind and one heart,—they lifted up their voice in one prayer; and straightway, without any hesitation and waiting, the answer came, the place was shaken, and they were filled with the Holy Spirit and spake the word of God with boldness. While that tells the whole story, let us examine more particularly the nature of the prayer, and the nature of the answer to the prayer.

We turn first to the prayer itself. Notice two things: first the convictions that created the prayer; and secondly the desire expressed, as it reveals the attitude of the men praying.

The convictions concerning God are indicated by the form of address, by what they stated concerning their own ancient Scriptures, and by what they said about the crucifixion of Christ.

The prayer opened with the words, " O Lord," and that word *Lord* is a very rare one in the New Testament. It is not the one usually translated Lord. It is a word which we might translate by using the word *despot*. Of course we have come to associate everything that is iniquitous with the word " despot "; but, as a matter of fact, it simply means *absolute ruler;* it indicates final sovereignty. Later, in the prayer they used the other and commoner word, but it opened with a *t*itle that indicated their attitude toward God and their conviction concerning Him. The first thought suggested is that of their belief in the sovereignty of God, and they illustrated the meaning of this form of address by saying " Thou that didst make the heaven and the earth and the sea, and all that in them is." They were confining themselves for illustration to the things nearest to them, to the very material world which the Sadducees said was everything. The Sadducees denied the existence of anything beyond that which was patent and self-evident; the heaven, that is, as a firmament with all its mystery; the solid earth; and the sea; these were the sum-total of the things which the Sadducee accepted or believed in. Now these men said, " O Lord, Thou that didst make the heaven and the earth and the sea." Evidently, therefore, to them God was more than all. This was the subconscious conviction that underlay the prayer of these men. Prayer always begins there. No man ever prays unless he has this conception of God, as being more than the sum-total of the things of which he is conscious in his philosophy and in his science. Underlying this prayer, therefore, which issued in boldness, was this conviction of the absolute sovereignty of God.

As we move on we find another conviction, or another phase of the one conviction. " Who by the Holy Spirit, by the mouth of our father David Thy servant, didst say:

> Why did the Gentiles rage,
> And the peoples imagine vain things?
> The kings of the earth set themselves in array,
> And the rulers were gathered together,
> Against the Lord, and against His Anointed."

Their quotation was taken from the second Psalm, which all Jewish expositors admitted, and admit, to be Messianic in its value. In all probability it was written by David in the midst of some local circumstances to which it referred, but it had larger applications and further meanings. Whether their conviction was false or true is not now under discussion. The point is that these men attributed the psalm to David, to the Spirit, to the foreknowledge of God; and consequently their conviction concerning God was not that of His sovereignty only, but also that of His wisdom. They believed that when David sang that psalm, he sang better than he knew, and fuller than he thought; that behind the singer was the inspiring Spirit; and that at the back of the wisdom that foresaw human events, was God Himself.

But there is yet another phase of conviction evident, perhaps in some senses more remarkable, more full of comfort and helpfulness. "For of a truth in this city against Thy holy Servant Jesus, Whom Thou didst anoint, both Herod and Pontius Pilate, with the Gentiles and the peoples of Israel, were gathered together." We must pause here to notice carefully how these men described what had happened in the city. Mark carefully their description of the forces massed " against Thy holy Servant Jesus, Whom Thou didst anoint." Herod, repre-

[130]

senting Hebrew authority; Pontius Pilate, the representative of Roman authority; " with the Gentiles," the nations outside the Covenant; " and the peoples of Israel," those of the Covenant; " were gathered together." These had been gathered together to destroy Jesus. That is quite true; but that is not what these men said. They said: " They were gathered together, *to do whatsoever Thy hand and Thy counsel foreordained to come to pass.*" That is the last phase of their conviction concerning God. It was the conviction, not merely of His sovereignty, not merely of His wisdom, but of His actual, definite, government and overruling, in the affairs of men.

These then were their conceptions of God. He made the heaven, and the earth, and the sea; and therefore He is before, and He is more than they. He foretold, through the singing of a man long centuries ago, the course of events; and therefore He is full of wisdom. But more, He presides over history. These men in the Upper Room were looking back to those sad, dismal, and awful days in Jerusalem when they arrested the Lord and Master Whom they loved; when He was bandied about between Herod and Pilate, when the outside nations and the chosen people combined to murder Him; but they did not speak about murder when they prayed. They would do that, when they were outside. They would charge His murder upon those who were guilty; but now they were in the secret place of prayer. They saw the people, assembled tumultuously together, but high over all they saw the Throne, and God governing and compelling.

Peter had given utterance to the same thought in the Pentecostal sermon when he put the two things into close connection saying " Him "—that is, Jesus,—" being delivered up by the determinate counsel and foreknowledge of God, ye by the hand of lawless men did crucify and slay." In this prayer there was only the recognition of the Divine overruling. These were the things in which

[Acts 4:23–31]

they believed: the sovereignty of God; the wisdom of God; the active government of God; and these convictions concerning God, inspired their prayer.

Their convictions concerning Jesus are as clearly revealed. First they believed in the sinlessness of Jesus. " Thy holy Servant Jesus." Twice they repeated the word. They believed in the Messiahship of Jesus. Having quoted the second psalm that referred to the economy of the Son, they said of Jesus, " Whom Thou didst anoint." They believed that through the Cross, He accomplished the purpose of God, for when they spoke of the things done by Herod and Pontius Pilate and the Gentiles and the Chosen, they spoke of the Cross not as defeat, but as victory.

The word " accomplishment " was surely used of set purpose. Peter and John were two of the men who had been on the Mount of Transfiguration. There they heard Jesus talk with Moses and Elijah about " The exodus that He should *accomplish*." These men recognized that He accomplished, even through that death that seemed so tragic, a definite purpose.

These then were the convictions that underlay the prayer of this apostolic band; convictions concerning God, His sovereignty, His wisdom, His government; convictions concerning Jesus, His sinlessness, His Messiahship, and His accomplishment through death of the Will of God.

Now let us turn to the desires expressed. Notice in the first place the evident consciousness of danger revealed in the actual petition. Their first petition was, " Look upon their threatenings." Their conviction concerning God was that He is sovereign, that He is All-wise, that He is governing the affairs of men, and making even the wrath of man to praise Him. They knew the threatening outside, and the only thing they could do with it was to remit it to Him. " Look upon their threatenings." They did not ask that the threatenings might cease, nor even that the threatenings might not be carried out. They did not ask that they might escape from the logical issue of persecution and death that they had seen. There was no such request. They asked that He would look upon their threatening; and then immediately that they might have boldness to speak the word, while God stretched out His hand to heal: "Grant unto Thy servants to speak Thy word with all boldness, while Thou stretchest forth Thy hand to heal." Thus they prayed for the continuance of that very activity which had produced the hostility. At the Beautiful Gate they had spoken the word with boldness, and God had stretched out His hand and healed the man; and all the hostility had come out of those facts. Now they prayed, and in effect they said: God help us to keep on in spite of everything, doing that which has produced the threatening. They had been charged not to speak in the Name again. They flung the caution aside. To the Sanhedrim Peter had said, "Whether it is right in the sight of God to hearken unto you rather than unto God, judge ye." Now, in the secret place, the men of courage came into the presence of the God in Whom they believed, and they had but one thing to ask, that they might still speak the word with boldness, while He stretched forth His hand to heal.

But there is another part to the prayer, revealing the deepest desire of the hearts of these men: "That signs and wonders may be done through the name of Thy holy Servant Jesus." Men of such conviction, are always men of such desire. Men who know such a God and such a Jesus, are always men who supremely desire,—not to escape from suffering, not to be spared all the toil and the travail of proclaiming the evangel,—but that His name should be vindicated and glorified by perpetual victory, and therefore that they may be kept bold in the preaching.

These praying men impress us, first as being consistent.

THE ACTS OF THE APOSTLES
[Acts 4:23-31]

This is a great word which we have largely misused. Some people think that to be *consistent* means that the same thing is said yesterday, to-day, and forever. A great consistency may make a man deny to-day what he said yesterday, because he finds out that what he said yesterday was not true. To be consistent is to be possessed and mastered by some one principle. Because these men were so possessed and mastered, they were strong. They were cautious also. This is seen in the fact that they were conscious of the peril, and therefore claimed the resources which were at their disposal in God. But supremely these men were courageous. There was no suggestion of retreat. The only passion in their hearts was to go forward, and their only fear was that they might fear, and so fail.

The answer to the prayer came immediately. There was first a sign: "the place was shaken." That was a response to their conviction concerning God. As Sovereign of the universe He laid His power upon the material house, and it was shaken. Do not be at all anxious if that kind of sign is not repeated in this century. The only infidelity to be feared is that which denies the possibility. Nevertheless, a material miracle is always a sign of dulness in the spiritual sense. All the miracles of the ancient days were necessary in order to lead on to the higher spiritual miracles which resulted. The Master said to His disciples: "Greater works than these shall ye do; because I go unto the Father." To read the context is to see that the "greater works" are the works of spiritual wonder. But to these people a material sign was granted, the shaking of the house. Then they were filled with the Spirit. This has sometimes been described as a New Pentecost. This is a most unfortunate expression. There can be no new Pentecost. Pentecost was once, and forever. The day of Pentecost was not a day of twenty-four hours. The day of Pentecost is the day of grace. This is the day of Pentecost. When the Spirit was outpoured in the Upper Room, the day dawned, which has not yet passed. This was no new Pentecost, but a new enduement, a new filling. A simple formula of New Testament terminology concerning the activities of the Holy Spirit will always help us to intelligent thinking: One baptism, many fillings, constant anointing These are all phrases of the New Testament. This was a new filling, a new enduement of power; perhaps because fulness had been interfered with by fear, while they were waiting for Peter and John. Personally I believe that the new filling was intended to prevent the development of incipient fear. They feared, and there was granted to them a new consciousness of the inrush of the Spirit. In Dr. Elder Cumming's wonderfully illuminative book *The Eternal Spirit,* he traced with accurate and scholarly precision the difference between the phrases " full of the Spirit " and " filled with the Spirit " as used in the New Testament. Some one full of the Spirit may nevertheless be filled to overflowing for specific service, and for work that waits to be done. These men were filled with a new consciousness, and a new actuality of the presence and the power of the Spirit; with the result that they went out, and spoke the word of God with boldness.

This study teaches us that if we would deliver the testimony of the risen Christ, characterized by the boldness of clarity and courage, we need right convictions concerning God, concerning His Son; and the constant reception of power by the inflow of the Holy Spirit. The last is the issue of the former. It is God, Who is the sovereign Lord, All-wise, actually governing, to Whom we must ever turn. It is Christ, Who is sinless, the anointed and appointed Messiah, Who accomplished through death the purpose of God, to Whom we must go. In proportion as we are submitted to Christ, and wait in prayer upon God, there will ever come to us that inflow of the Spirit, which will make us bold to proclaim

the evangel; and great results may and must follow where
the Church is thus convinced and Spirit-filled.

Acts 4: 32–37

We have been considering the infant Church in the
midst of hostile forces. We now come to a section of the
book which gives us a glimpse of the internal conditions
of her life at that time. This particular section falls
into two parts. There is first a picture of the Church's
fellowship, and then a picture of its discipline. We are
now to deal with the first of these.

Opinions held about this story by expositors and teachers are very divergent. They may generally be divided
into two main positions. There are those who count this
as a mistake—the first apostolic mistake. There are those
who believe it was Divinely ordered, and the inevitable
outcome of the Pentecostal effusion.

Those who declare that this was the first great mistake
made by the early Church do so for certain reasons which
we must briefly pass in review.

They affirm first, that the action of the early disciples
was due to their expectation of the speedy return of
Christ; that He would personally and actually return
within the generation; and that therefore there was no
need to retain possession of earthly goods. These early
disciples were certainly looking for the return of Christ,
as the disciples of to-day ought to be, and if they are not
—to quote Dr. Denny—the bloom is brushed from their
Christian experience; but we have no right to say that
these early disciples expected Him within a generation.
They expected Him all the time, and that was, and is,
the true attitude. In this story, however, not a word is
said to suggest that this expectation was the motive for
the selling of their lands and their houses.

Again, it is affirmed that this action was the cause of
that subsequent poverty of the Church in Jerusalem,
which made necessary the collections that were taken

through the Greek cities, and sent to Jerusalem. Such a statement is wholly gratuitous, and without a vestige of Biblical authority, probably the hypothesis of some one who approached the story with an anti-communistic prejudice.

That it is said that the action was a mistake is proved by the resulting experiences, those namely, of Ananias and Sapphira, and of the murmuring of the Hellenists because in the distribution certain of their widows were neglected. But the first lie, and the first discipline in the Church were due, not to the action chronicled here, but to the violation of the principles revealed here. The lie was the lie of a man and woman who were not true to the ideal; and the murmur of the Hellenists was against an unfair distribution.

Yet again it has been objected to by those who have treated the story as though the practice was one of indiscriminate charity, which as practised to-day, is so unquestionably unwise. But there is no similarity at all between the two things. This was wholly a Church activity. The material fellowship was merely the outward and visible sign of a spiritual fellowship, necessarily existing between regenerate men and women.

And yet once more, there are those who consider the action mistaken, because they treat it as though it were on the pattern of modern, legislative, social propaganda. As a matter of fact, it was not legislative at all. There was no law that any one should sell his land or house. In the case of Ananias and Sapphira the apostle said very definitely, While it was your own, it was your own; no one asked you to sell it. The action in each case was purely voluntary, and that of regenerate men.

A word of caution is necessary in the case of many who defend the story. Too often it is quoted in defence of a propaganda which fails to begin with Pentecost. That inclusively reveals the danger of taking this story, and preaching it promiscuously, as though it were a national idea, toward the realization of which we are to work to-day. Archbishop Magee, years ago, was severely criticized when he said that the British nation could not be governed on the principles of the Sermon on the Mount. But he was perfectly right. The Sermon on the Mount can be applied to England when England is a nation of regenerate men and women, and never until then. We are sometimes told to-day that the work of the preacher is to preach the Sermon on the Mount, and attempt to establish the Kingdom. Certainly it is, if we begin with Pentecost; but we must have Pentecost before we can have the condition of affairs described here. This condition of affairs was the immediate outcome of Pentecost, with all that it meant, of new vision, emotions, conceptions, power.

Let us attempt to look at the story of these few verses; first at the general description found in verses 32–35; and then at the particular illustration given in verses 36 and 37.

First, we have a general description of the condition of affairs obtaining among the members of the early Church. This was not a new departure in the case of the Church; it was not a new venture consequent upon new opposition. In chapter two, verses 44 and 45, we have an account of the things happening immediately after Pentecost. There at the very beginning, immediately upon the descent of the Spirit, and the filling of these people by the Spirit, these same conditions obtained. Notice the forty-second verse of that second chapter and then verses forty-three to forty-seven as they explain verse forty-two. The forty-second verse makes this declaration, " And they continued steadfastly in the apostles' teaching, and fellowship, in the breaking of bread and the prayers." Four things are named. The verses which follow simply break that verse up and show how they continued in these four things. First, The apostles' teaching: " And fear came upon every

THE ACTS OF THE APOSTLES

soul; and many wonders and signs were done through the
apostles." Secondly, Fellowship: "And all that believed
were together, and had all things common; and they sold
their possessions and goods, and parted them to all, according as any man had need." Thirdly, Breaking of
bread: "And day by day, continuing stedfastly with
one accord in the temple, and breaking bread at home,
they did take their food with gladness and singleness of
heart." Finally, Prayers: "Praising God, and having
favour with all the people. And the Lord added to them
day by day those that were being saved." These were
the conditions immediately following upon Pentecost.
The disciples, by the coming of the Spirit, baptized into
union with their Lord, continued steadfastly in the
apostles' doctrine, which does not merely mean that they
listened to the apostles, but that they supported the teaching of the apostles by the witness of their lives. Therefore, they continued steadfastly moreover in fellowship.
There is no richer word in the New Testament than the
Greek word so translated. *Koinonia* is translated in a
great many ways, because no single word can convey all
its richness. It and its cognate words are translated fellowship, communion, communication, distribution, contribution, partners, partakers. The root of the word is
found in the statement that they "had all things *common.*" The word translated *common* is the root out of
which the word *koinonia* comes. Fellowship therefore
is having all things in common. The great teaching of
the New Testament is that the child of God has fellowship with God, that is, all things in common with God.
All the resources of God are at the disposal of the child
of God. All the resources of the child of God are at the
disposal of God. These men of the early Church therefore, and necessarily, had all things in common with each
other. The conditions then that we find described in
this fourth chapter are exactly the conditions which inevitably followed the Pentecostal effusion, the baptism

of the Spirit, the indwelling of these men and women by Christ Himself through the Spirit. They were brought by that baptism into new relation with Christ, and so into new relation with God Himself. That inevitably meant new relationship with each other.

At the centre of the Ephesian letter, the apostle urged those Christians to whom he was writing, to walk worthily of the calling wherewith they were called. The first charge he laid upon them was this: " Giving diligence to keep the unity of the Spirit in the bond of peace." Having so written, he described what he meant by the unity of the Spirit in these stately words, " There is one body, and one Spirit." That one body is Christ, and all His people. He then showed how men come into that union: " One Lord," Christ; " One faith," fastening upon Him; " One baptism," that of the Spirit, making the trusting soul one with Him. Finally he described the result of that union: " One God and Father of all, Who is over all, and through all, and in all." That is *koinonia,* fellowship, all things in common. Men and women made partakers of the Divine nature, seeing in the Divine light, feeling with the Divine love, living with the Divine life. That is the basis of the communion of this chapter. The communism was not that of people who have signed articles, and decided to pool property. It was the communism of a new life, which, possessing all, made these attitudes and activities irresistible and necessary.

Let us now turn to a closer examination of the paragraph, and so of the fellowship; noticing first, its power; secondly, its principles; and thirdly, its practice.

The power of this fellowship is revealed in the words: " The multitude of them that believed were of one heart and soul." It does not matter for the moment whether these believers sold their houses and land, or not. That is not the important thing. Do not begin with the selling of a house, and the selling of land; begin with the fact that " they that believed were of one heart and soul."

THE ACTS OF THE APOSTLES

The initial fact is found in the phrase, "them that believed"; and the resultant fact in the statement that they "were of one heart and soul." These men were of one heart and soul because they had believed. Belief here must be interpreted by all the evangelical values of the New Testament. The people who believed, necessarily became men and women of one heart and soul. "Them that believed" is a phrase of inclusion and of exclusion. We cannot take this story, and apply it on the level of that crowd in Jerusalem which did not believe; and we must not attempt to apply the teaching of this story to the promiscuous multitudes to-day that do not believe. "Them that believed," were those who had yielded themselves to the Lordship of Jesus, to obedience to His teaching.

What was the result of their believing? "They were of one heart and soul." The two phrases are not carelessly selected. "One heart," reveals the emotional and inspirational centre; "One soul," reveals the new life as dynamic. This company of people, having believed in Him, submitted to His Lordship, being loyal thereto, were of one heart. They were moved by one great impulse, one love mastered them; they had one outlook, one inward consciousness, one inspirational motive. But more, infinitely more, they were of one soul. The word soul here is the word that indicates life; it is not the high word which means spirit, but the word which refers to life as a force, as a dynamic.

We can never have the flowers and the fruits of the garden of the Lord unless we have the roots; and we shall never be able to reproduce in any community, in any nation, all the fair and gracious beauty of this condition, save as we can realize anew the one heart and the one life of that early company of first disciples.

But now let us notice the principle of this activity. The first element was that of selflessness: "And not one of them said that aught of the things which he possessed was his own." The trouble with much social propaganda to-day is that every man says that what he has, is his own. Here no man said so, because no man thought so. The one heart and the one life had completely ended the selfishness of these people. They were self-less.

The second element was that of a corporate conscious-ness. "They had all things common." If we cannot un-derstand what that means, we must go to some of the apostolic writings, and listen to their descriptions of what the Church ought to be. If one member suffers, all the members talk about it, and attempt to be sympathetic, and decide to make a collection. That is not the idea at all. That is what we do to-day! This is it: "Whether one member suffereth all the members suffer with it; or one member is honoured, all the members rejoice with it." That is corporate consciousness. They had all things common. "Not one of them said aught of the things which he possessed was his own."

There is yet another element to be observed. These people lived in the conviction of the supremacy of the spiritual over the material. The very life of the Spirit in them made the question of property a secondary ques-tion. We may call them improvident. That is the word of the world, and I am not sure that it is not the word of the flesh and the devil also. These people were so mas-tered by the spiritual power that possessed them, so driven in this fresh and fragrant dawn of the Church's life by the reality of the eternal and the spiritual, that they held with light hands the things of the world. All material property was subservient to spiritual purpose, and so they said that nothing they had was their own.

Then observe carefully that there was no compulsion, neither rules, nor regulations, nor pledges! The mul-tiplication of pledges is always a sign of the decadence of the Church's life. There was a great spiritual impulse, but there was no compulsion other than that; these men were not compelled to give up anything; everything was voluntary. The distribution was apostolic, and according as every man had need. The movement was purely voluntary, wholly and absolutely spiritual, the answer of external activities to the inward dynamic. One heart, the emotional centre; one life, spiritual dynamic; one activity, all things belonging to all.

In the midst of the story we find the wider value of this great fellowship. Those who criticize this action of the early Church generally deal with this particular verse by omitting it. "And with great power gave the apostles their witness of the resurrection of the Lord Jesus; and great grace was upon them all." The apostolic witness to the resurrection was made powerful by the spirituality and the selflessness of the life of the Church in itself; it had the evidence of life in harmony with the life of Christ, the evidence of love as the master-passion of all activity. This was the supreme evidence in apostolic preaching to the resurrection of Jesus. And again " great grace was upon them all." We must not read that as though it meant that grace like some glorious, yet nebulous Divine cloud of benediction hung over them. " Great grace was upon them all," means that there was a beauty and a glory manifest in their own character; and that beauty and glory, or to use the word itself, that grace cooperated with the apostolic testimony to resurrection. The word was with power because it was incarnate in the life of that early Church.

Leave that general outline and turn to the particular illustration. Joseph was in all probability a wealthy man. We have met his relations before. He was the brother of Mary, that is, of Mary the wealthy woman who lived in Jerusalem, at whose house the early disciples gathered. Mary was the mother of Mark, so that Mark was a nephew of this man. He was by birth a man of Cyprus, which at that time was a great centre for Jewish people; and he was a Levite. But if we really want to know

[143]

something of the man, let us mark well the name which the apostles gave him: Barnabas. This was a name given, indicative of the supreme quality of this man. Bar-Nabas means son of prophecy. We have a translation in the text, "which being interpreted is, Son of Exhortation." The Authorized Version says, "The Son of Consolation," which the Revised Version has retained in the margin. The difference is the same as that obtaining in the translation of the word Paraclete. Did Jesus say, "I will send you a Comforter?" or did He say, "I will send you an Advocate?" He really said both. Actually He said, I will send you the Paraclete. The meaning of the word Paraclete is, one called to the side of another; and one called to the side of another for a twofold purpose, the Advocate, to argue, and the Comforter, to comfort. That the element of comfort was in His mind was evident by the fact that He said, I will not leave you orphans, I will send you the Paraclete. The fact that exhortation was in His mind was evident by the fact that He said, "When the Paraclete is come He will teach you all things." In the word Paraclete therefore we have the thoughts of exhortation and of consolation. Here is the same word—the son of Paraklesis, the son of exhortation, or consolation. The apostles surnamed him thus because of what he was in himself. This man was a man gifted in speech, but it was speech that while it was exhortative, was also full of comfort. If we follow his history through the book of the Acts, we shall see how true this was.

Now this man had land, and he sold it, and laid the proceeds at the feet of the apostles. Look at this story in the atmosphere of the present day. Men have such a passion for holding land, that they speak of it as *Real Estate*. The fact that this man had land and sold it, was remarkable. It was a great venture of faith. Here were the apostles, a few men with all the massed light and leading of their age against them. These men set up a fanatical communism, not by rule and regulation, but by the wild impulse of love; and here was a landowner who sold his land and brought the proceeds and laid it at the feet of the apostles. That is an illustration of the principle that underlay the whole movement. It was an act of love, for it was accomplished in the power of that great principle here enunciated. No man said that anything he possessed was his own. It was an outcome of life, he was compelled to it by the nature of the life he shared in common with the rest. This is an illustration of what all these men did in greater or less degree. Barnabas had land and he sold it. That was his investment. We have not reached the dividends yet. Those will be found later on in the book.

So in conclusion we observe two or three matters of supreme importance. First, we must remember that this is a picture of conditions obtaining only within the Church. We must remember secondly that these are conditions which ought to obtain within the Church. It may be said that this condition of affairs is very perilous. Ananias and Sapphira illustrate the peril of it. The Hellenist murmuring testifies to the peril of it. But in each case we must finish the story. In a Church that can establish that order, Ananias and Sapphira cannot live. In a Church that can establish that order, the murmuring of the Hellenists issues in the appointment of Spirit-filled deacons, and the trouble is settled. There is administrative power. Do not quote Ananias and Sapphira and the Hellenist murmuring as showing the impossibility of realizing this ideal. If it is not possible to-day, it is because we have lost the purity that makes the lie impossible within our borders; because we have lost the unity of Spirit that can administer in any hour of difficulty. Let us be honest! If that is a lost ideal, it is because the power realizing it is largely a lost power. The only restoration will be in the power of the preliminary things. In the Evangelical Revival how many wonderful things were said and sung. Call to mind one of the old hymns and this couplet therein:

> "Let the priests themselves believe,
> And put salvation on."

Go back to the apostolic writings, "Judgment must begin at the house of God." If we are ever able to return to that realization of fellowship, it will be in the power of the absolute filling of the Spirit. When we are of one heart, one inspirational centre; of one soul, one dynamic of life; then again, it will be true that not one of us will say that aught of the things which he possesses is his own. There will be no rules and regulations, but a great love. That is where the Church has most sadly failed. When Peter came to write his letter, he wrote words which to me are the most wonderful in all the apostolic writings, as setting forth one phase of truth about the Church. "Ye are an elect race," that is the life principle; "a royal priesthood"; that is our relation to God; "a holy nation," that is the social order. That is where we have failed.

We are not what we ought to be within the Church. I have no hope whatever of any social propaganda outside the Church. If we cannot realize this fair and fragrant vision of beauty within, at least let each soul see to it that it does believe; that the inspirational centre of its life is love, and the dynamic behind all its activities, that Spirit which makes things material forever subservient to things spiritual. The measure in which each does this will be the measure of the Church's approximation to the lost ideal. Let us pray for some measure of restoration; for therein lies the Church's safety, and her power of testimony to the resurrection of Christ in the world.

Acts 5: 1–16

The opening word of this section, "But," at once suggests a contrast. Interest still centres in the Church in

Jerusalem. We are still observing the first things in its history in that city. We have contemplated the first impression produced, the first message delivered, the first opposition manifested, and the first realization of fellowship. We have seen the hostility of rationalism, the Sadducean party opposed to the work of the apostles, preëminently because they proclaimed the Resurrection of Jesus from among the dead. Then following the hostility which manifested itself after the healing of the lame man at the Beautiful Gate, and expressed itself for the present only in examination and threatening, we saw the great and gracious and wonderful picture of the fellowship of spirituality; that first fascinating account of how these people—answering the impulse of love, walking in light, and energized by life, all of which things had come to them in new measure and method by the coming of Pentecost—had all things in common.

In this passage we are faced with a new peril, and a new manifestation of power. The passage opens with the tragic and awful story of Ananias and Sapphira; but it closes with the account of how all the sick who were brought to the apostles were healed. All that is here recorded of judgment and of blessing is the outcome of the One Presence in the Church. The blasting and the blessing were the acts of the Holy Spirit in His administration of the work and the will of Christ. The story therefore of the whole paragraph is that of the first discipline, and reveals its occasion, its operation, and its outcome. The occasion of discipline was the sin of Ananias and Sapphira; its operation was the direct, swift, and awful judgment of God; its outcome was a new fear and a new power resulting therefrom.

We need to understand exactly what this sin was. First let it be noted that it was a sin within the fellowship of the Church. There can be no doubt whatever that Ananias and Sapphira were already associated with that company of believing souls which constituted the infant

[147]

[Acts 5: 1-16]

Church in Jerusalem. The perils without we have seen; but this peril was within, and was far more insidious, far more subtle, far more dangerous, than all those from without. The Church has never been harmed or hindered by opposition from without; it has been perpetually harmed and hindered by perils from within.

Let it be carefully remembered that the sin of Ananias and Sapphira was not that of refusing to contribute. They brought a part of the price. Neither was it that of refusing to give all. It was not wrong that they should bring part of the price. We must insist again upon that which we emphasized in our last study, that the communism of the early Church was not by law, rule, regulation, requirement. It was the natural and beautiful outcome of the spirit-life by which all were mastered. Consequently when Ananias and Sapphira gave only part of the result of their selling of land, of their selling of their possession, there was no wrong in keeping back part of the price. There was no regulation in this early community that men should give, or that they should give all. This was not a requirement for fellowship or for service. Wherein then lay the sin? One must discover the nature of the sin by what Peter said both to Ananias and Sapphira. The sin of Ananias and Sapphira was the sin of pretending that part was all. It was the sin of hypocrisy, of attempting to appear what they really were not, of endeavouring to make it appear that they had done what they really had not. The sin was that of lying; so the apostle named it: "How is it that thou hast conceived this thing in thy heart? Thou hast not lied unto men, but unto God." This was the terrible nature of the sin; not that of refusing to give; not that of only giving part; but that of attempting to make men believe that they had given all, when they had only given part, and so that of lying to God.

We may illustrate this by the things of to-day. If a man attend a convention or a religious service, and sing

with fervour, "My all is on the altar" when it is not,
he is committing the sin of Ananias and Sapphira. The
Church's administration to-day is not what it was, or
there might be many dead men and women at the end of
some services. The sin of Ananias and Sapphira is that
of attempting, by confession of the mouth, or song of the
lips, to make it appear that things are, as they really are
not. The one thing that made Christ angry, the one thing
against which He uttered His severest words, was the sin
of hypocrisy. What severe things He said to the men
who pretended to be religious; what scorching, blasting
words fell from His lips against such. He had no attitude toward the hypocrite, but that of unsparing severity;
no language for the hypocrite, but the language of denunciation and of fire. Ye hypocrites who whiten the
external, and within "are full of dead men's bones and
of all uncleanness."

   This Divine attitude toward hypocrisy is revealed by
contrast in the story of God's dealings with His people
as recorded in the Old Testament, and in the accounts
of Christ's attitude toward honest men and women.
Honesty never made God angry, even when it seemed to
blaspheme, as in the case of Job. Christ was ever patient.
An angry protest might honestly be made against something He said, and if His terms of dealing with the protest were severe, the severity was with the mistake, and
not with the man who made it. Perhaps the simplest
illustration may be cited. When Martha faced Him upon
the day of her awful sorrow at the death of their brother,
she was angry. The story cannot be read without catching the accent of an honest, impatient anger. But He was
not angry. He patiently bore with it, shed light upon it,
and illuminated her mind. He led her into rest by answering the angry protest in such way as to astonish her.
If we are in the midst of sorrow, and feel that God has
done hardly by us, and then sing of resignation, that is
hypocrisy. But if we are in the midst of sorrow, and

tell Him all the hot anger of our hearts, He will be patient and gentle, and lead us into light. He Who said " I am the truth " never made any peace with a lie. This man and this woman lied. That was their sin.

But let us look at the sin a little more closely, in order that we may see what it really meant. We can only see it in the light of the previous story, that of the fellowship of the saints. Self instead of love was the impulse of the lying; darkness instead of light was its method; and an earthly possession instead of the fulness of life was the issue.

Self instead of love was the impulse. The marvel of the love existing among the Christians at that time we have seen illustrated in the picture of our last study; it was love that made men cease to say that anything they had was their own; love that made them feel each other's joys, and each other's sorrows in a holy communism. In the midst of that atmosphere of love, Satan was allowed to enter the heart; and the choice made was that of selfishness instead of that of love.

It was, moreover, the method of darkness instead of light. Wondrous light had come to these men; light in which the apostles themselves saw more clearly the meaning of Christ, and the ultimate issue of His mission, than they had done in the three years in which they had been disciples close at His side. It was a strange and mystic light that illuminated all the dark horizon, and led into life with all its new meaning. In the midst of that light, Ananias and Sapphira lived in the darkness, and walked in the darkness, and chose the method of deceit.

They chose, moreover, to retain earthly possessions for themselves, rather than enter into all the spacious issues of the life which they had received. Barnabas having land, sold it, and laid the proceeds at the feet of the apostles; and as we go on through the Acts of the Apostles, presently we find another thing recorded about him. He was " A man full of faith, and of the Holy

Spirit." That was the larger life. He flung the dusty
possessions away, and took hold upon the infinite things.
But these people clung to the thing that was material, and
in so doing denied the operation of the spiritual life.
That which is the price of honesty, is always the ruin
of a life. Judas may grasp his thirty pieces of silver,
but he will never spend them. There is no purchasing
power in the gain of dishonesty. Ananias and Sapphira
retained a part of their possession, but they lost even the
thing they sought to gain, when they were content to lose
the greater gain.

We turn next to consider the operation of discipline.
Here we have to do with matters which we must describe
as supernatural. Yet there is a sense in which they were
natural, rather than supernatural. If we interpret what
happened that day, by the higher law of the higher life
that had come to these men, it was natural. The un-
natural thing is that men should still live in the Church,
professedly in the name of Christ, and continue in their
impurity. This was the true nature of the new conditions. The discerning Spirit was at work, and the atmosphere was such that it was impossible for a man
with a lie in his heart to come in, without the lie being
known and detected. The tremendous, the overwhelming part of this picture, the thing that astonishes and
fills us with awe, is not the death of Ananias and Sapphira. It is rather that of the purity of the Church that
compelled that death; compelled it, not by law and control, but by the atmosphere of the Spirit in which the
Church was purified, and in which the Church was wholly
and absolutely at the disposal of the Spirit. There was
once a flaming sword that guarded the way to the tree of
life. How flaming, in the power of holiness, was this
atmosphere, into which if a man passed with the profession of generosity on his lips and a lie in his heart, he
was immediately arrested and smitten. I look back upon
the great scene, and it is not the death of a man that fills

me with awe, but that of the Church's condition. That little company of believing souls, a growing company all the time, but still comparatively a small company, was the Body of Christ, His instrument for the revealing of His will, and the carrying out of His will. It was dominated by the Spirit, and so was mastered by His love, walked in His light, and was energized by His life. There came into that assembly a man with a lie upon his lips; and in a moment one spokesman of the fellowship addressed him with a faithfulness that could only be the outcome of the Spirit's indwelling, inspiration, and interpretation. Peter had no mixed motive in his heart, he had no desire to retain the patronage of Ananias because he was a wealthy man; but being a man wholly at the disposal of the Spirit for the doing of the work of Christ, his word was that of terrific directness.

Then observe that Peter said no word to Ananias about his death. The sentence was not the calling down upon a man of a curse at the caprice of an ecclesiastical official. The death of Ananias was the act of God. It is probable that no man in that company was more surprised than Peter himself when Ananias fell dead. He "gave up the ghost." He could not live in that atmosphere.

It was also the purification of the Church. This was an act of discipline by which a man who would have spoiled the Church's fellowship, and paralyzed its power, by polluting its purity, was swept on one side. Through all the story of God's dealing with men, it will be found that the beginning of some new departure such as this, has been characterized by an act of sudden judgment. The question is often asked: Why has not this continued? If the Church had continued to live as a whole, in that atmosphere, that discipline would have been maintained. The Church has become dangerously weak in the matter of discipline. We have welcomed altogether too carelessly men into our fellowship who are not of us; and as the mixed multitude was the perpetual curse through all the years to the Hebrew nation; so the mixed multitude in the fellowship of the Christian Church has been, and still is, the supreme curse of the Christian Church. Far better the three hundred men that lapped, than the thirty-two thousand who first gathered about Gideon. I look back with wonder and astonishment and amazement and ever-increasing awe at that awful atmosphere of the purity of the early Church, in which a lie could not live; and in which the judgment was swift, sudden, sure, appalling, awful, direct, by the hand of God.

Finally the outcome is clearly revealed in the passage. Two words will express it: fear, and power. Luke is careful to say that the fear came upon the Church, and was felt outside it also. " Great fear came upon the whole Church." That is the first occurrence of the word Church in the Acts of the Apostles. Never before had the company been called the Church. Here she emerges in her conscious and corporate life. There fell upon them a new sense of fear, the revelation of the awful purity of the atmosphere of the Holy Spirit. They had felt the thrill of love, and had answered it in that holy fellowship described in the previous chapter. Now they were taught by this activity of the Holy Spirit in the case of Ananias and Sapphira, the purity of the Holy Spirit. The very Church itself fell into solemn and awful awe under the sense of that purity. Where the Spirit indwells and has full sway, the same awe forevermore abides. We have heard very much in recent years of the ministry of the Spirit. More books have been written on the work of the Holy Spirit during the last fifty years than in all the nineteen centuries preceding. Yet I am sometimes afraid, in reading books, in listening to addresses, in singing hymns about the Spirit, that we have been more impressed by the joy of the life, than by the awful solemnity of its purity. The early Church had to learn not only the love that made a man feel that nothing he possessed was his own, but that a lie could not live in the atmosphere of the Spirit. Either Ananias or the Spirit must go. The two cannot live side by side. Fear fell upon the Church, wholesome Godly fear; the Spirit of awe sweeping over the company of believers; the fear that made them investigate as to whether or not, perchance there were any lie in their own position and profession. Would God that such a baptism of fire might fall upon us to-day, the fear that drives us to a solemn enquiry as to whether our anthems are blasphemy, our hymns impertinence, and our profession a lie. I am passing no judgment upon any man, but I am bringing my life to the bar of the judgment of purity. It is only as we come there that we gain the full value of this story.

But the fear fell upon the community outside, as well as upon the Church; upon all the city, and upon all the leaders of men that thronged the city. That sudden and swift and awful judgment became a flaming sword barring the entrance, and holding men away. There is a sense in which the Church of God should always be spoken of as Mother Church, with her dear arms stretched out to take back the lost and wandering. But the Church must be a holy Church, a flame, a fire, and a scorching; so that while the wandering may come back, they know in their coming that the garments spotted by the flesh must be burned as they enter; that the unholy traffic must be left at the door; that no man or woman can hope to come into the fellowship of the Christian Church, whose hands are stained with unholy business; that no man or woman can hope to find refuge in the Church unless their lives are true and pure and consecrated to the highest of all ideals. It will be a good thing for the Church when she gets back so near to the Pentecostal manifestation and power, that fear falls upon the outside world. Why is it that the outside world does not fear in the presence of the Church? Why is it that parliaments and kings and emperors are not afraid of the Church? Because the Church has allowed to come within her borders the unclean thing; because she is not pure. If only the Church of God had maintained that level of purity that comes from absolute abandonment to the indwelling Spirit, so that His life might have flamed at her gates, men would have come for healing, but never for refuge for a lie.

But the result was not only fear; it was also power. "By the hands of the apostles were many signs and wonders wrought among the people; and they were all with one accord in Solomon's porch. But of the rest durst no man join himself to them; howbeit the people magnified them; and believers were the more added to the Lord." Then mark the peculiar evidence of power that follows. "Insomuch that they even carried out the sick into the streets and laid them on beds and couches, that, as Peter came by, at the least his shadow might overshadow some one of them. And there also came together the multitude from the cities round about Jerusalem, bringing sick folk, and them that were vexed with unclean spirits: and they were healed every one."

There are several things of importance in that paragraph. First of all notice that the paragraph does not say that the shadow of Peter healed any one of them, or that it did not. Do not let us deny the accuracy of the story, by denying the truth of something that is not affirmed. The phrase "the shadow of Peter" is a purely Eastern phrase; and in the Eastern lands to-day people will try to escape from the shadow of one man because there is an evil influence supposed to be in it; and they will try to come into the shadow of another in which there is supposed to be an influence for good. This is a purely Eastern picture, but see what it reveals; and see what these men thought of Peter. Sick people felt they would be healed if put in his shadow. It is a revelation of these people's conception of the power of the Christian Church. They were afraid, and yet they knew that

[155]

purity was at the heart of the fierce fire that scorched and blasted sin. The world always knows it. At the heart of the fire there is not only purity, but blessing. The world is keenly conscious of the fact that the only healing is the healing of purity and holiness, however much they may argue to the contrary. As they carried the sick out into the streets and laid them there, their doing so was evidence of the impression made upon them of that little company of pure souls, in the presence of whom no lie could live.

Then there was the actual healing of the multitudes. Observe how careful Luke the physician is. We can detect the touch of the physician in all his writings. He drew attention to the different kinds of sickness. " There also came together the multitudes from the cities round about Jerusalem, bringing sick folk, and them that were vexed with unclean spirits; and they were healed every one." That is to say there was bodily and mental healing, healing for the bodies of the sick, healing for the minds demon-possessed; and they were healed every one. The Church ought to face this problem and enquire as to whether we have not lost, with our loss of purity, an actual power which ought to have enabled us to deal with very much of physical and mental disease, which is still in our midst, and which baffles us on every hand. Take the story as written here, and the story of all healing in the New Testament, and it will at once be seen where the wrong emphasis is placed. Gifts were bestowed upon some in the Church and exercised by them. There is no case recorded where healing was made dependent upon a certain kind of faith, or even upon an attitude of faith on the part of the person who was sick.

What are the individual applications of the story? First surely this story speaks to us in the most solemn terms of the necessity for truth and holiness in the individual life. The need abides as much as ever. He requires truth in the inward parts.

THE ACTS OF THE APOSTLES

In making an application of the story so far as the Church is concerned, I repeat that here is a story that begins with destruction and ends in healing, but it is the one power in both cases. Hell and heaven are made by the selfsame presence. It depends upon what a man is, as to whether the presence of God to him be heaven or hell. "Who among us can dwell with the devouring fire? Who among us can dwell with everlasting burnings? He that walketh righteously; and speaketh uprightly." God is the one and final environment of man's soul, and He is heaven or hell to a man according to what the man is. The same mystic might in that early Church of the indwelling and abiding Spirit struck a lying man and woman to death, and healed the crowds that came. It is but one Presence, and indeed there is a very remarkable interrelation between the two effects. Through judgment in the Church the Spirit moved to the healing of all that were brought. It is when the Church is cleansed and pure that she is ready to be an instrument of His healing, whether it be of spirit or mind or body. Through judgment to healing is the movement of this narrative.

The Church pure is the Church powerful. Go back over her history and see how true that is. It has always been so. Mathematics have no place in the economy of God, numbers are nothing; quality is everything.

But the Church Spirit-filled is the Church pure. The only power equal to making a Church pure is that of the indwelling Spirit of God.

And the last thing is, the Church obedient is the Church Spirit-filled. In proportion as she is obedient to the light she has, she is filled not once and forever, but perpetually with the eternal inrush of the Spirit, which is also the eternal outflow of the Spirit's power. "Living water" said the Lord Himself. What is living water? Water that is not stagnant, simply that, and nothing more. The term does not suggest mineral properties, but a continual flow. If I gather from the bubbling spring some water, and say I will retain some of this living water for use, it ceases to be living water in the moment I have so gathered it. Living water is forevermore flowing in, and through, and out. The great and gracious river, figurative of the Spirit, is full of suggestiveness. The Church must be filled by the Spirit, Who ever fills, and ever purifies, and ever flows through. But if the Church by her worldliness, by her complicity with the world, the flesh, and the devil dams the flow of the river, she loses her power, because she loses her purity.

All the great principles revealed concerning the Church are true of the individual. It is the pure man who is the strong man. It is the Spirit-filled man who is the pure man. It is the man obedient to the light received, who is the Spirit-filled man.

Acts 5 : 17–42

We are still dealing with the first things of the Christian Church, and come now to the first definite persecution. We see the forces opposed to Christianity, gaining courage, most evidently the courage of desperation. The rulers were strangely perplexed by the new and remarkable victories that were being gained in the city. At the centre of our paragraph there is a statement which gives us a general outlook upon the condition of affairs in Jerusalem. This declaration is the more remarkable in that it was made, not by Peter, but by the high priest; not by one who stood in defence of the Christian movement, but by the chief leader of the opposition thereto. From the standpoint of the opposition it was surely a word spoken inadvisedly. I sometimes wonder if the high priest would have uttered such remarkable testimony to that little band of men arraigned before him, if he had known that it would be preserved for all time. He said to them: "We strictly charged you not to teach in this name; and behold, ye have filled Jerusalem with your teaching, and intend to bring this Man's blood upon us." This was, as we have said, most remarkable testimony to the growth of Christianity in Jerusalem at that time. It shows how profound an effect was being produced upon the city;—" Ye have filled Jerusalem with your teaching "; and more, ye " intend to bring this Man's blood upon us." This was a revelation of the fact that the testimony and teaching of the apostles were turning public opinion toward a true conception of the action of the rulers in encompassing the death of Christ.

As we read this chapter there are three standpoints from which we may consider the story profitably : first, that of the opposition :—its composition, its reason, and its methods ; secondly, that of the Church :—its master principle, the methods of its work, and its temper in the midst of opposition ; finally, that of seeing God amid the shadows, keeping watch above His own,—His methods, and His victories.

In order that we may follow this course, the simple facts of the story must be kept in mind. The apostles were imprisoned by the jealousy of the Sadducees. In the early morning, before daybreak, they were delivered supernaturally by the intervention of an angel. Immediately upon their release they returned—just as the sun was flushing the eastern sky, and as, in the Hebrew economy therefore, the ancient sacrifice was about to be offered in the temple—and carried on that work, for the doing of which they had been imprisoned. A little later in the day, but still in the morning, the Sanhedrim assembled, and they were perplexed because the apostles were lost. There is a touch of humour in the situation, in that trembling in the most august assembly of men that Jerusalem could produce. Luke describes that assembly on this occasion with careful accuracy as the senate and council, that is the greater and the lesser Sanhedrim. In imagination we see them assembled in their robes, and dignity, and glory; everything in readiness except the prisoners. They were not forthcoming While they waited, messengers were sent to the prison, only to discover their absolute helplessness in the presence of the Divine movement, for the messengers returned to tell them the prisoners had escaped. Then came another messenger, and there seems to be a touch of satire, whether intended or not, in his message: " The men whom ye put in the prison are in the temple standing and teaching the people." The apostles were at last brought, and placed in the centre of the council; arraigned on the charge of continuing to preach and teach in the name of Jesus. The apostolic defence followed, that address of Peter, a perfect example of courage and clearness and concise declaration of fundamental truths. It was a powerful statement, and the council decided to dismiss the men with a caution, and then violated their own order, by beating them. We then see them go forth, and a most illuminative thing is written of them: " They therefore departed from the presence of the council, rejoicing that they were counted worthy to suffer dishonour for the Name." Such is the story.

First then let us observe the opposition. A description is given in verse seventeen of those before whom the apostles were arraigned: " The high priest . . . and all they that were with him (which is the sect of the Sadducees)." Then in verse twenty-one: " The high priest . . . called the council together ";—that is the inner circle of the Sanhedrim, that which was known as the Lesser Sanhedrim, lesser not in importance but in numbers;—" and all the senate ";—that is the whole company of the Sanhedrim. Pharisees were included in that gathering. When we were considering the first opposition we saw how very careful the writer of the story was to show that the whole Sanhedrim was not in opposition; but now the complete Sanhedrim was gathered together. The full gathering was a revelation of keen interest. It was a rare thing in those days for the whole

of that great assembly to meet together. The Sanhedrim
was the constituted Hebrew authority, having limited
jurisdiction under the Roman rule, and they met occa·
sionally, a handful of them; but this whole gathering
was evidence of remarkably keen interest in the case
before them. This full gathering of the Sanhedrim was
a very important thing, showing the growth of the Christian movement in Jerusalem. So keenly interested were
the rulers of the people, that the whole Sanhedrim had
come together, gathering from far and near. They were
all there because they had felt the thrill of the new movement. The air was electric with it. The high priest,
spokesman of the rest, said, " Ye have filled Jerusalem
with your teaching." Men were talking in the assembly
courts, in the places of commerce, and everywhere, about
this new heresy, this new doctrine, this new teaching,
this new way, this new life, this new religion.

The real inspiration of the opposition is revealed quite
clearly in verse twenty-one; it was jealousy. Jealousy
is always an ugly word; and it means here exactly what
it means in our English tongue. Their jealousy is explained by verse twenty-eight. These rulers had discovered that their own authority was being set at nought
as the result of a new authority which was at work in the
city; an authority that had no central council, no police
to enforce it, no army behind it; but a mighty, spiritual
power, making itself felt in all the city. In consequence
of that new authority, theirs was being set on one side,
first by these very men who were arraigned before them,
and therefore by the people. They were " much perplexed concerning them whereunto this would grow."
They were unable to see the direction, and they were in
trouble as to the ultimate issue.

The final reason of the opposition was hatred. These
men did not understand this new movement. They could
not account for it. It was a great mystery to them that
they had not been able to end it when they crucified its

[Acts 5: 17-42]

Leader; and an even greater mystery, that when they laid a charge of silence upon a handful of Galilean fishermen, it proved to be absolutely and utterly without avail. Despite all their determination to stamp out the heresy of the Nazarene, Jerusalem was full of the doctrine. In the presence of that mystery their hearts were moved with hatred because they felt the reins of power slipping from their own fingers.

The methods of the opposition were those, first of intimidation; and finally of caution, according to the advice of Gamaliel. This advice was by no means strong, but preëminently weak. From the standpoint of the Church, the advice of Gamaliel to give them time was excellent; but from the standpoint of the opposition it was weak. The strong attitude is never that of allowing anything to drift, in order to see its result; but rather that of intellectual determination to examine and discover the meaning of that which is moving men. Saul of Tarsus was honest, intellectual, strong, mighty before he was converted, and he was so afterwards. His two attitudes of mind were these; first to crush the movement; and then, when he was arrested and compelled to come to the inner heart of the mystery, he discovered that the only attitude was that of toiling and suffering in order to put a crown upon the brow of Jesus Christ. The opposition to the Christian Church was mainly Sadducean, rationalistic, that which protests against the supernatural. In the presence of the supernatural it was strangely perplexed, and acting upon the advice of Gamaliel, decided to watch developments, rather than to face and solve the problem.

Let us now look at the Church. As we look back at the city of Jerusalem and accept this dictum of the high priest that it was full of the doctrine, we must feel a sense of contrast with the present times. To-day there are great multitudes of people gathering together to worship God. We thank God for all the assemblies of His saints. There is an atmosphere of fiery fervour and irresistible dynamic in these stories that we miss to-day. If we can see that early Church, we shall discover the reason of the difference. The opposition is exactly the same. It does not take the same forms to-day. It never will take the same form again. Physical imprisonment and torture are largely things of the past. They will not be tolerated to-day. But if the method of the opposition is different, the spirit is with us still. Sadduceeism is rampant, so is Pharisaism; they are represented to-day by rationalism and ritualism. These are the opponents of living, vital Christianity to-day, just as they were in Jerusalem.

How then is the Church to be victorious in the midst of these things? Let us go back to our story. Observe the principle upon which these men acted. It is expressed in one brief statement: " We must obey God rather than men." That was the master-principle of the early Church. The word translated *obey* is a rare word in the New Testament, occurring not more than four times altogether. It stands exclusively for obedience; it does not suggest anything except actual, absolute, unquestioning submission.

In his defence Peter affirmed three things concerning God: God raised Jesus; God exalted Jesus to His right hand; God gave the Spirit to them that obey Him. These were the great things which had brought these men into the position of absolute surrender to God; the resurrection, the ascension, and the outpouring of the Spirit on the day of Pentecost. In the power of these things Peter said, " We must obey God rather than men." We must put emphasis upon almost every word in that little sentence, in order to find the profound significance of it. " We must obey *God*." That is the language of a company of people who have come into fellowship with God, and have swept out from their lives all other mastership and all other authority. Or again, " We must *obey* God." Not we must consider Him, or patronize Him, or hold theories concerning Him, or defend the fact of His existence. Yet further, "We *must* obey God." It is when a man, or a company of men, says, I must, or, We must, that we listen with respect. When a man says, I ought, we are interested, but not moved. A man may know what he ought to do, and never do it. When a man says I must, and begins to interpret his rights or his beliefs in the terms of obligation, then he is passing into the realm of power. "We must." All these men are against you—"We must." You will be imprisoned— "We must." We are determined that you shall not— "We must." Finally, "*We* must obey God." They did not endeavour to persuade others to bear their responsibility, but took the burden upon themselves.

The proportion in which the Church and individual members of the Church say that, is the measure in which the old impressions can be made again, the old victories won, the old power be known. That may seem like a somewhat severe impeachment of the Christian Church to-day. If it be so then let us remember that whenever men say "We must obey God," and mean it, they safeguard themselves against the power of opposition, the peril of patronage and the paralysis of compromise. To ponder these three words is to see some of the reasons why the Church is not producing, and has not recently produced the old effects.

One is almost ashamed to speak of suffering for Christ to-day, there is so little of it. We see these men scarred, bruised, and battered; carrying in their bodies the stigmata of Jesus, the actual brutal scars and bruises in the flesh as the result of stones and stripes; when we put against all that, the suffering we have to endure to-day, one is almost ashamed to speak of it as suffering. But opposition is with us still, insidious, smiling, devilish opposition; and perhaps that kind of opposition is harder to fight than the other. How shall we be safeguarded against yielding to opposition? "We must obey God." The Church's gravest danger has never been created by opposition. When she has been opposed and persecuted she has been pure and strong. Never until she was patronized did she become weak. Wherever the Church is patronized and admired by the world, she becomes weak. How shall we safeguard against that? "We must obey God." So surely as the Church is obeying Him, she can never be weakened by patronage, and she never can be paralyzed by compromise. She must forevermore stand alone, bearing her testimony, opening her portals to receive the wounded in order that they may be healed, spreading her arms, great mother Church, to take the wanderers back again, and lead them to health and blessedness; but never permitting the standard of her ideals to be lowered, or her message of righteousness to be silenced, or her claim on behalf of God to be reckoned as of no account.

In this story we find not only the principle, but the methods of the early Church. These are revealed in the final word of Peter, "We are witnesses of these things; and so is the Holy Spirit, Whom God hath given to them that obey Him." What is a witness? Not a person who talks merely. Many people will talk who are not witnesses; and many people will witness, who do not talk. A witness is a martyr. A martyr is a confessor, not with the lip only, but with the life; a martyr is an evidence, a credential, a demonstration. I see Peter standing in the midst of the intellectual aristocracy of Jerusalem, saying in effect: You have no right to question the accuracy of what we say until you have accounted for what we are. "We are witnesses." See what we *were;* see what we *are;* and know that the change has been wrought because God raised Jesus, exalted Him to be a Prince and a Saviour, to give repentance and remission, and gave us the Spirit. We have followed Him; we have repented, our sins are remitted; we have the Spirit. "We are witnesses." See what we are. The Church is never powerful unless she can produce her witnesses; not her preachers merely. If men and women are listening to preaching and are incarnating the thing preached, and are becoming living witnesses, concrete, incarnate documents, that is the way of the Church's victory.

But observe the completion of the declaration. "We are witnesses . . . *and so is the Holy Spirit.*" That is the Church's final power. That is the mightiest fact of all. If we lack coöperation with the Holy Spirit, unless we are in business partnership with the Holy Spirit, we can do nothing to impress Jerusalem or London. Unless the preacher is touched with the unseen, unless the Church catches and flashes upon the world the mystic light of the infinite, which cannot be gathered in the academy or university, preacher and Church will be " Faultily faultless, icily regular, splendidly null." If we would fill London with our doctrine, we must be in partnership with the Holy Spirit. Then through joy and pain, the Church will move forward with God in continual victory.

Acts 6: 1-7

In these seven verses we have the account of the first organization within the Church. While this is a story which seems to be almost entirely local, yet it is full of value in its revelation of abiding principles. There is nothing more interesting in the study of this book, or indeed in the study of the whole New Testament, than the absence of anything like detailed instruction as to ecclesiastical arrangements. The incidental things are not apparent; but the essential things are clearly manifest. The incidental rearrangements are largely out of sight; the eternal things that admit of no rearrangement are perpetually in view.

Let us then look at this brief, human, natural story of the first organization of the Christian Church—not a full

[Acts 6: 1–7]

and final organization, but one in order to meet an immediate need; not so much that we may see the particular officers or system, but that we may see the underlying spirit and life and method.

It is necessary, however, that we should first see the local colouring; the occasion of the organization; and the men chosen for the particular work.

The occasion was that of the actual, or supposed, neglect of the Hellenist widows in the distribution of those funds which had resulted from the inspired communism of the early Church. This was not a quarrel between Jews and Gentiles; these people were all Jews; the Revised Version is careful to render the word *Hellenist*, which means " Grecian Jew." For an understanding of the distinction we must go back to the days of the Maccabees, and remember all that wonderful activity which had resulted in the creation, within Judaism, of two distinct and antagonistic parties. There were out-and-out Hebrews. They were dwellers in Palestine, and largely in Jerusalem, who spoke Hebrew or Aramaic, and observed all the customs and traditions of Hebraism. The Hellenist Jews still worshipped Jehovah, still followed the ritual of the ancient economy, but very largely spoke the Greek tongue, and had come under the influence of Greek thinking, apart altogether from Christianity. There was therefore a very clear line of division between the Hebrews, and the Hellenist Jews.

I am always thankful for the book of the Acts of the Apostles, and, among other reasons, because it takes away the false impression some people have that the early Church was absolutely perfect. I am perpetually hearing to-day that we need to go back to apostolic times. It is therefore a great comfort to me to see that in days of multiplication, success, and victory, there were difficulties within the Church, murmuring in the midst of development. These people had been baptized by the Spirit into union with Christ, and were living still in the glory of that Pentecostal effusion, which had wrought such wonders in individual lives, and had so impressed Jerusalem. Yet here into the company of the Church, into this sacred fellowship, there had come materialistic and social distinctions, that ought forever to have been destroyed at the doorway of the Church. I am not glad of the division—for all such divisions ought to cease the moment the threshold of the Church of Jesus Christ is crossed; but I am glad the story reveals it. The antagonism between Hellenist and Hebrew was within the Church. Here then we have a picture not of heresy, but of schism. If I may simply illustrate the difference, a schism is a rent, a sect is a piece torn off. There are no sects in Christianity; but alas, there is a great deal of schism. Never a piece has been torn off from the Church yet; would to God we all believed it. There is a great deal of schism, alas and alas, which ought not to be; but there are no sects in the Church. We still can sing Baring Gould's great hymn, " We are not divided "; and have loving pity for the man who cannot join us honestly in that singing. Here was a schism, a rent, a division, born of social distinction that ought never to have been recognized within the Christian Church.

What was the issue? Seven men were chosen; and all the names of these men were Greek names. There was not a Hebrew name amongst them. Almost certainly six of the men chosen were Hellenist Jews; one of them a proselyte, that is, a Greek who had become a Hebrew by religion. The remarkable thing about this, is that the difficulty was that the Hellenists imagined that the Hebrews inside the Church were neglecting them in the daily ministration, and when presently the issue of the spiritual and apostolic method was declared, the Church manifested not its weakness but its strength, in the fine and gracious act of electing seven men, not Hebrews but Hellenists, men from the very company of those who thought their widows were neglected. These men would henceforth have to do with the distribution of alms, not to the Hellenists only, but to the Hebrews also. That is the very spirit of Christianity. It overcomes prejudice by heaping upon those who imagine they have been neglected, all the honours and responsibilities of office. I am afraid we are a long way from apostolic times! Charles Haddon Spurgeon once said, If you have an angular, peculiar person in your church, always put him into office, and keep him at work. It was fine philosophy, warranted by this action of the early Church.

So much for that which is purely local. Through the local and the incidental, we discover the ideal and the essential. Perspective is the value of distance. From a distance then, let us look back at that picture, and observe three things: first, the organism; secondly, the organizing; finally, the organization.

First the organism. It is not described. There is no mention of unity here at all. Indeed, it is a paragraph that seems to deal with a quarrel, a schism; and yet, looking back at the whole company, there is revealed the Christian Church; not finally organized, but a great organism. The one Lord, and Hebrew and Hellenist Christians alike were loyal to the one Lord. The one faith, fastened upon that one selfsame Lord, and expressing itself—if in divergent opinions as between themselves—in common loyalty to the one Lord. Finally, the one Spirit, presiding over the whole company, and inspiring all of them, so that it was possible for the apostles to say, " Look ye out therefore, brethren, from among you seven men of good report, full of the Spirit."

Then we see not merely the one life, but all the organs in the one life, necessary for the fulfilling of the purpose of that life. They were all present. There were men there, quite capable of managing all the business enterprises of the Church; and there were men there, equally capable of proclaiming the great message of the Church. There were men there to whom had been committed the

[169]

service of the Word, the preaching of the Word. There were men there who had all the ability necessary for the serving of tables, for carrying out all the business side of the Church's work. In that company there were all the organs necessary for the fulfilment of the full meaning of the life of the Church. They had not been found, they had not been set in order; there was a little conflict between them; a little misunderstanding; but they were there. There existed a perfect organism, possessed of all the organs necessary for the fulfilling of the meaning of its own life.

The one purpose was that namely of the proclamation of the Evangel, the presentation to men of the Person of the world's Redeemer, the increase of the Word.

The sense of relation existing is manifest first in the complaint. These people complained because they recognized the unity, the inter-relationship, the mutual responsibility, and felt that it was not being realized. I leave out of count the question as to whether the complaint was warranted or not, as something which cannot be decided, because the story is silent concerning it. The fact of the complaint is demonstration of an underlying consciousness of unity. Those Hellenists who imagined that the Hellenist widows were being neglected, felt the neglect was a violation of that great fellowship, of which we have already spoken; and so the complaint was the manifestation of the underlying sense of unity. That unity has most clear manifestation in the organization of the Church, which resulted from this particular schism. Forget the murmuring of the Hellenists for a moment, and see in Jerusalem the one Church, an organism not completely organized, not perfectly working. There was a defect somewhere, but to use a medical distinction, it was a functional trouble, not an organic one. It is when we recognize the organism that we are able to organize. In proportion as we forget the organism, our organization is a mockery, a blunder, a disaster.

THE ACTS OF THE APOSTLES

We now turn to the subject of the organizing in the presence of the difficulty. This process consisted in the discovery of the organs, and their employment. Here comes out into prominence two orders of the Christian ministry. In the Congregational Church, we generally speak of this as the institution of the order of the diaconate. The word "deacon" is used in the Anglican Church in another sense to the sense in which we use it. It should be remembered that the word "deacon" never occurs in this passage. I believe these men were deacons; but the word does not occur here. The Greek word from which the word *deacon* comes is in this passage, but it is used not only of the seven but also of the apostles. The apostles were also deacons. It is important therefore to discover the meaning of the actual word. It simply means men who serve. Two orders emerge into view in this process of organizing; men who serve "the Word," and men who "serve tables." The twelve said, "It is not fit that we should forsake the Word of God, and serve tables," and presently the very word "service" is used of the work of preaching the Word. Consequently the first order is that of preaching of the Word, which includes apostolic, prophetic, evangelistic, and pastoral work, as Paul himself elaborated it, when he came to write the Ephesian letter. The preaching of the Word, whether apostolic, which is fundamental and authoritative; or prophetic, which makes application of principles to an age; or evangelistic, which woos and wins individuals; or pastoral, which teaches and instructs the saints that they may grow; all these are contained within the one great function of the preaching of the Word.

There is also another service which emerges at this point;—the service of tables. How did it originate? Mark carefully the simple order. As the result of the preaching of the Word new conditions of life were created. The numbers of those who believed in Jesus

[171]

multiplied, the Church grew in numbers, and whenever a Church grows in numbers it necessarily grows in necessity and need. All new conditions of life demand new arrangements, new care, new thought. These conditions demanded business attention. The business attention must be business attention in the spirit of the Word preached. Consequently this need for a new service was created. It was necessary that there should be an order of men, who should coöperate with the preachers of the Word, by caring for the new conditions arising as the result of the preaching of the Word. Therefore the office here revealed is not inferior to the apostolic office; it is separate from it, and yet complementary to it.

Notice in the second place the procedure. The first thing in this organism was the setting free of the apostles for their own work, setting them free from high work which nevertheless hindered them in the doing of their own. It was high and holy work, this work of caring for the distress existing among the members of the Church. It is always high and holy work, every part of the business of the Church—the swinging open of the door, the reception of the man who comes across the threshold, and placing him in relation to service and work. It is great in every detail, but the doing of it hinders the men who are called to the preaching of the Word. The apostles said, " It is not fit that we should forsake the Word of God "—not to do a low thing, a mean thing, a vulgar thing; but to do a high and holy thing, if the high and holy thing prevents our fulfilment of that which is our specific work. The first organization was designed to set the preacher of the Word free from everything except prayer and the preaching of the Word. " We will continue steadfastly in prayer and in the ministry of the Word."

Notice the process, the method, under the apostolic guidance. They instructed the people as to how they should act, and ratified their choice, but the appointment of the seven was a Church appointment. The whole multitude of disciples were gathered together; and they—the whole multitude, not the apostles—chose these men. The details of election are not given. This is in keeping with the utter absence of ecclesiastical detail which characterizes the apostolic records. The perpetual presence of the Holy Spirit was to be the safeguard of method and of choice. That which is final and necessary is the presence of the Spirit, His safeguarding of the organization, His selection of the proper men for the proper work, His making known of the will of the Lord for the whole company of disciples, under the direction of the apostolic teaching and apostolic authority. These are things that are very simple, and yet they are of supreme importance.

Mark very carefully the four things said concerning the men chosen to work in the Church. First, " Men from among you "; secondly, " of good report "; thirdly, " full of the Spirit "; finally, " full of . . . wisdom." These are not qualifications for preachers of the Word. This is the apostolic revelation of the conditions upon which men take office in the Christian Church. These are abiding conditions.

First, " from among you." This is the first law of Christian service, that those employed in serving the disciples of the Church should be of the number of the disciples. That condemns forever mixed finance committees, and shows that no Church has any business to bring on to its financial board a man who is not definitely and distinctively a Christian man.

Secondly, men " of good report," and the root of the word " report " is the same root as that for the apostolic word " witness "; martyrs; men of good witness. That is a twofold qualification; they are to be men well reported of; and they are to be men who have borne such witness as to create a good report. May I illustrate this by another passage that seems to be at a distance from this, and yet is closely akin to it; the apostolic charge which Paul delivered to Timothy, " Let no man despise thy youth." By that he did not mean that Timothy was to charge men not to despise his youth; he meant rather that he was to see to it that his youth was not despicable; that he was not a man that men could despise. These were men of good report, men of whom other men spoke excellent things; but in order to be that, they were men of excellent things, they were men who had borne good witness. This suggests the absolute necessity for the choice of men of character in the eyes of the world, for the carrying out of the functions of the Church.

Again, they were to be men " full of the Spirit "; that is, of full realization of Christian power and purpose. There are men who hold aloof from service, and say they cannot lay claim to that realization. Let us understand the meaning of the phrase. A man full of the Spirit is one who is living a normal Christian life. Fulness of the Spirit is not a state of spiritual aristocracy, to which few can attain. Anything less than the fulness of the Spirit for the Christian man is disease of his spiritual life, a low ebb of vitality. Fulness of the Spirit is not abnormal, but normal Christian life. Fulness of the Spirit does not necessarily mean, indeed it does not at all mean, the abandonment of interest in things of the earth; but it does mean that the things of this earth—home, business, profession, and all life, are touched by a hand which is Christ's hand; dealt with by heart and soul and will, under the dominion of the Christ. Such men, men of faith, of Christian devotion, and Christian life, are to hold office in the Church.

But there was yet another qualification, they were to be men, " full of . . . wisdom." It is interesting to notice here that whereas there are different Greek words, translated in our Bible " wisdom," the word here is σοφία, a word never used in Scripture save of God or of good men, except in one case where in evident irony, the practical apostle James says, " This wisdom is not a

wisdom that cometh down from above, but is earthly,
sensual, devilish." In this word "wisdom" there is a
moral quality, but infinitely more; it is a word that suggests the reaching of the best ends by the best means.
They were to be men of sanctified common sense. That
is not translation, but it is interpretation. The man who
holds office in the Church needs tact, and, if he lacks it,
he may have many other things and be of very little use.
He must be a disciple, a man of good report, a normal
Christian, full of the Spirit; but he must be full of wisdom. The very liberty which Christ creates is one of the
greatest perils threatening the Christian Church; a great
and gracious benediction but a perpetual peril, as all the
highest, noblest, and most beautiful things are the most
perilous things, because their adjustment is so delicate
and exquisite. The men who are to take office in the
Christian Church must be men of sanctified common
sense. An old story comes back to mind, the first application of which is in another direction. A Professor in a
Theological College on the American side of the Atlantic,
in his opening address to freshmen who had come up to
take the course, said, " Gentlemen, you need three things
if you are to be successful; gifts, grace, and gumption.
We can do nothing to help you as to the first; I believe
God has given you gifts; we can by training and prayer
help you to gain grace; but if you have not gumption
neither God nor man can help you, and I advise you not
to continue your studies." If this is true of theological
students, and ministers of the Word, it is more true of
the men who have to preside over the very delicate work
of serving the tables of the Christian Church.

We finally see the organization completed. The
organization of the Christian Church is its unified variety
at work; all the variety unified in order to work; the
whole Church obedient to one life-principle, which is
service; the whole Church working without friction,
which is strength; then the accomplishment of results,

which is success. " The Word of God increased." This is a most remarkable expression, showing that true growth of organization is a growth of capacity for revealing Jesus. " The number of the disciples multiplied," and that in the heart of opposition—Jerusalem. By fulfilment of function there was growth of the organism, and by growth of the organism there was increase of power and increase of work. Luke put the final touch upon the story when he wrote a most astonishing thing, " A great company of priests were obedient to the faith." The manifestation of the new exercise of spiritual priesthood destroyed in the best way possible false priestism, by bringing the priests themselves into the place of belief.

So finally we look back to that first organization and see that it was spiritual, simple, and sufficient; but it was not final. A great deal of subsequent organization is carnal, complex, and corrupt. We have to learn in the work of the Christian Church that we must get back to this ancient chapter, and its underlying principles, remembering forevermore that the external manifestation may change, and change perpetually. In the twelfth chapter of Paul's first letter to the Corinthians light may be found on this great theme. Some of the gifts that the apostle there enumerates are not in existence in the Church to-day; the reason for their non-existence being that He divided " to each one severally even as He will." Other gifts may be found in the Church to-day which the apostle did not name, because they were not then bestowed. To try to compress the activity of the Spirit of God in the Christian Church into a formula of a dead generation, even though the story be in the Bible, is to hinder the progress of the Kingdom of God. We must remember that the Spirit is living amongst us now. What we supremely need is to obey the Spirit's leading, and leave ourselves to His direction; always remembering that the work of the whole Church, whether it be the service of the Word or the service of tables, is holy work; and at the gate of the sanctuary service is a flaming sword, and no man must dare enter and lay unclean hands upon the holy vessels, or attempt out of an impure heart to accomplish results of purity.

Acts 6 : 8–15 and 7 : 54–60

We now come to the consideration of the eighth and last of these first things of the Christian Church;—the first martyr. I use the word martyr now in the sense in which it is usually employed. In the process of the centuries we have come to use the word only of such as seal their testimony with their blood. When we chant the *Te Deum* and sing, " The noble army of martyrs praise Thee," our minds turn back to the long and wonderful line of those who have been so true to truth, that they have died rather than violate it in life, or deny it in teaching. But those who have died for the truth were not made martyrs by their dying; they died because they were already martyrs. The fires of Smithfield in the olden days never made martyrs; they revealed them. No hurricane of persecution ever creates martyrs; it reveals them. Stephen was a martyr before they stoned him. He was the first martyr to seal his testimony with his blood.

The story of Stephen is full of strength and colour. The personality of the man arrests us first in that he breaks suddenly upon the view, and as suddenly passes out of sight. He was one of the seven allocated to the work of serving tables, a deacon in the Church. Almost immediately he flamed into a more remarkable prominence than any of the apostles themselves, by his stoning to death, in which there was the merging of tragedy and victory.

We gather from his name that he was either a Greek or a Hellenist, that is a Grecian Jew. His name indeed would have to have been prophetic. Stephen means a

[177]

crown. One can imagine that some fond mother named the boy thus, and so expressed her hope that he would come to some crowning; but little she knew the crowning to which he would come, the first to wear the crown of the martyr in the history of the catholic Church.

There are very many ways in which this story of Stephen might be profitably examined. I propose to deal with it as presenting the first clash of battle, even to the shedding of blood, between the forces of the world and the Christian Church. There had been one such clash of battle, even to the shedding of blood, before; but it was not between the world and the Church, but between the world and Christ. This story is preëminently remarkable for the fact that to that one "*Death-grapple in the darkness 'twixt old systems and the Word,*" this is in succession, continuity, and fellowship. We remember the opening phrase of the book of the Acts, " The former treatise I made, O Theophilus, concerning all that Jesus began both to do and to teach." By that very suggestive commencement, as we have already said, the writer gave character to his earlier treatise, and also a key to the second treatise. He connected them. The Gospel contained the account of the things that Jesus began to do and to teach, and that suggestive phrase indicates the fact that the ministry and mission of Jesus did not end with the things recorded in the Gospel. Therefore it becomes a key to the book of the Acts of the Apostles, which is the story of the things that Jesus continues to do and continues to teach through His Body, which is the Church, by the presidency and power of the Holy Spirit. Christ is seen, through His Body, carrying on the things He began to do and to teach. That is the supreme quality or quantity of interest in the picture presented by Luke, of Stephen in his confession and in his martyrdom. Here is a concrete illustration of what the apostle meant when he spoke of filling up " that which is lacking in the afflictions of Christ." By the use of that word *lacking,* the apostle did

[178]

not mean to infer that there was any absent element in the sufferings of Christ, something that had to be added, as to elemental value. The word *lacking* means the deficit, that is, that which comes later. The underlying thought of the apostle is that the sufferings of Christ are not over. Just as in the mystery of the Incarnation there has been granted to us a glimpse into the eternal fact of the nature of God, and the heart of God, and the suffering of God; so with the work of Jesus Christ and His suffering and His death. The actuality of His suffering did not cease; it is continued in all such as in fellowship with Him suffer shame for His name; their suffering is His, His suffering is theirs. To Stephen fell the singular honour of being the first member of the Body of Christ in whom this continual process of suffering was manifest, this travail that will never end until the ultimate purpose of God be achieved. We often speak of the hour that is to come, with hope and confidence, when " He shall see of the travail of His soul and be satisfied." Let us never forget that the travail itself is not ended; that God, and God in Christ, and God in Christ in His Church, are still travailing in the birth-pangs of redemption, toward the ultimate realization of His great Divine purpose. Here in this early story of the Church is a wonderful manifestation of a member of the Body of Christ making up that which is behindhand in His affliction, in fellowship with his Lord in nature, in testimony, in suffering, and in triumph. We learn the profound meanings of this whole succession of suffering in order to victory, by an examination of this first manifestation. There are two lines of thought; first, the fellowship between Stephen and Jesus; and secondly, the witness of Stephen to the world. The relation of these two things is patent. Stephen is first seen, filled with the Spirit, preaching with great wisdom, working wonders in Jerusalem. Then he is seen bearing his testimony before the Sanhedrim, that testimony which we speak of as his defence. It was the testimony

[179]

of Stephen to the world; and that testimony was the outcome of his fellowship with Jesus of Nazareth.

Let us first consider the fellowship between this man and Jesus. Those familiar with the life-story of Jesus cannot read this story of Stephen without feeling how remarkable are the notes of identification and similarity between the two. Here was a man walking along the very pathway of the Gospels with Christ. The attitude manifested toward him in Jerusalem and by the council, is almost identical with the attitude of the rulers toward Jesus. When we come to the dying of Stephen, the last thing that passed his lips was almost a quotation of some of the last things that Jesus said. Jesus in His dying said, " Father, into Thy hands I commend My Spirit." " Father, forgive them, for they know not what they do." Stephen in his dying said, " Lord Jesus, receive my spirit." " Lord, lay not this sin to their charge." There is perfect harmony between this story of how a man preached and wrought wonders and uttered his great address and went to death; and the story of how the Man of Nazareth preached and wrought wonders and uttered His great discourses and took His way to death.

Between Stephen and Jesus there was communion of nature, there was communion of testimony, there was communion of suffering, and finally there was communion of triumph.

Let us observe first of all the communion of nature. Stephen is described as being " full of grace and power." That is a comprehensive and final description of the nature of this man. Our minds go back to the earlier writing of Luke, and to his declaration concerning Jesus, that He grew in stature and in favour with God and with men. When Luke had to describe the nature of Jesus he always did so by the equivalents of those two words, grace and power. To express the underlying thought in the speech of our own day, I would say, Stephen was full of sweetness and strength. These words are really not so fine as the others, but they may help us for the moment. Sweetness, grace, all that is beautiful and tender and compassionate; and strength, power, all that suggests vigour and determination, dignity and authority. These two qualities were not in separated compartments, but merged in one personality, so that coming into the presence of this man one was welcomed by his grace, and at the same moment aware of his power. These same things were perpetually manifest in Jesus. We hear Him saying to the multitudes, " Come unto Me, all ye that labour and are heavy laden," with such sweet, wooing winsomeness that they crowded after Him; and then saying, " If any man would come after Me, let him deny himself and take up his cross and follow Me," with such sudden, awful solemnity that they hardly dare come at all. Here then was a man who shared the very nature of Jesus; a deacon of the early Church, a man serving tables; but so in fellowship with the nature of Christ that the impression he made upon the men and women who were round about him, was that of great grace and beauty of character, combined with great strength of purpose. These two things persisted to the end. Grace was manifested in his cry, " Lay not this sin to their charge "; and power in the words, " Lord Jesus, receive my spirit." The secret of Stephen's character was that he was in fellowship with Christ in nature, a partner of the very life of Christ.

Secondly, let us notice as briefly, their fellowship in testimony. Luke says of Stephen that he " wrought great wonders and signs " in Jerusalem. In the first Pentecostal sermon, Peter, speaking of Jesus, said of Him, " Jesus of Nazareth, a Man approved of God unto you by mighty works and wonders and signs, which God did by Him in the midst of you, even as ye yourselves know." Thus the very testimony of Jesus by wonders and signs as well as by word of mouth, was the testimony that Stephen had been bearing in Jerusalem. Luke here

[181]

speaks of the wisdom and the Spirit by which Stephen
spake; and in the second chapter of his first treatise he
speaks of the wisdom and Spirit by which Jesus spake,
in almost identical phrases. The selfsame words that he
used to describe the work and teaching of Jesus, he now
used to describe the work and teaching of Stephen.
Thus we see in Stephen a man, not only in fellowship
with the nature of Jesus, but also in fellowship with the
testimony of Jesus repeating His works, uttering His
words. In Stephen the Christ Who had communicated
to him His life, found an instrument for word and work;
and thus the things He began to do He still did.

Mark in the next place, the fellowship of suffering.
The cause of Stephen's suffering was that he had borne
testimony to the same things as had his Master. He had
strenuously rebuked sin. When we come to study his
defence we shall see with what fine art he led them over
their own history, until he came to the point where he
charged them with the murder of God's ultimate Servant,
Whom he designated "the Righteous One." The hatred
of their heart resulted from his rebuke of their sin.
Mark the course of that hatred; their suborning of witnesses, their attitude toward him throughout the whole of
his trial, and then the brutal sentence. The fellowship
of this man with his Lord was of the closest. Because
of the fellowship in nature fully realized, there was fellowship in testimony fully declared, and therefore there
was fellowship in suffering.

In the measure in which persecution still exists, this
law still operates. Men cannot live a Christian life without suffering. The old brutal methods of persecution are
forever at an end for us at least; but it is impossible to
share His nature and share His witness without coming
into fellowship with His sufferings in an ungodly and
antagonistic age.

Finally, the fellowship was that of His triumph. The
great secret is told when Luke says he was full of the

Spirit. Mark the manifestations of that triumph. It is seen in his outlook on his foes. He was full of pity for them, and so he prayed, " Lord, lay not this sin to their charge." That was the triumph of grace. It is seen also in his outlook on death. He was absolute master over it, as he said, " Lord Jesus, receive my spirit." That was the triumph of power. In that ultimate triumph there was fellowship with Jesus. Christ never spoke of His own death by any other term than that which indicated power and authority. Men still speak of death with the sense that there is defeat in it. No man loves death. For believers, death is irradiated with light, but it is the light of that which lies beyond it. Yet Jesus never spoke of death in the terms in which men speak of death. When He spoke of death He spoke of it as an *exodus,* as something He could accomplish, as something in the presence of which He said with defiant authority, " I lay down My life, that I may take it again. No one taketh it away from Me, but I lay it down of Myself." He suffered in its presence, because of the infinite mystery of its pain ; yet seeing through, He approached it with the tread of a Victor. Now His servant went out of the city, the brutal stones rained on him, he was dying; and in the final agony he spoke of death, not as of something mastering him, but as an experience in which he was able to commit his spirit to another. This was the triumph of perfect fellowship with Christ.

There was granted to this man in the final hour an unveiling; in order that he might know all the full and gracious experience of spiritual certainty, and that he might have the very help and encouragement needed. It was a vision of Christ's actual fellowship with him. Do I think he really saw that which he thought he saw? Surely yes. Other men would not see it. There are many things which *other men* can never see which yet are seen. It is well for us of the Christian faith to remember that, and face it perpetually. Do not let us try

[183]

to explain all our religion to the man who is not a Christian. It cannot be done. There is a statement in Hebrews, " He endured as seeing Him Who is invisible." We still talk of men who are far-sighted, and we usually mean men who see enough to arrange and combine for their own ends. Dying Stephen saw the heavens opened, and saw the glory of God. No one else saw that glory. What was it that Stephen's eyes looked upon? " The Son of Man." That is a description which no one had used of Jesus in the day of His flesh except Himself, save on one occasion in criticism. Stephen used of his Lord the tender title that He had so loved. Other writers speak of the risen and ascended Christ as sitting on the right hand of God. Stephen did not see Him sitting. Stephen saw Him standing. The two positions suggest the two activities of His Priesthood. He was a Priest after the order of Aaron, whose business it was to make Atonement. As such He sits at the right hand of God, because His work is accomplished. But He was also a priest after the order of Melchizedek. When Abraham was returning from conflict, Melchizedek brought forth bread and wine. Melchizedek was a priest of God who ministered to the failing strength of the warrior of faith. Stephen saw the heaven opened, and the glory of God, and the great Archetype doing Melchizedek's work, standing and ministering. Because a member of His Body was in pain and suffering, He stood to minister to him in the hour of his agony. The whole thing may be very simply explained by using Paul's words, " Whether one member suffereth, all the members suffer with it "; and linking with them other of his words, " The head cannot say to the foot, I have no need of you." When Stephen, a member of the great Body on the earth, was in pain, the agony was felt in heaven, and the Head of the Body stood. The dying Stephen saw the standing Christ. Wherever a saint of God in fellowship with the nature, testimony, and suffering of Christ is in pain, He stands, the great High Priest in sympathy and in ministry, until He welcomes that suffering one over the line, and into the eternal fellowship.

Acts 7: 2–60

We now turn to consider the testimony borne by Stephen as a witness of Jesus, in his apology, and by his dying. This word apology is one of the discrowned words in our language. We constantly misuse it in our daily speech. We say we apologize, when we confess that we are wrong. An apology is really an argument that we are right.

This address of Stephen was an apology, not for himself, but for his Master. His testimony in life and in death was Christo-centric; therefore it shared the clearness, authority, and influence of the testimony of Jesus. Just as we have seen in the previous study the wonderful unity between Stephen and his Lord; so here we shall see the same unity between the testimony of Stephen and the testimony of Jesus. Stephen's outlook was that of Christ. Stephen could have said as accurately as did Paul, " To me to live is Christ." We shall confine ourselves to the witness of his trial and death, recognizing that, being the outcome of his former testimony, it harmonized therewith.

Let us remind ourselves of the circumstances of this great apology. Stephen was arraigned before the Council, that is before the Sanhedrim; and the charge preferred against him was a strange mixture of truth and error. This is what they said of him, " We have heard him speak blasphemous words against Moses, and against God." That was their interpretation of what he had said. They suborned false witnesses who said: " This man ceaseth not to speak words against this holy place, and the law." These were their impressions of the results of his teaching.

[185]

THE ACTS OF THE APOSTLES

But the definite, specific charge—for a charge had to be formulated for the Sanhedrim—was this, "We have heard him say, that this Jesus of Nazareth shall destroy this place, and shall change the customs which Moses delivered unto us." That last statement was true undoubtedly; he had said that very thing. He had said that the mission of Jesus must culminate in the destruction of the temple, and the changing of the customs; but when they interpreted that to mean that he blasphemed Moses and God, that this man had set himself against all that was Divine in the origin of the Hebrew economy, they were wrong. He was arraigned upon a charge partially true and partially false. There is never any more serious situation than that:

"A lie which is all a lie may be met with and fought outright;
But a lie that is partly truth is a harder matter to fight."

Mark the answer of Stephen first, in general terms. It was not a defence. There was not in this whole speech of Stephen a single reply as to whether he had said the things they charged him with saying. The personal element is wholly absent. He was not careful for a single moment to defend himself even against misinterpretation. He did not attempt to show the difference between the formal charge and their interpretation of it. He was so utterly lost in the sense of God, and the spaciousness of his outlook in Jesus Christ, that he did not seem to think it worth while to reply to the actual words of the charge made against him. On the other hand, he did most definitely reply thereto, and defend the declaration that the temple must be destroyed, and would be destroyed without loss; and declared with new emphasis the necessity for the change of the customs established by Moses. From beginning to end however he made it perfectly patent that the last thing in his mind was any intention

[186]

of speaking against God or against Moses. Rather he argued that all that happened in the coming of Jesus was in fulfilment of the great central prophecy of their own lawgiver, Moses.

The apology of Stephen is therefore not in the nature of a defence, but of an arraignment. Looking back over the centuries at the great scene, we see Stephen, not so much as a prisoner at the bar, but as the vicegerent of God, the judge of the nation.

This was a great crisis in the national history. There had come such a crisis during the ministry of Jesus when He had said, " O Jerusalem, Jerusalem, that killeth the prophets, and stoneth them that are sent unto her! How often would I have gathered thy children together, even as a hen gathereth her chickens under her wings, and ye would not! Behold, your house is left unto you desolate." In the ministry of Jesus He first spoke of the temple as " My Father's house," but at the end He spoke of it as " your house . . . left unto you desolate." Now the second crisis had come in the history of the people. They had been given a Pentecostal opportunity. They had received a new spiritual presentation of the Evangel in the early mission of the apostles. All those first things which we have been considering constituted the witness of Christ by the Spirit in Jerusalem. Presently the mangled body of Stephen was Jerusalem's answer to this new opportunity. Ere he went out to death he stood, not as a prisoner at the bar, but as the judge of the people, declaring in the very terms of Christ, the doom of the city that had rejected Him.

His address was peculiarly Eastern. It is very difficult for the Western mind to follow the movement, and catch the cumulative force of its arraignment of the nation. At the close he said, " Ye stiffnecked and uncircumcized in heart and ears, ye do always resist the Holy Spirit." We of the West live lonely lives ; we speak of our fathers and our inheritance, but we hardly begin to feel the force of the relationship. The Easterner lives in the past as well as the present. Mr. Johnston Ross has said that no Westerner can ever understand the words: "Fill ye up the measure of your fathers." In that sense the whole method of this address, and the sweep of its argument, is Eastern. Stephen would not consent to deal with the immediate, save in relation to all that which had preceded it. He saw in events that were happening around him, not incidents, but movements in the rhythmic march of God, and revelations of the perpetual sin of his own people.

It was a great historic declaration, because it was the declaration of a man who looked out over history, and saw it in its highest values. There were few dates, and few names; and some of the names were mistakes, as will be gathered when the story is carefully considered; for instance, he said *Babylon,* where he ought to have said *Damascus,* when he quoted from the ancient prophets. Of course the mistakes may be due to copyists of the manuscripts.

The argument itself was an interpretation of history from the heights. Dr. Pierson said at the Ecumenical Conference of Foreign Missions in New York that "History is *His story,* if man can climb high enough to read it." Stephen had climbed the heights, and looking back over the history of his people he interpreted it in the light of the Divine method, and the Divine overruling. Beginning with Abraham, nay, beginning with the God of glory, and then in human history with Abraham, passing in review all the centuries after Abraham, he ended with Jesus. Their charges against him were, "We have heard him speak blasphemous words against Moses, and against God"; "We have heard him say, that this Jesus of Nazareth shall destroy this place, and shall change the customs which Moses delivered unto us." In answer, he gave them a general view of the whole history of that nation of which they were a part, and in which they made their boast. Beginning with Abraham he ended with Jesus.

Abraham was first mentioned as the man of faith. Joseph was mentioned, but only in connection with the attitude toward him of the patriarchs. The patriarchs sold Joseph. Moses they understood not, and refused. The test of testimony—mark the fine satire of it—was in the wilderness; and the forty years of their rebellion are in his mind. "Solomon built Him a house. Howbeit the Most High dwelleth not in houses made with hands." The prophets, their fathers persecuted them. Of the Righteous One they had become the betrayers and murderers. Through all the movement he emphasized the continuity of their failure.

Mark also how he pointed out to them through all the address the persistent purpose of God. "The God of glory" was the first phrase, and the glory of God was the perpetual theme. As we read this apology we see clearly that which Russell Lowell described, in the words,

> "   .   .   .   standeth God within the shadow
> Keeping watch above His own."

The apology may be read from beginning to end, losing sight of the nation, and watching only the goings of God through individuals; Abraham, a lonely man; Joseph, a lonely man; Moses, a lonely man; the prophets, one after another standing out in supreme and awful isolation; and at last the Righteous One, quite alone. Yet every individual is seen creating a new social opportunity and requirement, and marking perpetual progress in the Divine movement. As I read this defence, and watch the goings of God, I am impressed with the truth of Lloyd Garrison's word, "One with God is a majority." Therefore I learn also that one man can excommunicate a Church, one man can shut out a nation from national greatness; one man can set up an altar to which the Church returning,

[189]

may be redeemed; and one man can lift a standard around which the nation gathering, it can be remade. This man, standing arraigned before the Sanhedrim, led them back over their whole history, and the supreme note and glory of his apology was its revelation of the goings of God.

He was also impressing upon them the perpetual rebellion of man, man's hindrance to God's progress. It is one long story of man's utter inability to coöperate with God.

Yet again, not only is it the story of God's method, and of man's hindrance, it is the story from beginning to end of God's victory. God is revealed as forevermore moving a little further forward, from Abraham to whom He gave the promise of a seed; never resting in His march until the promise was fulfilled in the Person of the Righteous One.

He left them to make their own deduction. It was a self-evident one. He charged them with having rejected the last movement in the Divine progress. The argument from history was that they rejecting, were rejected; and that the rejected One was crowned. He admitted the partial truth of the charge they brought against him, by revealing to them the fact that the temple must be destroyed; but also insisting upon it that it might be destroyed without loss, because the throne of God remains, and the government of God is utterly unchanged; and explaining to them what he really meant by the testimony he had borne, and the truth he had declared. Stephen, standing before the Sanhedrim, interpreted the goings of God to a people who professed to know Him, and yet were perpetually hindering Him. In succession to his Lord he uttered again the things that Jesus had said, claiming that God had never been defeated, but that man had perpetually failed, as he had failed to understand and follow the Divine guidance.

The testimony that Stephen bore in his dying was that cf witness to the supremacy of the spiritual, to the reality of the unseen, and therefore, to the fact that the glory of God is essentially demonstrated by, and active in the grace of God.

First, it was a witness to the supremacy of the spiritual. Jesus had said: " Fear not them which kill the body, and after that have no more that they can do." " After that! " What can there be *after that?* The ultimate fear in the human heart that has lost its vision of God, and the sense of the spiritual, is the fear of death. A man may profess to believe that death does not end all, and yet in his underlying consciousness, his very fear of death is demonstration that he has no certainty of that which lies beyond, does not believe in the supremacy of the spiritual after death. The one great conflict of human life unilluminated by fellowship with God, is conflict with death, effort to postpone it, to evade it, to fight it off, so to live as not to hasten it. The materialist is forevermore saying, " Let us eat, and drink, for to-morrow we die." Therefore let to-morrow be postponed, for it is the final dread, the ultimate agony. Jesus said, " Fear not them which kill the body, and after that have no more that they can do," and in that word there flashed forth the light of His conception of essential personality; the body killed, but the man continuing. With softened footfall, and reverent demeanour, we come to the Cross. What does the Cross say? Among other things, profounder and mightier, it yet surely says, " Fear not them which kill the body, and after that have no more that they can do." I watch Christ Himself fastened to the Cross, and to my own heart there is profound and overwhelming significance in the word He uttered, " Father, into Thy hands I commend My spirit." They had killed the body —it was then ceasing to be, the life-blood was ebbing away, the vision was becoming dim, and as men looked on they said, He is dying; but He said, " I commend My spirit." " I lay down My life, that I may take it again. No one taketh it away from Me, but I lay it down of

Myself." That was the ultimate argument for the supremacy of the spiritual.

Stephen was a witness, a martyr of Jesus, an argument for the truth of the thing that he preached, taught, and lived; an evidence of Christianity, a credential. He went outside Jerusalem, and the stones fell thickly upon him. In the attitude of dying he was a witness to the supremacy of the spiritual. "Lord Jesus, receive my spirit." It is that conception and conviction of the supremacy of the spiritual which alone is equal to enabling a man to "fear not them which kill the body." The awakened sense of the reality of the spiritual makes cowards of us all. The courage that will face all opposition, and bear all bruising, and die, is courage born of the conviction of the reality of the spiritual. That day the Sadducean mob that largely composed the Sanhedrim (for the Pharisees were in the minority), as they watched this man die, saw how their theories were laughed out of court by a man who could bow in quietness and meekness to death, in the strength of his conviction of the supremacy of the spiritual.

How far do we know that conviction, and live in that power? It is a little difficult to answer this to-day, because no stones are waiting for us in the city. We may never be called upon, in this land at least, so to die as Stephen died. But there are subtler things than stones. Have I the courage that will make me true in the place of criticism and opposition, of supercilious disdain for the name of Christ? I have not, if Christ is to me but the name of a Teacher, high and noble though He may have been. But if I know the spiritual, if my life is circumferenced around the centre that is homed in eternity, then I shall have courage; courage enough to die for Christ perchance; but also that which is much more difficult, courage enough to live for Christ in places of subtle and insidious difficulty. The only courage that dares, is the courage born of the conviction of the supremacy of the spiritual. That was Stephen's dying witness.

Because it was that, it was also witness to the reality of the unseen. " I see the heavens opened, and the Son of man standing on the right hand of God." None other saw the vision in the crowd of people round about him. His murderers had no such vision. Saul of Tarsus did not see it; but I think Stephen's testimony haunted him, and constituted the very goads against which he tried to kick. This man saw the unseen; and by that dying word, and the triumph of his speech, and the light upon his face from the glory of a great vision, he testified in the Sadducean, rationalistic age in which he lived and died, to the reality of unseen things.

Finally, the most overwhelming testimony of his death was its witness to the glory of God as being grace. In that prayer of his, full of tenderness, there was an echo of the prayer of his Lord. Stephen died with a prayer upon his lips for the very men who were murdering him; and by that they knew that he believed, and lived in the power of the belief, that the glory of God, to which he had referred at the commencement of his argument, was the very grace of God. The prayer did not only reveal his desire for his enemies, but also his confidence in the pardon of God. He prayed to a God ready to pardon. There he lay, dying under the brutal stones, with the great consciousness of the failure of his own people in their past history filling his soul. He saw the outstanding places of their failure in their long rejection of the messengers of God, and he watched God's movement ever onward; and now when they had cast out the Righteous One, and were stoning him to death he prayed for their pardon.

The story ends with the mangled body of Stephen. No, it does not so end! It ends with the brief word written after, to stimulate interest, and suggest something still to come, " And Saul was consenting unto his death."

[Acts 8: 1-13]

The witness is dead; the truth lives; and in his very dying he has sown the seed of a mighty harvest in the heart of the hardest man in the crowd. So the first martyr sealing his testimony with his blood, reveals to us how true the thing is that has been said, and proven through all the centuries, " The blood of the martyrs is the seed of the Church."

Acts 8: 1-13

The martyrdom of Stephen created a crisis in the history of the Church. In reading the Acts, we find that from this point onward Jerusalem is no longer the centre of interest. It almost fades from the page. This is not loss; but great gain. When Jerusalem ceases to be the centre of interest, the record does not suffer in any way, nor does it reflect upon Jerusalem. The local, the temporal, the material, are of little importance in the Church of God. The universal, the eternal, the spiritual are supreme. It was of the very spirit of an old and past economy to fasten upon a geographical centre, and to depend upon material symbols. The Church now moves out upon the great pathway of her victorious business, independent of Jerusalem. That is the supreme revelation of this book of the Acts of the Apostles. Not easily did they learn the lesson, for the apostles clung to Jerusalem; but the great spiritual movement, independent of Jerusalem and of apostles, went forward; not slighting Jerusalem, not unmindful of Jerusalem, nor careless of its past history and early contribution; but far more influenced by the vision of Jerusalem from on high, the mother of us all, a spiritual ideal and victory. No longer hampered by localities and temporalities, the surging spiritual life of the Church swept them all away, and moved quietly and majestically on to new quests and new triumphs. Church failure has invariably resulted from an attempt to check that spiritual movement which is independent of locality, and of all things material.

Whenever the Church is governed from Jerusalem, or from Rome, or from anywhere else other than Heaven, it is hindered and hampered and prevented from fulfilling the great functions of its life.

The paragraph now under consideration falls into three parts; the events chronicled gather around three persons, Saul, Philip, and Simon; and three words suggest its values: persecution, power, and peril. The story of persecution, breaking out in Jerusalem and scattering the disciples, centres around Saul. The story of power, manifesting itself in strange circumstances and new surroundings and peculiar atmospheres, centres around Philip. The story of peril centres around Simon. Let us first examine the passage, and then attempt to observe its spiritual significance.

The story of persecution centres around Saul. In the seventh chapter, at verse fifty-eight, we find the words which introduce this man to our notice: " The witnesses laid down their garments at the feet of a young man named Saul." Then immediately follow the first words in the present paragraph: " And Saul was consenting unto his death." The question naturally arises: Who is this man? We find his own account of himself, as he was in those days, in his letter to the Philippians: " Circumcized the eighth day, of the stock of Israel, of the tribe of Benjamin, a Hebrew of Hebrews; as touching the law, a Pharisee; as touching zeal, persecuting the Church; as touching the righteousness which is in the law, found blameless." This account becomes the more remarkable when it is remembered that it was written not less than thirty years after his apprehension by Christ. After thirty years of Christian experience, thirty years' fellowship with the risen Lord, he looked back to what he was in the old days. Beginning on the level of the flesh, he indicated his relationship to the ancient economy. " Circumcized the eighth day." There was no carelessness in the matters of ritual observance on the part of his parents. "Of the stock of Israel, of the tribe of Benjamin." He was a Hebrew, purely and wholly so, of Hebrew parents. "As touching the law, a Pharisee." He was of the spiritual party in the Hebrew nation. "As touching zeal, persecuting the Church." He was intense in his devotion to what he believed to be true. "As touching the righteousness which is in the law, found blameless." He was true to the light as he saw it.

So Saul comes into view; a Hebrew of Hebrews; a spiritual ritualist; a zealous man; a man convinced; a man sincere; a man ardent and passionate; a man determined; a man with a clean moral record. Around this remarkable man the story of persecution gathers.

The words of Luke reveal the turmoil in the city. "Devout men buried Stephen and made great lamentation over him." I personally believe that Stephen was buried, not by Christian men, but by Hebrews. The phrase "Devout men" is peculiar and suggestive. Devout men, not believers or disciples, but the devout men in Hebraism carried Stephen to his burial. "But Saul laid waste the Church, entering into every house, and dragging men and women committed them to prison."

In that double declaration there is manifested a division of opinion, even among Hebrew people, concerning the death of Stephen. Some of them lamenting the brutality, tenderly buried him with great lamentation. Others, strangely stirred, broke out into wild and uproarious persecution of the Christians. Jerusalem was filled with the noise and the turmoil of persecution.

Two forces were in opposition in Jerusalem. They had been in opposition ever since the ministry of Jesus began. Now they were coming into conflict again most definitely. On the one hand was Sadducean Judaism, and on the other, spiritual Christianity. The remarkable fact here is, that Sadducean Judaism was being led in its opposition to Christianity by a Pharisee. Saul of Tarsus, a Pharisee, was already acting contrary to his deep relig-

ious convictions, perhaps unconsciously, when he led that
Sadducean opposition to Jesus Christ. He was no lover
of the Sadducean high priest. By virtue of his early
Pharisaic training, he was utterly opposed to the Sadducean philosophy. Moreover, he had seen Stephen die.
To all that we shall return when we come to the story
of his conversion.

All this turmoil grew out of Stephen's speech and
death. We see the base, attempting to rid itself of the
high; we see materialism, attempting to silence the voice
of spirituality. We see Calvary repeated. They put
Christ to death because His conceptions were spiritual
and theirs were material. They put Him to death because He insisted upon the supremacy of the spiritual,
while they grovelled in the dust of materialism. Now
these people, living by the impulse of His indwelling life,
must come to the same conflict.

As we watch that scattering crowd, we are observing
the progress of the Christian Church. They were entering into fellowship with His sufferings, and therefore
they were entering into the fulfilment of His purpose for
Judæa and Samaria. "There arose on that day a great
persecution against the Church which was in Jerusalem;
and they were all scattered abroad throughout the regions
of Judæa and Samaria." Thus were they scattered
through the regions which Jesus had told them to pass
over, and announce His Gospel, and they were going in
fellowship with His sufferings.

So we pass to the story of Philip, and of power. Philip
is introduced in chapter six, verses three to six, " Look
ye out therefore, brethren, from among you seven men of
good report, full of the Spirit and of wisdom, whom we
may appoint over this business . . . and they chose
Stephen, a man full of faith and of the Holy Spirit, and
Philip." In the twenty-first chapter, verse seven, we find
these words: "And when we had finished the voyage
from Tyre we arrived at Ptolemais; and saluted the

[197]

brethren, and abode with them one day. And on the morrow, we departed and came unto Cæsarea; and entering into the house of Philip the evangelist, who was one of the seven, we abode with him. Now this man had four daughters, virgins, who prophesied." Philip the deacon, one of the seven, became Philip the evangelist. He was among the number of those who were driven from Jerusalem by Saul's persecution. In the twenty-first chapter, Philip is seen entertaining Paul on his missionary journey. How they must have talked together of those early days, and of the martyred Stephen.

> " Saints, did I say? with your remembered faces,
> Dear men and women, whom I sought and slew!
> Ah, when we mingle in the heavenly places
> How will I weep to Stephen and to you!

> " Oh for the strain that rang through our reviling,
> Still, when the bruised limbs sank upon the sod,
> Oh for the eyes that looked their last in smiling,
> Last on this world here, but their first on God!"

I think they talked of that at Cæsarea.

This man Philip then was the centre of the wonderful movement in the city of Samaria. Jews have no dealings with Samaritans, but Christians have, and Philip came to Samaria. There he proclaimed the Messiah. In the course of this passage two great words for preaching are used in describing the work of Philip. He proclaimed the Christ—and that is the Greek word *kerusso*, which means to proclaim as a herald. We find later that Philip preached the Gospel, and that is the Greek word *euaggelizo*, which indicates the proclamation of good news. The message concerning Christ, delivered through the deacon-evangelist Philip, arrested Samaria. In Samaria the Christian preacher found a new atmosphere and a new outlook. Moreover, Samaria was at the time under the spell of Simon the sorcerer. To Samaria, driven by persecution, there came, not an apostle, but a man set apart to serve tables, in order that the apostles might be set apart to preach the Word. He proclaimed Christ, and his preaching was accompanied by mental and physical signs. Unclean spirits were cast out, and men were healed. The city was full of joy, resulting from these things; and in that attitude of amazement, of surprise, and of joy, they listened. This story of Philip is but an illustration of a much wider movement. The whole Church, driven by persecution, was proceeding in power.

So we come to the story of Simon, and of peril. Simon had amazed the city of Samaria with sorcery, and had gathered around him a great company of people. He had flung the spell of his personality over the city by his self-advertisement: " Giving out that himself was some great one." How is a city to be delivered from that kind of spell?

To Samaria Philip came, full of the Spirit, and driven by the indwelling life of the Christ, and there he proclaimed the Christ. Observe the difference: Philip proclaimed another, the Messiah; Simon proclaimed himself.

The third part of our paragraph elaborates the declaration of the second. The second says that " he proclaimed Christ "; the third that he preached " the Kingdom of God and the Name of Jesus Christ "; and this with power because he himself was submitted to it, and driven by it. " The Kingdom of God and the Name of Jesus Christ "; that was a new centre for a new society.

The people who had been under the spell of the sorcerer, listened. They believed, and they were baptized. The most marvellous victory in Samaria—for victory it was—was the belief and the baptism of Simon. We have no right to say that Simon was insincere. The very words used of the multitude are used also of Simon, and I believe his belief was as sincere as that of the rest, and his baptism was as valid as theirs.

THE ACTS OF THE APOSTLES

But there was a great incompleteness in the whole of this. The belief was intellectual assent, and the baptism was intellectual consent. In the fourteenth verse to which we come in our next study, we read that the apostles heard that they had "received the Word of God." That is to say that they had received it intellectually. They had not received the Spirit which brings regeneration, the beginning of the new life. This first victory broke the spell of the sorcerer. He himself was captured, and the city passed under the spell of the evangel. Great multitudes intellectually accepting the truth of what Philip had declared, submitted themselves to the rite of water baptism as an indication of their acceptance. It was a remarkable triumph.

The enquiry necessarily arises at this point, as to how it was that these people did not receive the Spirit immediately upon their intellectual assent to the truth. I have no answer. Whether the reason was spiritual or psychological is debatable. The story as it stands reminds us once more that we have no right to base a system or economy on any one picture given to us in the Acts of the Apostles. Here were people believing on Jesus, and subsequently receiving the gift of the Holy Spirit. There are other pictures where people believing received the Spirit immediately. We cannot, I repeat, base an economy or a system on any one instance. Our economy must be based rather on the whole revelation of the Acts of the Apostles. As in the Gospel stories, we see that Jesus did not fulfil His ministry in the souls of two men in the same way, that there was infinite variety in His method; so in the Acts of the Apostles we see that Christian experience cannot be tabulated and systematized in the case of any one, for all are different. God fulfils Himself in many ways. Let us make room for Him in the experience of other men, and not attempt to say that thus and so, and by sequence which we have systematized in our theology, must men pass into fullness of life. Here is a case, for some reason which cannot be discovered, in which men came into intellectual assent and consent, and yet lacked for a little while the real touch of life which made them members of the Church, and witnesses of the Christ. When presently the apostles came, they found Simon and the rest lacking the Spirit. Then came differentiation and discrimination, resulting from the next attitude taken up by Simon, and the rest.

What are the spiritual significances of this passage? First of all it is singularly impressive in its revelation of the sovereignty of the Lord Jesus. Note well His compelling power. He said to these men: " Ye shall be My witnesses in Jerusalem, Judea, Samaria and to the uttermost part of the earth." They halted, and waited, and failed to go forward. Then, through the fidelity of Stephen He ultimately compelled their teaching and preaching in Samaria, though He drove them out by persecution.

His sovereignty is seen, not only in His compelling power, but in His continued fellowship with these men. Persecution never for a moment weakened their consciousness of Christ, or their loyalty to Him. That is always so with martyrs, with witnesses, with those in whom He dwells. Here is a man, loud-voiced in his profession of loyalty to Christ, and when persecution begins, his testimony ceases. That man never really knew Christ in his inner life. Christ was external to his life. The one thing persecution can never do for a true witness, is to blur the vision of Christ, or change the loyalty of the witness to Him. One little word occurs here, which alone has no significance, but in its connection is full of most exquisite beauty. " They *therefore* that were scattered abroad went about preaching the Word." Wherefore? Because they were persecuted and driven out. How revealing is that! Persecuted and driven out, He yet held His throne in them; and secured their loyalty, for He never parted company with them in spiritual experience.

The next lesson is that of the universality of the Gospel. In Samaria we see the Gospel in a new atmosphere. That matters nothing. Christ arrests Samaria as easily as He arrested Jerusalem. The evangel brings conviction in Samaria, as surely as it brought it in Jerusalem.

Finally, we learn the lesson of the spirituality of the Church. Mark the obscurity of the apostles. All were driven from Jerusalem, except the apostles. The majority of expositors say that it was necessary that the apostles should remain at Jerusalem for purposes of government. I respect that view, but I am not sure. I am rather inclined to think that they should have been out on the highway of witness. When apostles stay at a geographical centre, they may do more harm than good. If they had been out upon the missionary pathway they would have been fulfilling the meaning of the word apostle, as they were not when remaining at a centre.

God is not, however, dependent upon apostles that stay at Jerusalem. He has Philip the deacon, the evangelist. The Christian Church in her spiritual conception is independent of localities and men. She fulfils her true function by the presence and power of the Spirit in all such as allow Him right of way to administer the affairs of the Christ.

Acts 8 : 14–25

This paragraph has still to do with the work of the early Church in Samaria, and is the sequel to our previous study. Samaria as a centre of operation was not chosen by the council of the apostles in Jerusalem. It was undoubtedly in the original intention of the Christ. Persecution had broken out in Jerusalem, and the saints were scattered here, there, and everywhere; and among the rest, Philip had come to Samaria and preached the Gospel.

THE ACTS OF THE APOSTLES

In this paragraph Jerusalem and the apostles reappear. The news reached Jerusalem that Samaria had received the Word of God, a statement which must have powerfully affected that group of men, who still retained some of their old Jewish prejudice against Samaria; for it is evident that Hebrew believers did carry over with them into their new relationship to Christ, the old prejudices against all things outside the Hebrew economy. Immediately, however, the apostles fell into line, and coöperated, sending two of their number to Samaria. We see here a new coöperation in spiritual ministry.

Another thing that impresses us is that the apostles themselves became evangelists. Peter and John having been to Samaria, having seen the work of God, having been the instruments for consolidating that work, and for purifying it at its very beginning by the exclusion of Simon, went back again to Jerusalem; but as they went, they "preached the Gospel to many villages of the Samaritans."

This paragraph then falls into three sections: first the apostolic visitation of Samaria; secondly the apostolic discipline in the case of Simon; and thirdly the apostolic evangelism through the villages of Samaria.

It is impossible to read this story without once more being impressed with something we have already noticed in an earlier chapter—the comradeship of these two men Peter and John. We shall not have occasion to refer to it again in the course of this book, because John here passes out of the record. He is never seen again in the New Testament history, save when Paul refers to his being in Jerusalem in the Galatian letter, and in his own references to his sojourn in Patmos in the Apocalypse. In this companionship of Peter and John, we see the spiritual fellowship of opposites in Christian service. How utterly and absolutely different they were! Peter the practical; John the poet. Peter the man of deeds; John the dreamer. When the work in Samaria had to be inspected,—for I think that was the first apostolic intention,—the Spirit, acting through the apostles, sent these two; the man of deeds, and the man of dreams.

The whole fiction of Petrine supremacy breaks down in the light of this story. If it be true that Peter was the chief, how comes it that he was *sent* by his brethren? Peter and John were sent in a holy fellowship by the Spirit of God Who in the Church at Jerusalem was still acting, and that as the Interpreter of the Will of Christ the only Head of the Church.

We turn our attention to the Samaritans. What is the story of these men in Samaria? First that they " received the Word of God." Secondly they were " baptized into the name of the Lord Jesus." Thirdly they had not received the Holy Spirit.

Let us institute a simple enquiry. Why did they not receive the Spirit of God immediately? In the paragraph concerning the teaching of Philip, we learned that he proclaimed Christ as Messiah; and that he preached good tidings of the Kingdom of God, and the name of Jesus. I lay emphasis upon those two statements because they cover the whole outlook of New Testament preaching. There are many words in the Greek New Testament translated *preach;* but there are two principal words, and both of them are used here about Philip. The two great ideals of preaching are discoverable in what Philip did in Samaria; the word *kerusso,* which suggests the proclamation of a herald; the word *euaggelizo* which suggests the declaration of good news. Philip did both. He proclaimed as a herald the Messiahship of Christ. He preached as an evangelist the good news of the Kingdom of God, and of the name of Jesus. This double declaration concerning the preaching of Philip shows that there was nothing lacking in his preaching. We must not account for the fact that when these people believed and were baptized they did not receive the Spirit, by saying that the preaching of Philip was faltering. Further on

[Acts 8:14-25]

in our studies we shall find that there were men in
Ephesus, who had not received the Spirit. The preaching of Apollos was faulty. Apollos had not known, but
Philip did know. Here was preaching which was preaching in the fullest New Testament sense of the word, the
authoritative proclamation of the Lordship of Jesus; the
glad telling of the good news of the Kingdom of God, and
of the name of Jesus—the name of Jesus being the symbol
of salvation. The preaching was complete. Why then
was it that when people believed into that very Name
which he preached, and evidently were baptized in water,
that they did not receive the Spirit? There is no answer.
There is no reason to be discovered in the Acts of the
Apostles for that delay. If that statement appears to be
most unsatisfactory, the fact that there is no answer, is an
answer. When the Church of God begins to recognize
that, strange and paradoxical as it may appear, we shall
be at the end of a vast amount of confusion in systematic
teaching concerning the work of the Holy Spirit. The
fact is of importance, and so we repeat it. There was a
full preaching, authoritative and evangelistic, of the
Messiahship of Jesus, of the Kingdom of God, of the
saving name of Christ. Men and women believing into
the Name—which is more than believing on it,—submitted themselves to all that the preaching claimed, and
were baptized. Yet they had not received the Spirit.

Peter and John came down to Samaria, and as a result
of their visitation these men did receive the Spirit. Let
us look then somewhat carefully at the story from that
standpoint. What did the apostles do? They prayed
for them; they laid their hands upon them; and then they
received the Holy Spirit.

In further explanation of the statement that there is
no answer to our enquiry; and in the presence of this
description of what happened, and of the method by
which these men received the Spirit; what light is there
upon our problem? We may be inclined to think that in

THE ACTS OF THE APOSTLES

[Acts 8: 14–25]

order to the reception of the Spirit it was necessary that there should be apostolic ministry; that while Philip the evangelist could preach a whole gospel and bring men into intellectual assent, and belief, and even to the obedience of baptism, yet because he was not an apostle there could be no reception of the Holy Spirit? If that be set up as a system, then we are face to face with a new problem. The mightiest missionary that ever existed in the early Church, Paul, received the gift of the Holy Spirit by the ministry, not of an apostle nor even of a deacon, but of Ananias a simple disciple. So we must be very careful not to set up a system that will break down presently. Or again we may be inclined to think that while this was not apostolic, yet it was the plan of God that men should only receive the Spirit as hands were laid upon them. We must not speak slightingly of any material ordinance, if it be in the economy of God. Was it then the laying on of hands which Philip had neglected, and the apostles fulfilled? Presently Cornelius received the Spirit, and the apostle Peter never laid hands on him. We must be careful not to create a system that does not hold good in all cases. If we say there must be some human intermediation, then why not in the case of Cornelius? The moment we become mystified in the presence of the operations of the Spirit, we have reached the heart of truth. "The wind bloweth where it will, and thou hearest the voice thereof, but knowest not whence it cometh, and whither it goeth." The moment in which any theologian, or school of theology, attempts to systematize the method of the coming of the Spirit into human lives, in that moment they are excluding a score of His operations, and including only one. These people had not received the Spirit. "The wind bloweth where it will;" and this is the supreme glory of the Christian Church. Its life and its power is not that of organization or ministry, but that of the indwelling Spirit.

[206]

THE ACTS OF THE APOSTLES

But what happened? They received the Holy Spirit. What difference did that make? In the first letter of Paul to the Corinthians, and in that twelfth chapter concerning spiritualities, is this verse—" For in one Spirit were we all baptized into one body." What then happened when the Spirit came to these men in Samaria? Exactly the same thing that happened when the Spirit came to the men in the Upper Room on the day of Pentecost. Exactly the same thing that happened when the Spirit came presently to Cornelius, falling upon him as upon those disciples at the first. Exactly what happened when the Spirit came to Saul of Tarsus. Exactly what happened when the Spirit came to the little handful of disciples at Ephesus. Exactly the same thing that happened when the Spirit of God came into our lives. They were baptized into the one Body of Christ. This is a figure of speech, but it is a supremely beautiful and fitting one. If we would know all the glory of it, and understand what happened to the Samaritan Christians, we must study carefully the teaching of the apostle, in which with inimitable art and matchless skill, he takes the figure of the body with its different parts and members and functions. Therein he speaks of "diversities of gifts." The word diversities may suggest division; so that we will use another word here, diæreses of gifts, diæreses of ministrations and of workings. The diæresis indicates a difference, and yet the running together of two letters in close connection as in the word naïve. Now in the body, the diversities in that sense, of gifts, of ministrations, of workings, are in one body; Christ, the Head, and all the members. That is what happened when the Spirit came. Samaritans were baptized into the one Body; that is to say from henceforth personality to them was to be Christian personality. Intellectually there was the outlook of Jesus; emotionally the passion of Jesus; volitionally the choices of their lives were the choices of Jesus. He in them, would think and love and

[207]

will. In that moment they were baptized into that one Body; and that meant membership in the Church; all their resources at the disposal of the Church, all the gifts in the Church, were gifts bestowed for their sake, whether they were gifts of the apostles, evangelists, prophets, teachers, or helpers. These people came into the mystic mystery of the one lonely and indivisible Church of Jesus Christ.

The picture that immediately follows emphasizes the teaching by way of contrast. What did Simon ask for, and what did Simon want? It is constantly imagined that he asked for the Holy Spirit, and wanted to buy the Holy Spirit, but the story does not say so. He said to Peter: " Give me also this power that on whomsoever I lay my hands, he may receive the Holy Spirit." He did not ask for the Holy Spirit; he asked for power to bestow Him. The whole city had been under the spell of this man's sorceries, and here was something that he lacked. What he craved was not the power of the Spirit, but the power to bestow the Spirit. There was born that which in the history of the Church has been described as simony, the buying and selling of position and office within the Church; the idea that ecclesiastical preferments can be procured in any denomination by money; the conception that the things of the Holy Spirit and of the Church can be purchased in current coin, of any state, or country. He asked for power to bestow the Spirit; to be admitted into the fellowship of the place in which the apostles stood; and to be brought to the position, where by the laying on of hands he also might confer power. The sin was a desire to possess spiritual power for personal ends. God deliver us from all Pharisaism, and all attempts to make application of that revelation of peril to any other communion than our own. Not merely the man who buys a living in some Church and sells it; but the man who in the great spiritual convention falls into line with certain suggestions of the speaker,

and professes, and seems to desire some spiritual blessing, in order to personal aggrandizement and fame; is
guilty of the same sin. A man does not receive the
Spirit in order to crowd his church, and if a man seeks
for a spiritual gift in order that he may enrich himself
at any point, in any way, he is attempting to traffic with
spiritual things for personal aggrandizement.

Think of the subtle peril of this suggestion to Peter.
He rose superior to the temptation, but still mark the
temptation, in order that we may learn this fact, that the
only way in which to resist this temptation is the way of
the fullness of spiritual life. Peter knew full well that
the Spirit had not fallen upon these men by the laying
on of his hands. That is what Simon thought he saw.
Peter knew, and declared that it was the gift of God. Yet
how easy it would have been to have agreed to the bar-
gain proposed. This was the peril confronting the early
Church, when a man asked to come into its office in return for money. Looking back over the history of the
Christian Church we see that she has not always resisted.
Mark well Peter's almost terrible severity; and I have no
explanation of that severity save as I believe that he
saw the peril to himself and to the Church: " Thy silver
perish with thee, because thou hast thought to obtain
the gift of God with money. Thou hast neither part nor
lot in this matter." Thou canst not invade the spiritualities with thy carnalities. If the Church believed that to-
day, and acted upon it, she might lack a good deal she
possesses, but would be richer for the lack. There is a
lack that means power; there is a possession that means
paralysis.

But observe the true spirit of the apostle, and the true
evidence of the indwelling Spirit in the tender sympathy
of Peter for the man, " Repent therefore of this thy
wickedness, and pray the Lord, if perhaps the thought
of thy heart shall be forgiven thee." Not in the thunder
of a final anathema did the apostolic speech end, but in

[209]

the tender hope of restoration. That is the Spirit of Christ. Some interpreters have said that when Simon said, " Pray ye for me to the Lord that none of the things which ye have spoken come upon me," he was impenitent, and only afraid of punishment. I do not think we have any right to say so. That is a subject better left where the record leaves it.

Our last paragraph deals with the apostolic evangelization. In this connection it is interesting to turn back to the Gospel of Luke. There, in the ninth chapter and at verse forty-nine, we read:

" And John answered and said, Master, we saw one casting out demons in Thy name; and we forbade him, because he followeth not with us. But Jesus said unto him, Forbid him not: for he that is not against you is for you. And it came to pass, when the days were well nigh come that He should be received up, He steadfastly set His face to go to Jerusalem, and sent messengers before His face, and they went and entered into a village of the Samaritans to make ready for Him; and they did not receive Him because His face was as though He were going to Jerusalem. And when His disciples James and John saw this, they said, Lord, wilt Thou that we bid fire to come down from heaven and consume them? But He turned and rebuked them."

John would have destroyed the Samaritan village by fire in those early days, but now he is seen preaching the Gospel in the Samaritan village. No comment is necessary. It is such a wonderful revelation of what the spiritual life really is. The man was completely changed. He was still Boanerges, a son of thunder, a man of resolute and determined endeavour; only the whole force of his nature had been turned in another direction. That is the story of the fullness of spiritual life. Let us be careful not to imagine that when the Spirit takes hold of man or woman He makes them all of one pattern. He

takes the man and turns the whole force of his life into
a constructive instead of a destructive direction.

The abiding truths we have surely seen as we have
passed the story in survey. As we read of the coming of
the apostles to Samaria, and the reception of the Samaritans of the gift of the Spirit, we learn the truth anew,
that nothing short of the actual reception of the Spirit
is Christianity. Men may come very near, they may be
intellectually convinced of the supremacy of Jesus; they
may even decide that they will adopt His ethical ideal;
they may go so far as to determine that they will imitate
the perfection of His example. But these things do not
make men Christians. The whole evangel of the authoritative Christ, of the Kingdom of God, of the saving
Name, may be understood, but there may be no touch of
life. If men have not received the Holy Spirit, they are
not members of the Christ. No man has entered into
true Christianity, save as there has come to him that life
which is illumination, which is emotion, which is volition, and all which are Christian. "If any man hath
not the Spirit of Christ, he is none of His."

We learn also from this story, what Christian life
really means. There was glorious coöperation in service;
apostles and evangelists working together. There is perfect fellowship in all the orders of the Christian ministry
in the fullness of the Spirit. Peter and John the apostles,
are glad to go down and help consummate the work of
Philip the evangelist. There is no antagonism in the
heart of Philip against the work of Peter and John.

Again, by the awful and solemn exclusion of Simon,
we learn that the Spirit-filled Church is a Church in
which simony cannot live.

Finally we have a further illustration of the marvellous
power of the Church. One sentence is enough to illustrate it; victory was gained in Samaria. This Judaism
had never won. How near the Samaritans had come to
Judaism—the Samaritan Pentateuch, the Samaritan cir-

cumcision, the Samaritan rite and symbol; but ritualism approximating to ritualism never brings the ritualists together; and Judaism and Samaritanism never merged. Judaism never conquered Samaritanism, but the Word of God won in Samaria. So the triumph of the Church must be that of the Word proclaimed in the power of the Spirit.

Acts 8:26-40

While this paragraph commences with words that suggest intimate relation with what has preceded, there is nevertheless a very definite and decided break in the narrative at this point. The verse begins: " But an angel of the Lord spake unto Philip." The work of Philip is still in view, and yet, here commenced that wider movement in the activity of the Christian Church, of the beginnings of which, the remainder of this book of the Acts of the Apostles tells the story. It only tells the story of beginnings, because this wider movement in the work of the Church is not yet completed.

We have seen the first movements, indicated in the commission of Jesus, " In Jerusalem, in Judæa and Samaria." Now we have the first movement beyond, toward " the uttermost part of the earth." We almost invariably speak of the opening of the door to the Gentiles as having taken place in the house of Cornelius, and of Peter being the first messenger of the evangel to the Gentiles. That may be true, or it may not. There is a question as to what the Ethiopian's nationality really was. I believe that by race he was Ethiopian, that is a Gentile; and therefore, that not to Peter the apostle, but to Philip the deacon was given the work of first expanding the commission of Jesus so as to win one for Him from among the number of those who by the Jews were looked upon as outside the covenant of promise.

Of the issues of this movement toward Africa, we have no record. There are legends, interesting, but quite unre-

liable. Our interest in this story is in the movement itself, as this account reveals its direction and methods.
So we shall first examine the story, and then attempt to
observe its abiding teaching.

Let us first look more carefully at this Ethiopian
Eunuch. We are told quite clearly certain things about
him. He was " a man of Ethiopia," he was " a eunuch
of great authority under Candace, queen of the Ethiopians "; he " was over all her treasure." It has been
suggested that he was a proselyte to Judaism, a proselyte
of the Gate, a proselyte of righteousness. If this was
so, he would not be admitted to the inner sanctuary at
Jerusalem, but would be allowed to stand in an outer
court, in order to worship. There are those who hold
that this expression, " a man of Ethiopia " simply means
that, being a Jew, he was nevertheless born in Ethiopia,
and had risen there to this position of power and eminence. Probably he was indeed a man of Ethiopia in
the full sense of the word, a son of Africa, himself one
of the race of Ham, a negro. That is my own personal
conviction. I believe he was the first of the African
race to become a Christian. It is now established that
at least three centuries before Christ Greek literature and
thought had permeated that central African district, and
that a most remarkable civilization was realized under
Candace. Probably this word Candace is not the name
of a woman, but rather a title, like Pharaoh. The
Egyptian portraiture of the Ethiopians shows the distinct
negro type.

I never read this story without wondering how it came
about, that seeing this man passed down into Ethiopia so
early in the history of the Christian Church, Africa is
where she is to-day. In the earliest churches in existence
in Africa, we find that they failed to translate the Scriptures into their own language, failed to give the Bible
to their own people. The story of missions the whole
wide world over, shows that the success or failure of such

missions has always been dependent on whether those brought to Christ had the Scriptures in their own language or not.

This man had been to Jerusalem to worship, and he was now on his way back. What had he found in Jerusalem? He went to the Hebrew centre of worship, to the Hebrew priesthood, to the Hebrew temple. He went to that system of worship, a portion of the sacred literature of which he held in his hand, and was reading on his way home. In Jerusalem he found that whole system of worship materialized, under Sadducean influence; materialized, ritualistic, dead.

In some of the things this man said to Philip on his return journey, one can hear the echo of his discontent with everything he had found in Jerusalem. The statement, " He was returning and sitting in his chariot, and was reading the prophet Isaiah," shows his interest in some of the profoundest things of the Hebrew religion. Philip had said to him, " Understandest thou what thou readest? " In his answer I can detect the restlessness of a great disappointment and discontent. " How can I, except some one shall guide me? " The word " guide " there is a very technical word. It is used again and again with reference to authoritative teaching and interpretation. Christ described the authoritative teachers of His time as " blind guides."

This man, profoundly interested in the deepest things of the Hebrew religion—for Hebrew expositors will agree that the great prophecy of Isaiah was reckoned by themselves to be the finest and profoundest of their writings and literature—had found his way back to that writing, and therein to that strange and mystic chapter, telling the story of the Servant of God, suffering, bruised, and through travail proceeding to triumph.

While profoundly interested, he was equally ignorant. Said he, " How can I understand, except some one shall *guide* me? " . . . " I pray thee, of whom speaketh the prophet this? of himself, or of some other?" If the fact that he read proved his interest, and his confession proved his ignorance; this question proved his intelligence. It was the question of the hour among the expositors. Was that portraiture of the latter part of the prophecy of Isaiah, which at that particular point becomes the portrait of a suffering, bruised, and broken Servant nevertheless emerging into triumph, Isaiah's account of himself? Or was he speaking of some one else? "Who hath believed our report? and to whom hath the arm of the Lord been revealed?" Was Isaiah uttering a lamentation about the failure of his own ministry, or was he speaking of some One Who should come and should fail? That, moreover, is the question which is still being debated concerning this chapter. There are those to-day who are a little more inclined to be dogmatic than was the Ethiopian Eunuch. It is affirmed that Isaiah had no view and no vision of the ultimate suffering of the Servant of God, but that the whole meaning of the passage was exhausted in his own experience, or possibly in that of Jeremiah. But that is not our subject now. We are interested in the man. A man of authority, he had been to Jerusalem, seeking to worship; to satisfy in the city of holy associations, in the very central place of worship, the deepest, profoundest, and holiest cravings of his life. This man laden with honour, overwhelmed with responsibility, sitting in his chariot, read aloud as men did in those days, the prophecy of Isaiah, pondering over it, perplexed by it, catching the music in it, and yet wondering what it all meant. He was a hungry soul!

Let us now look at Philip in these new circumstances. "But an angel of the Lord spake unto Philip, saying, Arise, and go toward the south unto the way that goeth down from Jerusalem unto Gaza; the same is desert." The word "But" suggests change in the circumstances of Philip's ministry. From Samaria, the city crowded

THE ACTS OF THE APOSTLES
with interests, and crowded with men, he was sent to the lonely road, that winds away from civilization across the desert, toward another civilization, foreign, alien, different. From a ministry among multitudes, with all its thrill and fascination, to a conversation with one man. Philip did not even know he was going to one man. He only knew he was going to the Desert! Samaria was the city of fellowship, new fellowship, glad fellowship, the fellowship of souls won for his Lord. Philip the beloved evangelist had been in the midst of that sacred fellowship. He was now disturbed, and sent into loneliness: "Go toward the south unto the way that goeth down from Jerusalem unto Gaza; the same is desert."

But that is only part of the story. It was an angel who told him to go. When obeying, and having arrived, he saw the retinue passing along the road, and this man sitting in the chariot, it was the Spirit Who whispered in his heart, "Go near, and join thyself to this chariot." With the company of angels, in fellowship with the Holy Spirit there is no loneliness. In this great life and movement and service of which Philip was an honoured instrument, there are heavenly guidances, and eternal illuminations, and spiritual comradeships, which make men forevermore independent of crowds, or anything else that the world holds to be sacred.

Both the Eunuch and Philip were prepared for this interview. The preparation of the Eunuch consisted in the fact that he had the prophetic writings, and a sense of his own ignorance. The preparation of Philip, in that he knew the historic fulfilment of the writing, and was indwelt by the Spirit of knowledge. On the one hand was a man poring over most wonderful writings, seeing glimpses of light, catching strains of music; but unable to find his way into the fullness of life, unable to catch all the music of the great song. On the other hand was a man who had seen the ancient prophecy wrought out in the experience of One upon Whom his eyes had in all probability rested, and Whom he had come to know more perfectly by the fulfilment in him of the Christ life by the Holy Spirit.

Let us now look at the method of Philip's approach. He did so with an enquiry, and with a play on words, which cannot easily be translated into English. The Greek word for reading, quite literally, means " to know again." When a man reads, he is supposed to be knowing again, repeating over again. Some one else had known, had written, and the man reading, knows it again. There is a fine philosophy of how to read suggested by the Greek word for " reading." The word " understandest " was really the second part of his second word. It is as though he had said, Knowest thou what thou knowest again? That is a very imperfect way of suggesting the play upon words. In the method there was a gentle raillery, intended to arrest the mind. The question meant, Is there any use in your reading? Do you know what you are reading? Do you know what you are knowing again?

Then mark the answering question, " How can I, except some one shall guide me? " This was the expression of a great discontent. He besought Philip to come up and sit with him. If he was filled with discontent, he was also full of desire for instruction.

Philip had no doubt as to whether the prophet spoke of himself, or of some other. Philip would not have denied that the prophet spoke of himself; but he knew that when he began to speak of himself, " Who hath believed our report? and to whom hath the arm of the Lord been revealed? " he climbed upon that suggestion of the Divine authority of his own mission, and saw through the centuries another Servant of God. He saw the great ultimate working out of the things that he had felt in his own soul. Philip therefore declared that it was Jesus of Whom the prophet wrote. The questions of the

[217]

[Acts 8: 26–40]

Eunuch were answered, as this man, not an apostle, not directed by Jerusalem, but instructed by the Spirit, and guided by the Christ, sat in the chariot, and explained the ancient writing.

What was the issue? On the part of the Eunuch, obedience, implicit and immediate. " Behold, here is water; what doth hinder me to be baptized?" The gloss which was in the text as a verse, now rightly relegated to the margin, may throw some light upon the fact that in preaching Jesus, Philip had led him also toward those final things which Jesus had said concerning conditions; and so he went down into the water, and was baptized.

Philip, having done his work, was caught away by the Spirit, and " was found at Azotus." It is not at all necessary that this should be accounted a miracle. I am never anxious to read miracles in, where they are not; any more than I am anxious to rule miracles out, where they are in. " The Spirit of the Lord caught away Philip; and the Eunuch saw him no more for he went on his way rejoicing." He was quite independent of Philip. The picture is not that of the Eunuch left dazed, upon the highway, wondering what had become of Philip. He had forgotten Philip, for he had found all for which his soul was hungry. " He went on his way rejoicing," the new light upon his brow, the new life thrilling through his spirit, the new love mastering him. He was independent of Jerusalem now, he was independent even of the messenger; because he had found the Master.

The abiding teaching of the story is patent. It is the story of the victorious Christ at work immediately among men. Sang the ancient Psalmist:

" Thou hast ascended on high, Thou hast led away captives;
Thou hast received gifts among men,
Yea, among the rebellious also."

I go further on in the Psalm, and find these words:

" Ethiopia shall haste to stretch out her hands unto God."

It was the One that had ascended on high, Who had led captivity captive, Who saw Ethiopia stretching out her hands to God. Nay He it was by the Spirit Who caused that stretching out of the hands. He was at work by the Spirit in the heart of the Ethiopian Eunuch before Philip reached him. The Spirit was ahead of Philip, making this man discontented, giving him to know his own ignorance. So we see the Christ preparing this Ethiopian Eunuch; commanding His servant to leave the city for the desert, the crowds for loneliness, the fellowship for isolation. As we see the meeting between these two men, we realize anew that this Christ is He Who opens, and no man shuts; Who shuts, and no man opens. He is still carrying on these same things in these same ways. He opens doors, and then through His people, enters the doors He opens. Long e'er the missionary comes to the land we call benighted, He is preparing for the coming of the missionary. It is not always by Isaiah that He prepares, but by the fetish, that the Ethiopian carries with him to-day. Happy indeed is that missionary who can do what Philip did, begin just where the enquirer is, and preach Jesus. There is no gleam of light in the world's religions but that Christ fulfils it; and no discontent of the human heart but that He meets it.

The last thing this story has for us is a revelation of the responsibilities of His own. It may be dismissed in a sentence as to statement! *If Christ is hindered, it is because some Philip is not willing to go!* It may be pondered long and carefully in application!

Acts 9:1–9

We now turn to the more definite and systematic ex-

[219]

pansion of the Christian movement beyond the first circles, and follow the growth of the Christian Churches
among those Asian cities which were so largely under
Greek influence. This movement is the more remarkable
when we remember the antagonism between Hebraism
and Hellenism.

This particular paragraph contains the story of the
conversion of Saul of Tarsus. It must, however, be related to the whole triumphant movement of Christ, by
His Spirit, through His Church. It was not difficult in
some senses for Christian Hebrews to evangelize Judæa.
Their brethren, after the flesh, dwelt in Judæa, and while
it is perfectly true that they were slow to do it, and did
not set to work at all systematically until they were driven
forth by persecution, still there was no religious revulsion produced in the minds of any as they preached their
great evangel through Judæa.

It was a little more difficult to preach in Samaria, for
there existed the influences of the ancient traditions, and
the habits of long centuries, which were expressed in the
familiar words: " Jews have no dealings with Samaritans." That antagonism to everything Samaritan had
manifested itself in the request proffered by one of the
sons of thunder when they would have called down fire
out of heaven to destroy the Samaritan village which had
refused to receive Jesus. But under the conviction of
the Spirit, a man full of the Spirit had gone down to
Samaria, and had preached, and Samaria had received
the Gospel, and the triumph had been won.

But now by far the most difficult work awaited these
men. Once they stepped over the boundary-line, and began to touch these ancient cities, with their Jewish customs and Greek influences, they were in a new atmosphere, and one far more difficult for them than any in
which they had so far preached the evangel.

The last three prophecies of the Old Testament, those
of Haggai, Zechariah, and Malachi, were undoubtedly

post-exilic. In the course of the prophecy of Zechariah, with its wonderful visions and strange foretellings of the coming of a King to be rejected, and yet ultimately to be crowned, these words occur, " I will stir up thy sons, O Zion, against thy sons, O Greece." These words were not mere rhetoric. They are for us revealing words. They had immediate reference to the Greek aggressiveness under Alexander the Great; and they had their first fulfilment in the victory of Judas Maccabæus over Antiochus Epiphanes. These facts are matters of history. Yet, while the words of Zechariah had such fulfilment, they had a deeper significance, for they suggested the diametrically opposed ideals of Hebraism and Hellenism.

We must recognize this antagonism between the two ideals. The ideal of Hebraism was that of the moral, the righteous, the religious, and it insisted upon law. The ideal of Hellenism was that of the culture and freedom of human life, the perfection of the powers of nature, the full play of all the forces of individual life. As we put these two ideals thus into contradistinction, in the measure in which we are Christian we see that they are not really contradictory, but complementary. But for ages this antagonism was very manifest.

To quote from Dr. Hugh Black's *Culture and Restraint:* " The policy of Alexander aimed at unifying the various elements that made up his world-wide empire, by the diffusion of a common language and civilization. To this end the Oriental races were to be saturated with Hellenic culture by means of the Greek colonies that followed in the wake of the victorious army. Entirely new Greek towns were founded, while the older cities were leavened by Greek settlements. Thus over one-half of Asia a network of Greek culture was stretched, which had as its object the reducing under its influence of the whole surrounding regions."

To take one glance again at the Maccabæan rising and

victory. Onias, the High Priest, contemporary with Judas Maccabæus, opposed with all the force of his religious fervour the Hellenizing influences which were spreading through the whole region.

Turning to the time of Christ we find the opposing forces represented in the two parties, of the Sadducees and the Pharisees. The Jewish nation had become largely Sadducean. The Sadducees were Hellenists. The Pharisees stood for Hebraism. There, in the last analysis, was the conflict between the Hebrew ideal, which the Pharisee represented, and for which he fought, and for which he made his traditions a safeguard; and the Greek ideal of culture and freedom, the glorification of human life, and the denial of the supernatural, for which the Sadducee stood. This then was the atmosphere at this time. Away beyond Judæa, Galilee, and Samaria, lay these ancient cities that had become Hellenized; and in the midst of them were colonies of Jews; Hellenized Jews; and to these also the Gospel must be preached.

This introduction has been necessary background to a right understanding of the apprehension of Saul of Tarsus. In the very word Tarsus there is significance. He was born there, a Hebrew of Hebrews, as he tells us in one of his epistles. Both his father and mother were Hebrews; there was no mixture in his blood. Timothy was born of Greek and Hebrew parents, but not so Saul. Nevertheless Saul was of Tarsus, a Greek city, the great university city of the time. At about fourteen years of age his parents were anxious that he should not pass under the Hellenizing influences of Tarsus; so they did not send him to the university there, but to Jerusalem; and he was brought up at the feet of Gamaliel.

This man, born in Tarsus, received the earliest and mightiest impressions in the atmosphere of Hellenism. He received his religious education from father and mother, Hebrews, not Sadducees, but Pharisees; and then was sent up to Jerusalem to complete that education at the feet of Gamaliel. This was a wonderful merging; indeed a coming together of opposing forces. The boy had spent his play-time in a Greek atmosphere, and had gained his earliest impressions there, the impressions that will abide, even though the snows of innumerable winters are upon the brow. This man, a Hebrew of Hebrews, a Pharisee, was also a Hellenist. Greece had touched him with its culture, its refinement, its poetry, and all its glory, and his zealous, godly, and much to be reverenced teacher, Gamaliel, was utterly unable to eradicate the poetry and passion of Greece, for he had been too long in Tarsus.

With all that in mind, we turn to our story. It gives the account of the apprehension by Christ of the man who was to be His special instrument in carrying His Gospel to these cities under the influence of Greek culture. We see the wonderful fitness of the choice. Whereas, it is perfectly true, that when the Master has a piece of work to be done, He can take hold of a man devoid of equipment, and bestow upon him fitness for service; again and again the past is taken into account; and the preparation of the earliest years is perpetually preparation within the will of God for the accomplishment of a great purpose. As to natural fitness, Peter would not have been successful, John would have been altogether out of place, James would certainly have failed. But this man Saul was one whose preparation consisted in his blood relationships, and all those years spent in Tarsus. The choosing of the Holy Spirit is not capricious.

Briefly then let us look at the man to be apprehended; at the apprehension itself; and at the man after the apprehension.

The man to be apprehended. There are previous glimpses of him in the eighth chapter. He is there seen minding the clothes of the men who are hurling the stones upon Stephen. The next statement concerning him is

THE ACTS OF THE APOSTLES

that he was "consenting unto his (Stephen's) **death.**" In that declaration, which means that he gave his vote for the death of Stephen, is a revelation of the fact that he was a member of the Sanhedrim. He was a man saturated with Greek ideals; yet even bitterly devoted to Hebraism; a man at war with the Sadducean philosophy, profoundly convinced of the divinity of Pharisaism, having given his vote for the dying of Stephen and of others, minding the clothes of such as cast the stones. We are further told, and can dismiss the whole tragic story in the words of the sacred narrative, that "he laid waste the Church."

Now let us take up the story as it is written: "But Saul, yet breathing threatening and slaughter against the disciples of the Lord, went unto the high priest." Let us see the mental mood of this man, so far as we are able. Take that verse again. Vincent translates thus, "Breathing hard, out of threatening and murderous desire." The Greek form there certainly warrants that translation. It is the picture of a man fiercely opposed, breathing hard, out of threatening and murderous desire. That is too familiar a picture to need exposition. But we have omitted a word. "But Saul yet breathing out threatening and murderous desire," or "But Saul *still* breathing out threatening." That is a small word, which seems as though it mattered little, yet it is full of profound significance. Surely there is nothing lost by the omission of this word. To omit it is still to have the picture of a fierce man, determined to stamp out the Nazarene heresy. a man definitely appointed as the public prosecutor of Christianity. But that is not all the picture. The word "yet" or "still," is one which suggests continuity in an attitude, in spite of something. In this passage certain words are omitted in the Revised Version which appeared in the Authorized. There is no question that they are accurately omitted; but in the twenty-sixth chapter and the fourteenth verse, when Paul was telling the story

of his conversion, he quoted words which Jesus addressed
to him, which are not chronicled in this paragraph: " It
is hard for thee to kick against the goad? " The answer
of Paul, " What shall I do, Lord? " is also omitted. This
is found in the twenty-second chapter, and the tenth
verse, where Paul was again narrating the fact of his
conversion. When Christ said to him, " It is hard for
thee to kick against the goad," what did He mean?
Surely He meant, Saul, there are forces playing about
you, that would drive you in one direction; and you are
kicking against them. This man, a Hebrew of Hebrews,
was determined to stamp out the Nazarene heresy, and he
had obtained letters of the high priest, and was on his
way to Damascus, to hale men and women to prison;
but he was kicking against the goads, he was fighting
against conviction.

Let us go back again to the sixth chapter, and to verses
eight and nine:

" And Stephen, full of grace and power, wrought great
wonders and signs among the people. But there arose
certain of them that were of the synagogue called the
synagogue of the Libertines, and of the Cyrenians, and
of the Alexandrians, and of them of Cilicia and Asia,
disputing with Stephen."

This means that Stephen's conflict was with the Hellenists, not with the Hebrews. The whole of his marvellous
address was a protest against Hellenism. Stephen's fight
was not with Pharisaism. We must be fair to Pharisaism. The rags of Pharisaism were its self-sufficiency,
its boastfulness, its contempt for others; but the heart of
Pharisaism was spiritual, a defence of spiritual religion
against rationalism. Stephen's fight was with Sadduceeism. Probably Saul had heard that great defence of
Stephen; and all his Pharisaic sympathy would be with
Stephen. As this man listened to Stephen, he heard a
man emphasizing the spirituality of religion, and charg-

ing upon them that they were turning from spiritual things. Yet he had consented to his death, had seen him die, and there had been manifested to him, his own belief in the supernaturalism of religion. He had seen a man bloody from the stones, bruised and battered and beaten, going out of life, with his face lit with a glorious light, and had heard his declaration that he had seen into the world beyond, a living Lord and Master. It was the vindication of his own philosophy and profoundest conviction. " *Yet* breathing threatening and slaughter." This man was fighting against a strange turmoil of mind, in which mental questionings, enquiries, wonderings, amazement, mingled.

Moreover he had now been to the Sadducean high priest, sacrificing his own deepest religious principle in going; and had asked and obtained from him letters, empowering him to hale to prison and to death men and women who, however much they might seem to be antagonistic to the ancient ritual of his people, did nevertheless hold the spiritual verities which he himself held. So, troubled by all these forces of the past, and this mental turmoil, revealed in a white-hot passion. partly born of the fact that he was violating a growing conviction, Christ apprehended him.

By the omissions here from the text of the words of Christ, Luke fastened attention on the actual person of Christ, without deflecting the thought of the reader more than necessary to Saul. The first phase in the apprehension of Saul was that of a great light shining round about him out of heaven, above the brightness of the sun. It was a moment fraught with tremendous issues in the whole programme of Christ in the world. Then came the enquiry. A voice spoke, not in the Greek, but in the Hebrew tongue, " Saul, Saul, why persecutest thou Me?" It was a voice out of heaven, out of the light, asking him, a man on the earth, why he persecuted the One Who spoke. What a strange thing, what a star-

tling thing! "Who art Thou, Lord?" cried the astonished Saul. Oh, the revolution, the convulsion, the up-
heaval in the soul of Saul. Then came the most arresting thing. The voice replied: "I am Jesus Whom thou
persecutest." Then there broke upon his consciousness,
dimly and indistinctly, more perfectly apprehended in
after days, the great truth that Christ and the Church
were one. How Paul wrought out this truth in those
great letters afterwards, as he insisted upon this unity
of the living Lord with His people. It is as though Christ
had said to him, Those men and women whom you have
haled to prison have suffered; but it is I Who have suffered in their suffering, Saul. The brutal stones that
you saw hurled upon Stephen, cutting into his flesh, and
giving him physical pain, reached Me, hurt Me. I felt
every throb of Stephen's pain.

But there was another meaning in the words. "Why
persecutest thou Me?" I am above thee in the heavens;
thou canst not undo My work; that against which thou
art fighting, is not the fanaticism of a mistaken fanatic;
it is the march of God through human history. "Why
persecutest thou Me?" In that moment, nebulously as
yet, not perfectly apprehended, the truth was breaking
upon the mind of this man, and by implication, ere he
knew it, he had yielded himself to the One Who had
spoken out of the eternal light, and Who had addressed
him by name. "Who art Thou, Lord?" That use of
the word Lord revealed a fine recognition of a trained
mind, in the presence of such a manifestation of supremacy. When the light came, and the voice spoke,
prejudices went, and all the antagonism that created the
fever heat of his hostility ended. He was in the presence
of supremacy, and he admitted it as he said, Lord!

Then came the revealing words, "I am Jesus." Again
Paul told the story, and in doing so spoke of the answer
coming in the form, "I am Jesus of Nazareth." Who
was Jesus to Saul of Tarsus? A dead man, disgraced,

and hated! Then there came the light and a voice. In the presence of it he said, " Who art Thou, Lord?" The answer came, " I am Jesus." The Jesus that he thought dead was alive. The Jesus that he thought disgraced was at the centre of heavenly glory. The Jesus that he hated, spoke to him in the language of an ineffable love. We do not wonder that this man never looked back! It was a great arrest, a great apprehension.

He was then commanded to do one thing, and that the most simple: " Rise, and enter into the city, and it shall be told thee what thou must do." That is always the Master's method. Was it a simple thing? It was a very severe thing. They were expecting him in Damascus; those opposed to Christ were expecting him as their leader; and those with Christ were expecting him as a great enemy. Christ said, Go into the city, and wait.

So he came to Damascus. Damascus was one of the first cities that Alexander had conquered, and into which he had brought his great influence. Paul came into Damascus led, for he was blind, defeated, and captured. I think when I get to heaven I shall want to know what became of the high priest's letters. He who had come armed with official authority to end the Nazarene heresy, was led in, the blind slave of the Christ. Those were wonderful days, the three days and nights that the blindness continued! We are not surprised to read that he ate and drank nothing. What happened in his thinking? One little word in the Philippian letter helps us. " What things were gain to me, these have I counted loss for Christ." He was finding the balance of things. What things were gain, I counted loss; my Hebrew birthright, for I had been born into Christ; the Hebrew rite of circumcision, and all the observance of the ritual, for I had entered into life in Christ. Did you count the Pharisee's supernaturalism loss, Paul? Yes, because I gained the spiritualities in Christ. I think through those three days of blindness and fasting, he was taking stock of the situation, and every hour there came to him a new consciousness, not of loss, but of gain.

Mark again the Master's fitness in the choice of the instrument. To see the Hebraism and Hellenism merging in Paul read in the Galatian letter these words: " I have been crucified with Christ," that is Hebraism, restraint; " and it is no longer I that live," that is Hellenism, culture. Then he merged the two, " but Christ liveth in me," and that is Christianity. In that final sentence Hebraism and Hellenism have joined hands; culture is seen resulting from restraint, and restraint merging into culture. In this story then, we see Heaven's arrest of the apostle who passed through the Asian cities to carry the evangel to these regions beyond.

Acts 9: 10-22

The opening words of the paragraph suggest continuity. In the first nine verses of this chapter we saw, first the man to be apprehended, Saul of Tarsus; secondly, his apprehension, as on the way to Damascus the light shone round about him and the voice of Jesus spoke to him; and thirdly, the man after his apprehension, in Damascus. The man who had set his face toward Damascus, having obtained letters from the Sadducean high priest in order that he might hale to prison and to death all who were followers of the Nazarene, was led into Damascus weakened, silent, and blind.

We now come to the second stage in the preparation of this man for his work. The contrast is very remarkable between the condition in which we left him in our last study, and that in which we shall leave him at the close of this one. We left him blind; we shall leave him with the scales fallen from his eyes, seeing. We left him silent, we shall leave him in the midst of the Jews of Damascus, preaching and proving that Jesus is the Christ. We left him weakened by the way, broken down, with prejudices swept away as by a hurricane; we

[229]

shall leave him growing stronger as his face is set toward his great work.

The paragraph presents us with three pictures. The first is that of Ananias and the Lord Jesus. The second is that of Ananias in his dealings with Saul. The third is that of Saul in the synagogues. Let us examine the pictures, and then attempt to gather up the spiritual significance of them.

We are at once arrested by the man Ananias. Nothing is known about him other than that which is revealed in this book of the Acts; and the poverty of the revelation is the richness of the unveiling. He is comparatively obscure. He passes before our vision at this point and never again, save as he is referred to by Paul, and save as his influence can be discovered in the writings and thought of Paul. It is certain that the influence of the first things Ananias said to Saul, and the first things he did for Saul, permeated all the writings of Paul, and had a bearing on all his missionary endeavour. When this man Saul was to be dealt with, and his face set toward the line of his life-work, and when he was to be brought into the reception of all those spiritual forces which were necessary thereto, the instrument employed by God was an obscure man. We spoil the picture of Ananias which the Spirit has given us, when we add to it the daubing of legends. Ananias is named as a disciple, and nothing more. He held no official position. He was not an apostle. We have already seen how independent the Holy Spirit was, and is, of apostles. He sent the deacon Philip to Samaria. We now see that He is not even dependent upon deacons, a most salutary lesson, even for the present age. He employed a disciple, neither an apostle, nor a deacon, and made him the instrument through whom the fullness of spiritual blessing came to the man who was to be the pioneer missionary; not only to bring individual men in Asian cities to Christ, but in capturing Hellenism and bringing it to the rebirth, through his profound and Spirit-inspired ministry.

Another thing we must not omit here, although it is found in Paul's first record of his conversion in chapter twenty-two. In making his defence he referred to this man thus: " One Ananias, a devout man according to the law." Now this was not a description of his Christian character, but of his Hebrew character. Paul was the last man to describe a Christian as a devout man according to the law. He was " a devout man according to the law, well reported of by all the Jews that dwelt there." This meant that Ananias was not a Hellenist, but a Hebrew. Saul, who by religious education was preëminently a Hebrew, but who by all the influences of childhood was a Hellenist, was now to be sent to the Greek cities; and the man sent to lead him into fullness of life was a Hebrew, having the Hebrew ideal as the master ideal of his Christianity.

Jesus spoke in a vision to this man Ananias, calling him by name. His response was quick and immediate, " Behold, I am here, Lord." Jesus told him what He would have him do, listened patiently to his protest, and urged him to obedience.

This story impresses us with the naturalness of the supernatural to those early Christians. Luke writes it without any defence, does not for a single moment think it necessary to explain, or to account for it. No surprise is expressed that the voice of the Lord was actually heard by this man, that there was direct and immediate communication between them. Jesus was alive from the dead, and Ananias was not surprised when he heard Him speak. Moreover Ananias did not get ready to reply, he *was* ready. It is a glorious picture of wonderfully tender, direct, and immediate familiarity between Christ and His own.

Jesus speaking to Ananias referred to " Saul, *a man of Tarsus*." Tarsus was the centre of Hellenistic educa-

[231]

tion, and to name it to such a man was to suggest that
against which the whole of his philosophy was at war.
The objection of Ananias was a perfectly natural one.
Saul's reputation had preceded him. The purpose of
Saul's mission to Damascus was known. Ananias said,
"I have heard from many of this man, how much evil
he did to Thy saints at Jerusalem; and here he hath
authority from the chief priests to bind all that call upon
Thy name." It is interesting to notice in passing that
the word *saints* has only been used once before in the
New Testament. It is found in the Gospel of Matthew,
but there it is applied to men of the old economy, as it
speaks of the saints who came out of their graves. It
had never been applied to Christians until now. It is
peculiarly a Pauline word. I think he learned it from
Ananias. It is followed by a definition of saints, "All
that call upon Thy name." The Corinthian letter,—a
letter peculiarly written for the sake of Christians living
in the midst of Hellenist Judaism,—commenced, " Paul,
called an apostle . . . unto the Church of God which
is at Corinth . . . called *saints,* with *all that call
upon the name."* The similarity is at least significant.

To Ananias the Lord gave the secret of His own heart
about Saul in the words: " He is a chosen vessel unto
Me, to bear My name before the Gentiles and kings, and
the children of Israel." So Ananias was sent.

The next picture is that of Ananias and Saul. Saul
spent three days in the " street which is called Straight."
Visitors to Damascus know the street. It is still there,
and constitutes the main highway. Along that street he
passed, led blind to the house of one Judas, which now
lies below the rubbish. That street in Damascus stretched
from the western to the eastern gate. In the days of
Saul it was very beautiful, typical in every way of that
Greek movement to which we have made so many references; a great highway through the city of Damascus,
the principal highway, divided by Corinthian columns

into three avenues, along the centre one of which the footmen walked, while along that on one side all the traffic proceeded to the western gate, and along the other moved the traffic to the eastern gate. There, in one of the principal residences, as befitted the reception of the representative of the high priest in Jerusalem, Saul of Tarsus was received; and there in his blindness he spent three days. The attempt to identify the Judas of that house with a Judas of the New Testament is utterly unwarranted. The Judas who entertained Saul entertained him as the ambassador of the high priest, and was full of amazement at the strange thing that had happened to him in those days.

To that house, befitting the reception of the representative of the high priest in Jerusalem, Ananias made his way. When he arrived he laid his hands upon him, and said, " Saul, brother." He thus immediately recognized the new relationship. Then, proceeding he referred to "the Lord." That was the word which Saul had used on the way to Damascus, when he said, " Who art Thou, Lord?" The answer given to him was: " I am Jesus Whom thou persecutest." Now Ananias said: " The Lord, even Jesus, Who appeared unto thee in the way which thou camest, hath sent me, that thou mayest receive thy sight, and be filled with the Holy Spirit." That message was delivered, while the hands of Ananias lay upon Saul.

Then, " Straightway there fell from his eyes as it were scales, and he received his sight." We are certainly warranted in believing that while only the falling of the scales is mentioned, the full experience came to him, to which Ananias had referred; he received his sight, and the fullness of the Holy Spirit. Carefully observe that these were not the hands of an apostle, not the hands of a deacon, but the hands of a disciple. Christ sent a disciple, he laid his hands upon this chosen vessel who was to bear Christ's name before kings and Gentiles. In

[233]

simple address, with nothing in it that was official, with all brotherliness, and in simple obedience he put his hands upon him, and said to him, " Saul, brother, the Lord, even Jesus . . . hath sent me that thou mayest receive thy sight, and be filled with the Holy Spirit "; and immediately he received the fullness of the Spirit.

From subsequent stories we learn that Ananias commanded him to be baptized, and to wash away his sins after he had received the fullness of the Spirit. This of course was the baptism of water, and was the sign of a break with the past, and in all external things, a falling into line with the spiritual change that had been wrought in him. The baptism of the Spirit in this case, was followed by the baptism which was for outward confession.

The last picture is that of Saul in the synagogues. But between the picture of Saul and Ananias and this one, at least two years had elapsed, during which Saul had been in Arabia. This we learn from his letter to the Galatians. From that period of solemn solitude under the shadow of Sinai he returned to Damascus. He had started forth from Jerusalem to reach these syngagogues as the persecutor; he now came as the preacher. He started for them in order to put an end to the Nazarene heresy; he reached them as the great apostle of the Way of Life through the Nazarene. " Straightway in the synagogues he proclaimed Jesus,' and mark carefully what follows, he preached that Jesus " is the Son of God." That was a new departure, an enlargement of the evangel. It is interesting to discover when we turn to the writings of the apostles, that the phrase " the Son of God " is peculiarly that of Paul and of John. Preëminently it is that of John, for in his brief epistles in which there are seven chapters, the phrase is found twenty-three times. In all of Paul's writings, including the Hebrews for the sake of this argument, it occurs twenty-nine times. Peter was the first to use it at Cæsarea Philippi, but it is only found once in his letters. It is the full statement of the mystery of the Person of the Lord Jesus Christ, and straightway this man commenced to preach that. What a wonderful contrast between this proclamation of Saul in the synagogues that Jesus is the Son of God, and the intention with which he had come there! He started, a sincere man, to persecute those who differed from him. He stood in the synagogues, a sincere man, but with no thought of persecuting those who differed from him now. He would preach to them, persuade them, argue with them, but there was no persecution.

As we review the whole paragraph, what are its supreme spiritual values? First, its revelation of the living Christ dealing immediately with His own, accomplishing His purposes through His own, enlarging His operations in the world by joining others to Himself. The living Lord, the risen Lord, is seen carrying on His own work; in a vision appearing to Ananias; in a vision appearing to Saul; and so bringing them together. The living Christ was at work. Oh for a recovery of this lost sense! How often we seem to put Him at a distance. We pray to Him as though we had to travel leagues to find Him. We treat Him as though from some high altitude He had committed the work to us, and was unmindful of it, save as we persuaded Him to look at it. The picture here is that of the overruling and living Person, knowing the right man for the right place, and the right message for the right man.

And once again we have an illustration of the truth of the words Jesus uttered: " the Spirit bloweth where He will." We cannot compel this Spirit into any particular line of action. No apostle, no deacon, but a disciple, laid hands upon this man, and the fullness of the Spirit was received.

Observe also the first thing Paul did after receiving the fullness of the Spirit. " He took food." He fasted until he received the Spirit, but the first thing he did after re-

ceiving the Spirit was to eat a meal. Do not let us imagine that we demonstrate the fact that we are full of the
Spirit when we trifle with our physical life. He ate his
meal, and then in the strength of the fullness of the Spirit
and a meal, he left for Arabia. That is the whole philosophy of common-sense Christianity.

Acts 9: 23–30

We now come to the third, and last section, in the account of the apprehension of Saul of Tarsus, in which
there are four stages. The first is covered by the words,
" When many days were fulfilled." During those days,
Saul passed into Arabia and tarried there probably for
two years. The second is that of his return to Damascus.
The third is that of his return to Jerusalem. The fourth
is that of his return to Tarsus.

At once the supreme interest of the story becomes
manifest. At the commencement of the chapter we saw
Saul leaving Jerusalem for Damascus, and read of the
happening by the way. We looked at him in those hours
of darkness, when all external things being excluded by
the beneficence of his blindness, his thoughts were inevitably turned to his inner and deeper life. We saw
him receiving the fullness of the Holy Spirit in that hour
of the coming of Ananias.

We shall now attempt to see him in that period over
which a veil is drawn to a very large extent; the period
of the sojourn in Arabia. Then we shall watch him
moving back over the pathway; first to Damascus; then
to Jerusalem, from which he had started as the officially
appointed prosecutor of such as named the name of
Jesus; and so back to Tarsus, to the home of his boyhood. We see nothing more of him, until, because of the
new movement in Antioch, Barnabas went down to
Tarsus, and found him.

Between the apprehension on the Damascus road and
his return to Jerusalem three years elapsed. " He was

certain days with the disciples which were at Damascus"
(verse 19). "And when *many days* were fulfilled"
(verse 23).

What happened within the compass of the "many
days" with which this paragraph opens? The answer is
to be found in the Galatian letter, chapter one, verse
seventeen, "Neither went I up to Jerusalem to them
that were apostles before me; but I went away into
Arabia; and again I returned unto Damascus." Within
the compass of that indefinite phrase "many days" Saul
went into Arabia. There are chronological uncertainties
here. Some think the visit to Arabia was one of brief
duration, and that he returned almost immediately to
spend the greater part of the three years in Damascus.
That may be so. A careful reading of the story leads
me to the belief that the greater part of that time was
spent in Arabia, in quietness, in seclusion. This man,
arrested for special work, for further preparation passed
almost immediately after the arrest, and the filling with
the Spirit, into the lonely, splendid region of Arabia.
What associations the place must have had for Saul!
Under the shadow of Sinai the great lawgiver of the
people to whom he also belonged, had spent forty years
of preparation for service. In the same country, majestic
by reason of its rugged splendour and lonely grandeur,
he had received the law. Moreover it was from that
same district that the next outstanding figure in the
history of the people, Elijah the prophet, had suddenly
appeared. These two, Moses and Elijah, the great lawgiver, and the great reformer, had spoken upon the
mount with Jesus of His exodus; and these men had received the training of the desert for their ministry among
the multitudes.

Some ancient expositors believe that Saul went to
Arabia and evangelized, that he was busy among the
scattered and wild peoples inhabiting the district. All
that is quite uncertain. I believe that F. W. H. Myers

came nearer to the truth about that period when he wrote, as though they were the words of Paul himself,

" How have I seen in Araby, Orion,
    Seen without seeing, till he set again,
Known the night noise and thunder of the lion,
    Silence and sounds of the prodigious plain!

How have I knelt with arms of my aspiring
    Lifted all night in irresponsive air.
Dazed and amazed with overmuch desiring,
    Blank with the utter agony of prayer!"

Paul makes two references to this period. Both are in Galatians; the first in 1 : 17, and the other in 4 : 25. In writing to the Galatian Christians he states that he " went away into Arabia "; and later, in the course of the argument there is another incidental reference, merely geographical, " Now this Hagar is mount Sinai in Arabia." Ambiguous as the references seem to be, there is much light in them. It should be remembered that this Galatian letter is one which reveals the conflict between Jerusalem and Antioch; and Paul's contempt for the officialism which had manifested itself in the college of the apostles is patent throughout. One touch shows how he felt. Writing of those whom he had met in Jerusalem, in a parenthesis he described them as " they who were reputed to be pillars." Throughout the letter he was defending his apostleship, and his gospel, against the influence of Judaizing teachers. With that background in mind, notice where these references to Arabia occur. He first declared to those to whom he wrote, that he did not receive his apostleship from men, that his appointment to apostleship was not mediated, but immediate. He declared moreover that he did not receive his gospel from men, but directly from the Lord Christ. In order to emphasize this fact he gave the history of his missionary days, introducing it with the word that showed how he recognized the Divine government:

[238]

THE ACTS OF THE APOSTLES

[Acts 9 : 23-30]

" When it was the good pleasure of God, Who separated me from my mother's womb, and called me through
His grace, to reveal His Son in me, that I might preach
Him among the Gentiles; immediately I conferred not
with flesh and blood: neither went I up to Jerusalem to
them which were apostles before me; but I went away
into Arabia."

The contrast in the paragraph immediately throws light
upon the sojourn in Arabia. He did not confer with
flesh and blood; he went into Arabia to confer with his
Lord. Remembering the Hellenistic atmosphere of his
boyhood's days in Tarsus; the religious convictions
created by his Hebrew blood and training; and the strange
experience through which he had passed in his apprehension by the One Whom he had thought dead and disgraced, but Whom he had discovered to be alive and
glorified; what was more natural than that he should
desire a period of reconstruction? The arrest had been
an earthquake, and the whole superstructure of past years
had tottered and fallen, and lay in ruins about him. He
was quite certain that the One Whom he had persecuted
was the risen Lord; but he wanted time now to confer
with Him alone. We can follow him in imagination
back to the desert, to the splendour of its loneliness; and
see him entering into conference, into consultation with
Christ. In his letters we find how often he referred to
things he had received from Christ. In writing to the
Corinthians he said, " I received of the Lord that which
also I delivered unto you." That is but a simple illustration, but it is full of light. I believe in that period in
Arabia there was close, intimate, personal, definite and
clear conference between this man and Christ.

But the second reference, in the fourth chapter, is
equally interesting and illuminating. He wrote:

" Tell me, ye that desire to be under the law, do ye not

[239]

hear the law? For it is written, that Abraham had two
sons, one by the handmaid, and one by the freewoman."

Then he went back to Arabia, to Sinai, to the place where
the law was given, to the place where the great founder
of the nation received instructions concerning the ritual
of worship. Sinai stood for Hebraism; and he went back
to the shadow of that mountain, back into all the lonely
splendour of that very area where Moses had received
the law directly from God. He went back to put Hebraism in the light of the new revelation. The result was
that he looked at Jerusalem, and declared that Jerusalem
as he found her, was in bondage. But a little while before, he had left Jerusalem, the appointed prosecutor of
a heresy which seemed to threaten Hebraism. Now from
Arabia, looking back upon Jerusalem in the light of the
revelation that had come to him upon the Damascene
road, he saw Hebraism in bondage; but he saw that the
Jerusalem above, the mother of us all, is free.

In the argument of this fourth chapter of the Galatian
letter we discover the results of the sojourn in Arabia.
There, through the illumination of that Spirit which he
had received in fullness; and as the result of his conference, not with flesh and blood, but with the living
Christ through the Spirit, this man saw the old in the
light of the new. In the figures of speech which he employed, and which mean little if we depart from the
atmosphere in which he lived, but which meant very
much to the men who read them as they came from Paul's
pen, we discover the merging in his consciousness of the
two values which had contributed to the making of his
life before he met Christ, the freedom of Tarsus, and the
bondage of Jerusalem. Under the shadow of Arabia's
mountain, in conference with Christ, in the light of the
Holy Spirit, the two things merged. He still saw Jerusalem, as the city of God, the city of government, the
city of righteousness, the city of worship; but he saw

[240]

Jerusalem free, with her gates open to the four points of
the compass, with all the nations of the world pouring
their riches into her. He saw no longer a restraint that
destroys essential humanity, but a redemption that re-
news. All the forces that as a Hebrew he had considered
wrong, he now saw redeemed, renewed, and incorporated
in the great purpose of God; so that presently, when
correcting Corinthian disputes, he could say, " All things
are yours; whether Paul, or Apollos, or Cephas, or the
world, or life, or death, or things present, or things to
come; all are yours; and ye are Christ's, and Christ is
God's." There in Arabia, in conference with Christ, by
the illumination of the Spirit, in the atmosphere in which
Hebraism was born, he came to discover that in the two
ideals that he had always considered as being opposed to
each other, there were elements of truth; so that when he
wrote to the Galatians in defence of freedom, it was in
defence of a freedom within the law of love for Christ.
He learned those things in the quietness of Arabia; he saw
the rough and rugged magnificence of Sinai clothed with
asphodel and flowers; he saw the stern element of Judaism laughing into the breadth and beauty of Hellenism.
Hellenism was cleansed by Christ from its impurities;
Hebraism was delivered by Christ from its austerities.

From Arabia he went back to Damascus, where
hostility was stirred up by the Jews, aided by the Damas-
cenes. The burden of his preaching there we have already
referred to. It brought persecution upon him. In writing his second letter to the Corinthians he distinctly asserts that those who guarded the gates were under the
order of the officers of the King. But the disciples, those
very men whom he had come to hale to prison, helped
him to escape from prison. Those whom he had come
determined to put to death, now aided him to escape from
death. These contrasts are very remarkable. Observe
the indignity of the method by which he left Damascus.
After Arabia, with its magnificence and revelations, the

apostle to the Gentiles escaped from Damascus in a
basket, let down over the wall. Yet in that very contrast
is the glory of this story. He was not delivered by some
miracle, or by some whirlwind, although these were possible in the economy of that God Who had borne away
into the land of great distances and silences a prophet in
a whirlwind of fire; or Who by the Spirit had swiftly
transported Philip from the desert. In this story is a
revelation of the tender love of these disciples; and of the
fact that the man who passes from a period of conference
with Christ may have to exercise his work in the most
commonplace way, and sometimes find himself in circumstances which lack dignity.

He then went back to Jerusalem. There is also a touch
here full of beauty. Arrived there, he sought out the
disciples. In the old days he would have been a welcome
guest in the houses of the men of light and leading. Now
he did not seek them, but the disciples. Their fear of
him was perfectly natural. Three years had passed since
his conversion, and they had not seen him. They had
however heard the report of him, and were afraid to receive him; until Barnabas found him and introduced him
to the little company. Perchance Barnabas had known
Saul before this; for he was a Levite and a native of
Cyprus, near to the coast of Cilicia, where Saul had been
born. Saul was thus introduced to the little company,
and became the guest of Peter for fifteen days, not to
seek from him any authority, but to confer with him; as
he was careful to state in his Galatian letter.

Then he went straight to the assembly of the Hellenistic
Jews, and disputed with them. This word *disputed* only
occurs in this book of the Acts in one other place, in
chapter six, and verse nine. Stephen disputed with the
Hellenized Jews. Saul had listened in all likelihood, had
seen the result when the Jews turned upon him, flung
him out, and stoned him to death. He had watched
Stephen die, himself consenting to his death. Now when

he came back to Jerusalem, he went to the same company of Hellenistic Jews, and did the same thing that Stephen had done. He took up the ministry of the man to whose death he had consented. The ministry of Stephen had been peculiarly an argument against the Sadducean influence of the hour. Saul, the Hebrew, had violated his deepest religious convictions, when he had agreed to the death of Stephen. Now arrested by Christ, he attempted to make amends for past folly and sin, and so sought out the very place where Stephen had argued, and continued the argument as he disputed with them. The result was that he shared that hostility which brought about Stephen's death, for "they went about to kill him." Later on in this book we find that Paul tells us something about this, which Luke does not insert at this point. In the twenty-second chapter, when reviewing his story, he says that the Lord appeared to him here in a trance, in an ecstasy, and bade him depart, for He had other work for him to do.

Once more, aided by the disciples, we see him leaving Jerusalem; going back through Cæsarea to Tarsus; back to the old scenes after the new vision, back to the old atmosphere in the power of the new life. There we leave him, until Barnabas presently finds him and leads him back to Antioch.

In our study we have attempted to watch the movement as part of the whole of the activity of the Spirit of God through the Church, in those early days of her history. We have seen the apprehension of this man as part of the Lord's method for that new campaign. Jerusalem had heard the evangel. It had been preached in Judæa and through Samaria. Now there lay waiting for the Gospel, that wider district of Asia, with those Asian cities, and their strange mixture of Jewish synagogues and Hellenistic thinking. For the doing of that work this man was selected by the Holy Spirit. As we contemplate this story, we see how the Spirit of God selects the right

THE ACTS OF THE APOSTLES

man, when unhindered by the pride, arrogance, and self-satisfaction of men. Here was a man, in whose preparation we can trace Tarsus and Jerusalem; and more, Rome also. He was not only Hebrew and Greek; he was also Roman, with a passion for empire. So the Spirit of God selects for peculiar work those who are peculiarly fitted for it by their first creation.

But that is not all the equipment needed for the special work. He could not do the work that was to be done, because of Tarsus, because of Jerusalem, or because of Roman imperialism. He must first know the risen Lord. That stands forevermore as the first qualification for Christian service. That was the master note in all his preaching and teaching. Secondly he must receive the Spirit's fullness. Then there must be Arabia, the desert, and quietness. The peril of much work to-day is that of imagining that any man, immediately he has been converted can break the bread of life, and tell out the deep things of God, and fulfil a great ministry. It may not always be Arabia as a geographical location, but God never uses for the great work of interpreting His Kingdom any man who has not been definitely called and spiritually trained. Reverently to illustrate here from the life of our Lord, for that is always superlative and therefore final; the Lord Jesus Christ preached for about three years, but there was the long preparation of eighteen years preceding that preaching, in the carpenter's shop. Even when He came to the hour of His ministry, He was halted again for forty days in the wilderness. Saul began to preach in Damascus immediately after his conversion; but because God had some fuller ministry for him, he had to leave Damascus and go into Arabia. There must be the preparation that comes from conference with Christ, and waiting upon Him.

What did this man leave behind him? Both Hebraism and Hellenism. What did he carry over with him into the new life and ministry? His own personality, re-

deemed and renewed. Henceforth he was neither Hebrew nor Hellenist, but Christian; a man who in fellowship with the character of Christ had discovered the value
of Hebraism, and had sloughed off the things therein that
were worthless; a man who in fellowship with the risen
Christ, had grasped the secret of Hellenism, and flung
away the things that were worthless.

So we leave him for the present in Tarsus, presently
to see him again upon the high road of his work for God;
having seen in this study how wondrously the Spirit of
God selects, equips, prepares.

Acts 9: 31

This one verse is of great importance, because it marks
a new departure in the story as it gathers up suggestively,
certain unrecorded facts. The first word necessarily
arrests attention, "*So* the Church throughout all Judæa
and Galilee and Samaria had peace, being edified." That
simple word "so," suggests the statement of result, and
the relation of the result to the cause.

The statement of this verse is generally treated as
though the result to which Luke desired to draw attention was that of peace, and as though the cause was the
conversion of Saul. I believe that the verse includes
much more in each case; that the result referred to is far
larger than that of peace, indeed that peace was temporary
and incidental. The essential result is, " Being edified."
Peace very soon passed away, and persecution broke out
again; but the edification went on and has continued in
the Church until this hour. As to the cause, it certainly
is not inaccurate to include Christ's apprehension of Saul
of Tarsus therein, but a great deal more must be included.
To get the suggestiveness of this introductory word " so "
we must turn back in the story, and call to mind ground
which we have already traversed. The last statement of
this verse is that the Church "was multiplied." In
chapter six at the first verse we read, " Now in these

days, when the number of the disciples was multiplying, there arose a murmuring of the Grecian Jews ";
and there follows an account of the setting apart of seven
men to the office and dignity of the serving of tables in
the power and fullness of the Spirit of God. After that
we read that " the Word of God increased ; and the number of the disciples multiplied in Jerusalem exceedingly ;
and a great company of the priests were obedient to the
faith." The story of Stephen occupies the remainder of
chapter six and the whole of chapter seven. At the commencement of chapter eight we read, " There arose on
that day a great persecution against the Church which was
in Jerusalem ; and they were all scattered abroad throughout the regions of Judæa and Samaria, except the
apostles ; and devout men buried Stephen, and made great
lamentation over him ; but Saul laid waste the Church,
entering into every house, and dragging men and women
committed them to prison." We are familiar with all the
recorded happenings following that statement up to this
thirty-first verse, " So the Church throughout all Judæa
and Galilee and Samaria had peace, being edified." Much,
however, had happened which is not chronicled. A
much wider work was going on than is recorded in this
book. Certain outstanding and vital incidents in connection with the movements have been noted ; the persecution and scattering of the disciples, and its use by the Holy
Spirit. Our attention has been focused upon the apprehension of Saul of Tarsus. But as we have said, much
more had been going on ; and in this phrase, suggestively
and remarkably, Luke draws attention to the much more.

Here we read of " The Church throughout all Judæa
and Galilee and Samaria." That is an entirely new conception, not found in the book of Acts before. This is
the first occasion on which the word " Church " is used
in that spacious sense. When persecution broke out, the
Church at Jerusalem was almost wasted ; there, as it
seemed, most havoc was wrought ; and the disciples were

[246]

scattered everywhere. We saw the persecution scattering them, and the evangelization of the whole region round about which resulted from the scattering. We noticed carefully the apprehension of one man, the central figure Saul; and now as the result of the persecution which scattered, and as the result of the evangelization that followed, as the result of the arrest of one man who was leading the opposition and his apprehension by Jesus Christ; " The Church throughout all Judæa and Galilee and Samaria had peace, being edified." The " so " with which the verse opens encompasses the whole movement.

From this verse to the end of the twelfth chapter, Peter again becomes the central figure. Here at the parting of the ways between that vital story of the apprehension of Saul, and the interesting account of Peter's work, we have a picture of the Church such as has not appeared before. The statement of Luke concerning the Church is a most careful one.

In examining this verse we must bear in mind its completeness as a paragraph. It stands alone in the record, rightly placed. Let us, moreover, carefully notice the divisions of this paragraph. The Text of Westcott and Hort separates it carefully from the following verse; and its punctuation divides it into two parts, by placing a comma after the word " edified." The punctuation of the Revised Version follows this idea, though with English fullness. Therefore I find that this text has two distinct parts; first, " The Church throughout all Judæa and Galilee and Samaria had peace, being edified"; and secondly, " and, walking in the fear of the Lord, and in the comfort of the Holy Spirit, was multiplied." There are then, two phases of revelation; first of the Church in itself; and secondly, of the Church in its service.

Let us first take time to consider the essential meaning of the word " Church." The word *ecclesia* literally means called out. The picture of the Church suggested by the word is that of a company of those who are separated from the nation, and from the race, an entirely new company.

The use of the word is interesting. In the seventh chapter of this book it is used in a way, to notice which, will help us: "This is he that was in the *church* in the wilderness." That might be translated quite accurately, "the *assembly* in the wilderness." The phrase has reference to the ancient people of God; and in that verse we discover the Hebrew use of the word. When Jesus first made use of it at Cæsarea Philippi, saying to Peter, "Upon this rock I will build My Church," He used a not uncommon word. Those who heard it were arrested not by the use of the word *ecclesia*, but by the authoritative and possessive pronoun, "*My* ecclesia," by the use of which He indicated something with which they were familiar, and something with which they were entirely unfamiliar. The Hebrews understood the word *ecclesia* as referring to the peculiar people, the chosen nation, the Theocracy, the Divinely-governed people.

But the word had also a Greek meaning, and in this book of the Acts of the Apostles it is used in the Greek sense in the nineteenth chapter and the thirty-second verse: "Some therefore cried one thing, and some another: for the *assembly* was in confusion." There the reference was to the special gathering of the craftsmen. Then there is the account of the uproar in Ephesus, and twice the *assembly* is mentioned, where the reference is to the Civic Authority. What then were the peculiarities of the Greek *ecclesia?* It was composed entirely of free men, no slave was allowed to be a member of the Greek *ecclesia;* and its function was that of government.

Two ideas are therefore suggested by the word; the Hebrew idea which was that of a God-governed people; and the Greek idea, which was that of a governing community. When Jesus said at Cæsarea Philippi "My ecclesia," He was doubtless perfectly familiar with the

[248]

two ideas, and He included them both. The word appears upon the pages of this book of the Acts, and refers to the company of those who are following the name of Jesus; and are first, the God-governed people; and secondly, the governing people; the people who hold the keys, not of themselves, the Church, but of the Kingdom; the moral interpreters, those who are to state the standards of life, and who are to insist upon the ethical ideas of Jesus.

Now observe the enlarged conception at this point. The word " Church " had occurred only two or three times previously. In the second chapter it is said, " The Lord added to them," the Authorized Version renders it " The Lord added to the Church." The real meaning is that He added to Himself, and so to the Church. Then a little further on, in the fifth chapter we read, " Great fear came upon the whole Church." In the eighth chapter, again, " There arose on that day a great persecution against the Church. . . . Saul laid waste the Church." These occasions are grouped in order to note the fact that up to this point every reference to the Church had been to the Church at Jerusalem. But now it is employed with a wider outlook: " The Church throughout all Judæa and Galilee and Samaria." In the Authorized Version the passage reads " the Churches throughout." I have no hesitation in saying that the change is not only necessary, but vital to an understanding of this passage. Later on, there will be recognition of local centres; but here a greater, grander idea than that breaks upon the vision. The preposition is significant, not the church of, but " the Church throughout." Whenever we lay emphasis upon the preposition of, we wrong the catholic ideal. The Church of Scotland, the Church of England. There is really no such Church. There is the Church throughout Scotland, England, Ireland, the World! A great spiritual vision breaks upon the sight at this point, of a united Church. Mark

[249]

the wonderful comprehensiveness of this; Judæa,
Galilee, and Samaria were included; and the movement
was about to spread. Go back to the Gospel history, and
remember how the men of Judæa held in contempt the
men of Galilee, as they called it, Galilee of the Gentiles.
Between Judæa and Samaria there was perpetual feud;
" The Jews have no dealings with the Samaritans." Yet
here we read "the Church throughout all Judæa and
Galilee and Samaria"; not one for Judæa, one for Galilee,
and one for Samaria, continuing race prejudice, per-
petuating bitterness, establishing local geographical
centres. This great movement was sweeping all these
things away forever. One *ecclesia* called out from
Judæa, Galilee, Samaria; brought from prejudice, pride,
and geographical limitation, into the unity of the Spirit.
Here then for the first time there appears upon the page
of the Acts of the Apostles, the spacious catholic conception of the Christian Church.

Then let us notice the edification of that Church. I am
not careful to dwell upon the "peace," for, as I have
said, that was transitory; the essential thing is "being
edified." This suggests the incompleteness of the Church.
The man who wrote that word had no idea that the
Church was complete. It was being built. The word
also indicates progress; he saw the work going forward.
Moreover it looks to finality; that which is building will
yet be completed. Luke, as he wrote, saw not only the
spiritual conception of the Church, but its invincibility,
the fact that nothing can destroy it. Through opposition
and persecution he saw it growing up into the holy Assembly of the Lord; and he saw growing into that whole
Assembly the several buildings, the individual churches.
Yet he lost sight of the individuality of the local churches,
in view of the supreme glory of that ultimate Church
which is to be the very Assembly of the living God.

Thus these people are seen passing away from the
temple at a centre, and becoming themselves the temple

wherever they are. The larger spiritual ideal is emerging, and being realized, the ideal expressed by Christ Himself to one individual,—not a Hebrew, not even a Galilean, but a Samaritan, and more wonderful still, a Samaritan woman, and still more remarkable, a Samaritan woman who was a sinner;—" The hour cometh, when neither in this mountain, nor in Jerusalem, shall ye worship the Father . . . the hour cometh, and now is, when the true worshippers shall worship the Father in spirit and in truth." That is the catholic Church, independent of locality, sweeping over all geographical boundaries.

Where are we to-day? The Church is still being built. If only we could remember, that it is as we discover the simplicities, that we reach the sublimities, we should cease our criticism of parts of the Church. No man has seen the Church; it is not built, it is being built, but it is not completed. Half the things about which we quarrel to-day are scaffolding, rather than essential building.

We turn now to a brief examination of the second part of the verse: " And walking in the fear of the Lord, and in the comfort of the Holy Spirit, was multiplied." That word " walking " has certainly no reference here merely to the habits of life; it is a far profounder word. In Rotherham's translation it is rendered " the Church . . . *going on its way* in the fear of the Lord and in the comfort of the Holy Spirit." The particular word here translated " walking," is one that always suggests purpose as opposed to aimlessness. There is another Greek word found in the New Testament which is not necessarily that of purpose or finality, and from that word we have derived our word " peripatetic," which may describe quite an aimless walking around. Not so this word. This is the word that Jesus made use of in the great commission recorded by Matthew, " *Go* ye therefore and disciple the nations." He used the same word in the commission as Mark records it, " *Go* ye into all the cosmos." At this point Luke takes up that word, a word full of these sacred associations. He was not now describing the habits of individual members of the Church, but the service of the whole Church, *going on its way*. The Lord's intention for His Church, is that it should be an ambassage, a corporation of living souls, sent out upon the King's business. Luke sees the Church fulfilling this function, going on its way.

The twofold condition of that going is stated. First, "Going in the fear of the Lord." The Lord had thus commissioned His Church: "Go ye therefore, and disciple the nations, baptizing them into the name of the Father and of the Son and of the Holy Spirit: teaching them to observe all things whatsoever I commanded you"; and again: "Go ye into all the cosmos, and preach the gospel to the whole creation." The Lordship of Christ to those early disciples was twofold in its application: He was the Lord of life, the authoritative and final one; and He was the greatest of all servants, Himself leading those who serve in places of suffering and toil and travail. Here then we see the Church; a spiritual Body, including all who believe within its boundaries; going on its way in the fear of the Lord. This meant that its life was yielded to His dominion, and itself was forevermore proclaiming His authority, and insisting upon it. It meant also that its life was at the disposal of His suffering ones: as it entered into the cosmos, and placed itself against the wounds and weariness of humanity, touching the degradation of life everywhere, so as to heal it. That is to "go in the fear of the Lord."

But all this was done "In the comfort of the Holy Spirit." The word "comfort" is palpably inadequate. The Holy Spirit was spoken of by our Lord as the Paraclete, the One called to the side of His people when He was about to leave them. He came first for comfort, to disannul orphanage, to fill the gap, to console those who were left behind; but He came to be an Exhorter, as well as Comforter, the Advocate Who should plead the cause of the absent Lord. The Greek word here covers the two values, and we may render it walking in the comforting advocacy of the Holy Spirit. In the ministry of the Holy Spirit the Church went forth to work. That ministry was that of making the Lord Himself real to the consciousness of those who went, for witness, for preaching, for insistence upon the Lordship of Christ; for proclamation of His authority over all life, and for revelation of the power of His Saviourhood.

In view of all this we are not surprised to read the last phrase, brief though it is, that the Church " was multiplied." The idea is not merely that of the numbering of units; it is that of fullness; the Church was made to abound. The Church went forth in abounding power, itself growing and multiplying because of the two facts of its life: the master-principle of the Lordship of Jesus, and the power and comfort of the Holy Spirit.

As we look back to this ancient picture, we earnestly desire new realization in the day in which we live. There are two things we gather from our examination of this verse. First, the spiritual conception of the Church. This is suggested by the phrase " the Church throughout." By that phrase all geographical boundaries are ignored, all race prejudices are destroyed, all ancient feuds are ended, all religious centres are abolished. Nineteen centuries have gone, and we still have our geographical boundaries, and name our Churches according to them; race prejudices still divide the Church; ancient feuds are still maintained within the Church; and we still go up to some special centre to worship. Let us more carefully contemplate the great ideal. In proportion as our eyes behold it and our hearts desire it, and we in individual life conform to it; we shall hasten the perfecting of the Church, and the accomplishment of the will of God.

It is impossible to read this verse without being re-

minded of the missionary vocation of the Church. Here
the Church is seen going on its way, going in the way the
Lord commanded it, going to the nations to disciple them,
going into the cosmos to suffer in order to save; and
going on its way in the fear of the Lord, and in the comfort of the Holy Spirit. These two things are closely
united. The first part of the verse ends " being edified ";
the second part ends " was multiplied." The underlying
thought is exactly the same. Consequently if the Church
is to be missionary, she must be spiritual; and if the
Church is to be spiritual, she must be missionary.

Acts 9: 32-43

This paragraph constitutes a link between the story of
Saul and that of Cornelius. It is complete in itself, and
yet is closely related to that which has preceded it, and
that which is to follow.

As to its relation to the preceding one, we remember
that Saul was at Tarsus; and that, as the introductory
declaration of this paragraph reveals, Peter was going
throughout all parts. Saul is now left for a little while
at Tarsus, and we have no record of his doings; but are
brought back again from this point, and on to the end of
the twelfth chapter, to Peter.

This paragraph is related to that which follows in that
the last word of this chapter declares that Peter " abode
many days in Joppa with one Simon, a tanner "; and immediately following is the account of Cornelius. Peter
came to Joppa, which was to be to him a place of new
and revolutionary vision.

The paragraph to be considered is of the nature of a
page of illustrations. Peter is seen travelling everywhere,
exercising his ministry. Certain facts are recorded;
those of the healing of Æneas, and the raising of Dorcas;
and finally and most significantly, that of Peter lodging
in the house of a tanner. These pictures gather up much
that has gone before, and illuminate it. As we ponder

the pictures there are three things impressed upon the mind, with which we may deal in an ascending order; first, the communion of the saints; secondly, the operations of the Spirit; and thirdly, the victories of the Lord. Beginning on the lowest level, that which is simplest and most apparent; let us see what this paragraph reveals of the communion of saints; then looking behind that manifestation, what it reveals of the operations of the Spirit; and finally that which is the supreme matter, what it reveals of the victories of the Lord.

First then as to the communion of the saints. Reading this story carefully, we are conscious of the influence of a man who is not named. It is a simple and natural question to ask, Whence came there to be saints at Lydda? Let us turn back to chapter eight, to the story of the Ethiopian Eunuch, and all that followed. The last verse reads, " Philip was found at Azotus; and passing through, he preached the gospel to all the cities, till he came to Cæsarea." If we trace Philip's journey from Azotus to Cæsarea on a map, we shall find that the direct road went through Lydda. I think it is a fair conclusion that Lydda was one of the cities where Philip preached. He had preached in Samaria and a Church had been formed. He had preached to the Ethiopian Eunuch, and had won him for Christ. He had been borne by the Spirit to Azotus, and then started preaching through the cities. It is probable that his preaching in Lydda had been the means of gathering together a number of those who believed on Christ. Here then were the saints at Lydda, as I believe, the result of Philip's preaching.

Then at Joppa lived Dorcas, whose ministry was that of deft fingers, inspired by a full heart. It was a great ministry. When presently Peter came into that chamber, and the widows about him were lamenting, and handling the garments she had made, what a beautiful revelation we have of the woman! She gave herself to making garments for the poor. It is of course true that her

work sprang out of the mastery of the Christ-love, for
that is always anxious to clothe the naked. I think however that here are results of Philip's ministry. When
the dispute arose in Jerusalem in the early days concerning the distribution of alms, the Hellenist widows complained that they were being neglected, and seven deacons
were elected, men full of the Holy Spirit and full of wisdom, to set this matter in order, Philip was the second
man chosen. When he passed through the cities, I believe he not only preached the Gospel, so that men might
be saved, but he showed the lines and directions along
which the new Christian life should be used for the blessing of others. I think there is proof of Philip's ministry
in the saints at Lydda, and in Dorcas and her beneficent
operations in Joppa. Peter now passed over the ground,
and entered into the result of Philip's ministry. This
was part of the communion of saints. Wherever Peter
went, he entered into the labours of another. Such
ministry as Peter exercised in Samaria would have been
utterly out of place had it not been for the preparatory
ministry of Philip. There was no antagonism between
the evangelist and the apostle; and wherever it is found
to-day it is because either the evangelist or the apostle is
out of harmony with the Lord. There was communion
of ministry here.

At Joppa we have this wonderful picture of Dorcas.
Luke says concerning her that she " was full of good
works and almsdeeds." One would have thought that the
story was complete there; but I think that there was
Divine purpose in the addition of three small words
" which she did." So many people think of good works
and almsdeeds, and dream of them; but she did them.
She not only pitied the poor when the sharp wind blew;
she ministered with deft fingers to their need. This
again is a picture of the communion of saints. These
two phases are most suggestive; the communion of saints
in the ministries of the Church, that of the evangelist and

that of the apostle; that of the proclamation of the first things of salvation, and that of the man who instructs and edifies; that is the communion of ministry. Then we see that little homely group of women, around one who is known forevermore as the one who made coats and garments for the poor. The communion in each case is the same. The master-principle underlying the comradeship between evangelist and apostle is the same as that which underlies the companionship that exists between the woman of heart and leisure and ability, who makes garments, and the widows who in poverty and need, wear them.

The communion of saints always expresses itself in service. Wherever the apostle urges the saints to be true to the communion, fellowship, the expression of communion must be in service of some kind. The Church does not express its communion when it gathers together in assembly, and asserts it. The Church expresses its communion when in all types and kinds of its manifold ministry, it coöperates and ministers in helpfulness and love.

Then we come to the deeper and underlying matter, of which all that we have seen is but the fruit. Mark the operations of the Spirit as revealed here. The twelfth chapter of I Corinthians is an exposition of this paragraph. Take these little pictures of the condition of things in the early days, and then read that great, and magnificent statement of truth concerning the Church's relation to its Head, and its inter-relationship, and we can account for all we find in these pictures. Or we may account for the clear vision of that statement in the Corinthian letter by the fact that it was written by a man who had entered into this great life of the communion of saints.

First of all there are evidences of the Spirit's operation in the guidance of the apostle, as he went " throughout all parts "; to the saints at Lydda, to Joppa by the invitation of two men who represented the assembly in trouble because Dorcas was dead; then tarrying in the house of Simon the tanner. Nothing is stated about the activity of the Spirit. This man is travelling throughout all parts, no longer because of persecution, for the Church at this time had peace. Persecution will attack it again presently. The apostles tarried at Jerusalem until they were driven out by persecution; but the period of persecution had passed for the moment. Peter went through Lydda, incidentally, from the human standpoint. He went to Joppa because two men invited him. He went to lodge with Simon the tanner. This is not the story of haphazard journeying. The Spirit was guiding this man throughout all parts. Whence the liberty, the freedom, the ability to pass from place to place? "Where the Spirit of the Lord is there is liberty." All the bondage that results from separation, division, as between Christian people, is due to the absence of, or disobedience to, the guidance of the Spirit of God. The operation of the Spirit is plainly manifest, and it becomes the more beautiful when it is seen that the Spirit was guiding the apostle through the simplest human methods. Two men called him from Joppa, and he went, and entering into the house of Simon the tanner, he lodged there.

The working of the Spirit is manifested in the exercise of gifts; the gift of miracles, the healing of Æneas, a man outside the Church; the raising of Dorcas, a disciple inside the Church. The gift of miracles is not the only gift of the Spirit to be found there. At the conclusion of the Corinthian chapter when the apostle was dealing with the subject of gifts, enumerating them, among other things he referred to "helps." That gift is illustrated in the case of Dorcas. That is the meaning of helps; to be quite simple and literal it means gifts of relief. When Dorcas was using her deft fingers to make garments, she was doing it in the power of that gift which the Holy Spirit had bestowed; just as surely as Peter raised

[Acts 9: 32-43]

Dorcas, and healed Æneas, as the result of gifts bestowed by the Spirit. Much of the force of Christian testimony is lost in the world because we forget that such a gift as this is also of the Holy Spirit. In that Corinthian 12: chapter the apostle gives two lists of the gifts of the Spirit, in the first part one and in the second part another; from the second some of those in the first list are absent, and in the first list some that are in the second are not named. If we refer to other lists in the New Testament of the gifts of the Spirit we shall find that no two are the same. All of which is of profound significance. What are the gifts of the Spirit? No man can answer. The Church to-day has gifts that she had not in the apostolic age. She had gifts in the apostolic age that she has not now. There are two master statements in the Corinthian letter; the Spirit " dividing to each one severally as He will "; and " God set the members each one of them in the body, even as it pleased Him." We have no business to be wasting time wondering why we have not the gifts that the early Church possessed. He giveth as He will. If He withdraw the gift of healing which Peter had, I have nothing to do with it, but to be thankful that He still bestows the gift of helps. If we are tempted to think they are so different; that the one is so small, and the other so great, we are entirely wrong. While men are wondering and hankering after something that is more spectacular, more likely to make them notorious, they neglect the gifts of the Spirit which will make them helpful, and they are hindering the work of God. He gives as He will. If He does not to-day bestow certain gifts, He is always bestowing some. Let us take the gifts He gives, and use them, and not sigh for other gifts that are withheld in wisdom. This is the age of the Spirit. We are to act, not in imitation of the methods of the apostolic age, but in obedience to the present work and power of the Holy Spirit. When the Spirit of infinite wisdom, giving as it pleases Him, bestows a gift upon a man, the

[259]

simplest of them all according to the language of human, incompetent thinking; he makes his contribution toward the accomplishment of God's purpose in the world by using that gift, rather than by sitting down and sighing for the possession of some gift not bestowed. It may be argued that the apostle finished that very chapter in Corinthians by saying " Desire earnestly the greater gifts," but if we read on, he also wrote, " And a most excellent way show I unto you," which was the way of love. Passing through the thirteenth chapter, and on into the fourteenth, we find that he distinctly announced his conviction that the gift of tongues is infinitely inferior to some of the simpler gifts which men have held to be o less value and of less importance. Let us attempt to fre ourselves from these false divisions, as between great an small service, important and minor work. The membe of the great Church of Christ who out of the welling lov of her heart for the poor and needy, sits in a Dorca meeting making garments for the poor, is rendering serv ice as sacred as that of the man who ministers to he in holy things. Let us have done with this false idea i the Church that the man who is notorious is great. The peril of life is that of being conspicuous. We are perpetually in danger of losing the very freshness of the Spirit, because of what men call great opportunities. Garments made by Christian women, members of the perpetual Dorcas Guild, contribute to the victories of the Christ, and the enterprises of the catholicity of the Church, quite as surely as the sermon and argument in defence of the Evangel.

Let us take one other glance over the whole story, at that supreme matter, the victories of the Lord. It would be quite possible to imagine as the story is read, that we were back again in the Gospels. There is first the story of the healing of the body. How careful the apostle was in speaking to Æneas to make clear what happened! " Jesus Christ healeth thee: arise, and make thy bed."

We hear again the very echo of the voice of Jesus. The appeal was to the will: Arise. The command was laid upon him to do in his healing what he could not apart from the healing, " Arise, and make thy bed." There was no condition of faith on the part of the man who was healed. It was a gift of healing bestowed without condition, except that he would rise. He was only asked to exercise his will, which was to express itself in walking. We go back again to the first verse of the book of the Acts, " The former treatise I made, O Theophilus, concerning all that Jesus began to do and to teach." He said to a man, " Arise, take up thy bed and walk." He was still doing it through a member of His body, Peter the apostle.

Then we come to the raising of the dead. Once again the picture is so like what Jesus did, that some of the ancient commentators have suggested that Peter did actually make use of the very words of Christ, for there is but a letter different. Jesus said, " Talitha cumi." Peter said, " Tabitha cumi."

The question may be asked, How is it that men do not still raise the dead? Think again how rarely Christ raised the dead. It is recorded that He only did so on three occasions. What was the immediate purpose in His raising of the dead? In every case, the raising of the little damsel, the young man of Nain, and Lazarus, there is one answer. He raised them for the comfort of those that mourned. But every one He brought back, came back to suffering. The little damsel came back out of peace into turmoil; the young man came back out of eternal youth, to grow old; Lazarus came back out of infinite peace to conflict. Thank God He did not raise more; and we will not ask for our dear ones back. Notice what Peter did with Dorcas. He gave her back to the saints and widows. It is the same Lord of life on this side Pentecost as on the other; not Peter, not an apostle, but the same Christ. Why does He not heal so now? Why does He not raise the dead so now? **The** question can only be answered by Himself. I decline to place any blame for the withholding of this gift upon the Church. I recognize that He is doing His work in other ways, and so my heart rests there.

The last wonder of all in the victory of the Lord is not that of healing the sick, or raising the dead; but the spiritual emancipation of a disciple. Peter went and lodged with one Simon, a tanner. We know the abhorrence the Jew felt for a tanner, and the fact that the tanner was not allowed to follow his calling save at a set, legally defined distance from the city's limits. But Peter went in to lodge with one Simon, a tanner. That is the victory of Jesus over prejudice. We go back again to a story on the other side of Pentecost, and see the Lord going in to lodge with the very kind of man that the Jew hated, the publican, Zacchæus; as the Pharisees said in their technical cleanness, which was of the essence of pollution: " He is gone in to lodge with a man that is a sinner." Peter went in to lodge with one Simon, a tanner. It was a movement toward the larger vision, which was immediately to follow.

So we leave the page of pictures, attempting to gather up the great conclusion. The communion of saints is created by the operation of the Spirit, and issues in the victories of the Lord. The operations of the Spirit are for the victories of the Lord through the communion of the saints. Once again the victories of the Lord follow the communion of saints by the operations of the Spirit.

A threefold responsibility is suggested; that we cultivate the communion of the saints; that we do it by submission to the indwelling Spirit; and that the reason shall forever be, our desire to crown Him Lord of all.

Acts 10: 1-23

We now begin the study of a wonderful movement of

inclusion. Here the door was opened to the Gentiles, and the first representative Gentile entered the Church.

We cannot affirm that no other Gentile during the eight years since Pentecost had found his way to Christ. In all probability others had been brought to the sound of the Name, and to obedience to the claim of Christ. This, however, is the record of the particular case which arrested attention, provoked controversy, and finally brought the apostles and the Church to a recognition of the larger meaning of the work of Christ.

In order to understand the wonder which was created by the conversion of Cornelius, we must appreciate certain facts. The Christian movement was distinctively Hebrew. Christ Himself after the flesh was a Hebrew. His chosen apostles were all Hebrews. His ministry was exercised among Hebrews. Indeed there were occasions when He made that very evident in some of the things He said. That was the meaning of the almost strange word He spoke to one seeking soul: " It is not meet to take the children's bread and cast it to the dogs." There were prophetic exceptions in the midst of His ministry; indeed, the one already cited was such an exception; for although He said that His ministry was exercised among the Hebrew people exclusively, He nevertheless granted to the seeking soul the blessing sought. All His ministry harmonized with His understanding that God's intention in the Hebrew people was always that of reaching the people beyond that race; and so bringing blessing to them. Yet in order to understand the prejudices of the earliest members of the Christian Church, we must remember that Christianity was an outgrowth of Judaism, a development of Hebraism, and the early disciples had heard Jesus speak of God as the God of Abraham, and of Isaac, and of Jacob. He had distinctly told them that He had not come to destroy the law, but to fulfil it. He had insisted upon it in their hearing, that neither jot nor tittle of that law should pass till all was fulfilled.

[Acts 10: 1-23]

Beyond the Pentecostal effusion, the Church growth had been almost exclusively Hebrew. There may have been exceptions, as scattered disciples preached Christ here and there, and Gentiles had heard and obeyed. But the general movement had been Hebrew. The disciples in Jerusalem had not ceased to observe the worship of the Hebrews. They still gathered in the courts of the Temple. Peter was still observing the Hebrew habit of prayer even in Joppa. He went up at the sixth hour of the day, which was the midday hour for prayer. Even Cornelius, in Cæsarea had adopted the forms of Hebrew method in his religious life, and observed the ninth hour, another Hebrew hour of prayer.

There had, however, been a gradual approach to a wider understanding. The inclusion of Samaria was remarkable. When Philip reached Samaria and preached, and the news came to the apostles that the Samaritans had received the Word, there was an element of surprise in their attitude; but they recognized the movement as of God.

Moreover there had been the definite reception into the fellowship of a Gentile who undoubtedly was a proselyte, in the case of the Ethiopian Eunuch. The future apostle to the Gentiles had been apprehended, had spent those lonely months or years in Arabia, had gone back to Jerusalem, had continued the ministry of Stephen to the Hellenist Jews, had been persecuted; and at the very time was in Tarsus of Cilicia. But so far, no Gentile, as entirely separated from Hebraism, had been admitted on apostolic sanction to the fellowship of the Christian Church. The admission of this man Cornelius rocked the Church to its very centre, threatening to divide it in twain. It was the beginning of a long-continued controversy, in the process of which the man now in Tarsus had to fight over and over again for the right of his apostleship, and for the larger ministry that he exercised.

Our present study is preparatory, and is occupied with

[264]

the story of two visions, and of a meeting between the men who had come from Cæsarea and Peter in the house of Simon the tanner. In this study we shall not attempt to dwell upon the final significance of the vision which was granted to Peter, for he had not come to a full understanding of it in the house of Simon the tanner. That broke upon him later in the house of Cornelius. Let us then consider these two visions; as to the two men, and as to the two results produced.

There is nothing whatever here to warrant the view that this man Cornelius was a proselyte in the full sense of the word. There were full proselytes, and proselytes of the gate; and the distinction was a very real one. Full proselytes of Judaism were such as submitted themselves entirely to all its rites and ordinances, were circumcized, and thus entered into all the privileges of the covenant people. Cornelius was not one of these. He may in all probability have been a proselyte of the gate, but such an one remained a Gentile in the thinking of the Hebrew. A proselyte of the gate was considered by the Hebrew as outside the covenant, outside the place of privilege; for he had not submitted to the ceremonial rites, and ordinances, even though he professed sympathy with the one master-idea of the Hebrew religion, that of its monotheistic philosophy. We know certainly that Cornelius was a Roman soldier. He may have been a patrician or a plebeian. There was a great Roman family of the Cornelian patricians; and there was also a great family of enfranchised slaves, Cornelii, for an emperor had enfranchised a number of slaves, and had given them his own name. This man may have been of one or the other family; which, we cannot tell.

His religion arrests us. He was a centurion serving under Herod Agrippa, the representative of Roman power in that district. Stationed with his cohort at Cæsarea, he was thus the representative of Rome for the quelling of tumults if they arose, for the insistence on

[265]

order; a part of Rome's great police force. He was an officer, moreover, of the Italian band, that is of a band made up of soldiers from Rome, entirely outside the influence of Judaism. He was a man of faith, faith in the one God, which he expressed in his life. He was devout in all the full and rich sense of that word. His faith in God was expressed in his gifts, for he gave alms to all the people. His faith in God was expressed supremely in his prayer, for he was a man who prayed alway. Here then was a man outside the ancient economy, very largely uninfluenced by it in all probability in the earliest days of his life; himself a Roman, a centurion, of the Roman cohort, saturated with Roman ideas and ideals of government; and a man of faith in the one God, expressing his faith in the devotion of his life, in his almsgiving, in his prayer. Moreover he was a man whose godliness was such that the whole of his household had been influenced thereby. To go a little ahead of our present paragraph, we find that revealed in a remarkable way. When the angel visitation came to him, he called into conference " two of his household servants, and a devout soldier of them that waited on him continually." Those under him shared his faith. This is a remarkable picture of a little household governed by a godly man outside Hebraism. This man Cornelius stands out, an interesting and unique figure, not to be accounted for as we first meet him, by Christianity, or by Judaism. He is an evidence of the truth to which John draws attention in the introductory chapter of his Gospel, that there is a " light that lighteth every man." He is an illustration by contrast of the truth to which Paul draws attention in the Roman epistle when he charges the Gentiles with this peculiar sin, that they held down the truth in unrighteousness; that is, that they had not obeyed the light they had; that whereas in the creation they might verily see the Divinity and the wisdom of God, instead of following that light and worshipping God, they worshipped the creature more than the Creator, made to themselves images and worshipped these. There was the Gentile sin. But here was a man standing in contrast to that description, one who had been true to the light that was within him. He had followed it, yielded himself to it, and had become a worshipper of the one true living God.

But he had not passed into the fullness of life or of light. He also needed Christ. He also needed spiritual enduement. That is the key to the situation. The most remarkable thing about this story is the wonderful character of Cornelius before he became a Christian. Just as Jesus said, " Ye must be born anew " not to a man vile and contemptible and notorious in vulgar sin; but to Nicodemus, the highest product of Judaism, the man who, sincere and true and devout and enquiring, was seeking the teaching of every messenger from heaven; so also here, the first Gentile admitted into the recognized fellowship of the Christian Church was a Gentile who had come as far as he could, apart from the evangel. There is no suggestion that in the mind of the Spirit, and presently in the mind of the Christian apostle, or in the mind of those early Christian thinkers, Cornelius was all he might be. Had there been no Christ, no evangel, had he never heard the message, then he would have been judged by the light he had, and his obedience to it; but he needed the fuller light, and his obedience to the early light was the condition upon which the angel came to him and said: Thy prayers and thine alms are gone up for a memorial before God. And now send men to Joppa, and fetch one Simon. He shall tell thee what to do; the other things waiting for thee, and the larger life opening its doors before thee.

To return to Joppa. Let us notice the other man, Peter. In all likelihood he might have said with Saul of Tarsus, that he was " a Hebrew of Hebrews," of pure Hebrew parentage. The prejudices of the past were still strong within him. He had seen something wider. Illuminated by the Holy Spirit on the day of Pentecost, he had interpreted the fact of the coming of the Spirit when he had said to the listening multitudes, "This is that which hath been spoken through the prophet Joel." He had declared that the Spirit should be poured upon "all flesh." That little phrase is the most inclusive possible; "all flesh." Had he yet come to full understanding of the significance of the thing he himself had said? It is very unlikely. In our previous study we left him in the house of Simon the tanner; and that in itself was an evidence of the fact that prejudice was being broken down. Prior to his coming to Christ, and his baptism of the Spirit, Peter, the Hebrew, would not have lodged in the house of Simon the tanner. The trade of the tanner was held in such supreme contempt that if a girl was betrothed to a tanner without knowing that he followed that calling, the betrothal was void. A tanner had to build his house fifty cubits outside the city. But this man Peter's prejudices were so far broken down that he was content to lodge in the house of Simon a tanner; assuredly in the house of a man who loved Christ, a fellow-disciple. The first outworking of prejudice was gone; and yet it was still in his heart. He still thought of Hebraism as so Divine, that its rites must be submitted to by those who were coming into the larger life from the Gentile world. It was necessary that he, and those associated with him, should discover the fact that the old economy had been swept away by fulfilment; and that now without rite, ceremonial, or ordinance of Hebraism, men might come into living relationship with Christ.

So the two men are seen; one in Cæsarea, the product of the light that the Gentile had apart from Judaism; and one in Joppa, a man who had been brought up in Judaism, had been brought into relation with Christ, but had not yet come to a full understanding of the glory of the light in which he lived, of the power of the life which was throbbing through his own soul.

Let us now turn to the visions that came to these men. To Cornelius it was an open vision, a definite and actual visitation. To this man, an angel came in the hour of his meditating. That which is of supreme importance is not the presence of the angel, but what he said. In the angel's message to this man Cornelius, there was a recognition of everything that had gone before. " Thy prayers and thine alms are gone up for a memorial before God." Here the truth of a subsequent statement that " God is no respecter of persons " is made manifest. The angel came to an uncircumcized Gentile, with no part in the fleshly covenant, with no privileges within Hebraism. It was an object lesson not only to Peter, but for all time. In the words of the angel there was a recognition of the past, no word of blame, no word that charged him with sin, but a recognition of the fact that he had been true to the light he had received. " Thy prayers and thine alms are gone up for a memorial before God."

But the angel brought not only recognition, but instruction. " Send men to Joppa, and fetch one Simon, who is surnamed Peter: he lodgeth with one Simon a tanner, whose house is by the seaside." In the word of the angel we have a revelation of the line of Cornelius' prayer. He shall tell thee what to do. That surely implies that Cornelius was anxious, was enquiring, that he had come to some place of perplexity in his life. It may have been he was hesitating as to whether he would become a proselyte, and enter into that religion; for he had discovered that the God of the Hebrew was a mighty God. It may have been that he also had come under the influence of Philip, and the wonderful preaching that had made its way through Samaria and Judea. It may be he was wondering whether he could enter into fellowship with that Christ Whom Philip had preached, save through Judaism. It may be that this actual problem was in his mind which was confronting the Church. Be all that as it may, the fact remains that to this man, sin-

cere and enquiring, the angel came, recognizing his sincerity, and indicating the line of progress.

In our return to Joppa we have an entirely new vision,
no longer objective, but wholly subjective. Peter had
gone to the housetop at the hour of prayer, and there
is a human touch in the story; he was very hungry, and
fell into a trance, into a condition of ecstasy, for that
is the meaning of the word. While in that condition he
saw the vision. To Cornelius an angel came; to Peter a
vision was granted, while he was in a state of trance.
As this Jew looked at that vision he saw a strange vessel
in the form of a great canvas, filled with all kinds of
animals. There would necessarily be the revulsion of
the Hebrew against them. Then a voice sounded, " Rise,
Peter; kill and eat." His answer rendered, " Not so,
Lord," is hardly emphatic enough. It is not distinctively
Petrine. To translate bluntly, this is what he said:
" Lord, by no means ! " He is the same man we knew
in the Gospel, the man who said, " That be far from
Thee, Lord," " Thou shalt never wash my feet." By no
means, Lord, I have never eaten anything common or
unclean. That was the Hebrew speaking. Then came
this remarkable word to him, " What God hath cleansed,
make not thou common." The voice did not say, " What
God hath cleansed that *call not thou common*"; but
" *make not thou common,*" which is a far stronger word.
The idea conveyed was that of the cleansing of all, and
therefore the putting away forevermore of those ceremonial limitations which had cursed the Hebrew religion.
Do not make common, do not defile by your attitude
toward it, that which God hath cleansed. We are no
longer to speak of animals as unclean, and put them into
a place of degradation, if God has cleansed them. We
may naturally enquire if the Divine commandments re-
garding certain foods have been abrogated. So far as
the commandments against certain forms of animal life
were ceremonial, they are swept away; but so far as

they were laws of health, they abide. It should, how‑
ever, be remembered that the laws of health in that land
and in this may be different. The general health law of
Hebraism is that of Christianity; that the body must be
cared for as the property of God, and nothing be eaten
or drunk which harms it, and makes it an unfit instru‑
ment of the spirit. That tabulation of clean and unclean
has now passed away forever; but the law of health
abides. This is what astonished Peter. He had no right
to call them unclean, for they were cleansed. Some‑
thing had taken place in the history of religion, that
revolutionized all the habits and methods of religion.
Henceforth men were not to make anything profane
which God had now taken within the circle of that which
is sacred.

So the two results are seen. In Cæsarea there was
conference between the centurion and his trusted serv‑
ants, two of them household servants and one a soldier.
There followed the obedience of faith, and Cornelius is
seen waiting, while the men take their journey of thirty
miles, tarrying perhaps for a night at Appolonias. In
Joppa we see this man Peter, in his perplexity and his
open‑mindedness. While Peter pondered there on the
housetop, the Spirit spoke to him. This was no longer
a vision, nor an ecstasy. This is one of those almost
amazing declarations of this book, revealing the intimacy
between those early disciples and the Holy Spirit. To
this man, with all his prejudices, and his magnificent
loyalty the Spirit said, " Behold, three men seek thee.
But arise, and get thee down, and go with them, nothing
doubting." There was no explanation of the vision yet.
Peter was now about to tread an unknown pathway, he
was coming to new revelation. He was perplexed with
the vision, but the solution awaited him. In order to
discover the solution of this perplexing vision, he was
commanded not to be afraid. Then with the perplexing
vision in his mind, and the voice of the Spirit in his

soul, he heard the cry of the men outside that Eastern house, and he went down and said, " Behold, I am he whom ye seek: what is the cause wherefore ye are come?" They then delivered their message, and " he called them in, and lodged them."

This is a great picture. The house of a tanner; and inside it, the tanner himself, the apostle of Christianity, two household servants who are Gentiles, and a soldier. They all stayed together that night. The unifying Spirit, breaking down barriers, sweeping out prejudices, was at work more powerfully than those men knew. When the traveller visits Joppa to-day he is still shown the house of the tanner. There it stands, the waters lapping the shore close by. I think angels watched that house that night, with the despised tanner a fellow-disciple, the great apostle, the three Gentiles as they lodged there.

As Peter had not yet come to an understanding of his vision we postpone that consideration, confining ourselves to Cornelius, and the general values of the study. All that Cornelius was, resulted from his obedience to the light he had received. But all that was preparatory. Because he walked in the light that had come to him, he was led presently into fuller light.

The general values of this story are those of its revelation of the progress of the Divine movement, and of the mosaic of details. Every detail is part of the larger whole. Two men are thirty miles apart. They must be brought together. In order that they may meet, while Joppa is busy with its trade, and Cæsarea with its great shipping interests, and will know nothing of what is going on; God within the shadows keeping watch above His own, sends the angel to Cæsarea, and grants the ecstatic trance in Joppa. Thus they were brought together. Presently as the result of that meeting, the infant Church, with its lingering prejudices, will be compelled to a recognition that in Christ there is neither Jew nor Gentile; that the Christian movement includes all who come through faith in Christ, into fellowship with Him; and before its onward march pride and prejudice must forever give way.

Acts 10 : 23–48

In this paragraph we have an account of the things resulting from the two visions: the vision of an angel which came to Cornelius openly; the vision of Peter, which came in the form of a trance.

The vision of Cornelius was objective, and needed no explanation, for the instructions given to the Gentile soldier were perfectly clear and definite. All that was necessary was that Cornelius should obey, and discover the issues of the revelation. That of Peter, on the other hand, was subjective, and needed interpretation. Herein then we have an account of what followed the visit of the angel in the case of Cornelius; and the interpretation of the trance, which was granted to Peter.

In the meeting between these two men, the detailed story of which is told in this passage, there was mutual value. Peter's visit, and the message he delivered, explained to Cornelius the reason of the angel's visit. Cornelius' experience explained to Peter the meaning of the trance. When this Jew, who was Christian also, came into the household of Cornelius, and saw all the things that happened there, he understood the vision that had come to him on the housetop in Joppa. We shall first consider the story, and therefrom attempt to learn the lessons.

The story may be divided into three parts. First there was the enquiry. Peter, arrived at the house of Cornelius, said, " I ask with what intent ye sent for me? " The second part of the story gives the evangel. It is found in the address which Peter commenced to deliver, for as we shall see, he did not finish it. The third part of the story deals with the enduement, as it tells of the coming of the Holy Spirit upon the Gentiles.

The company who journeyed for those thirty miles from Joppa to Cæsarea was composed of ten men; the three who had been sent,—two household servants and a soldier; the apostle himself; and six men whom he took with him—Christian Jews, who are designated as "they of the circumcision." In the taking of these men, there is detected the anxiety of Peter, his wonder, and his perplexity. He had seen the vision; some gleam of light had broken upon his mind, and he was quite conscious that the journey toward the house of the Gentile was an entirely new movement; so he took with him six brethren, Hebrews, who were Christians.

The company waiting for them consisted of Cornelius, and his kinsmen and friends. When Peter arrived, Cornelius did him obeisance. The word "worship" there must not be misinterpreted. It simply declares that Cornelius gave him full honour, according to the custom of the East. Peter's refusal becomes more significant when we see it was not an act of worship, but merely an act of obeisance. There was surely dawning upon him the great truth, "I myself also am a man." In that word in which he refused the obeisance, he recognized the manhood of Cornelius.

Peter then declared in the presence of the company his difficulty in coming. He told them how contrary it was to law and tradition and custom for a Jew to enter the house of a Gentile and eat; and in that statement we see his lingering prejudice. He still described himself as a Jew, as an apostle of Jesus Christ; but he had not come to the full consciousness of what Christianity really meant, or he would never have said such a thing. Cornelius answered his enquiry by repeating the facts of the story which have been considered in our last study, of the visit of the angel to him.

Peter's address commenced with that preliminary word: "I perceive that God is no Respecter of persons, but in every nation he that feareth Him, and worketh righteousness, is acceptable to Him." He then proceeded to deliver his message. He began by admitting that the word which he had to declare, was a word committed to Israel, but in the parenthesis, "He is Lord of all," he revealed the fact that he was coming, as he stood there in the midst of those circumstances so new and strange to him, to a fuller understanding of the meaning of Christianity. The word was sent to the children of Israel. The preaching of peace by Jesus Christ was to the children of Israel. But the uttering of the words, "He is Lord of all," shows that the light was breaking upon his spirit, and he was coming to the fuller understanding of the meaning of his Master's work; and consequently of the Church's responsibility. In the study of these discourses of the New Testament, those of Peter, or of any of the apostles, we are always impressed with the wonderful way in which they covered the whole ground of the work of Jesus. Mark the things that he now said. He made passing reference to the baptism of John, to the message of the forerunner and herald. He then named the Lord, by that familiar phrase Jesus of Nazareth, which set Him on the common level of everyday life. He next distinguished Him from all the men among whom he placed Him, by the remarkable declaration that God anointed Him with the Holy Spirit, and with power. He then told the story of His public ministry, "Who went about doing good, and healing all that were oppressed of the devil; for God was with Him." He then referred to His crucifixion, "Whom also they slew, hanging Him on a tree"; and immediately as was the custom of apostolic preaching, he illuminated the Cross by the Resurrection, "Him God raised up the third day, and gave Him to be made manifest." Again, He is "the Judge of quick and dead," not merely the Judge Who is to sit upon a throne in some dim and distant time as the Judge of the dead; but the Judge to-day, the Criterion of conduct, the One before Whose bar men are forever standing. Finally he proclaimed the great and gracious message of the evangel, " Through His name every one that believeth on Him shall receive remission of sins."

In the declaration of the evangel Peter was careful to emphasize the fact that it was witnessed. " We are witnesses of these things." He used that expression twice, and around the two occasions he grouped the essential notes of the mission of Jesus. Witnesses of His life and death; of the anointed Man, the beneficent ministry, and the violent death. Witnesses of His resurrection and supremacy; the resurrection itself was so definite, that they sat and ate and drank with Him; His supremacy was revealed in the fact that He had charged them to declare His Gospel. Finally he said that to Him the whole of the prophets gave witness.

But the speech of Peter was interrupted. He was not allowed to finish. As he spoke, there fell on those assembled Gentiles the selfsame gift that the disciples had received at Pentecost. The evidence was in the gift of tongues; glad and ecstatic utterances of praise, not necessarily in different languages, for there is no reference to such. The gift of tongues is not only to be interpreted by the second chapter of the Acts, but also by the first Corinthian letter. It was the gift of praise. Mark the words, " They heard them speak with tongues, and magnify God." The same effect was produced upon these Jewish Christians from Joppa which had been produced upon the Hebrew crowd in Jerusalem. They were amazed as they listened to the utterances of praise, to the glad words that magnified God. They heard these men with loosened tongues giving utterance to the fact of the new life which had come to them. Observe that these men received the gift of the Holy Spirit before baptism in water, without the laying on of apostolic hands. Some had received the Spirit because the apostles laid their hands on them. Some had received the gift of the Spirit after water baptism. Here was another irregu-

larity, and the value of this story of the Acts of the
Apostles is that it is forevermore revealing the fact that
"The wind bloweth where it will." The Spirit interrupted the apostle in his discourse, falling upon the
listening men and women, when they had heard enough
of the message to believe into the Christ. So the Spirit
fell; and they of the circumcision were amazed as they
heard them magnify God.

What are the supreme lessons that this story teaches?
We will confine our answer entirely to those of the enquiry and the evangel. They may be at once indicated
by three points in the narrative. Peter first said, " Unto
me hath God showed that I should not call any man
common or unclean." That is the first lesson of value.
Again, " I perceive that God is no Respecter of persons;
but in every nation he that feareth Him, and worketh
righteousness, is acceptable to Him." That is the second
lesson. The third lesson is that of the suggestiveness of
the interrupted speech of the apostle.

In the words, " Unto me hath God showed that I should
not call any man common or unclean " we find the first
significance of the vision, as they reveal Peter's understanding of the meaning of the vision of the vessel let
down, with all kinds of animals therein, which he was
ordered to rise, and slay, and eat. In that moment the
apostle came to an understanding of the truth that in the
Christian economy there was to be no race superiority,
and no religious superiority: " That I should call no man
common or unclean." Who was the speaker? He was
first of all a man who from birth, naturally, and in some
senses perhaps properly, had been proud of his race; a
man who, passing away from Judæa into any other country, would everywhere, whatever other men had thought,
have been in his own heart proud of his national relationship; a man who looked upon himself as of a superior
race to all others. Now God had said to him that this
was to be so no longer; that there is no race superiority.

[277]

THE ACTS OF THE APOSTLES

But the speaker was by religion originally a Hebrew; and at the moment a Christian. Yet Peter was not to consider his religion as a Jew superior to the religion of Cornelius. Peter was also to remember that his religion as a Christian gave him no right to call any man common or unclean.

How far has the Church understood this fact? How far have we learned that lesson? Has our Christianity taught us that our race relationship gives us no superiority in the world? Or do we not even yet imagine that God has a chosen people, and that people the Anglo-Saxon race? It is an appalling heresy, which cuts the nerve of Christian work, which makes impossible full devotion to missionary enterprise. There is no race superiority, there are no inferior races.

But even beyond that, more astonishing, and more unbelievable, it is true that the Christian preacher or teacher must call no man common or unclean. He has no right to look with contempt upon any man because he does not share his religious doctrine or creed. To change the word "unclean," and render the passage more literally: "God hath showed me that I should not call any man *common* or *uncleansed.*" The remarkable thing about the word "common" is that it is the root, *koinos,* from which we derive our rich word *koinonia,* fellowship. "God hath showed me that I should not call any man common." Here is a strange and apparent contradiction. There is no finer explanation of the word than that of its use in the beginning of this book, "having all things in common." That means the ending of all degrees, the breaking down of all castes, the coming to a realization of the unity of life. That is the true idea of the word. But Peter said, "God hath showed me that I should not call any man common." In that statement we have an instance of the false use of the word. The Gentile is common clay; we are a spiritual aristocracy! So the Hebrew had said for generations; and so says the Chris-

[278]

tian Church altogether too often at the present hour.
The man outside is common, not within the sacred circle,
shut off from privileges. Peter said God had taught him
that he should call no man common, outside the circle.

How is that false conception of the meaning of the
word " common," to be corrected? By a discovery of the
fact that all men in the sight of God, for some wonderful reason occupy the same position. Let us go back to
the vision. There was the vessel let down, containing
all kinds of animals. Peter, commanded to slay and eat
said, " Lord, by no means, I have never eaten anything
that is common or unclean." The answer was, " What
God hath cleansed make not thou common." In that
word there was a recognition of the fact that there was a
process by which the thing that was unclean had been
made clean. In the infinite and mysterious and overwhelming economy of the grace of God, by the Cross of
the Christ, the whole race is redeemed. The race is not
saved. The New Testament makes a clear distinction
between salvation and redemption. Salvation is always
referred to as following the act of faith; redemption
never. Redemption is independent of faith. Upon the
brow of every man there is the sign of the Cross; and
on every human life there rests the sacred enduement of
the mystery of sacrifice,—God's sacrifice wrought out
into visibility by Calvary. This man came at that moment to the recognition of the fact that he had no race
superiority, that all questions of race were swept away as
by a flood, submerged in the new fact that men everywhere are redeemed, and that therefore there is no common man, in the false sense of the world.

That is the Christian outlook. Paul declared the same
truth when he said, " There can be neither Jew nor Greek,
there can be neither bond nor free, there can be no male
and female: for ye are all one in Christ Jesus." By the
side of that great passage we might put one of the prayers
of the Talmud, which Paul had doubtless said every

[279]

day for years, " Oh God, I thank Thee that I am not a
Gentile, that I am not a slave, that I am not a woman."
Humanity in the sight of God stands on redemption
ground; and when we perpetuate within the Church of
God our race prejudices, or when we show to the world
our race prejudices; and imagine that God is caring for
the elect inner circle, and is careless about the vast multitudes, then we violate the first principle that this great
lesson teaches.

The second lesson is but the enlargement of the one
idea or one truth included within the first. Peter said,
" I perceive," and the word is one that indicates the coming to a clear comprehension. It is the very word Paul
used about his conversion when Christ apprehended him.
Here it is used in the realm of the mind. It indicates the
sudden grasping of ideas. He had come to a new view,
to a larger understanding, fresh light had broken in upon
him. " I perceive that God is no Respecter of persons."
Those familiar with the Greek New Testament remember that " Respecter of persons " is one word, and that a
very suggestive one. I am not sure that it is not a play-
ful word, with a touch of satire in it; that Peter had
now come to such revelation of God's attitude as to use
the word, " I perceive that God is no Accepter-of-a-face."
Imagine a Jew saying that; the Jew who had thought
that his very face was the hall-mark of Divine election.
Now he said, God is no Respecter-of-a-face. Of course
it means infinitely more than that; it means all that the
thought suggested to a Jew. " But in every nation he
that feareth Him, and worketh righteousness, is acceptable to Him." That is not the same verb. It is a stronger
one; carrying with it the idea of closer relationship with
men everywhere, who walk in the light they possess.
Men that fear Him work righteousness. The apostle
did not mean to say that man is received upon the basis
of his morality. God has cleansed, and God's reception
of the race is based upon the passion of God, as wrought

out in the Cross, according to this great evangel. But no man is to be saved because he understands the doctrine of the Atonement. He is saved, not by understanding it, but because he fears God, and works righteousness. Oh, the glad and glorious surprise of those ultimate days when we find that there will be those who walked in the light they had, and wrought righteousness, and were acceptable to Him; not because of their morality, but by the infinite merit of the Cross, and by the fact that they yielded themselves to the light they possessed. The sin of the Gentile is not that he does not believe the thing of which he never heard. It is that he holds down the truth which he knows, in unrighteousness. This was the great advance for Peter. He had not quite cut loose from the old prejudices. Paul had to withstand him one day a little later on. This story is not merely the story of the emancipation of a man, it is light for the Christian Church to the end of time.

Finally in chapter eleven, Peter in telling the story in Jerusalem, of this visit to Cornelius, said, "As I began to speak, the Holy Spirit fell on them" (verse 15). One can imagine when Peter reached this point, that he had but laid down the lines of his address and indicated the outstanding facts, and that he was intending to elaborate them; but his was an interrupted speech. But it was yet a complete speech; complete in its matter, for it spoke of Christ only, fully, and clearly. It was complete in its method. It was a message delivered in obedience to the instruction of the Spirit, for the Spirit had said, "Go with these men, nothing doubting." It was a message delivered by a witness, one who in his own life knew of the power of the things he spoke. It was a message accompanied by the Spirit, and at the very moment when the things of Christ had been presented by this Spirit-filled man to the multitude, the work was done.

To read that address and note its interruption, and the sudden falling of the Spirit upon its hearers is to be re-

buked. We labour so hard to make the Gospel plain.
We so constantly imagine that it is necessary for us not
to preach Christ only, but to defend Christ, and vindicate
Christ, and explain Christ. We leave so little room in
our preaching and teaching for this coöperative ministry
of the Holy Spirit. It is a great and sacred ministry to
speak only and briefly of the ministry of the Christ. As
we do so the Spirit Himself will carry the message, fall
upon the multitudes; and the work of bringing men into
fullness of life be accomplished.

Acts 11

This chapter falls into two parts. The first eighteen
verses are almost exclusively occupied with a recapitula-
tion of the story told in chapter ten; the last twelve deal
with the growth of the movement among the Gentiles.
It is only necessary to note the first part of the chapter,
as to its connection with what follows, in order to see
how it prepares the way for that wider and most remarkable movement which commenced at Antioch.

The report reached Jerusalem that the Gentiles had
received the Word of God, and the attitude of the
apostles toward the news is indicated in the declaration
that they " contended with " Peter, not for preaching the
Word to the Gentiles, but for eating with them. In the
previous chapter, at the twentieth verse, these words occur, " Arise, and get thee down, and go with them, *nothing doubting:* for I have sent them." Such was the word
of the Spirit to Peter on the housetop in Joppa. Again,
in this eleventh chapter, at the twelfth verse, Peter says,
" And the Spirit bade me go with them, *making no distinction."* The verb " contended with them " is exactly
the same as that translated in those two passages, " nothing doubting," and " making no distinction." The word
doubting is an insufficient word. The Spirit of God commanded Peter to go with these men, without wavering.

without discrimination, without making distinction.
When he came to Jerusalem the brethren there did this
very thing. They discriminated with him, debated with
him, contended with him; and he told them that the Spirit
had charged him to go with these men doing nothing
of the kind. It is quite evident that these men in Jerusalem were passing through the mental experience
through which Peter had passed. It was perfectly natural that he should waver, that he should discriminate, as
between Gentiles and Hebrews; but the Spirit had
charged him to make no such distinction, to go without
wavering or contention. When he came to Jerusalem
he found that the apostles, his brethren, were experienc-
ing the same mental difficulty. They were making distinctions between themselves and the Gentiles. In a
word, they were doing what the Spirit had charged Peter
not to do. In order to help them, he told them the story
of the experience through which he had passed, and
by which he had been delivered from making such distinctions. He told the story of his visit to the house of
Cornelius, told how before he had delivered the message
he had intended to deliver, before he had fully declared
to them all that which was in his heart, while he yet
spoke, without his intervention, not by the laying on of
hands, not even as the result of his interpretation, nor in
answer to his intercession, the Holy Spirit fell on the men
who listened. Having told his story to the brethren in
Jerusalem, Peter said—and the whole matter was
summed up in his enquiry—"Who was I, that I could
withstand God?"

The wisdom and graciousness of the Jerusalem
brethren were manifested in the fact that when he said
this, they held their peace; their contending was over.
They could not deny the evident activity of God Himself, by which the Spirit had been poured upon these
Gentiles; and therefore they could no longer argue for
difference or distinction or discrimination. They praised

THE ACTS OF THE APOSTLES

God that the Gentiles also were to receive like gifts with themselves.

All this prepared the apostles in Jerusalem for coöperation with the wider movement, and now therefore we may turn immediately to the last twelve verses of the chapter. This paragraph falls into four clearly marked sections. In verses nineteen to twenty-one we have an account of the initiation of this new movement. In verses twenty-two to twenty-four we see the confirmation of the movement by the apostles and the Church at Jerusalem. In verses twenty-five and twenty-six is contained the story of the consolidation of the work. In verses twenty-seven to thirty we see the coöperation of the new with the old.

The story of continuity is in the nineteenth verse. The outstanding words to note are these: " *scattered* " through " *tribulation.* " That is the beginning of the new work. Surely God works in ways we never would have chosen. The next words that arrest the attention are these: they " *travelled . . . speaking.* " This passage is rich in words descriptive of the methods by which the early disciples witnessed. It contains no less than four Greek words, and every one of them is significant. This is the word for simple speech, the common harangue, or conversation of travelling people. They travelled, speaking the Word, not preaching it in certain acceptations of that word, but talking it. Scattered through tribulation, these people passed through all the regions round about, travelling here, there, and everywhere; but they were careful to speak of this sacred thing of their life only to Jews. This method began when they martyred Stephen, and Hebrew opposition breaking out, believers were scattered by tribulation. If the saints are scattered, and if they are Spirit-filled, they do but scatter the seed of the Kingdom, which is the Word of God.

We come in the next verse to the new departure. Men of Cyprus and Cyrene, reaching Antioch, began to preach. Now another word is employed, the word that is stamped upon the page of these New Testament stories, the word *euaggelizo*, the declaration of the evangel, the definite proclamation of the Gospel. These men of Cyprus and Cyrene began to preach the Gospel to Greeks. That was the new beginning. This had not been done before. Stephen had held disputation with Greek Jews, with the Hellenists in Jerusalem; but these men, reaching Antioch, having travelled there from Cyprus and Cyrene, talked, not to the Grecian Jews only, but to the Greeks. Antioch was wealthy and magnificent, and was described as one of the " eyes " of Asia, the third great city of the world at that time; Rome being first, and Alexandria second. Antioch was the residence of a Roman prefect and his court. It was also the place of a large Jewish colony. But it was supremely Greek. There was the grove of Daphne, and heathenism appeared in its most tempting and debasing form. It was of such magnificence, that its main street ran for four miles through the length of the city. These men from Cyprus and Cyrene preached there to Greeks; not in an obscure village, but in this great city, which for strategical purposes in the economy of God at that moment was more central and available than either Alexandria or Rome, and was free from the limitation imposed upon thinking by Hebraism in Jerusalem.

The work in Antioch resulted from no immediate action of the apostles. These pioneers of the new missionary movement, these instruments chosen by the Spirit and sent to Antioch for the initiation of the larger fulfilment of the purpose of God, are unnamed. Speculation has been busy trying to name them. Surely such speculations miss the value of the fact that the names were not given. The teaching of the passage is that the Spirit of God ever moves out in new directions, apart from all officialism; a lesson which always needs to be borne in mind, forgetting which has often been our hindrance. Simple men of Cyprus and Cyrene, unnamed pioneers,

THE ACTS OF THE APOSTLES

travelling, found themselves in magnificent, voluptuous, and sinful Antioch; and they determined, without consultation with any one, to preach the Gospel not merely to the Jew, but to the Greek also. So began the new movement.

The next few verses tell the story of the confirmation of that movement by Jerusalem. The report that the Gospel had been preached to Gentiles reached the apostles. They had been prepared, by Peter's experience, for this report; and so they immediately sent Barnabas. Mark the wisdom of the choice. He was not an apostle, though the intimate of the apostolic band. He was a man of Cyprus; and men of Cyprus and Cyrene had begun this work in Antioch. Yet one cannot read this story without feeling that their sending of Barnabas was that of doubt. They had hardly reached Peter's understanding that no distinction was to be made.

But when Barnabas reached Antioch, he saw " the grace of God." There can be no question that when he came into the midst of the company of believing Greeks in Antioch, into the fellowship of those who had been gathered about these men of Cyprus and Cyrene, he detected the supreme spiritual evidences of the divinity of their work in the tone and temper of the men in the midst of whom he found himself. A little later on in this book we shall come to an occasion when Paul came to Ephesus, and missed such marks, and said in astonishment to the men, " Did ye receive the Holy Spirit when ye believed? " Barnabas, on the other hand, coming to Antioch found the evidences of grace, a new tone and disposition, evidences of joy, light, and happiness; all that which characterized the presence of the Spirit, and the grace of God. He gave these disciples no apostolic and authoritative instruction; but he *exhorted* them. This is yet another word, which is akin to the word Paraclete. It may also indicate the reason why the apostles gave this man his name, Barnabas; for he was a son of comfort, a son of exhortation. "He exhorted them all, that with purpose of heart they would cleave unto the Lord."

Thus the work grew and developed. Barnabas is described, not in an official capacity, for he had none, but as to his character. He "was a good man, and full of the Holy Spirit and of faith." We saw in the first few verses that this movement was entirely apart from officialism; now we see that there was to be no schism in the body of Christ. The new movement was not to continue in separation from Jerusalem. The independent beginning was part of a spiritual unity, and that unity was manifested and maintained. In this visit of Barnabas to Antioch we see the linking of Jerusalem with Antioch, in the underlying inspiration and enduement of the Spirit. The work in Antioch commenced without Jerusalem; but Jerusalem and Antioch were united by the visit of Barnabas. Thus there was not merely the new departure in independence of Jerusalem; there was also the new sense of fellowship in interrelation with Jerusalem.

Next in order we have an arresting picture: that of Barnabas leaving Antioch, not for Jerusalem, but for Tarsus. Years before, he had helped Saul to escape from Jerusalem when the Hellenists were persecuting him; and he had sent him up the country, and across to Tarsus. Since then Saul had been in Tarsus, probably travelling round the district, and preaching in Cilicia, but no details of such work are given. Now Barnabas went to seek him. It has been said that he knew where to seek him. The word suggests rather that he did not. Quite literally it says that he went *to hunt him up.* Saul had been waiting and preparing for greater work. Recognizing the fact that no ministry is complete in itself, that it must ever seek the coöperation of others; seeing in that centre of Antioch work that he could not do, Barnabas was heroic and Christly enough, to be obedient to the Spirit, and to seek for Saul.

[Acts 11]

There, for one year at least, Saul was the assistant of Barnabas. They gathered with the Church, *teaching*. Here we have another word, which means quite simply teaching. As we look back on this work, we are impressed by that little group of people gathered together. Antioch would pass and perish with the running of the centuries; but that new movement, the inclusion of the Greek within the work of the Spirit through the Church of Christ, was destined to spread through all the neighbourhood, and eventually to capture the whole world.

It was at Antioch that the disciples were first called Christians. Professor Lumby has pointed out that the word is hybrid. It is a Greek word with a Latin termination. In that I think is evidence of the fact that it was a name given to these men by Antioch. It was certainly not chosen by the Jew; for to him Christian would have meant a man of the Messiah; and he would object entirely to that description of those of the Nazarene sect. It was certainly not a name chosen by the Christians themselves, for they designated themselves " disciples," " brethren," " those of the Way." It has been said that it was a nickname, and that it was given to them as a title of contempt. That may be so. In any case, the giving of the name in Antioch reveals two things. It shows first that Antioch recognized the Church no longer as a sect or part of Hebraism, but as a new society, which could not be named by Hebraism, but must be known by a name of its own. I think also that Antioch named these people by what Antioch saw in them. They were the people of the Christ, Whomsoever He might have been. It was of the Christ they spoke, of the Christ they sang, for the Christ they lived.

In all this the free operation of the Spirit of God is again manifested. The man of the apostolic confidence, Barnabas, sought the man born out of due season, Saul. Barnabas acted evidently upon his own initiative, and yet in response to the indwelling and guiding Spirit of

God. On that action the seal of the Divine blessing was set, and their year's work was formative and preparatory to the larger movements of which the rest of this book is the chronicle.

In the last section, we see the enlarging coöperation. Agabus was a prophet. This is the first mention of a prophet in the New Testament economy, and the predictive element of the work was evidenced as this man foretold the coming of a great famine.

The impressive fact, however, in this last paragraph is that of its revelation of the sense of unity. These Greeks had heard and believed in the Gospel; and there were evidences of the grace of God, which evidences Barnabas had seen. Barnabas and Saul had been teaching and instructing them, and they had been growing in grace. When therefore Agabus foretold the coming of the famine, these Christian men at once recognized that the famine would bring distress to the brethren in Judæa. Spontaneously they began to care for those brethren, not under the direction of the apostles, but out of that new life which has love at its heart. So important did they conceive the work of relief to be, that they set their two teachers apart for the carrying of their gifts to Jerusalem. This is a glorious and gracious revelation of the consciousness of oneness in the Spirit; obedience to prophecy, expressing itself in love; and love taking the practical form of definite help sent to those in Judea who would suffer most as the result of the coming famine.

The true notes of development are revealed in this study. First there is the note of continuity. Every movement is the outcome of an earlier one. Secondly, there is the note of an absolute freedom. Every movement is a new departure. Thirdly there is the note of an unbroken unity. Every movement is part of one great whole. Finally there is the note of a perpetual variety.

First, every movement is the outcome of an earlier one. Stephen's martyrdom was Antioch's opportunity

THE ACTS OF THE APOSTLES

Through his martyrdom tribulation broke out, and the Christians were scattered, travelling everywhere, and coming at last to Antioch. In the economy of God we cannot see all the issues of the thing we suffer, or the thing we do to-day. When we imagine that we can, then we become restless. Or again, Peter's vision became the Church's eyesight. Or again, Saul's apprehension on the way to Damascus was Antioch's supply. Or again, Antioch's spiritual blessing became Judæa's material succour in the hour of famine. These things of God are all linked together.

But again, every movement is a new departure. Mark the freedom. Men of Cyprus and Cyrene preached to Greeks. That was a new movement. The sending of Barnabas by the apostles was a new official action. The finding of Saul by Barnabas was an independent action. Some ecclesiastical courts to-day would have summoned Barnabas back to Jerusalem, to investigate. The collection for Judæa was spontaneous. The movement is always manifesting itself in a new way; linked to the preceding things but always independent.

Then again, every movement is part of one whole. Mark the unity of it. We cannot better express this than by citation of Paul's words written to Ephesus: " One Lord, one faith, one baptism; one God and Father of all, Who is in all, and through all." That apostolic word is stamped upon this paragraph. One Lord is preached, whether it be by the travellers who talk, or by men of Cyprus and Cyrene who preach, or by Barnabas who exhorts, or by Agabus who prophesies. One faith is exercised, whether it be the faith of the men who first heard and believed, or the constant faith of the men who believing, obeyed, and allowed the Spirit to lead and guide them independently of all prejudice. One baptism is shared, the baptism of the Holy Spirit. One God is glorified. These are the great things of unity; and they are the things of unity for the Church to-day.

Finally there was a great variety of gifts; the apostolic gift, the evangelistic gift, the prophetic gift, and the pastoral gift. Paul enumerated these in that same passage in the Ephesian letter, " He gave some to be apostles, and some, prophets; and some, evangelists; and some, pastors and teachers." They are seen at work here in this new departure and new movement. There was also a variety of methods. Four or five words describe the method by which the Word was preached.

In that paragraph we have the microcosmic revelation of true Christian work, and missionary development. Every new departure is a continuation of something which has gone before. No one can act in independence of Christ and His Church in work for Christ. No one man can win a soul. How many prayers, and long hours of patient teaching, and many other ministries, are needed to the making of one soul anew? How can we fulfil any Christian service that is not linked to the magnificent past? I believe in the holy catholic Church, and that every piece of work to-day is linked to the things that have gone before. But there must be freedom from the restraint of the past, freedom from the interferences of hoary and ancient traditions; for where the Spirit of the Lord is, there is liberty. There must also be absolute freedom. Every new departure is independent, in that it is under the impulse and inspiration of the Spirit, and is the test of the Church's unity. The essential things of unity are not those of ecclesiastical management, or of human creeds. These are they. One Lord to be preached; one faith to be exercised; one baptism, that of the Spirit, to be received; one God to be glorified. In proportion as we come to a recognition of these underlying things we shall be able to sing truthfully:

> " We are not divided,
>   All one body we,
>   One in hope and doctrine,
>   One in charity."

There are also varieties of gifts. The Spirit of God is
still bestowing gifts. Men are still receiving gifts of the
Spirit, for apostolic, pioneer work in distant lands; for
prophetic declaration of God's truth to their own age;
for evangelistic calling of men to Christ; or for the
patient teaching and training of the saints. The Spirit
is with us yet, and the method of His operation is that
of diversity, while He Himself is the unifying life of the
Church.

Acts 12

This chapter is supremely interesting because with it
Jerusalem, as the centre of the Church's operations, passes
out of sight. It only appears twice again in the history
of this book; once as the meeting-place of the council
which set the Gentiles free from all the obligations of
Judaism; and once, when Paul revisited it, and for the
saving of his life was compelled to seek the protection
of the Roman power.

It is also an interesting fact that the words in the
seventeenth verse, " Peter departed, and went to another
place," are the last concerning him in this history. In
Galatians there is an account of his contention with Paul;
and his letters were certainly written at a later date; but
here he passes out of sight in Luke's history.

We have been tracing the story of the development of
the work among the Gentiles. The outstanding facts in
that development were: first the apprehension of Saul of
Tarsus; secondly the vision of Peter, and the reception of
Cornelius; and thirdly, the establishment of the new
centre of operations in Antioch. Antioch will now become the centre, not Jerusalem. All those wonderful
missionary journeys which remain to be considered,
started from Antioch; and the returning apostles and
missionaries reported there. It became God's new centre
for the fulfilment of the commission which Jesus gave
to His disciples, that they should be witnesses unto Him,

not only in Jerusalem, Judæa, and Samaria, but also
unto the uttermost part of the earth.

The story contained in this chapter is quite simple and
straightforward. The supreme interest is that of conflict
between the godless theocracy and the new nation. Those
terms need some definition. The term " godless theocracy " in itself is a contradiction. The nation of Israel
was created by God in order to be a theocracy, a people
governed, not by man, but by Himself. To recall the
facts of the history of Israel from Abraham, will be
sufficient to illuminate the thought;—Abraham called,
Abraham answering; the growth of the people, their organization into national life by the way of exodus from
Egypt; the appointing of the leader and the lawgiver;
the giving of the law, and the establishment of the ritual.
These are but landmarks. Then there came an hour in
which they said,—and mark the profound significance of
the word, " Make us a king like unto the nations." In
that hour God said to Samuel that they had rejected
Him from being King. That was the hour of their supreme failure. From that moment there was steady
degeneration. God made the nation in order that all
other nations might in it see the breadth, the beauty, the
beneficence of the government of God. The nation was
to be, not a monarchy, not a democracy,—and each is an
equal tyranny,—but a theocracy, a God-governed people.
Luke describes Herod as king. Those familiar with
Paley's " Horæ Paulinæ " will remember that he quotes
this reference as proving the historic accuracy of Luke.
This man Herod was king of the Jews, the first to bear
the title for long time. He represented in his own person, as he acted on behalf of the nation, the theocracy
without God. That is one side of this picture.

On the other side was the new nation; and again the
term may need explanation. It may be suggested that
we substitute the word " Church," for nation; but in this
connection I adopt that word " nation " from Peter's

definition of the Church as a holy nation. This reveals one side of truth concerning the Church which we are perpetually in danger of forgetting. I am inclined to think that the Church has most signally failed in that she has forgotten she is God's theocracy, God's nation. What is a nation? A nation consists of all those who live under one sole authority, and in mutual inter-relationships; and the Church in the will of God is not merely an elect race, not only a royal priesthood, not only a people for God's possession, not only a people having a heavenly vocation that can only be fulfilled in ages yet unborn; that is all true, but she is also a nation, in the world for the same purpose for which the Hebrew nation was created, for the revelation to the world of the beauty, breadth, and beneficence of the Divine government. Here then, is the picture of that nation, with no earthly king, and without a parliament; but with one governing King. These two forces come into conflict in this chapter. The Church, the holy nation, will come into conflict with other of the world forces presently. She has been doing so ever since. Here, however, is the last clash of the conflict between the theocracy God-created, which had failed; and the theocracy God-created, which was yet upon its trial.

In that way we will consider it; dealing with the opposition and defeat of the false; and the strength and victory of the true. Such division is based upon a recognition of the one central matter of the Kingship of God. For the realization and manifestation of that Kingship Israel was created. For the realization and manifestation of that Kingship the Church exists as to its earthly responsibility. The supreme matter in life is not the saving of man's spirit; nor better dwellings. Those are parts of the supreme matter, which is the establishment of the Kingdom of God. Even that is a phrase which I sometimes think we have devitalized by using too commonly. What is meant by the establishment of the Kingdom of

God? It means that the matter of importance for every soul, for every nation, for the world is that God should govern. The will of God was the master-passion in the life and ministry of Jesus. The ancient people of Israel was created a nation to realize that will, and to manifest it. The Church of God was created to realize it, and to manifest it.

In noticing then the opposition and defeat of the false, our attention is necessarily fixed in the first place, upon this man Herod, Agrippa the first, a nephew of that Herod Antipas who murdered John, and a grandson of Herod called the Great, the murderer of the innocents at the time of the birth of our Lord. This man was of Roman habits, for he had lived in Rome for thirty years, the boon companion in every kind of vice of the son of an emperor. He was, however, strangely enough, even throughout those days of dissolute habits, a man having Jewish interests. It is confidently affirmed, and accurately undoubtedly, in contemporary history, that it was through his intervention that Caius was prevented from setting up an image of himself in the very Temple of God. He had always been interested in Jewish people. Josephus says of this man:

" He loved to live continually at Jerusalem, and was exactly careful in the observance of the laws of his country. He therefore kept himself entirely pure, nor did any day pass over his head without its appointed sacrifice."

It is impossible to read that without seeing that Josephus defended Herod, because of his sympathy for that which was purely Jewish. Then we must remember that there was Edomite taint in his blood, just as in the case of the Herod with whom Jesus came into contact. Finally, he was a man of Greek learning. Leaving Jerusalem, at the end of this campaign, he found his way to Cæsarea, and set up a throne, and as Josephus tells us, sat thereon in glittering garments of silver, receiving the homage of

[295]

THE ACTS OF THE APOSTLES

the crowd until he received the homage which put him in the place of God. This was the man who now stretched forth his hand to vex certain of the Church.

Luke tells us in this chapter that he "put forth his hands to afflict certain of the Church. And he killed James the brother of John with the sword. And when he saw that it pleased the Jews, he proceeded to seize Peter also." This man was preëminently a politician; one who had no strong antagonism to the Christian movement within his own country, but who had very little interest therein; a man who desired to retain his own position and footing, and who in order to do it, found it was necessary to hold the Jews and please them. So the last movement against Christianity by the organized nation of Israel, through the person of their king, was a political movement.

All this is of no value save as it is set in the light of the fact that this was a people made for the exhibition of the Divine government. Here was their last king, the sycophant of a child of Roman voluptuousness, an Edomite, attempting for political purposes to retain Jewish power, supremely given over to all manner of Greek frivolity; and this man is the representative of the people whom God had created. This was the man who stretched forth his hand to vex the Church.

In the activity of the opposition two things must be noted. First, James, the brother of John, was slain by the sword. He was surnamed by his Lord, Boanerges, a son of thunder, and only appears beyond the Gospel narratives in two places. He is named among the apostles who received the Holy Spirit on the Day of Pentecost, and again in this one sentence, as being murdered by Herod. That sentence reminds us of an occasion when he and John found their way to Christ, and said, "Grant unto us that we may sit, one on Thy right hand, and one on Thy left hand, in Thy glory." Our Lord said to them, "Ye know not what ye ask. Are ye able to drink

the cup that I drink? or to be baptized with the baptism
that I am baptized with?" And they said that they
could, little knowing what they said. In that matchless
and infinite grace, which is ever patient with His people,
He did not laugh at them, but said with a tender note of
loving sarcasm, which yet thrilled with infinite grace,
"The cup that I drink ye shall drink; and with the baptism that I am baptized withal shall ye be baptized; but
to sit on My right hand or on My left hand is not Mine
to give: but it is for them for whom it hath been prepared." Now Herod stretched forth his hand to vex the
Church, and slew James with the sword. So he was
baptized with his Master's baptism. And what of John?
He lived on until the last of the apostolic band had
crossed over. So we may be baptized with the baptism
of fellowship in the sufferings of Christ by life, as well
as by death. The opposition, however, fastened upon
James, and then upon Peter, who was imprisoned and
guarded, the intention being to bring him forth and slay
him.

Now mark the end of the opposition. It was entirely
baffled. The empty prison was the end of it. In the fifth
verse of the chapter we read, "Peter therefore was kept
in prison: but prayer was made earnestly of the Church
unto God for him." There were the two forces at war.
Peter kept in prison by Herod; a Church at prayer for
him. "Simon, Simon, behold, Satan asked to have you,
that he might sift you as wheat: but I made supplication
for thee, that thy faith fail not." Mark the continuity
of the Acts. Peter was kept in prison, but the Church
prayed. The empty prison tells the sequel; the opposition
failed, and the Church won. Herod left Jerusalem for
Cæsarea, in all likelihood in anger; and then within a
few days, or weeks at most, there was the final manifestation of his supreme sin; rebellion against God. That final
manifestation was the assumption of the functions of
God. This is no distant story. These are living things

to-day. If a man dethrone God he always makes himself God. If God do not occupy the throne of every life then man will assume for himself the very functions of Deity. So there was wrought out in the person of Herod Agrippa the sin that ruined a nation in the hour when he allowed a fickle shouting crowd to declare, " The voice of a god, and not of a man," and received homage as such. Swiftly and awfully the touch of the Divine wrath was upon him, and he gave up the ghost.

Turn to the other side of this picture. There are three things to be noted in considering the strength and victory of the Church: first, the Divine government itself; secondly, the instruments made use of; and finally, the issue of the conflict.

As this story is studied, two things impress us concerning the Divine government: first, the mystery of it; and secondly, its clear manifestation. It is impossible to read the story and declare that God's government can be finally explained. Why did God permit James to be slain, and deliver Peter? Why did He allow Herod to arrest James and slay him; and then, to use the word that is always indicative of our human limitation, miraculously deliver Peter? There is no answer to these questions. I also have seen James slain when I thought we could not spare him. I also have seen a man full of fire and enthusiasm and force, removed swiftly and suddenly, by a way of pain; and I have said, What is God doing? His is a government which does not attempt to explain itself finally to watching men, but which manifests itself so that watching men cannot deny it.

James is slain, and if men are in the midst of the troublous days when Herod is stretching out his hands, they will say they are coming to the crisis when they are powerless. God did not deliver James, but immediately afterwards He delivered Peter. That reveals the fact that if He can deliver Peter, He could have delivered James. There is infinite comfort in that; the comfort of the revelation of the fact that One Who could deliver Peter, and in wisdom did so, was equally wise when He did not deliver James. Life can never be perfectly understood in the process of its living; we must wait. Just beyond the gleam and flash of the sword, and the overwhelming agony of the moment James came to the explanation. God doeth all things well; and the release of Peter illuminates the death of James, as we come to rest in the infinite wisdom of the Divine government.

The instruments of the Divine government revealed in this chapter are two: first, a praying people; and secondly, ministering angels. A praying people that is the supreme thing, so far as human responsibility is concerned. Mark two things about these praying people. They prayed earnestly, and the word is a very strong one, "without ceasing" it is translated; "earnestly" is more accurate; but still better, they prayed "with agony." He was not released until the very night before execution. I think they prayed through all the day and night; one group gathered in the house of the mother of Mark, and perhaps others in other places. Herod Agrippa, pervert of Rome, with Hebrew national aspirations, an Edomite, and a Greek, cleverest of all the Herods in certain ways, stretched out his hand to vex the Church. What shall we put against this new force? A praying Church is against this force.

But another thing about their praying is that they prayed doubtingly. That has been strenuously denied, but I think the story cannot be read without seeing it. When Peter knocked at the door, Rhoda, the girl with the sweet and fragrant name, heard his voice, and she forgot to open for very delight, and left him standing outside. When she came and said, Peter is without, they said, "Thou art mad." But they had been praying? Yes, and believing; and yet wondering how God could do it; and when the answer came they were surprised. Do

[299]

not criticize them. I am thankful for the story. It cheers me in my praying. I pray, and God knows I believe in Him, and I desire, and I wonder whether He can. If I challenge my unbelief, it vanishes. These people prayed earnestly and doubtingly, and yet that force of earnest, halting prayer was mightier than Herod, and mightier than hell.

Then notice the ministry of angels. If we are tempted to say that does not happen now, I affirm that the only thing that does not happen is the smallest thing in the story. Peter did not know it was an angel who delivered him, and did not know he was out of the prison until the angel had gone. He thought he was dreaming, and it was not until the angel had taken him the length of one street and had departed,—to use the word of Luke, translated differently,—he collected himself together. He gathered up all the impressions, and then discovered that the Lord had delivered him. The only thing that does not happen now is the small thing, the material part of the story, the chains removed from the wrists, and the opening of a door. Those soldiers did not see that angel. There is an older story which helps us at this point. There was a servant who said to his master, Lo, my master, what shall we do? His master prayed, " O Jehovah, open his eyes." When his eyes were opened, lo, sweeping up the mountain he saw hosts of angels. It is not well that we should see them to-day, for this is not the age of sight; it is the age of faith. But they are here! Are they not all ministering spirits, sent forth to do service for the sake of them that shall inherit salvation? I still believe in angels, and many a prison door the angel opens still, and many an hour of darkness is illuminated by something that we do not understand. It is the ministry of the angels. The material manifestation may be denied to-day, but that only proves that we are living in a clearer spiritual atmosphere, for when the spirit must be instructed by the thing that appeals to the senses it is because men are in the twilight. In proportion as we rise into the larger and higher and fuller day, the material signs will pass; but it is still true that " the angel of Jehovah encampeth round about them that fear Him."

And how did this end? " And immediately an angel of the Lord smote him, because he gave not God the glory; and he was eaten of worms, and gave up the ghost. But the Word of God grew and multiplied," in spite of kings and peoples and prisons. Then the chapter ends with the little part of the great whole, a small touch, full of beauty. Barnabas and Saul are seen going over to Antioch. Behold Jerusalem for the last time; the whole of the godlessness manifested in Herod, who stretched out his hand to prevent the growth of this spiritual movement; and this victory of the new nation. The opposition ends in defeat. Who are these three men going off down that road? They have three hundred miles before they reach Antioch; Barnabas, Saul, and Mark. Herod is dead, but the Word of God is living; and the messengers are on the highroad.

Let the story fling its light on present circumstances; on all oppositions, of kings, peoples, prisons.

> " Why do the nations rage,
> And the peoples imagine a vain thing?
> The kings of the earth set themselves,
> And the rulers take counsel together,
> Against Jehovah, and against His Anointed,
>   saying,
> Let us break their bonds asunder,
> And cast away their cords from us.
> He that sitteth in the heavens will laugh:
> The Lord will have them in derision.
> Then will He speak unto them in His wrath,
> And vex them in His sore displeasure;
> Yet have I set My King
> Upon My holy hill of Zion."

THE ACTS OF THE APOSTLES

Do not treat that as ancient literature; it is the matin of the morning, it is the evangel of eventide. Sooner or later godlessness assumes the functions of God, and then immediately is blasted and broken.

Let the light of this study fall, not only upon all opposition, but upon the people of His purpose. James is still slain, and Peter spared; or to take another illustration from the same story, a prison door that striving men cannot open, is opened without hands, and Peter passes through. A house door, that a maiden could open, Peter has to knock at, and then cannot open it. We are in the midst of these mysteries. God knows they are in our lives. Let us thank God that He Who opens one door shuts the other; and the door He shuts is as great a beneficence as the door He opens. Prayer is still our one and only resource. Not federation even among ourselves, if we are prayerless; not policy or art, or cunning, but prayer is the resource of the Church; and angels are still ministering spirits; and the Word of God still grows and multiplies.

Yet is there not a warning here? Israel, Jerusalem, Herod! Go back to the twenty-third chapter of Matthew, and listen again to the words of Jesus, " Behold, your house is left unto you desolate." There is a perpetual principle involved. For what is the Church created? If we fail, that word will be spoken to us as surely as it was spoken to Israel.

Yet note the encouragement of it all. God, the Church, and the Word! Said Paul, when writing to Timothy near the end of his ministry, " I suffer hardship unto bonds, as a malefactor; but the Word of God is not bound. Therefore I endure all things." In the spirit of that government of God as revealed in our study, be it ours to work and toil, to suffer and to sing, until He calls us home by the swift and sudden call, or after the long day's work is done; from the shadows of eventide into the light that never faiis.

Acts 13: 1-3

This paragraph is a brief one, but of great importance. It may be spoken of as the watershed of this book. We now enter upon a study of that wonderful movement, of which Paul was the central figure. In this story, without any announcement or reason given, Saul's name is changed to Paul.

These three verses give the account of the beginning of the great missionary movement. In the first sentence there is the recognition of matters already considered in previous studies: " Now there were at Antioch, in the Church." The twelfth chapter took us back to Jerusalem, and we saw it pass out of the record of the history of the Christian Church. It is only seen once more in the course of this book, when the council was held at which the Gentiles were set free from all obligations to Judaism. In that chapter moreover we saw the last national Jewish hostility to Christianity, centralized in Herod. In the story of the movement of the Church of God, according to her Lord's will, toward the uttermost part of the earth, chapter twelve is an interpolation, necessary for the understanding of the whole story.

The story now resumed, takes us again to Antioch, to which we were introduced in chapter eleven. First of all we saw the initiation of the movement. Men of Cyprus and Cyrene preached the evangel to the Greeks, turning aside from the ordinary custom of preaching only to the Jew. There was also the story of its confirmation, when the apostles sent Barnabas to visit the work; and he, preaching the grace of God, was glad, and charged them to remain steadfast to the Lord. Then followed the story of its consolidation, as Barnabas sought Saul of Tarsus, and brought him to Antioch, that he might share with him in the work of teaching and instructing these people. We also had the account of coöperation, when the new Christian Greek believers in Antioch recognized their relationship with their brethren in Jerusalem, and

ministered to them in material things. The movement
in Antioch was in continuation of everything that had
gone before, but it was characterized by a most remarkable independence. This work was not apostolic, if by
apostolic is meant a work under the authority of apostles,
for they were not consulted. Men of Cyprus and Cyrene,
unnamed men, began the great and gracious work. It
was characterized moreover, by unity, for it was again
the one Lord, and the one faith, and the one baptism, and
the one God glorified. It was finally characterized by
infinite variety, for in chapter eleven we have four different words employed to express the method of preaching, and four offices of the Christian Church are all recognized as at work.

The last verse of the previous chapter reads thus,
" And Barnabas and Saul returned from Jerusalem, when
they had fulfilled their ministration, taking with them
John whose surname was Mark." Paul and Barnabas
had been to Jerusalem, carrying the gifts of the Antioch
Church for the relief of the suffering saints in Jerusalem.
Thence they had returned, bringing Mark with them.
From this point Antioch was the new base, the new
centre of the Divine operations. From it, the messengers
were sent forth; to it they returned. In considering the
missionary journeyings of Paul, we shall see that in each
case he started from Antioch, and reported there. In
Antioch the conflict with Judaizing teachers presently
became acute. It was in Antioch also that Peter dissembled, and Paul rebuked him. It was in Antioch that
the proclamation of Gentile freedom was made, resulting
from the findings of the council in Jerusalem.

To this assembly, this Church in Antioch, the Spirit
made known His will; and in responsive coöperation
this Church set free Barnabas and Saul, the messengers
who were to begin that great missionary work throughout all the district. Of that important event this brief
paragraph gives a suggestive account.

There are three lines of consideration which demand our attention. First, that which is central in the paragraph, the declared activity of the Spirit of God: "The Holy Spirit said, Separate Me Barnabas and Saul for the work whereunto I have called them." Secondly, the preliminary conditions that made possible this activity of the Spirit. These are revealed in the first phrase, "The Church in Antioch"; and the following description of prophets and teachers ministering to the Lord, and fasting. Thirdly and finally, the resulting coöperation of the Church with the Spirit: "Then, when they had fasted and prayed, and laid their hands on them, they sent them away."

First then, as to the action of the Spirit. Observe carefully the definiteness of this declaration as to the activity of the Spirit: "The Holy Spirit said." He made known His will to these people, so that they had neither doubt nor uncertainty in their minds. Moreover this is not the picture of a Church choosing men to be sent forth on missionary enterprise. This is not the picture of a Church discussing the fitness of men for the doing of any particular work. There is a sense in which it would be perfectly accurate to say that the Church had no voice in the selection of these men. The choice was not left to the Church. The choice was based upon a prior fact in the activity of the Spirit: "Separate Me Barnabas and Saul for the work whereunto *I have called them*." It would be idle to speculate as to when these men had been called; but in the second letter to the Corinthians, the twelfth chapter, in the first brief paragraph of four verses we have an account from the pen of Paul of an experience which he had, and one which most certainly affected all his life. He wrote: "I knew a man in Christ, fourteen years ago (whether in the body I know not; God knoweth) such an one caught up even to the third heaven . . . and heard unspeakable words, which it is not lawful for a man to utter." From the date of that Corin-

thian letter, which can be placed with comparative accuracy, we know that this wonderful vision of which he
never could speak with anything like detail, occurred in
Tarsus, before Barnabas sought him. It may be that it
was in that hour, when he was caught into the third
heaven, and heard the things he could not utter, that the
Holy Spirit called him to all the suffering, the travail,
and the triumph of these wonderful missionary journeyings. In the case of Barnabas we have no hint as to the
time or manner in which he was called. Looking back
over the ground traversed, there may be a clue, in the
friendship of these two men. Saul apprehended on the
way to Damascus, hurrying away into Arabia, and spending long time in solitude and preparation, appeared at
last at Jerusalem. Barnabas was the man who welcomed
him, shielding him from the opposition of those likely to
misunderstand him. He took care of him, set him on
his way back to Tarsus, and left him there. Directly
Barnabas arrived at Antioch, and saw the necessities of
the case, without consulting the college of the apostles,
he went to Tarsus and sought for Saul. Evidently there
was an affinity of mind and thought and purpose between
these two men; and the Spirit now said, I have called
them, separate them unto Me.

The method of the Spirit with the Church, the assembly in Antioch, is revealed in the command, " Separate Me." Thereby He called the Church into definite
activity with Himself. It has often been affirmed that
this message of the Spirit was one delivered only to the
little group of men whose names occur here in the passage, the names of men who were either prophets or
teachers. I do not so understand the statement. The
word of the Spirit was a word through the prophet most
likely, to the whole Christian assembly in Antioch; but
the Spirit called the Church to separate these men. He
called the men to the work, but before they went forth,
He called the Church into definite coöperation with Him-

self in separating them. "Separate Me Barnabas and
Saul," that is, give them freedom and give them authority.
Send them forth in the freedom of My own call to them.
Send them forth under the authority of that call, recognized by the will of the assembly in Antioch. The
activity of the Church was to be that of submission to
the Holy Spirit, not an independent activity. Their
freedom and their authority as they went were to be
gained through their absolute surrender to, and obedience
to the Holy Spirit. "There is one body, and one Spirit."
The Spirit is the life of the body; the body is the instrument of the Spirit. The Spirit is the Holy Spirit of
God; the body is the assembly of the saints. The Spirit
works through the assembly; but the assembly has no
power to move save under the inspiration and impulse of
the Spirit. There is one body, and the body must
coöperate with the Spirit in separating its members for
particular service. "There is one Spirit," and that
Spirit must direct, control, suggest, choose, elect, equip,
all who are to do its work.

As we look back to this activity of the Spirit, we have
a great revelation of the purpose of God in His Church.
It is the picture of the Spirit of God, able to make known
His will perfectly to an assembly. It is the picture of
an assembly, able to discover His will without doubt,
without uncertainty. It is the picture of the Spirit and
the assembly, working in perfect harmony, and the results
are seen in all the missionary triumphs which followed.

That immediately leads us to enquire, What were the
conditions under which it was possible for the Spirit of
God thus to make His great and gracious and perfect
will known? In the first verse three matters are revealed.
The first thing is the Church. "There were at Antioch,
in the Church." The second thing is that of the gifts
resident in the Church, "Prophets and teachers." The
third is that of the activity of the Church: "They ministered to the Lord, and fasted."

The very phrases carry their own exposition. What is the Church? The ecclesia, the called out company. Not to Antioch could the Spirit speak, but to the Church in Antioch; not to the promiscuous crowd thronging the streets of the fair and wonderful city, not to the merchants in the market-place, not to the legislators in their ecclesia—the Greek town council—could the Spirit speak, but to the Christian Church.

How was the Christian Church in Antioch constituted? Certain men of Cyprus and Cyrene had preached in Antioch to these Greek men the Gospel of the Lord Christ; and these men hearing the Gospel of the Lord Christ had believed, and had been baptized by the Holy Ghost. That company of men and women, in living union with the living Christ by the baptism of the Holy Spirit, constituted the Church. There had been no consecration of a building. There had been no apostolic visitation. The Church was not the result of official action; but of the proclamation of the Lord, and belief in Him, and baptism into His life, by the overruling of God. The catholic Church is not Anglican, nor Roman, nor Greek, nor Free; but that whole company of men and women baptized by the Holy Spirit into living association with the living Lord. Wherever there is such a company of people, there also is the Church. There was the Church in Antioch. Presently they coöperated with the Church in Jerusalem; but Antioch was independent of Jerusalem; and the Holy Spirit could speak to the Church in Antioch.

In that Church in Antioch were gifts directly bestowed by the Spirit; "prophets and teachers." Prophets are men of insight and foresight, who seeing into the heart of truth, and far on into the economy of God, as the result of personal fellowship with Him, speak forth the words of God. "Teachers" are men of understanding, who having that understanding, are able to impart their knowledge to others. The Lord, when He ascended on high,

received gifts; "He gave some apostles,"—they are not
mentioned here; " Prophets," such were here in Antioch;
" Evangelists,"—they are not mentioned here; " Pastors
and teachers,"—such were here. Whence came the
gifts? From the Lord Himself. How? By the bestowment of the Holy Spirit.

Some of the men are named. Barnabas, whom we
know well, was a man of Cyprus. Symeon was called
Niger. Not much can be based upon that designation.
It may mean that he was a Jew, and that the surname was
given to him on account of the swarthiness of his com-
plexion. It may be, as some believe, that he was an
Ethiopian, a proselyte, who had taken a Jewish name.
Lucius was of Cyrene. This was a man with a Latin
name. Manaen was the foster-brother of the Herod
who had murdered John. He was in this company, gifted
either as a prophet or a teacher. And finally Saul.
What a fine and glorious blend there was in this company! Thus the Spirit bestows gifts upon men. In
Judaism, the son of the high priest succeeded to the
priesthood. That is so no longer. There is no succession, because the living Lord is always present. Succession means distance, but the Lord is ever in the midst
of His Church.

The activity of the Church is declared in the words,
" They ministered to the Lord, and fasted." The word
translated " ministered," is a most suggestive one, being
that from which we derive our word " liturgy." The
Greek word was first employed of civil service in Athenian law. It came to be used in religion and of priestly
service. It specially described eucharistic service, that is,
the service of praise. Gradually it became the word that
indicated set forms of worship. The real thought in it,
is that of the exercise of the proper functions of organs
in the power of life, the exercise of the organs under the
dominion of the spirit of man, intellectual, emotional,
volitional. These men in Antioch, not the prophets and

[Acts 13:1-3]

teachers only, but the whole Church, were engaged in this sacred ministry to the Lord. In the epistle to the Hebrews (1:14) it is said of the angels, " Are they not all ministering spirits; sent forth to do service for the sake of them that shall inherit salvation?" The ministering is related to the service. The angels are ministering spirits, that is, those who worship and offer to God; but they are sent forth from that worship to do service. Isaiah saw the vision of God high and lifted up. He heard the chanting of the seraphim. They were proclaiming the holiness of God. They were fulfilling the function of their angelic life in praising. Then the song of one of these angelic beings was silenced; he was sent forth to do service to the man who needed cleansing. Ministering to the Lord is the function of a worshipping people. They recognize that work is not everything, but that worship is a prime and fundamental necessity. The Church in Antioch had not lost the art of worship. The outcome of worship is always readiness to obey the Spirit when He sends us forth to work. The Church is an institution for worship, its members minister to the Lord, and then they are sent forth to be of service. Worship and work are always intimately associated. If we try and work without worship, we shall disastrously fail. If we worship and never work, we shall become ritualists. The attitude to which the Spirit can reveal Himself is that of worship.

"They ministered to the Lord, and fasted." The word "fasted" indicates a special season of spiritual exercise, in which the Church, His body, is separated from all activity save that of ministering to the Lord. To a Church in that attitude the Spirit can speak, and the Church will not mistake His voice.

The last matter revealed here is that of the resulting coöperation. Luke writes, " Then," that is after the Spirit had spoken, and therefore in answer to His word. How did the Spirit speak? We ask these questions still and fain would discover the answer. One cannot say definitely how the Spirit spoke to the Church at Antioch. At the same time we may surmise, illustrating the story by His methods on other occasions. I do not for a moment imagine that the assembly heard a voice. That is the mistake we too often make. We try to force ourselves into ecstasies in order to hear the voice, and then we imagine we hear it! That is not the suggestion here. He made known His will to the assembly, probably through one spokesman, whose word produced agreement. We see now the reason of the naming of the prophets and teachers here; Barnabas, Symeon, Lucius, Manaen, Saul. But we are not told through which of them the Spirit spoke. The method of the Spirit is ever that of obscuring the instrument. In these days of worship and of fasting, one of their number probably rose and spoke, and immediately in the whole assembly there was unanimity, absolute conviction that this was the mind of the Spirit. If we will place ourselves at the disposal of the Spirit He will lead and guide us to-day in the same way as He has ever done, guiding definitely, immediately, positively making known His will. " The Spirit said." Oh the dignity, the grandeur of this statement! Are we listening for His voice, as these men listened?

When the Spirit had spoken, the work was done decently and in order. They fasted and prayed, this time for the men who were to be separated; and they laid their hands on them. Who laid hands on them? Not apostles, for there was not an apostle amongst them. Consequently the laying on of these hands was the laying on of the hands of prophets and teachers, possibly of members of the Church who were neither. In this great Church every believer stands on an equality with every other believer.

Then they let them go. " They sent them away " is a faulty translation. In the next verse we read: " So they, being *sent* forth by the Holy Spirit." That is not the

[311]

same word as in this statement. What did they really do? They released them. What did the Spirit do? He sent them. The Church could not send these men forth. The Church could release them, set them free, by caring for all other obligations, by taking responsibility for all that they would need.

The Spirit still directs the Church upon fulfilment of conditions. His choices are those of infinite wisdom. Some must stay in Antioch, and some must go. The Church can be directed by the Spirit on fulfilment of conditions; and when directed, her obedience must be immediate and complete.

The final word is for the individual. No man can go unless the Spirit call him. This is the high doctrine of the ministry. Men cannot make a minister; not even the Church, nor her theological halls. He must be called of the Spirit. Unless he hear that call sounding in his soul, ringing like a trumpet night and day, giving him no rest until he is compelled to say, Woe is me if I preach not; then in God's name let him stay where he is, in his present calling. But if he hear the call, then let him remember that it is his business to go forward within the fellowship and under the guidance of the Church.

Acts 13:4-12

The method of Luke from this point, perhaps even more markedly than before, is that of selection. Only occasional incidents are recorded. In this paragraph few details are given. These men were sent down to Seleucia, a port of Antioch. They then sailed to Cyprus. At Salamis they proclaimed the Word of God in the synagogues of the Jews, and then they passed through the whole island to Paphos. There is no doubt that they fulfilled their ministry in every place at which they touched; but there are no details, no account of what they did, or of the victories that were won. Luke has selected certain important incidents, in order to illustrate the method of the Spirit of God in the carrying on of His work. In order to gain the values, we need to give special attention in each case to the principal event, glancing only at the incidental matters.

The first incidental matter in this paragraph is that of Elymas the sorcerer. We know nothing either of his earlier career or of what happened to him afterwards. The blindness that came upon him was for a season. Possibly he came from that blindness, as Paul himself had done, to fuller and more glorious light.

Sergius Paulus is also incidental. We have no knowledge of his earlier career, nor of his subsequent history.

The change of name from Saul to Paul occurs in this paragraph. From this point to the end of the book Luke speaks of him by the Gentile name, Paul, instead of the Jewish name, Saul. At the point when he started forth, set free by the Church at Antioch, sent by the Holy Spirit to the fulfilment of that great ministry for which he had been apprehended, and for which he had been fitted by long training—his ministry to the Gentiles, Luke recorded that his name was also Paul, and from thence he proceeded to speak of him by the Gentile name only.

Another incidental matter at this point is that Paul now comes into prominence. His action when they came to the court of Sergius Paulus was that of a man taking the lead in the great new movement; and we read, " Now Paul and his company set sail from Paphos." Until that moment it had been " Barnabas and Saul," but from now on, and until the end of the story, Paul is most evidently the leader of his company; and when the two names are put together, it is no longer Barnabas and Saul, but Paul and Barnabas.

There is still another incidental matter; that of the journeying. They touched at Seleucia, the port from which it was possible for them to sail to Cyprus. Arriving at Salamis they preached the Gospel to the Jews in the synagogues, and then journeyed through the whole island. We know nothing of those journeyings; of the trials and triumphs, of the sadnesses and gladnesses that came to them. " When they had gone through the whole island unto Paphos," something happened which Luke has carefully chronicled.

Let us then fasten our attention upon this central matter of the paragraph. Two phrases give us the key. The first is found in the fourth verse, " Sent forth by the Holy Spirit"; and the second in the ninth verse, " Filled with the Holy Spirit." The first links the story with all that has preceded it. They were sent forth by the Spirit, and released by the Church at Antioch. The context of this second phrase, " Paul, filled with the Spirit," reveals an activity of the Spirit which had not been manifested before. Note the startling sternness of the words he employed to Elymas the sorcerer: " O full of all guile and all villany, thou son of the devil, thou enemy of all righteousness, wilt thou not cease to pervert the right ways of the Lord? " These are the words that follow the declaration that Paul was filled with the Spirit. These are the words which were the outcome of that special filling. This is something entirely new. In the case of Ananias and Sapphira, that swift and sudden and awful discipline, the Spirit was seen to be a Spirit of fiery discipline in the Church. It was the first manifestation of the fact that ought to be the abiding fact, but which, alas, is not an abiding fact, that the atmosphere of the Church of God should be one in which a lie cannot live. Here, however, we have an activity of the Spirit which was that of a fiery attack upon something outside the Church. Let us consider the story in its deepest value, as revealing the activity of the Holy Spirit; observing first the reason of this strange and fiery activity; noticing secondly its method; and finally, its issue.

What was the reason of this attack upon Elymas? The very words of Paul rather startle the age in which we are living. We are not accustomed to such language;

we never think now of addressing to any man outside or
inside the Church, such words as these, " O full of all
guile and all villany." Remember Paul did not say this
about him, but *to* him. He looked into his face, he fastened his eyes upon him. This is quite definite. This
man Paul, contemptible of bodily presence according to
his own estimate, looked into the eyes of another man, a
Jew, keen, subtle, clever, occult; and looking straight into
his face, said: " O full of all guile and all villany, thou
son of the devil, thou enemy of all righteousness, wilt
thou not cease to pervert the right ways of the Lord?"
Let us carefully bear in mind that this follows immediately upon the declaration that he was filled with the
Spirit. There is no doubt that he was specially filled with
the Spirit for the saying of this very thing. Why this
anger? Why the fierceness of these words? The
answer is that another man was involved, Sergius Paulus.

Let us then look at this man. His name would lead us
to believe that he was a Roman. He was certainly a
representative of Roman government, and for some
reason not declared, he was a man enquiring after truth.
Perhaps he was weary at heart of all the materialism in
the midst of which as a Roman soldier he lived. His
enquiry for truth will probably account for the presence
of Elymas at his court. There were at that time very
many sorcerers travelling through these cities, and finding their way into places of power on profession of their
wisdom in things occult, and their ability to work wonders and signs. Sergius Paulus was seeking for something above the dust, something a little higher than the
material world, asking if there were any reality in the
things which men described as supernatural. Then there
came to him the story of the arrival and journeying
through the island of two men who claimed to preach
the Word of God. He desired to hear the Word of God,
and therefore sent for Barnabas and Saul. Luke tells
us that he was a man of understanding, that is quite

[315]

simply, a man of thought. There is nothing in this world the devil dreads like a man who dares to think. Such a man will inevitably touch the realm of the spiritual and the supernatural. He may not come to certainty on these matters, but he will face their possibility. Here was a man of thought, therefore Bar-Jesus was there, and therefore also, he sent for Barnabas and Saul. He is seen between these two forces.

Look for a moment at Elymas. He was a sorcerer. The word may have a rougher suggestion than is warranted. Like Simon Magus, Bar-Jesus was one of the magi, one of the wise men of the time. Things true and false were strangely mixed among these men. The accurate science of to-day was born in the midst of them. Chemistry is the outcome of their alchemy, as astronomy is the outcome of their astrology. It is not easy to discover how far these men were deceived, and how far they were right. Elymas was a man dwelling on the borderline of the occult, able to touch it, professing to be able to work wonders by it.

But he was also a false prophet; and immediately following that statement we are told that he was a Jew. Here then was a man who had been brought up with a knowledge of Hebrew literature, and the things of Hebrew religion; a man who by birth and training had been brought into closest understanding of the highest things in religion. But he was a false prophet, he was uttering things that were not true. Go back to the Old Testament, and discover its teaching about false prophets, as to the nature of the sin committed, as to the judgment that fell upon them. There might have been excuse for Bar-Jesus if he were merely one of the magi, for there was much of light in their teaching, as well as error. But that a Jew should become a false prophet, by professing to be able to do the things he was doing, was sin. When Paul looked at him and spoke so sternly to him, on the human side the very vehemence of what he said

was born of the fact, not that he was a sorcerer, but that
he was a Jew trafficking with unholy things, in order to
win position in the house of Sergius Paulus.

This man withstood Barnabas and Saul, and the word
" withstood " suggests a systematic endeavour, as Luke
records, to turn aside Sergius Paulus from the faith. We
are immediately brought face to face with the reason for
this activity of the Spirit. Filled with the Spirit, Paul
uttered those strange, startling, burning, scorching words,
because Sergius Paulus was in danger. The severest
words of the Bible, Old and New Testaments, are reserved for those who stand between men and truth, for
those who stand between men and God. Perhaps the
supreme chapter in the whole of the Old Testament is
that wonderful chapter in the prophecy of Ezekiel, the
prophet of the exile, the prophet of light and hope by the
river Chebar, seeing visions of God, diagnosing the actual
disease of the scattered people to a remnant to whom he
was a minister. He described the false prophets as under
the severest judgment of God. At the close of our
Lord's public ministry He pronounced eight great woes;
not one upon sinning men, but all upon those who were
false teachers and guides, false interpreters of the will
of God. Christ never said anything hard or severe to a
sinning man or woman. His severity was reserved for
men who failed to guide, when they professed to do so.
The noble sarcasm of John Milton expressed the whole
wrong, when he described false shepherds as " blind
mouths." Ruskin's exposition of that phrase was, that
shepherds should watch, and they are blind; shepherds
should feed, and they only desire to be fed—" blind
mouths." That which called forth the fiery protest of the
Holy Spirit through Paul was that this man, a Jew, a
prophet, was standing in the way, or attempting to do so,
of the soul of a man finding truth, and finding life.
That was the reason of the fiercely burning fire.

Notice in the next place the method. The immediate

equipment of Paul for this particular work was that he was filled with the Holy Spirit. That opens the whole question of New Testament terminology concerning the work of the Holy Spirit, a most prolific and interesting subject, the neglect of which has caused infinite confusion. These phrases of the New Testament are never used interchangeably; the baptism of the Spirit, the anointing of the Spirit, the sealing of the Spirit, the filling of the Spirit. We perpetually mix them, and speak of baptism as a second filling, which the New Testament never does. There are in the New Testament two phrases, very much alike, and yet separate in intention. The first is " full of the Spirit," and this indicates that fullness of the Spirit, which is the true life of the believer. The normal life of the believer should be that of being full of the Spirit. Paul undoubtedly was at this moment, baptized by the Spirit into living union with the Lord, anointed by the Spirit for the service which His will appointed, sealed by the Spirit as the property of the Lord unto the day of redemption, having the fullness of the Spirit for the living of all his life. Then there came a moment when there was a special work to be done, and he was filled, suddenly filled by the Spirit, in the sense of being specially equipped for a special work; specially prepared for a special emergency.

What was the result of this filling? Clear discernment; he knew this man through and through, not by his own cleverness, not by mere intuition, but by that immediate filling of the Spirit which became illumination, enabling him to see to the very heart of the man who stood confronting him. He described him in character, " Full of all guile and all villany, son of the devil, enemy of righteousness." Then he described his sin, " Wilt thou not cease to pervert the right ways of the Lord? " So this sudden enduement of power meant discernment and speech, speech that was definite, attacking, vehement. We speak of the wooing winsomeness of the Spirit, and

thank God, we cannot say too much thereof. " The fruit
of the Spirit is love." The final and perfected issue of
the work of the Spirit in the heart of man is love. But
the Spirit of love is a Spirit of fire, and that for very
love. Why the fierceness of this description? Why the
blunt speech that fell like scorching fire upon the heart of
the man who listened? For love of Sergius Paulus;
because this man by his teaching, his greed, and by his
endeavour to retain position at the court, would " pervert the right ways of the Lord," withstand the Word of
God, attempt to prevent this man entering into the fullness of life. For the sake of Sergius Paulus this Spirit of
God immediately equipped Paul, so that he saw and knew
and spoke, and became the instrument of judgment.

Yet there is a touch of wonderful tenderness discoverable at the heart of the fierce fire. Paul said to him,
" The hand of the Lord is upon thee, and thou shalt be
blind, not seeing the sun for a season." The blindness
was the material symbol of the man's spiritual condition;
and Paul, speaking not of his own will, or of his own
choice, not pronouncing upon him a doom which he
thought he deserved, but becoming the very voice of the
Spirit of God speaking out of that sudden equipment,
pronounced upon him that judgment of blindness " *for a
season.*" How long it lasted no one knows. What was
the issue in the case of Elymas, no one can tell. We
must leave it at the point where it is left in the narrative.

What then was the issue of this activity of the Spirit?
First, the vindication of truth. Paulus desired to hear
the Word of God. For that reason he sent for Barnabas
and Saul. The last thing recorded is that he was " astonished at the teaching of the Lord." Thus this method
of the Spirit vindicated the truth which Paul and Barnabas were declaring. But that is not the final word as to
issue. It is this—he believed. The fiery method of the
Holy Spirit as here revealed is vindicated in the fact that
Sergius Paulus was brought into the light, and received

all the gifts and graces of the Spirit in Whose power these men had come with the message of that great evangel.

In conclusion, to look at this story in its entirety; two things arrest attention; the new opposition, and the new manifestation of the Spirit's repelling power.

This was a new opposition. The opposition in the earlier part of the Acts against Christianity was not the opposition of Elymas the sorcerer. That earlier opposition was that of the rationalism that denied resurrection, spirit, and angel. From here to the end of the story the opposition was of a different kind. Not that the old Sadducean opposition ceased, but that another antagonism to the Christian Church was manifested. The inspiration of this opposition was love of gain; its weapons were those of a false supernaturalism. This has run through all the centuries, and is abroad in the world to-day. Trafficking with the occult in the name of religion will always attract the attention of men: and it is one of the grave perils which at this hour is threatening Christian evangelism. The aim of it is to turn men aside from the faith. Perchance it is not consciously the aim of some who practise that which is false in supernaturalism; but it is the aim of the prince of the power of the air, who worketh through the children of disobedience, to prevent the spread of the Gospel. Those who work in heathen lands discover the awful power of this opposition, and it is active in our own land also. There are hundreds who are being moved from the faith delivered to the saints, or prevented from obedience to it, by the charm and the glamour of a supernaturalism which is not according to the revelation of the Word of God.

The repelling force is the force of the Spirit. Elymas the sorcerer was a lover of gain; but in this fiery action of the Spirit there was a love of man. In the case of Elymas, there was a false supernaturalism; but in the case of the Spirit, there was the true supernaturalism. Paul was filled by the Spirit, and then conducted a definite and daring warfare against the thing that was false. The aim of Elymas the sorcerer was to turn aside from the faith; the aim of the Spirit in His repelling activity was to establish this man in the faith.

The opposition of the supernatural and occult is one of the gravest perils threatening the Christian faith. So it ever has been. So it remains at this moment. The Sadducean philosophy which is popular to-day is dying, as it must die. It is true that man cannot live by bread alone. Man cannot be fed on dust. What we need to fear is traffic with the occult, base spiritualism, and all mental forms of healing, which are apart from the Word of God. Men must be brought into relationship with the Lord Jesus Christ. Anything and everything that denies Him as perfect Saviour, while offering in His place some substitute of spiritual ideal or occult influence, is the gravest peril of all. There are moments when it is necessary that the Spirit of God should speak in stern denunciation. Let us, however, remember that the only reason for anything of this kind in preaching, and teaching, in speech, must be the reason of our love for man; not because the doctrine is not ours, not because the false view is not in agreement with our mental convictions, but because the false view is hindering men and women from coming into relationship with Jesus Christ. It must be the heart that loves Sergius Paulus that speaks in anger to Elymas the sorcerer.

Acts 13: 13-41

In this passage we have Paul's first recorded address, not by any means the first message which he delivered, but the first which has been preserved for us in the records. In those early days, after his apprehension by Christ, in Damascus he reasoned with the Jews. Then later, in Jerusalem he dealt especially with the Jews of the Greek synagogues. When taken away by the brethren from Jerusalem to Tarsus, where he remained

for a number of years, there can be no doubt that he still
continued to speak of the things that had become more
to him than life.

It is interesting to remember that when Barnabas discovered the grace of God in Antioch of Syria, " He went
forth to Tarsus to seek for Saul: and when he had found
him, he brought him unto Antioch." That is a statement
that may be read easily and its suggestiveness missed.
Dr. Christie has drawn attention to this, pointing out that
the word means that it was not easy to find Saul; that
when Barnabas arrived in Tarsus he had to seek for
him. He suggests that Paul was busily occupied with
evangelistic work. Recent investigations prove that
through all the region of Tarsus there are remains of
Christian Churches. In all probability during those years
spent in Tarsus, Paul was passing through the villages,
preaching the great Gospel of his Lord and Saviour
Jesus Christ. Then at Antioch in Syria he had been for
a long period with Barnabas, teaching and instructing.

In this paragraph we find that Paul passed through,
from Paphos to Perga in Pamphylia, and it is chronicled
quite briefly, " John departed from them, and returned
to Jerusalem." Luke, with a fine delicacy, gives no
reason for the going of John Mark. There has been
much speculation as to why Mark left Paul at that point.
Subsequently he tells us that " Barnabas was minded to
take with them John also, who was called Mark. But
Paul thought not good to take with them him who with-
drew from them from Pamphylia, and went not with
them to the work " (15:38). Again no reason is as-
signed, but that at least shows that Paul considered there
had been some deflection on the part of John Mark from
the clear line indicated by the Holy Spirit, as they were
moving out into the larger work that lay before them.
The journey from Perga in Pamphylia to Antioch in
Pisidia was one beset with much difficulty. No account
of that difficulty is given here. It is probable that on

that very journey, the apostle and Barnabas, and perchance Luke also, had to face those perils of robbers to which he made reference in one of his letters. It may be that Mark knew the peril of the journey, and shrank therefrom. It may be that Mark had not yet escaped from Peter's influence, even as Peter had not yet escaped from his own more unworthy self. Be that as it may, there came a time when Mark was restored to full fellowship. In that final letter to Timothy, written from the last imprisonment in the Mamertime prison, this man Paul, from whom Mark now parted, and who declined fellowship with him a little later because he feared his fidelity, wrote, " Take Mark, and bring him with thee: for he is useful to me for ministering."

Arrived in Antioch of Pisidia, Paul uttered the first message which has been preserved for us in outline. It is of great interest in view of the fact which we have noted in our earlier studies, that this man Paul was Hebrew of Hebrews, and was also saturated by early training, with an intense sympathy for the Gentile world, and for the Greek method of thought. The ideals of Hebraism and Hellenism were both active in him.

There are senses in which it is unnecessary for us to consider this address in detail. It was largely historic. In it he stated God's method with His ancient people up to, and including, the coming of Jesus, His rejection, crucifixion, and resurrection. We are familiar with the details. That which is of interest is the method of the grouping of those details, as standing in a Hebrew synagogue, having other than Hebrews in his audience, he delivered this message. It was a great hour in the history of the Church when Paul rose to deliver this message in the synagogue at Antioch in Pisidia. Let us consider first, its atmosphere; secondly, its argument; and finally note its appeal.

Antioch in Pisidia was a city of Greek origin, founded by colonists from Magnesia. At the moment when Paul stood there, it was a city under Roman government, part of the great empire; the seat of proconsular government. Moreover it was a city having a Hebrew synagogue, in which this address was given. In that city the three great world-powers and forces dominant at the time, were all represented; and they were the three elements merging in the mental make-up of Paul. There was the fundamental fact of the Greek mental mood; there was the governing force of Rome; and at the centre there was the religious influence of the Hebrew synagogue. Into that synagogue, in the midst of these forces creating the atmosphere, came this man Paul, himself a Hebrew of Hebrews, in profound sympathy with Hebraism; Paul of Tarsus, who had spent his early years in the midst of Greek ideals; Paul, the Roman citizen, freeman of the Roman Empire, with a passion for government. All these forces were incorporated in his interpretation of Christianity. This was the new missionary.

Think of the atmosphere as created by the audience who listened to him. Notice first, his own company. The phrase " Paul and his company " in the thirteenth verse should not be passed over lightly. Paul had been the assistant of Barnabas, but now he had become the central figure. Barnabas was there; and perhaps Luke was there also, as Dean Alford suggests. There may have been two or three others, but we do not know who they were. As we think of that company, we are reminded of the words, " Where two or three are gathered together in My name, there am I in the midst of them." There, in the Hebrew synagogue, was a Christian Church, the two or three gathered in the Name. I think when Paul delivered this first message, he looked at Barnabas and Luke more often than at the crowd. He spoke in the atmosphere of believing souls, in fellowship with his Lord, and so in fellowship with himself.

Then there were the men of Israel, his own people after the flesh, the people of God, the men of privilege.

[Acts 13: 13-41]

They had the oracles; to them pertained the covenants, to them were given the promises. As the eyes of this man, Christ-illumined, passed from the little company about him, and saw the men of Israel, he was looking into the faces of people who were peculiarly the people of God.

But there were also others. "And ye that fear God." That is not a second description of the men of Israel. In the midst of the address he again made a distinction, "Brethren, children of the stock of Abraham, and those among you that fear God" (verse 26). In explanation of these two references we may glance at a verse beyond this paragraph: "Now when the synagogue broke up, many of the Jews and of the devout proselytes followed Paul and Barnabas" (verse 43). There the other men are described as "devout proselytes." These were Greeks, Romans perchance, men who out of the midst of polytheism had been attracted to the religion of the Hebrew, because it was the religion of the one God.

Yet further, in order to understand the atmosphere, we must look, not only at the city of Antioch and at the audience, but at the preacher also. His address was modelled upon the address of Stephen. If we compare the address of Peter, delivered on the day of Pentecost, with this of Paul, their similarity is created by the fact that they had the same truth to proclaim. Both declared the Cross. Both affirmed the resurrection. When that is said, however, the similarity ends. But to read the address of Stephen which immediately preceded his martyrdom, and then to read this address of Paul, is to see that Paul consciously, or unconsciously, modelled his speech in this synagogue in Antioch of Pisidia, upon the address of Stephen. That is a matter full of interest. Paul had heard Stephen's defence, and had never escaped the power of it. Stephen, full of faith, and of the Holy Spirit, had passed in review the history of God's ancient people, until he had charged them with sin and folly, and

[325]

THE ACTS OF THE APOSTLES

had roused their anger. When they hounded Stephen to his death, Saul had consented, given his vote as a member of the Sanhedrim, had stood, minding the clothes of the men who stoned him. I believe that even then in the heart of Saul the appeal of Stephen sounded like a clarion cry. It was with him yet; and its power and persuasiveness moved him as he delivered this message in the synagogue at Antioch.

Again notice, that throughout this address Paul spoke from the standpoint of separation from Israel. He spoke to the men of Israel, and all that fear God; and once or twice only in the course of his address did he identify himself with them. For the most part he spoke as separated from them. Moreover, he was in intense sympathy with the Greek outlook. But in Christ, he stood apart from Hebraism and Hellenism, in order that he might demonstrate the glorious comprehensiveness of the Christian message which included both.

Paul declared two things in his argument; first, the Divine government; and secondly, the Divine grace. His message was that God is the One governor; and that the government of the one God is the government of a continuous and overwhelming grace.

The fact of the Divine government was not argued; nor was it presented as a doctrine. It was, however, so constantly referred to, as to make the whole statement an argument and a doctrine. He dealt with the people of Israel from the moment of their deliverance from Egypt. He traced the history of the people, showing how they came out of Egypt into the wilderness. He referred to them as coming into the land of promise, and dealt with their sojourn in the land, until the time of David. Then he omitted entirely their history from Solomon to Nehemiah and Malachi; but linked the history to the Christian movement when he said, " Of this man's (David) seed, hath God according to promise brought unto Israel a Saviour, Jesus." That long period of degeneracy, de-

[326]

terioration, despair, and disaster, that dark gulf of human failure between David and Jesus, he bridged by the pronoun " He " which had reference to God. Out of David's seed " He," God, brought this Man Jesus. In all his dealing with the history of the people he insisted upon the Divine government. As to the coming out of Egypt, " God chose this people," God " exalted the people," God " led them forth." Concerning the forty years in the wilderness, " Suffered He their manners." The change the revisers suggest in the margin is possible by the alteration of one letter in the Greek, and that form is found in some of the manuscripts. The weight of argument may still be in favour of the rendering, " suffered He their manners "; but if the change be adopted, then what Paul said here was, " He bare them as a nursing Father." We find the same tender, compassionate thought of patience, in the other rendering, but whichever rendering is taken the emphasis is upon the pronoun " He," " *He* suffered their manners," " *He* bare them as a nursing Father." We see the people coming into the land, and Paul says, " He destroyed seven nations before them," and " He gave them their land for an inheritance, for about four hundred and fifty years." That period in which they were without a king, governed in hours of crisis by dictators and judges, he interpreted thus, " He gave them judges until Samuel." Then of the hour of change, at the commencement of the breakdown in the national history, when they clamoured for a king, Paul says, " He gave them Saul." When presently the history tells of this man's death, Paul says, " He . . . removed him." Next in the history we see David the king, and again he says, " He raised up David to be their king: to whom also He bare witness." Finally, " He " the same God, " according to promise, from the seed of David, brought this Man, Jesus." Then these men of Israel, because they did not understand their own prophets, did not understand Jesus when He came; and

they slew Him, and put Him in the tomb. But Paul says,
" God raised Him from the dead."

Thus the Government of God was the fundamental
note in the message of this speech in the synagogue at
Antioch. God chose, exalted, and led forth a people.
God suffered them, or bare them as a nursing Father, in
the wilderness. God destroyed nations before them, and
gave them the land. God raised up judges in the hours
of their difficulty. God gave them Saul when they clamoured for a king. God removed him from his position.
God raised up David. Then came the history of Solomon,
the break-up of the kingdom: Judah, Israel, captivity,
defeat, and disaster. There was no king, no priest, no
prophet. The remnant of the people was living under
the Roman yoke. God brought forth Jesus. The one
God is thus declared ever moving forward, in spite
of all human failure, toward an ultimate purpose of
blessing.

Wonderfully the Divine grace is also revealed in this
word of Paul in the synagogue at Antioch. This is the
central Christian message to Israel, and to the Gentile.
Human failure is recognized. Paul recognized the descent as he reviewed the history of Israel. First there
was the weakness of these people in those early days in
the wilderness, when He suffered their manners, or bare
them as a nursing Father. Then came their waywardness, when they clamoured for a king, and rejected Him.
Lastly their wickedness is seen when they asked that
Jesus should be slain, and they laid Him in a tomb. All
that is a dark picture, of the failure of a people called,
chosen, and exalted by God for privilege and purpose.

But that is background only. Paul would impress
upon these men of Israel, and the proselytes gathered in
the synagogue, not the failure, but the grace that was
above it, beyond it, mastering it, moving through it toward the accomplishment of Divine purpose. The
Divine grace was original, for He chose them. It was

patient grace; He suffered them, or bare with them as a
nursing Father. It was disciplinary grace; He gave
them Saul that they might understand at the commencement the real meaning of their failure and desire for a
king; and He gave them David, who took hold of the
kingdom, and represented the will of God to men. It
was fulfilling grace, in spite of Solomon, in spite of
Ahab, in spite of Ahaz, in spite of Nebuchadnezzar, in
spite of Assyria, in spite of Egypt, in spite of all circumstances and forces and disaster and defeat, He brought
a Saviour. That is the infinite music of the Gospel.
When He brought the Saviour into darkness and blindness even among the people of His own choice and exaltation and government they did not know Him. They
read the law and the prophets, which led up to, and
promised this great Saviour; but when He came they
were blind, and did not understand Him. There is no
more wonderfully illuminating word, revealing at once
the Divine government and the Divine grace, than that
in which the apostle declared that God compelled the
folly and sin of these people to fulfil His purpose. They
fulfilled the Scriptures they did not understand, by con-
demning Him Who stood in their midst, according to the
purpose of God. Peter declared the same great truth in
his first sermon when he said of Jesus, "Him, being
delivered up by the determinate counsel and foreknowledge of God, ye by the hand of lawless men did crucify
and slay." Paul said they "fulfilled them by condemn-
ing Him." Finally it was accomplishing grace; and by
three facts he set Jesus before them, as fulfilling the
highest expectation, aspiration, and prophesying of the
past. The second psalm presents the King. This is the
King. Paul then linked a reference from Isaiah, to the
sixteenth psalm, which Peter also quoted in his first
sermon; that psalm which predicted that the Holy One
should never see corruption. He declared that by the
raising of Jesus, He was demonstrated as the King, ac-

cepted, and proved to be the hope of Israel and the Saviour of the world. Such was his argument.

Finally he uttered his appeal. He proclaimed " This Man," the King, the crucified, the risen Man. Peter had told his hearers in Jerusalem that there was remission of sins. Paul did the same, but he employed another word, the word " justified." Here a new word came into the language of the Christian Church. Our Lord had employed it in the parable of the Pharisee and Publican. It became Paul's great word, and to know all its meaning we must study his letter to the Romans. " Justification " is a mightier word than " remission of sins." It is a word that explains remission of sins, and glorifies that idea. There in the synagogue in Antioch in Pisidia, to men of Israel, and to Greeks attracted by the doctrine of the one God, this man affirmed His government, and His grace; and proclaimed Jesus as fulfilling both, and providing the possibility of justification for every one that believes.

From that proclamation he passed to a word of warning. " Beware." He quoted from the prophecy of Habakkuk, the prophecy of the man of faith, that revealed the principle of faith as the one principle upon which man must live. So he revealed to these people the fact that it is by faith in this Man that men are justified.

To summarize. This first recorded speech of the great missionary apostle declared the one God, the one purpose of God, the one Saviour. He proclaimed the evangel, which may be summarized in one word, justification by faith. The proof that there is such justification is in the resurrection of Jesus Christ. This proclamation was for Hebrew and Gentile. Separating himself from each, he included both in his great message; because in Christ he was neither Jew nor Greek. In Christ he had found the One Who brings the Jew and the Greek into life, and into harmony with the will and purpose of God.

Acts 13: 42-52

This paragraph contains the account of the things immediately following upon the delivery of Paul's address in the synagogue at Antioch. It is the story of a strange commotion in the city, of conflict, and of movement; the story of an emotional manifestation, of an intellectual difficulty, and of strange volitional processes. The story is bounded by Sabbath days, but the atmosphere is that of strife.

We have considered the address of the apostle; here we see the results of that address. Imaginatively we can fill in those days between the Sabbaths. We can understand how these men, who had listened to the message in the synagogue, went their way in the schools and in the market-places, and among their friends, talking of the strange, remarkable, and arresting words that they had heard from the lips of this stranger in the city. When the next Sabbath came, and this man was to deliver another message, nearly the whole city gathered together. Antioch in Pisidia was stirred to its very centre. Let us attempt to discover the cause of the unrest, and see how this conflict illustrates certain great principles concerning the preaching of the evangel of Christ.

What then was the cause of this unrest in Antioch in Pisidia? The forty-second verse reads, " And as they went out "—these people who had listened in the synagogue—" they besought that *these words* might be spoken to them the next Sabbath." In verse forty-four, we read, " And the next sabbath almost the whole city was gathered together to hear *the Word of God.*" In the forty-sixth verse Paul, addressing the Hebrews, said, " It was necessary that the *Word of God* should first be spoken to you." The forty-eighth verse reads, " The Gentiles . . . glorified *the Word of God.*" In these statements we discover the secret of the unrest in Antioch. A city was moved to its very centre, divided into conflicting camps of thought, emotion, and volition, by the message of one man; a message characterized in that opening verse by the men who first heard it as "these words"; and described by Luke as "the Word of God," that being a direct reference to Paul's discourse.

Therefore if we would understand that which had so profoundly moved Antioch in Pisidia, we must remind ourselves once again of the notes in that discourse. Its unargued supposition was that of the one God. Undoubtedly that was the note that attracted and held the attention of the proselytes in the synagogue, and which appealed to the men of Antioch. The truths which he had affirmed concerning the one God, were those of His perpetual government and His unfailing grace. He traced the history of the Hebrew people, from the original call of Jehovah, through their exodus from Egypt, and the period in the wilderness, to the possession of the land, and the giving of the kings; first Saul, for purposes of discipline; and then David, for purposes of illumination. He passed over the whole period from Solomon to Nehemiah, taking the story up again with the coming of Jesus.

The fundamental truth declared was that of the one God, Who governs. He chose, He exalted, He bore with the patience of a nursing Father the waywardness of the people He had created; He appointed kings and dethroned them; and through the long and dark years of deterioration and degeneration in national life, He prosecuted His own purpose, until at last, from the seed of David after the flesh, He brought Jesus the Saviour.

Paul further showed that the action of the one God in government was always that of an infinite grace; that the inspiration of the activity of the throne was that of undying love.

Thus he had uttered his central teaching; and if he had attracted and held these people by the affirmation of the unity of the Deity, and by the declaration of the perpetual government and grace of God, surely he had strangely startled them as he had declared the Cross of Jesus, and His resurrection. He explained the Cross by the resurrection.

He then made the great affirmation in the hearing of these men that it was possible that they should have remission of sins; and he used the word that occurs for the first time in the history of the Church, which he subsequently elaborated in his great Roman letter, the word "justified." He ended with this note, that every one that believed in Jesus might receive remission of sins, and be justified freely; Hebrew and Greek, the people of his own blood relationship, and those strangers, men of another type, and another method of mind, and of separate convictions.

These were the things to which the men of Antioch listened in that first discourse, and the result was that of conflicting views, conflicting emotions, conflicting decisions. The conflicting views are revealed in the conflicting emotions.

How was it that a message like this so profoundly moved the city? Because it was a message that touched the deepest things of human life; the truth about God; the question of an age-abiding life, a life that cannot be destroyed, a life that persists through every age and possesses it, but is never influenced by the passing of an age; the fact of sin, and the remission of sins, justification. The address of Paul in the synagogue was not occupied with material things. He did not discuss physical culture, food reform, dress reform, or housing reform. His message was not one that dealt preëminently with questions of the intellect. He did not discuss that difference at which we have looked, and of which he was conscious, between Hebraism and Hellenism. He entered into no political discussion as to the question of Roman authority. He dealt with the central facts of every human life: God, life, and sin. I do not suggest that this man was ignoring the mental mood in the midst

[333]

THE ACTS OF THE APOSTLES
of which he found himself, or that he was uninterested in the mental processes going on around him. He did not hold in contempt the things of the material life: food, raiment, and dwellings. But he did not stay to deal with things accidental, and transient, the things of every human life; but passed to the inspirational centres. When he spoke of God, of age-abiding life, and of sins, and the possibility of true remission, he was dealing with facts which forevermore make their appeal to men, arrest their attention, produce unrest, produce division, intellectual division, emotional division, volitional division. These are the things that produce the effects to be found through all this book of the Acts of the Apostles.

Let us observe the conflict a little more carefully. First of all it is said that these men were "filled with jealousy," and then we read, "As the Gentiles heard this, they were glad." Notice the difference: "filled with jealousy," filled with gladness. Observe another contrast: "They . . . contradicted the things which were spoken . . . and blasphemed"; "They . . . glorified the Word of God." Or again, some counted themselves "unworthy of age-abiding life"; others "were ordained to eternal life." These two declarations are mutually interpretative. In the statement, "As many as were ordained to eternal life believed," the word ordained has no reference whatever to any act of God. It refers to the attitude of the men themselves. In the "Emphasized Bible" Mr. Rotherham has changed the word with great advantage, so that it now reads, they that were *disposed* to eternal life. Finally some "blasphemed"; while others "believed." This set of contrasts reveals conflict, division, difference, following upon the preaching of the Word, and produced by the preaching of the Word.

What were the reasons of refusal? Prejudice and selfishness. The intellectual activity of the men who refused the Word, ceased. The refusal of the Word

[334]

was not intellectual, it was the refusal of prejudice.
They listened on the first Sabbath; and there is evidence
that they were objecting intellectually. It is found in the
fact that as Paul drew to the conclusion of his sermon,
he said to them, "Beware, therefore, lest that come upon
you, which is spoken in the prophets: Behold, ye despis-
ers, and wonder, and perish."

But no word was spoken by them of their difficulty, or
objection, on the first Sabbath. Indeed it is written
that "As they went out, they besought that these words
might be spoken to them the next Sabbath." Why then
this attitude of refusal? It was not the attitude of intellectual difficulty, but the attitude of prejudice. These
men saw that the Gentiles also were listening with eagerness, and that Paul was proclaiming to them the same
possibility of privilege as he was proclaiming to the Hebrew. They were prejudiced, selfish; the question of
truth was forgotten, and the question of personal privilege became paramount. Out of that closing of the mind
against truth, in favour of an ancient prejudice, they
counted themselves unworthy of life, they contradicted
the things that he said, they blasphemed.

But look at the others. Just as in the first case we
saw that prejudice was the outcome of the closing of the
mind to truth, so on the other side we see the open mind.
These men listened to the Word of this One God, governing in grace, and providing a Saviour, and proclaiming
justification, and they allowed the truth to make its appeal
to them. To these men truth was supreme, and therefore the true sense of the new privilege was created.
The effect of truth in every individual life is conditioned
by the opening or the closing of the mind. There is a
very significant phrase in the Gospel according to John,
"the honest heart." When there is the honest heart,
the open mind, the willingness to receive the truth, to
know truth, to follow truth at all costs, the result of the
preaching of this doctrine of the apostle is always that of

[335]

life. But where for any reason the mind is closed against the truth, where prejudice enters in, and arguments are created as the outcome of prejudice, then the result is that of death.

What followed these things? First, "The Word of the Lord was spread abroad throughout all the region." Secondly, persecution broke out that dogged the steps of Paul through all the rest of his journeyings. Thirdly, the disciples were filled with joy and the Holy Spirit. In the city conflict, intellectual, emotional, volitional; and then the Word of God spread through the whole region. A persecuting city may fling out the messengers, but it can never fling out the work they have done. Left in the city of Antioch in Pisidia was a little group of those who had heard, and had believed, and had received the new gift, and had been made members of the Christ; and they were filled with joy.

Let us glance back over the story for our own profit. Observe first the Christian preachers. The work of the preacher is forevermore to declare the deepest things in the life of man. Christian preachers are not careless concerning material life, or mental matters; but their business is to bring men and women into right relationship with God, to deal with the essential in human nature. Notice also the work following the preaching. Paul and Barnabas urged those who believed to continue; but they definitely turned from the Hebrew to the Gentile. Said they: "Seeing ye . . . judge yourselves unworthy of the age-abiding life, lo, we turn to the Gentiles." How the love of his brethren followed Paul. How it sobbed in tears, and breathed in agony, in his subsequent epistles. He never ceased to love his brethren after the flesh, who never did anything for him after the hour of his conversion to Christ, except persecute him and cause him suffering. Yet mark very carefully his words: "It was necessary that the Word of God should first be spoken to you. Seeing ye thrust it from you, and judge

[336]

yourselves unworthy of eternal life, lo, we turn to the Gentiles." The principle involved in that statement is that when people have heard the offer of the age-abiding life through the crucified Christ, if they will not accept it, it is the duty of the prophet, the apostle, the evangelist, to turn to others. If that principle of Paul's action in the synagogue in Antioch of Pisidia were applied to our land to-day, would there not be a great exodus of preachers, an abandonment of pulpits, and of going to the distant lands where men are eagerly waiting for the message? How far ought this principle to apply? It is a searching question that comes to the soul in pondering this story. It was the action of a splendid courage, an action that appals the soul, and compels pause; but moreover, an action justified by the results.

Again, note the effect of the Christian message; it is life unto life, or death unto death. It produces jealousy or joy, blasphemy or belief; the spirit of hell which persecutes, or the Spirit of holiness which seeks to save. The preaching of the Cross forevermore appeals to the intellect of men, and divides them. It stirs the emotional life, producing opposite and conflicting emotions. It storms the will, and demands belief, or blasphemy. The preaching of the Word divides as nothing else in the wide world can divide.

What is the personal enquiry that grows out of such a meditation? On the one side are those who judge themselves unworthy of age-abiding life; on the other are those who are disposed to the age-abiding life. These will blaspheme, these will believe. On which side do I stand? That question must be answered in the secrecy of the soul.

Acts 14: 1-20

In this paragraph we follow Paul and his company to the furthest outward limit of their first missionary journey. The remainder of the chapter is occupied with the revisitation of the churches on the return journey. We follow the movement, first at Iconium; then at Lystra; and then for a brief period at Derbe, concerning which nothing of importance is recorded, but which was evidently a period of quietness and peace in the work of evangelization. From Derbe they turned back again, traversing the route already taken, instead of crossing immediately home, as they might have done.

The chief interest in this story for us centres in the continuity of the work. This is best seen in the observation of the workers, by watching Paul and his little company as they arrived at Iconium, and at last escaped from there under pressure, and found their way to Lystra, where Paul was stoned and left for dead. There are four matters of interest: first the methods of their ministry; secondly the manifestations of power that accompanied their ministry, particularly the fact of the diversity of manifestations; thirdly the diversity of their experiences; and finally, the perils that threatened them.

In order to observe the methods of the ministry of these men, we must get back into the atmosphere, into the actual surroundings where the work was carried on. At Antioch in Pisidia there was a large Hebrew synagogue where the apostle first preached. He left Antioch because he was flung out of the city, and he took his way fifty miles to the east. There he certainly found a synagogue, but not so many Hebrews. He was coming gradually into the more definitely Gentile atmosphere. Hearing there was a plot on foot for the taking of his life, he left Iconium, and travelled forty miles to the southeast, and came to Lystra, where there was no synagogue. He had now come into the most pronounced atmosphere of Gentile life and thought. Thus we follow the movement of the Christian faith into an entirely new atmosphere, being further removed from the influences of Hebraism.

In the third verse of this chapter there is a phrase

THE ACTS OF THE APOSTLES

which we must specially note, "*Long time therefore* they tarried there," that is, at Iconium. "Speaking boldly in the Lord, Who bare witness unto the Word of His grace." That was the one theme of these men as they travelled. In this book of the Acts of the Apostles, wherever that word Word occurs in this connection, the first letter should be capitalized. "The Word of His grace" was the theme of the preaching. These men went into the new cities with no new message, but with the same message; adapting their method of presentation, but never changing the truth. They came to Lystra at last, and even there, as in Antioch of Pisidia, as in Antioch of Syria, as at Jerusalem at the beginning, they had one message, "The Word of His grace." The phrase stands for all the facts concerning Jesus of Nazareth, which these men were telling as they went. Presently we shall come to an account of how certain men said of Paul, Let us hear what this babbler says. A babbler was a teller of tales. There were men travelling through those Greek cities who gained their living by telling tales. They were public entertainers; they gathered people round them, and told stories of the things they had seen. Paul was a teller of tales. So also were his companions. They told what we speak of as "the old, old story." They told the story of the life of Jesus; they told the story of His death; they told the story of His resurrection, because by His resurrection everything else was transfigured, illuminated, interpreted. They were tellers of tales; and the message was always the same, "The Word of His grace."

At the beginning of this chapter there is one of those small words of the New Testament, which are so often full of light. A small and insignificant word it appears to be at first, and yet it is the light centre of the whole verse. "And it came to pass in Iconium, that they entered together into the synagogue of the Jews, and so spake, that a great multitude believed." "They so

spake." The word immediately suggests the manner of
the delivery of the message. It was not only the thing
they said, it was the way they said it. "They *so* spake."
Some expositors in dealing with this have laid emphasis
upon the fact that the apostles were careful in preparation. Another lays emphasis upon the fact of Paul's
logical mind, by which he compelled men to agree to the
things he spoke. That little word " so " arrests the spirit,
and grips it, and says to all teachers and preachers, Can
you *so* speak that men will believe? Paul I think gives
his own explanation of the meaning of the word " so."
When writing to the Corinthians, in his first letter, speaking of his coming to them, he said, " I came unto you
. . . not with excellency of speech or of wisdom."
Then it was not his eloquence, it was not his logical
faculty. "And I was with you in weakness, and in fear,
and in much trembling." Paul was always a man intrepid, courageous, dogmatic, daring; but the intensive
force of his intrepidity and courage is there revealed, " I
was with you in weakness and in fear, and in much trembling." Continuing he said: "And my speech and my
preaching were not in persuasive words of wisdom, but
in demonstration of the Spirit and of power." There we
discover the secret of the " so," " They *so* spake." That
is the secret of the preaching that prevails, and that wins;
the preaching that is authoritative, definite, positive, and
without apology, as the result of a sense of weakness
and trembling and fear in the mind of the preacher; but
which weakness and trembling and fear are all overcome by the preacher's fellowship with the Holy Spirit.
The true preacher says the thing that seems to have no
force in it, and which carries no conviction merely as
the result of his eloquence, or his argument; but when
he says it, it becomes a fire and a searching and a burning, because the Holy Spirit catches it up, and bears it
in upon the inner consciousness of men.

In the fourteenth chapter, and the early part of the

third verse, we read, "Long time *therefore.*" Wherever we find the word "therefore" we enquire "wherefore?" Let us glance at the preceding verse: "The Jews that were disobedient stirred up the souls of the Gentiles, and made them evil affected against the brethren." *Therefore,* the apostles stayed for a long time in Iconium. The reason of the long tarrying was not the success of the work, but its difficulties. The reason why they stayed was that persecution was abroad against those first gathered disciples. This reveals the persistence of their method. All new difficulties did but inspire these men to continuity and perseverance.

Yet once again, as we watch the methods of this ministry here, we have one of the first illustrations of the wonderful power of adaptation. At Lystra we have the picture of these people desiring to sacrifice to him, and the story of what happened at Lystra is an unconscious but very powerful evidence of the authenticity of this book. Ovid tells of a legend of the coming into that very region of Jupiter and Mercury long before. That city of Lystra had at its very gates a temple erected to Jupiter, in memory of the fact that Jupiter and Mercury had there descended. Immediately these people said, This is another epiphany of the deities; the gods have come again, as our fathers told us they came long before. That was the occasion for Paul's speech. In Antioch of Pisidia he had in the synagogue Jews and Greeks, men who in their hunger for one God, had turned to Hebraism. His speech there indicated the unity of Deity, and the government of God in grace. Now in Lystra there was not a single reference in his address to the Hebrew Scriptures, or Hebrew history. He began where the men of Lystra were, discovered the elements of religion present in their actual consciousness, and upon that based his appeal. His address, a brief and wonderful one, was delivered to men who had never had the light of revelation.

THE ACTS OF THE APOSTLES

When these men were suggesting to offer sacrifices to him, even the priests of Jupiter bringing sacrifices and garlands, he said to them, " We also are men of like passions with you." There, in a flash, idolatry is revealed, in contrast to the religion of revelation. All the gods that men worship are gods of like passions to themselves. Think of all the systems of religion that the world has, the highest and best, as well as the lowest and most degraded; and the deity worshipped is of like passions with humanity. In those words Paul put the falsity of idolatry before the attention of these men; and declared to them the living God, the One Whose very Being lies in a realm far removed from the rage and jealousy of human passion. He drew their attention to the fact that He had never left Himself without witness, even in their midst; calling them to a realization of the fact that if they had the light of Nature, if they had taken time to think, they might have discovered the power and wisdom of God. There he began his appeal; and then he preached to them " good tidings." Luke, giving the record, did not repeat the story of the evangel; but he did emphasize the method of the apostle, who recognized the element of religious life that there was in the basest people, and endeavoured to correct it, and so instruct the people toward the truth.

Having thus glanced at the methods of the work, let us look over the story again, observing the manifestations of power. At Iconium the Lord wrought signs and wonders by their hands. There is no detailed list of these given; but the words employed, " signs and wonders," are familiar. They were miraculous manifestations. We have no account of such signs and wonders in Antioch of Pisidia. Observe the diversity of the Spirit's activity. In Antioch in Pisidia there was preaching, and nothing else is recorded. In Iconium there was the preaching of the same Word of grace, and an accompaniment of signs and wonders. It may be said, Why draw such emphatic attention to this? In order that we may be reminded that we cannot base a system of procedure upon any single occurrence in any given place. That is a peril always threatening the Christian Church. In Iconium there were signs and wonders; therefore there must be signs and wonders everywhere. By no means. On the method of the Holy Spirit at any given hour and place, we have no right to base a doctrine of perpetuity. When men, sincere souls, attempt to teach that the one sign of the gift of the Spirit is the gift of tongues, they are departing from apostolic history. The Holy Spirit can surely bestow the gift of tongues to-day, so that a man can speak in another language; but He will as surely supply the interpreter also for the man so speaking. We supremely need to-day to get back into such fellowship with the Spirit of God, as to remember that He can do what He wills, giving gifts as He pleases. I am sure that the gift of healing is still within the power of Jesus Christ, and that He can bestow it upon men for the purposes of His will; but I believe that when a man has that gift, he will lay hands on men, and they will be healed. We cannot compel the Spirit of God to a line of activity, which He takes upon occasion, and declare that is His perpetual method.

At Lystra there was another revelation. Paul was preaching, and in his audience there was a cripple. Paul spoke to him, and commanded him to stand up because of what he saw in his face. He saw that he had faith to believe. Two things are revealed in that story: the faith of the man created by the preacher, as listening to the story of the risen Christ he applied that story to his own peculiar need; and a preacher interpreting the faith in the face of his listener. Every preacher knows the man who listens, and who looking through the preacher, sees the truth, grasps it, begins to apply it; the light of it is in his eye, eagerness is manifested in his face. There was a great and magnificent irregularity in Paul's preaching.

THE ACTS OF THE APOSTLES

[Acts 14: 1–20]

He dared to stop, and say to the man, " Stand upright on thy feet." Then the man leaped up and walked. The men of Lystra looked upon it as a great material miracle, but the deeper fact was the spiritual miracle that lay behind it; that man's apprehension of the truth, and the application of it to his own case; the preacher's knowledge of it, and his keenness of sight in the man's operation of faith in the living Lord. That was the wonderful thing.

Then " they stoned Paul, and dragged him out of the city, supposing that he was dead "; and to the astonishment of his own company, presently he rose and walked back into the city. Do not miss the miraculous here. It may be said he swooned and recovered. That may be true: but the men of Lystra and the disciples took him for dead. As the stones fell thick and fast upon him, I think he remembered Stephen. Personally I think he was dead; and quite literally and actually was restored to life, and had a positive resurrection, in order to the fulfilment of his life's work.

Looking over the ground once more, we mark the diversity of the apostle's experiences. How differently God deals with His workers. From Antioch Paul was allowed to escape, and was preserved. At Iconium God overruled circumstances, he was warned, and escaped. But he did not escape from Lystra. We cannot say that God took care of him at Antioch, and at Iconium, and that He did not take care of him at Lystra. That would be blasphemy. Paul was writing to Timothy, the young minister, his last letter, and said to him, You know the persecutions I endured at Antioch, at Iconium, at Lystra, but out of them all the Lord delivered me. At Antioch and Iconium He delivered him by saving him from the stones. At Lystra He delivered him through stoning. How often we are tempted to say: God delivered in the past, but He has not done so this time. Calamity has come, we are bruised and broken. Wait a little. Pres-

[344]

ently we shall be able to say, Out of them all He delivered me. Sometimes the only deliverance God can work for us is by the way of the stones, and by furnace experiences.

We note finally the perils threatening these men. There were the perils of opposition. Disobedience produced the spirit of opposition; hatred, plotting, stoning. But the gravest peril threatening these men was that which came to them in the hour when men suggested that they should worship them. That is the supreme peril to the Christian worker. It would have been so easy to gain power and notoriety; to take this worship, and abandon the pathway of persecution and of the stones. That is the peril of the prophet. When men bring garlands to worship, when men suggest his deification, he is in extreme danger. If men would help the prophet, they should pray that he may never accept the garland, or the worship of men. This was a most insidious hour. I would not suggest that there was any trembling on the part of Paul. He was not seduced, because he was living in such fellowship with his Lord that it was impossible.

This is the end of the first missionary journey on the outward march. As we look over the movement we are impressed by the fiery sword of the Christian evangel. Wherever these men came they brought a disturbing, dividing force. Every city was shaken to its centre, and men driven into opposite camps. As we watch, we remember the word of Jesus, "Think not that I came to send peace on the earth: I came not to send peace, but a sword!" Unless the Christian evangel of to-day is a fiery, dividing, separating influence, flinging men into opposite camps, it is not the evangel of the apostles. It is always a disturbing element, because it makes no compromise. This evangel comes into human life, and removes and casts out the devil in human life. This evangel has no soft phrases for sin, no rose-water method with iniquity. It is the evangel of blood and fire; and those who object to such terminology are those who are without the evangel.

Moreover we are impressed with the fiery spirit of the evangelists. Authority, insistence, courage, invincibility. They came to no city to discuss philosophies, but they came to preach Christ. They came into the midst of all forms of religious life to recognize the elements of truth, but not to leave men in gloom. They came to correct the mistake, to redeem the truth from error, and to set men upon the highway. They were great intrepid daring fiery spirits; and it is only thus that the kingdom is ever to be won for our God and His Christ.

Acts 14:21–28

This is the story of the return journey, after the first missionary campaign of Paul. The last place visited in his outward march was Derbe. I think we are warranted in supposing that his work there was characterized by quietness and peace. No details are preserved, but it is recorded in the first verse of this paragraph, that when they had preached the Gospel to that city, and had made many disciples, they returned. From other writings we know that in Derbe the apostle gained a friend, a companion, a fellow-helper, in Gaius. Up to this point the whole journey had been characterized by stress and strain. It may be that the persecuting Jews did not know where Paul and his company had gone. Certainly they do not seem to have followed him to Derbe.

From Derbe the great eastern road ran through the passes of the Taurus range of mountains straight to Tarsus, from whence Paul and his company could have taken ship, and crossed quickly over to Seleucia, and so would have arrived at Antioch in Syria. That was the easy way back to the Church that had sent them forth. That would have been the most speedy and safe method of return; most speedy certainly, for the distance was very little in comparison with the route now taken. In-

stead of that they traversed the twenty miles back to
Lystra, the forty on to Iconium, the sixty on to Antioch;
and then came along the southern coast. The crossing
of swollen rivers and the presence of robbers might have
made the mountain passes dangerous. Nevertheless perils
from robbers and rivers are always easier than perils
from antagonistic fanatics. Along the way by which
they had come, they had left companies of angry men
in every city, determined to deal with them, and if possible to put them to death. Instead of taking what appeared to be the speedy and safe way Paul turned back
again, called at Lystra, and tarried there, how long we
do not know; moved on to Iconium, tarried there, doing
definite and specific work; went back again to Antioch
in Pisidia, journeyed down through Pisidia, and stayed to
preach at Perga. From thence he took ship, and sailed
home.

The fact of this backward journey is significant. The
outward journey had been one of missionary enterprise;
it was the journey of a pioneer, the going into new terri-
tory, with a new evangel. He created division, bringing
the sword wherever he came, dividing cities and men into
two camps, believers and blasphemers, men full of jealousy, men filled with joy. Let us then survey this journey back; considering first the fact of that journey; secondly, its values; and finally, its consummation, as they
rehearsed to the Church all the things that had been fulfilled.

As we think of the fact of that backward journey, the
courage of it impresses us; and we are driven to enquire
its cause. First of all Paul went from Derbe, the place
of peaceful work, over the twenty miles of "wild and
dusty plain," to Lystra, the place of the stones. At this
long distance of time from the actual happenings we
are in danger of forgetting all the facts of the case. The
end of his previous work in Lystra is very briefly told;
they stoned him and left him for dead. So far as Lystra

was concerned, that was the end of his ministry. It is easily read, but to understand it a little exercise of the imagination is necessary. Twenty years after, the memory of that stoning was with him still: "Once was I stoned." Such an experience was one that undoubtedly left its stamp upon him physically, to the end of his days. The journey completed, Derbe being evangelized in peace and in power, there was the short way home through the Taurus ranges, by Seleucia, to Antioch. But he did not take it, he went back to the place of the stones, back to the place of the suffering, back to the places where the hatred of his fellow countrymen, and the opposition of the new men whom he was seeking to lead to light, had broken out into fierceness, where they had rained stones upon him, and left him for dead.

Then he went back still further forty miles, to Iconium. He had left that city in haste. There had been perils and dangers in Iconium from the first of his preaching there; and he had tarried a long while because of the perils and the dangers. At last his friends had discovered there was a plot hatching to end his life, and under their advice he left in haste. Because the plot had failed when he was there before, it was not at all likely that those men had lost their resentment.

Once again, he went still further back to Antioch, over another sixty miles, through all the perils of that strange and wild country of Lycaonia, among men of strange speech. That was the city from which, at the end of his ministry, he had been cast out. He had to leave Antioch because Antioch would have him no longer.

We cannot read this paragraph, then, without seeing the wonderful courage of this man and his little company. If there was no good cause for this backward journey, it was the courage of foolhardiness. Why did he thus go back? The answer is to be found in the discovery of what he did. He went back to Lystra to find the little group of disciples; back to Iconium to see those

who had believed; back to Antioch for the same purpose. He went back, confirming, exhorting, organizing.

Paul was driven back first by his consciousness of the
importance of the truth which he had declared, the great
Gospel of which he was not ashamed, which he knew to
be the power of God unto salvation. The first visit
through these cities had been that of proclamation; but
in all the things he had said there were implications
and applications, which it was necessary these early disciples should understand. He had passed through these
cities preaching two things supremely: first, the risen
Christ; and secondly, the possibility of man's justification
by faith in the risen Christ. These were great truths,
arresting men, compelling attention, constraining belief in
certain cases, and blasphemy in others.

But those who had been won by the words, constrained
by them, and had believed, did not understand the full
value of them. There were implications in the doctrines
of resurrection and of justification. If these little groups
of men, situated in an atmosphere so antagonistic to life,
were not to be overcome, and devastated, it was necessary that they should be instructed. It was his passion
for truth, and for its perfect understanding, that drove
him back over the way. When years later, from prison
he wrote the greatest of his letters—letters we had never
had humanly speaking, apart from the limitation of the
prison house—one thing he repeatedly said, in writing to
his children in this very region, in Ephesus, Colossæ, and
Philippi, was that the supreme passion of his heart for
them was always that they might have full knowledge.
Full knowledge makes faith mightier, and hope burn
more brightly, and love more profound. On the outward
way he proclaimed the central verities, and gathered men
in the first act of faith; but he went back, in order that
the truth might have its full triumph in the lives of those
who had believed.

Then he was drawn, not only by passion for truth

but by the fellowship of the saints. There in the cities were the companies, the assemblies, of separated souls. Think of those little groups in the different cities. In Lystra they had left the apostle for dead; but there were disciples there, among them probably Timothy. At Iconium was another group, so much alone, Jew and Gentile alike hating them. At Antioch were those proselytes of the gate, and those Hebrews who had dared to enter the larger life, very much alone. The lure of the lonely saints compelled him to turn his back upon the Taurus passes, and the quick way home, to tramp the long distances, that he might minister a new courage to them. And what courage he must have brought when he came and stood in the midst of that little group at Lystra, and they saw the brands of the Lord Jesus upon his face, the brutal bruising of the stones still there. I think the fellowship of the saints drew him the long way home again.

But we do not touch the deepest note until we hear one word falling from his lips in the course of his confirmation and exhortation. He charged them that they should " continue in the faith; and that through many tribulations we must enter into the Kingdom of God." The master passion of all his work is disclosed in the words: " the Kingdom of God." The way into the Kingdom of God was declared, it is the way of tribulation. The meaning of that declaration is not that through tribulations individual men enter into the Kingdom of God. It is rather that through tribulation we realize the Kingdom of God, set up the Kingdom of God. This man, in common with all the great seers of God, recognized that the Kingdom of God is already established, but needing to be realized. The Kingdom of God is established, and no man escapes it. We do not understand the buffeting of the tempest, and the mystery of the battle, and the strange perplexities in conflict of the saints as they march toward the ultimate; but we know that it is all within the

Kingdom of God. No army marches across the face of the world, but that He marshalls the battalions, and over-rules the movement. But to enter the Kingdom, and bring men into relation with it, to establish it in the world, to cast out the forces that spoil, can only be done through tribulations. Did not this man know now, as he had not known before, that the Kingdom of God was established through the tribulations of the Lord Christ Himself? Only through tribulations can God enter into His Kingdom, and realize it in this world, with its sin and suffering and sorrow. Paul himself had felt the stones raining on him at Lystra, the physical agony and the mental disappointment; but he knew that by the process of that pain, he was helping to establish the Kingdom. It was the passion for the Kingdom that drove him on the outward journey through perils oft. It was the passion for the Kingdom that drove him back with fine statesmanship and consecration, to strengthen the little companies of men, who in their turn, through trial and tribulation should coöperate with God for the establishment of the Kingdom. This was the courage of faith, and of a great knowledge; courage born of a true conception of the methods by which God would establish His Kingdom.

The values of that journey back to the Churches may be expressed in three words: confirmation, exhortation, and organization.

Confirmation means reëstablishment, or perhaps even better, further support. He went back to give further support to these Churches, to interpret to them the meaning of their life in Christ; a most important part of all Christian enterprise. Having seen the flaming glory, and heard the wooing winsomeness of the infinite music of the evangel of a risen Lord, and of justification, the young child of God must be taught the meaning of life in Christ. Paul went back to further establish, to support, to confirm.

But he went back for exhortation. He exhorted them

to continue in the faith. In those cities the seen things were antagonistic. Go back to Lystra, Iconium, Antioch in Pisidia, get right into the midst of the city, and look around, and you will see temples, idols, shrines, lasciviousness, lust, luxury. That is a description of all cities, ancient and modern. Cities never change. These people were living in the midst of these things. Oh, this lure of the near. How is a man to be victor over the things that can be seen and touched and handled, of which he is quite sure? By faith, which is the assurance of the unseen things. Faith is the venture that steps off the tangible; and in the doing of it, demonstrates to its own soul the reality of the intangible. Paul said to these men as he went back, Do not look at the seen things in Lystra, Iconium, and Antioch; continue in the faith. This is the great word that ever needs to be uttered for the establishment of Christian life. He exhorted them to patience in tribulation, because that was the way of victory.

Then organization. He appointed elders, or presbyters, in all the Churches, by prayer with fasting, in the company of the Church. Finally he commended them, Church and elders, to the Lord in Whom they had believed. This was the first organization of the Church outside the area of Judaism.

So far all the emphasis of the declaration has been upon the Church. Was there any value in the return journey to the apostle? That return journey, and all such return journeys, gave him an exposition of the very doctrines which he had preached. Paul did not study theology before he began preaching, but learned his theology as he preached. It was when he had seen the effect produced by the evangel on life that he knew what justification and sanctification really meant. Seeing the effect of the Gospel on the lives of men, he came to an understanding of its power and method; and it was after such observation that he was able to say, " I am not ashamed of the Gospel, because it is the power of God."

[352]

The return journey was thus also one of confirmation of his own Gospel. He saw its power, and was growingly convinced of its value. He was also confirmed in his purpose to continue in the great work.

I think there was also another value. When he had confirmed and exhorted and organized at Lystra, Iconium, and Antioch, and after he had preached in Perga, and reached Attalia, there emerged another value of the long journey home. Watch the progress of that little ship along the coast, to the north of Cyprus, and observe that man on deck, bruised and battered, weakened physically by the perils of the journeys, and the brutality and cruelty. Look at his eyes, sore eyes, weak eyes perchance; but eyes through which on that sea voyage there flamed the glory of a triumph. I think the quiet restfulness of that sea voyage was great gain. Thank God this apostle was a man, who knew the weariness of work; and there was great value to him in the longer journey by sea, as he took his way back.

One brief glance at the consummation of the journey. The Church at Antioch had commended him to the grace of God. They had sent him forth with Barnabas to the work whereunto the Holy Spirit had called them. There at Antioch they had waited for his return, and had prayed. At last he came back to them, the work fulfilled, and they awaited the report.

That was a wonderful meeting when the Spirit had said, " Separate Me Barnabas and Saul "; and the Church had separated them, and sent them on their way. This also was a wonderful meeting, full of expectation, and the glory of a new enterprise. The men they had separated are there; one of them is bruised and weakened; he is carrying the brands of Jesus in his body. What will they talk about? " They rehearsed." Did they tell about the difficulties, the stones and the bruises? Yes, but how did they tell them? Listen to the brief ring of triumph. " They rehearsed all things that God had done

with them, and how that He opened a door of faith
unto the Gentiles." Their view-point was that of the
Divine activity. Other things were out of sight, or set
in relation to it. But the supreme thing they said to the
Church was this, that " God had opened a door of faith
unto the Gentiles." That was the report.

As we close this meditation there is one sentence of
supreme value to all Christian men and women.
" Through many tribulations we must enter into the
Kingdom of God." The form and fashion of the tribulations change with changing years, but the principle
abides. The places of suffering are the places of power.
Lystra, the place of stones, is the dynamic centre. " I
will tarry at Ephesus until Pentecost; for a great door
and effectual is opened unto me, *and there are many adversaries.*" That is the reason why he stayed. The place
of power is where the adversaries are, and the stones,
and the tribulations. It is the process of tribulation that
brings the victory.

> " Far down the ages now,
> Her journey well-nigh done,
> The pilgrim Church pursues her way
> In haste to reach the crown.
> The story of the past
> Comes up before her view;
> How well it seems to suit her still,
> Old, and yet ever new!

> " 'Tis the same story still,
> Of sin and weariness;
> Of grace and love still flowing down
> To pardon and to bless:
> No wider is the gate,
> No broader is the way,
> No smoother is the ancient path,
> That leads to light and day.

" No sweeter is the cup,
No less our lot of ill;
'Twas tribulation ages since,
'Tis tribulation still:
No slacker grows the fight,
No feebler is the foe,
No less the need of armour tried
Of shield and spear and bow.

" Thus onward still we press,
Through evil and through good,
Through pain and poverty and want,
Through peril and through blood;
Still faithful to our God,
And to our Captain true;
We follow where He leads the way,
The Kingdom in our view."

Acts 15 : 1-35

This has sometimes been called the story of the first
council of the Christian Church. To that description of
the gathering in Jerusalem Farrar in his " Life and Work
of St. Paul " objected, for excellent reasons. He showed
that the council in Jerusalem was not a convention of
delegates, but a meeting of the Church at Jerusalem, to
receive a deputation from the Church at Antioch, and to
consider a subject of grave importance in the matter of
missionary enterprise. He pointed out moreover, that
this gathering in Jerusalem was for purposes of consultation, and not for final and dogmatic decision. Yet
it may be good to retain the name of council, if we would
understand what a council should be, and see wherein the
grave errors of many subsequent councils have consisted.

Almost all councils subsequent to the first have attempted to fix some habit of ritual, or to give final form
to the expression of some great truth. Neither of these
things was attempted in the gathering in Jerusalem.
The true function of a council as herein revealed, is that
of considering an immediate subject, and finding an im-

[355]

mediate application of principle. Nevertheless such consideration and such finding must necessarily have a most
important bearing on future development. When the
council met in Jerusalem, it gathered to consider a problem that was immediate, which was created at Antioch,
the new centre of missionary enterprise; a problem created by the arrival there of men of Judæa, who were
charging these new Gentile converts,—mark this most
particularly,—not that they should be circumcized; but
that unless they were circumcized they could not be
saved. The council met to consider this matter, to hear
the report of those who were sent by the Church at
Antioch; not in order to learn what the Church at Jerusalem had to say authoritatively and finally, in order that
it should be obeyed; but for purposes of conference, and
that the larger fellowship of Christian people might be
taken into account when facing so grave a situation.

Luke's picture must be interpreted by Paul's letter to
the Galatians. Without suggesting that either account
is untrue, it is quite certain that if they be read together
we shall catch a different tone. There is a touch in
Paul's account of the story, which reveals how keenly
he felt certain attitudes taken up toward him, even on
the part of the apostolic band. We cannot read Paul's
account of the council, and of its findings, without seeing that had they been other than they were, he would
not have obeyed them. He was not seeking the authority
of the Church at Jerusalem. He was not asking for an
expression of truth by James or by Peter, ex cathedra.
He was there for purposes of consultation; and had the
finding been one that put the Gentiles into bondage, he
would have broken with Jerusalem, and all the apostles,
in the interests of truth. There are evidences in his account of the story, of the fact that there was a good deal
of dissension, and difference. and argument, before finality was reached.

But when the history is read as Luke has recorded it,

then we discover not so much the details of difference, as the ultimate harmony of decision. The story becomes the more interesting when we recognize these two things; when we see that in the first assembly, and in subsequent discussions, there were very many differences, and some touch perhaps of bitterness. Yet at last, there came a great and holy and wonderful moment, when that assembly of Christian believers, with different opinions, after discussion, based upon a master-principle, were able to say, " It seemed good to the Holy Spirit, and to us."

Let us first observe the story of the council, and then attempt an application of its findings to our own day.

It is well that we should first enquire what the difference of opinion was, that gave rise to the council. When we have discovered it, we may consider the discussion that ensued, and finally look briefly at the decision arrived at. To get back into the atmosphere is to understand the naturalness of the difficulty. To the Jew, Christianity was the fulfilment and continuity of the old economy. Therein he was distinguished entirely in his mental attitude from the mental attitude of the new converts in Antioch, Iconium, Lystra, and throughout that district. The religion of Jesus Christ to the mind of the Hebrew believing into Him, was not a religion that destroyed the religion of his fathers, but fulfilled it. The religion of Jesus Christ had grown out of the religion of his fathers, was the continuity of one Divine movement. Paul's address in the synagogue at Antioch in Pisidia dealt with the great doctrines of the unity of God in order to capture the mind of the Greek; but he spoke also of the whole Hebrew movement, and saw its fulfilment in Christ and in His evangel.

But the new movement in Antioch of Syria was a movement not influenced by that tradition. Indeed, the movement at Antioch had not even an apostolic tradition behind it; it began with Christ, and the men of Antioch therefore were quite careless as to the things preceding, and had no interest in them.

Mark these differences. The Christian Jew, looking upon his Christianity as the direct outcome, continuity, and fulfilment, of the august religion of his fathers, came to Antioch and into all these cities; and found Greek Christians, who had no relation with the Hebrew religion or tradition; whose Christianity began in their knowledge of Christ. Immediately we see the naturalness of the difficulty. These men, many of them perfectly sincere, said that these Greek Christians could not be saved by beginning in the middle of a process; that it was not enough that they began with Christ. They must also be brought to everything that prepared the way for the Christ. They must conform to the law of Moses, and the ritual of Moses.

This difficulty was serious, for it was one which would be repeated in new centres. It would accentuate within the Christian fact, a conflict between Hebraism and Hellenism, which had been so profound and bitter in the years prior to that fact. When Saul of Tarsus was apprehended by Jesus Christ for a special purpose, it was the apprehension of a man in whom the two ideals of Hebraism and Hellenism met, in whom they had been at conflict until Christ found him, but in whom they were now merged into one great Christian mental attitude. He was Hebrew of Hebrews, but he was Saul of Tarsus. The idea of bondage and denial and sacrifice, was the idea of Hebraism; the idea of liberty and culture and the fulfilment of life, was the idea of Hellenism. In Christ he had found that through bondage men come into liberty; that through death men come into life; that through all that Hebraism stood for, men realize all that Hellenism suggests. That was the victory won in Saul of Tarsus. Now if through these new Churches in the midst of Hellenism, Hebraism was to reassert certain of its old rites, there would be cleavage in the Christian movement. That was the peril of the situation. If these teachers from Judæa had been victorious, then through those earliest years, lasting until now, there would have been division between the Hebrew Church of Christ, and the Gentile Church of Christ; and the bitterness caused by such division would have been mutually destructive, and the testimony of Christ to the world would have been lost. So that it was not merely a dispute about a rite or ceremony, but something far profounder that gave rise to this council in Jerusalem.

Before passing from this contemplation of the difficulty, having touched upon its naturalness and its seriousness, there is yet another element to be noticed in the danger that threatened the Church. Circumcision in the original purpose of God was ordained for the cure of self-righteousness. It was an outward and visible sign or symbol of the fact that this people was separated to God, and dependent upon God; that all they were, and were able to do in the world, arose from the activity and the government of God. At once we see wherein the Hebrew people in the process of the ages had entirely missed the meaning of the rite, for which they were now prepared to fight. Circumcision was now being made the instrument of self-righteousness. That which was intended to mark its destruction, or to indicate its absence, had become the sign and the cause of its possession. Circumcision, and all the rites and ceremonials of Hebrew observance, had become evasions of the true purpose of God; opiates by the use of which men drugged their souls to the clamant cry of righteousness. That is always the danger of ritualism. The religion of the most high God had been made subservient to the observance of external rites. Paul saw the peril of grafting a ritual on to the Christian Church, putting a rite or a ceremony in the place of essential spiritual life and communion. That was the inspiration of his anger and passion; and presently, of his strong and stern denunciation of Peter, when subsequently to the council, Peter went down to Antioch and dissembled. These were not small matters. They were fundamental matters. This was a difference involving the very genius of religion, as to the profoundest things of Christianity.

Concerning the discussion, the two passages, this fifteenth chapter of the Acts, and Paul's story in Galatians, are mutually interpretive. Evidently Paul and Barnabas were graciously received by the Church. Evidently also there was a private conference between Paul and Barnabas and the elders. That is admitted in the sixth verse of this fifteenth chapter, " And the apostles and elders were gathered together to consider of this matter." It is quite briefly stated by Luke. What happened in that conference we are not told, but it was a quiet and private conference. The deputation from Antioch in Syria consisted of Paul, Barnabas, and Titus, and perchance two or three others. The story of their reception is told in verse four: They " were received of the church and the apostles and the elders, and they rehearsed " in Jerusalem what they had been doing all the way. They told how they had left Antioch rejoicing in the triumphs won; they told the story of Perga and Attalia. Arrived in Jerusalem, they simply rehearsed the triumphs of the Gospel, they did not raise the difficulty.

In the Galatian letter Paul is careful to state what happened at this point. In the second chapter and second verse he says, " I went up by revelation; and I laid before them the Gospel which I preach among the Gentiles, but *privately* before them who were of repute, lest by any means I should be running, or had run, in vain." That is Paul's account of what happened when the apostles and the elders were gathered together with the deputation, the church not being present. Paul laid before them, not the story of his triumphs, but his Gospel. At the first reception he rehearsed the story of all God had been doing in the district; but to that smaller select company, he rehearsed the Gospel, he told what he had been preaching, he went over the ground of the truth he had been proclaiming.

Having discussed his Gospel with the apostles, and having, as we learn in Galatians, won the approval of Peter, James, and John, the church assembled again; and there followed the discussion in the council. In this there are three things to notice: first, the address of Peter; secondly, the address of Barnabas and Paul (which was the speaker it is impossible to say, for the speech is not reported); and finally, the address of James.

Peter contributed two things to the discussion: a fact, and a deduction. The speech of Peter is not that of the theologian. He was not arguing about a doctrine. He was not entering into the delicate and difficult discussion as to rites and ceremonies. Peter, bold, blunt, and magnificent, said in effect, Here is a fact, and here is a deduction. The fact was that God had sent him to the Gentiles, and gave to the Gentiles in the house of Cornelius the Spirit of God, "making no distinction." The deduction he made was that they should not tempt God. On the sin of tempting God there is light in the history of the Old Testament; there is light in Hebrews and in Corinthians; and supremely there is light in the temptation of our Lord in the wilderness. To tempt God is to refuse to follow His guidance. Said the tempter to Jesus, "If Thou art the Son of God, cast Thyself down"; and Jesus said, "Thou shalt not tempt the Lord thy God"; that is, thou shalt not refuse to wait for His guidance and direction, thou shalt not initiate adventures in order to see whether or not He will help in circumstances which are not of His will. Said Peter, Here is the fact, God has already given the Gentile all grace without ceremony, ritual, rite, and observance. Here is the deduction: do not be afraid to follow God, even though He seems to be breaking through things dear to our heart; do not tempt God, by refusing His guidance.

Paul and Barnabas simply rehearsed, saying in effect that Peter's fact had been multiplied by facts throughout all these cities. They had been sent by that Church in Antioch, upon which some men now would superimpose a bondage and a yoke, through Seleucia, and Cyprus, from Salamis to Paphos, from Perga in Pamphylia into the new Antioch in Pisidia, away on through Iconium and Lystra, to Derbe; and everywhere facts had been multiplied, God had given the gifts of grace, and the gift of the Spirit, without rite and without ceremony.

The final speaker was James. He first referred to Peter's fact, admitting it, reëmphasizing its importance and value. " Symeon hath rehearsed." He then showed how Peter's fact, and the facts of Paul and Barnabas were in perfect harmony with prophetic foretelling. He quoted the great word from the prophecy of Amos, in which it is predicted that through the triumph and restoration of Israel the Gentiles also should receive blessing;—a prophecy not perfectly fulfilled even until this hour; to be fulfilled undoubtedly, in the economy of God; —a prophecy fulfilled in principle on the day of Pentecost when that little Hebrew community became the true Israel of God; and immediately following, when the prophetic promise was fulfilled in the experience of the Gentiles. Then James said, " Wherefore my judgment is, that we trouble not them." Before proceeding to consider the judgment, note the particular emphasis of that word. To translate quite literally, James said, " Wherefore I decide," or " I think "; and we must interpret the word *decide* by the word *think*. Much has been based upon that " I decide " of James. It has been said that he was the bishop of Jerusalem, that he was in authority over the Church in Jerusalem; but there is not a vestige of proof in the narrative itself, and for the traditions that have gathered round the story, I am bound to say I have no respect. It has been pointed out that the pronoun " I," " *I* decide " is emphatic in the Greek. An emphatic pronoun depends after all upon the tone and emphasis. The emphatic *I* must be interpreted in harmony with the rest of the New Testament and the Bible. It is absurd to believe that James at this moment gave his personal opinion as the final word, from which there could be no appeal. He, the practical man, the writer of the epistle, the brother of the Lord, spoke last; and in his speaking gave with due reserve, and with a consciousness of the importance of the views of others, his strong opinion. The very emphasis on the I shows that he was only expressing a personal conviction. Nevertheless with that opinion the Church agreed. The decision to which they came was not the decision of a man. It was such a decision that when they registered it and wrote it and sent it to Antioch, they did not say, After consultation, James, the bishop, speaking ex cathedra, has decided. They said something far more full of dignity, " It seemed good to the Holy Spirit and to us."

The decision was first of all characterized by unanimity. It was the expression of the conviction of the apostles and the elders and the Church; and the secret of the unanimity was that of the presidency of the Holy Spirit in the assembly. " It seemed good to the Holy Spirit and to us."

The terms of the decision may be stated in other language, because this record is so much the language of that particular time. The decision immediately was that they would not trouble the Greek Christians any further, but that they charged them concerning things they were not to do. The decision for all time was first, that no ceremony is needed to make men Christ's; and secondly, that observances are necessary on the part of men who are Christ's. They would not trouble them further, would not harass them, crowd them, jostle them, press them, put them into difficulty, with habits and observances which were not essential to salvation,—the things of ritual. Nevertheless they charged them that being

Christ's men, they must observe the attitudes and habits of loyalty to His moral standards; they must abstain from the pollution of idols, from fornication, from things strangled, and from blood. Such were the decisions.

What then were the results? They may thus be summarized: rest in Antioch; and a period of preparation for future work. This council came between the first and second missionary journeys of the apostle, and constituted a necessary pause, the passing of a difficulty that had risen, its settlement once and forever, so that whenever Judaizing teachers in days to come should pass through that district and teach these doctrines, they would be known as not having apostolic or Christian authority. It was an important decision, one that affects the whole history of the Church from that moment unto this.

In conclusion, what are the applications of this story to ourselves? There is something we do well to consider in the method of the findings. The supreme word flames with light upon this page: " It seemed good to the Holy Spirit and to us." It marks a progression or development from a centre to something external. Communion with Christ by the Holy Spirit lies at the very root of that word. The second thing is the outcome of the first; that of the unity of the Church by the Spirit. The final thing is that of the unanimity of the Spirit and the Church. There will never be unanimity unless it be based on unity. There never will be the realization of unity save in response to a fundamental union; a union between the members of the Church and the living Lord by the Holy Spirit. This picture of the council in Jerusalem is that of a company of men and women, sharing the life of Christ, desiring only to know the mind of the Lord, having no selfish views for which to contend. These are the conditions upon which it is possible for any such assembly to say, " It seemed good to the Holy Spirit and to us." The Church does not seem to be able to say it to-day, either a local church, or the great councils of the

Church. We must freely admit we very seldom hear this language. We do read that a matter was carried by an overwhelming majority, but that is a very different thing. An overwhelming majority often leaves behind it a minority disaffected and dangerous. We shall come to unanimity when we are prepared to discuss freely, frankly, our absolute differences, on the basis of a common desire to know the mind of the Lord. If we come to a meeting of diaconate or Church, a Christian council, having made our minds up that so it must be, then we hinder the Holy Spirit, and make it impossible for Him to make known His mind and will. But if we come, perfectly sure in our minds, but wanting to know what the Lord's mind is, then ere the council ends, to-day as yesterday, the moment will come when we shall be able to say with a fine dignity and a splendid force, It seems good to the Holy Spirit and to us.

If that be the lesson of the method of the findings, what is the message of the findings? What has this council of the long ago to say to us to-day? Its first lesson is that the Christian man and the Christian Church is free from the bondage of Hebraism. There is a sense in which we are not influenced by Hebraism. There is a sense in which Judaism makes no appeal to us. Therefore to state the principle in other words: nothing is necessary to salvation, other than faith in Christ, and consequent life in the Spirit; neither baptism, nor the Lord's Supper, nor the observance of any ordinance, or ceremony. Let us decide as did this council, that we will trouble men no further, that we will no more insist upon this rite or that ceremony in order to salvation.

The second lesson is that of the necessity for bondage to the law of the Spirit of life. There must be, on the part of all Christian souls, abstention from the haunts and the habits of idolatry; abstention from many practices, not in themselves unlawful, in order to a testimony of separation; and the observance of the laws of humanity.

[Acts 15: 36-16: 10]

These Gentiles must abstain from things strangled, and from blood. That was not Hebraism. That was not the law of Moses. It was said long before Moses. In the covenant of God with Noah, when humanity started out again upon a new movement, the law was given. So for these Judaizing teachers, James' quotation was one full of wisdom. He stepped outside the Hebrew economy, and referred to the laws that regulated human life, apart from Hebraism, and said these people were to observe the human law.

So the findings of the council which have perpetual application are those of freedom from rites and ceremonies as means of salvation; observance of all habits that mark us as separate from idolatry, and from the practices of idolatry; and devotion to the Divine ideal of human life, and to the keeping of the laws for the well-being of human life.

Acts 15: 36-16: 10

It is quite evident that there is a gap in the history between verses thirty-five and thirty-six. The last words in the previous paragraph declared that " Paul and Barnabas tarried in Antioch, teaching and preaching the Word of the Lord, with many others also." That gap is supplied by a brief paragraph in the Galatian letter (2: 11-21). Peter visited Antioch, and when he came, acted in the true spirit of the findings of the council, in that he sat at meat with the Gentiles, making, to use his own words, " no distinction." Evidently a little later on there came down from Jerusalem men influenced by the Judaizers. When they came, they were not told of the dispute, but Peter—to use Paul's very strong word— " dissimulated," in that, in the presence of these men he ceased to eat with the Gentiles. Against that activity, in which Barnabas evidently sympathized for the moment, Paul made the vigorous protest recorded in the Galatian passage. The ending, however, was evidently one of peace. Rebuked by Paul, the dissimulation of Peter ended, and no bitterness remained in the heart of either.

When the difficulty was settled, and the future line of action was clearly defined, Paul began to prepare immediately for further journeyings, and work. The subject of supreme interest in the second missionary journey of Paul is that of the invasion of Europe. Once again the circle widens, and we see the apostle crossing the boundary line into Europe. The call of the man of Macedonia was answered, and the evangel carried yet further afield.

In this paragraph we finally reach Troas, full of historic interest; Troas on the coast line, washed by that sea which, at its other extremity, touches the Continent beyond; Troy, the historic battleground between Europe and Asia. The story of those battles we have read in Homer and in Virgil. It was to that point the great apostle came at the end of the present paragraph.

That invasion of Europe was not in the mind of Paul, but it was evidently in the mind of the Spirit. He did not start from Antioch on this second journey with any intention of going to Europe. The closing words of the paragraph read thus: " And when he had seen the vision, straightway we sought to go forth into Macedonia, concluding that God had called us to preach the Gospel unto them." That little word " concluding " is full of interest and value. It marks the ultimate result of processes. Paul began the journey by desiring to revisit churches already founded. He ended at Troas with a vision, a surprise, a new call, an open door, and vast expanses stretching out before his eyes, of the possibility of new work, and with the conviction that this was the mind of the Lord.

The period of time covered by this paragraph (15 : 36–16 : 10) must have been considerable; but in reading the condensed narrative of Luke, it is evident that everything leading up to the vision was tentative, preliminary, and that some greater movement was ahead. The " conclusion " referred to in the final words was the result of all the preceding incidents.

An analysis of the passage brings into prominence certain separated incidents of personal experience. There is the story first, of contention and of the separation between Paul and Barnabas. Then follows the account of how Paul started on his journey in the comradeship of Silas, and found Timothy at Lystra. Then we have the record of a further movement, on to Troas, and we see Paul and the man of Macedonia. The supreme value of the paragraph, however, is to be found in synthesis, rather than analysis. When we look at these separated incidents in the light of certain declarations concerning the guidance of the Holy Spirit, we shall see the strange and contradictory and troublesome events merging into a mosaic, until the pattern stands clear and beautiful upon the page, of the Divine overruling and the Divine government.

Let us therefore consider the paragraph in these two ways, glancing at the incidents of human experience, and endeavouring particularly to observe the unifying Divine guidance. This is the great value of this paragraph. There is something full of conflict here. The smooth and rhythmic movement of the earlier part of the book for a moment seems to end. Here are cross-currents, and difficulties, dissension between two men whose union had been one full of value, and force. Then purposes were frustrated, intentions thwarted; Paul wanted to revisit those cities to which he had already been with Barnabas; but he never reached them on this journey. He did visit cities where the Gospel had been preached, but not the cities where he had founded churches. Instead of following a course through Perga and Pamphylia, he was driven through Syria and Cilicia. When presently, that work being accomplished, he crossed through the Taurus ranges, and came to Derbe and Lystra, then he fain would have moved in a certain direction, but the Spirit hindered him, and drove him yet another way. When again his face was set toward the northern country of Bithynia, and he would have evangelized there, the Spirit again drove him in another direction. The sweep of the river is troubled, but it moves forward in the counsel of God. The spiritual value of the paragraph is evidently that of its revelation of the guidance of the Spirit of God, by the hindrances of the people of God.

To glance at the incidents first. It was Paul's purpose to return to the cities already visited, to see how they fared. Concern for his children was in his heart, but infinitely more than that. He had concern for those churches because they were centres from which the Gospel was to be sent yet further afield. It was an eminent teacher who once said that he would rather perfect one saint to the work of ministering, than call hundreds of people to the beginnings of Christian life. This man also felt the enormous importance of making the Church what it ought to be in any given centre, in order that the Church might fulfil its true function in that centre. The underlying passion of the apostle was not merely to see his brethren, but to see how the churches fared, because of his conception of the importance of their work. As they were about to start, there occurred the contention between Paul and Barnabas; and we must not smooth this down and say that it was a quiet discussion. The Greek word translated " contention " is the word from which we derive our word paroxysm. I am greatly comforted whenever I read this. I am thankful for the revelation of the humanity of these men. If I had never read that Paul withstood Peter to the face, and that Paul and Barnabas had a contention, I should have been afraid. These men were not angels, they were men. It is very interesting to study the differing opinions as to who was to blame. There are most eloquent defences of Paul and of Barnabas, as to who was right, and who was wrong. Amid differing opinions, a man may have one of his own. My own sympathy is entirely with Barnabas, notwithstanding the fact that the Church at Antioch sent Paul and Silas out by the grace of God; and the account does not say that they gave a benediction to Barnabas and Mark. Perhaps they were both right. Paul was severe, because Mark had failed them once, and he felt that no man could go to this work, who having put his hand to the plough had looked back. Mark had gone away from them when their faces were set toward the difficulties of Perga and Pamphylia. He had not gone with them to the work. Barnabas felt that Mark should have another chance. Perhaps there is a sense in which Paul and Barnabas were both right. Mark profited by the actions of both. Mark sailed away to Cyprus with Barnabas, and they pass out of the story in the Acts of the Apostles. We do know something more of Mark. When he had been with Barnabas some time, he was restored to Paul's fellowship; for when Paul wrote to the Colossian Church, he spoke of him as his " fellow-worker," commended him to the Church; and in his last hours, besought that Timothy would bring him with him. The last thing we know about Mark, the " servant of Jesus," whom Paul for a time would not trust, but to whom Barnabas gave a second chance, is that it was he who wrote the Gospel of the perfect Servant. Perhaps his moral courage was stiffened by Paul's severity, and confirmed by the tenderness of Barnabas.

Paul now went forward to the churches of Syria and Cilicia. We have had no account of the planting of any churches in Cilicia. Tarsus was the chief city of Cilicia. Paul may have planted them in those years before Barnabas found him. At any rate he went there now, confirming the churches of Cilicia.

So we reach the second incident. It is evident that Paul moved away from Cilicia, from Tarsus, through those Taurus ranges, and went to Derbe. It is difficult to measure the journeys by time limits, but it was probably five years since he was at Derbe, the place of peaceful evangelism, at the end of a troublesome campaign. No details are given.

At last Paul came to Lystra, the place of the stones, the scars of which were still upon his body; the memories of the day when they beat fast and furiously upon him were still with him. At Lystra he found Timothy. How often God's servants return, after years of absence, to some rough and rugged place of battle, and of blood, and of agony, and find the fruitage. When did Timothy become a disciple? The question cannot be answered dogmatically, but the probability is that he became a disciple in those days of Paul's previous visit. Paul had once been a young man, and had watched the stoning of a saint called Stephen, minding the clothes of such as stoned him. He had heard the dying prayer, and the vision of the face of Stephen had fastened like goads in his heart and life. At Lystra he had gone through Stephen's experience; and perchance another man had seen the stones hurled. Now he went back to find Timothy in the place of stones, and from that moment there was formed that rare and beautiful friendship, the friendship of an old man for a young man.

Timothy was the son of a Jewess. His father was a Greek. We have seen how in all this movement, the ideals of Hebraism and Hellenism were merged and fulfilled in the teaching of Jesus. Paul had now found a man in whose very blood the two fires mingled, in whose mental calibre the two ideas were found, a man by nature at once Hebrew and Greek; and by grace he was well reported of by the brethren. From that moment a companion was found for Paul; and he was found at Lystra, the place of the stones.

We know certain facts concerning his service. Two of Paul's letters were addressed to him. Six of Paul's letters have this man associated with him in the superscription, those of the second epistle to the Corinthians, Philippians, Colossians, the first and second letters to the Thessalonians, and Philemon. Timothy was with him on this second missionary journey. Timothy was at Ephesus with him in the days of strife. Timothy accompanied him on his last journey to Jerusalem. Timothy was with him in his first imprisonment. For Timothy he sent, in the loneliness of the second imprisonment. He became his son, his child, his comrade in the fight, and so the stoning of years ago now blossomed into this great benediction of a new comrade in the work that lay before him.

So they passed on. Here we might dwell upon the apparently strange act of Paul in taking this man Timothy, and submitting him to the rite of circumcision. Notice carefully what immediately followed. After the rite Timothy and Silas went with him through the churches, taking the decrees of the council at Jerusalem, which provided that the Gentiles were not to be compelled to submit to circumcision as necessary to salvation. This is surely an illustration of the wonderful adaptability of this man. Paul has been criticized for this action, but I do not believe that such criticism is justified. This was a case of expediency, in order to the fulfilment of ministry. Paul knew that the Jew would criticize. Very well then, not for his sake, but for the sake of his becoming all things to all men, if by any chance he may win some, let this man who had been brought up in the Hebrew religion, submit to the rite of the Jew, and so create his opportunity for speaking to the Jew also.

So we come to the last incident, and to the things immediately preceding it. Paul was prevented from preaching by the action of the Holy Spirit. He would have preached in proconsular Asia, one of the provinces, and he was prevented. The Holy Spirit forbade him. He therefore turned in the other direction, and went through the region of Phrygia and Galatia. That was the beginning of the work in Galatia. In the Galatian letter, in chapter four, we have the account of how he first came to preach in Galatia: " Ye know that because of an infirmity of the flesh I preached the Gospel unto you the first time." Luke says the Holy Spirit forbade him preaching in Asia, and he preached in Galatia. Paul says because of an infirmity of the flesh he came first to Galatia. In this letter we have that which was local and incidental. In Luke's account there is the recognition of the government and driving of the Spirit. It is not necessary for us to imagine that Paul heard the voice of the Holy Spirit forbidding him. That was not the method of the Divine government or guidance. The local and the incidental fact was some affliction, some illness, which made it impossible for him to travel through proconsular Asia, and which turned him aside, perchance for rest and quietness, with the issue that he preached in Galatia.

Then presently they again moved forward, and their hearts were set on Bithynia, where they fain would have preached. Then the phrasing alters, not that they were forbidden by the Holy Spirit, but by the Spirit of Jesus. This was not another Spirit. It is but another way of referring to the Holy Spirit. The truth declared is that these men, in fellowship with Christ, simply could not go to Bithynia. They were driven on. There are many who will understand this story from their own experience. Paul wanted to preach in Bithynia, but somehow he could not. The Spirit of Jesus drove him on. There seemed no value in this long journey, striking west. The north was luring him. Bithynia with its scattered tribes, was there. He would fain preach, but he could not. So he was driven west, until he came to Troy. There was given to him the vision of a man of Macedonia, and at Troy Luke joined him, for there the language of the narrative passes from the singular to the plural. Paul saw the vision, and straightway hastened toward Macedonia. I sometimes wonder whether Luke was not the man of Macedonia,

[373]

whether he did not come to call him, and ask that he would join him. I do not deny the vision. Peter saw a vision, and then saw the real man. Perchance the vision of the night was granted to this man at Troy, and then came Luke the actual man. Now the whole journey was explained. The new door was opened. Such are the incidents.

I think we shall miss the value of the story entirely if we commence with the declarations of the guidance of the Spirit. When Luke wrote the book he put in those declarations, and he was quite right; but if we get back into the actual atmosphere of this paragraph we shall surely see Paul strangely puzzled. Quarrelling with Barnabas, parting from him, he wanted to preach the Gospel; and so he passed through Syria and Cilicia, and came to Derbe and Lystra, and there he met Timothy. Then he fain would go on to proconsular Asia, and he could not do it; he was sick, he was ill, an infirmity of the flesh was upon him; and he could not go on. It was necessary that he should take another direction, and he went into Galatia, and preached there. Then he turned back again. There was no reason that he could understand. It is a picture of cross currents, of difficulty, perplexity, and darkness. Then he felt the lure of Bithynia, and he would go there. No, he must go west, and on he went, perplexed. Then came the vision of the man of Macedonia; and when he talked it over with Luke in other days, and Luke would write the story, he told that which at the moment he did not know. The Spirit forbade him preaching in Asia. The Spirit of Jesus drove him ever and ever on toward Troas. Thus upon the paragraph there is stamped first the fact of the guidance of the Holy Spirit. The fact for us is demonstrated by all that follows—Philippi, Thessalonica, Berœa, Athens, Corinth. All these resulted. If this man had preached in proconsular Asia, had gone up to Bithynia, what of Philippi, what of Thessalonica, what of Berœa, what of

Athens, and what of Corinth? The guidance of the Spirit was subsequently recognized by these men.

Notice too, that the declarations concerning the driving of the Spirit, and the guidance of the Spirit, are put in at the points of supreme difficulty, where the guidance of the Spirit conflicted with their own intentions. Here is a wonderful outlook on life. A man can look back and say: There was the point where I desired to go a certain way, and circumstances prevented. But these men say the Holy Spirit prevented. Here was a moment when I was moved to a service that drew me north, and I could not go; something forbade me. But these men say, the Spirit of Jesus drove me against my own inclination.

The supreme value of this story is its revelation of the fact of the guidance of the Spirit, when there is no revelation of the method of that guidance. In our attempt to interpret what seems to be the supreme value, our only peril is lest we try and explain the method, whereas as a matter of fact the method is hidden.

How far can we see the method? Only so far as to know no method is revealed. The Spirit overruled the separation between Paul and Barnabas. With what issues? The separation gave two missionaries for work, for their revisiting of the churches, and the regions beyond. The Spirit guided through Paul's illness, which necessitated his taking another direction. The Spirit guided by the consciousness of this man's fellowship with Jesus, so that he was driven in that fellowship in a westerly course. The Spirit guided by the vision of the man of Macedonia. Here is the revelation of the fact that the Spirit guides, not by flaming visions always, not by words articulate in human ears; but by circumstances, by commonplace things, by difficult things, by dark things, by disappointing things. The Spirit guides and moulds and fashions all the pathway.

The important thing, however, is that the man whom the Spirit will guide is the man who is in the attitude in

[375]

which it is possible for the Spirit to guide him. So we look again at this man, and we find an attitude of life revealed. It is that of loyalty to the Lord, faith in the guidance of the Holy Spirit, and constant watchfulness. There is where we too often fail. It is when a man is in fellowship with the Lord that he sees that the disappointment and the difficulty are also under the guidance of the Holy Spirit. It is the watcher for the Lord who sees the Lord. If we make up our minds that the way of guidance is the way of flaming vision, and rolling thunder, and an articulate voice, and a lifting to a height of ecstasy, then we may never be guided. But if we are watching for Him, we shall find Him guiding us in the day of difficulty and the day of disappointment, and the day of darkness; when it seems as though the rhythmic and majestic flow of the river has ceased, and we are in cross currents, and are tempest-tossed. The Holy Spirit forbade proconsular Asia, by permitting the apostle to be so sick, that he had to travel another way. What we need then, is confidence in the guidance of the Spirit in the hours when no voice is heard, and no vision is seen. If we will follow then, the hour of vindication will come, there will come the vision, there will come the man of Macedonia. His voice will be distinctly heard, and then we shall conclude that God would have us go into Macedonia. Then we shall understand the strange experiences. Why does He drive us west when we would go north? I do not know. At the limit of the west so far as land is concerned, a man of Macedonia came to him. Then he understood the denial, the pressure, and the disappointment, and why he could not go to Bithynia.

The beauty of this paragraph for us is that it presents conditions with which we are most familiar. It shows how the Holy Spirit guides still in the line of the Divine purpose, even when we see no supernatural sign. Faber sang a song of truth that he is the greatest of victors who knows that God is on the field when He is most invisible.

Whether it be that the individual life is filled with sorrows, or whether the perplexity of life is overwhelming, or whether the strife of national crisis is about us, God's in His heaven, and He is overruling and guiding, and out of the chaos He is bringing the cosmos. The Spirit leads men and women who look and watch and wait and follow. It was a time of groping and uncertainty. Ways which they desired were shut against them. It was a time of direction and a time of certainty. The route was marked in the economy of God to Troas, to Macedonia, Philippi, Thessalonica, Berœa, Athens, Corinth. If Paul had gone to Bithynia he might have stayed there. Oh, to go, not where I may choose, even by my love of the Lord, but where I am driven by the Lord's command. Circumstances of difficulty are opportunities for faith, and the measure of our perplexity in service and in Christian life is the measure of our opportunity. Let us follow the gleam, though the darkness threaten to envelop. Let us be true to the inward monitor, and if in being true, suddenly illness prevent, and we cannot follow, then rest in the Lord in the darkness, and know that God's shortest way to Troas may be athwart our inclinations and purposes. It is better to go to Troas with God, than anywhere else without Him.

Acts 16: 11–24

This paragraph constitutes the first page in the history of all that resulted from the strange method of the Spirit in preventing and hindering, and so guiding Paul. Immediately following the vision of the man of Macedonia, Luke says: " Setting sail therefore from Troas, we made a straight course to Samothrace." " A straight course " is a nautical phrase, meaning quite literally, sailing before the wind. The voyage occupied two days only, because the wind was with them. A little later on, we shall find that this same voyage occupied five days, against a contrary wind. Sometimes upon the King's business, **the** wind is with us, and sometimes it is against us.

Beginning with this statement, we find that the contrast to everything in the last study is remarkable. We have seen this man hindered, perplexed, driven, buffeted, and the first word now is that " we sailed before the wind." Thus the wind blowing ever where it listeth, coöperated with that Spirit of Whom it is the symbol, in driving the missionaries on. The change in method and experience is marked, but it is the same Spirit Who perplexed and hindered him, and so gave opportunity for the activity of faith, Who is now seen coöperating, even in the direction of the wind, as it drives these men along the pathway of the Divine appointment.

This consciousness that the very forces of Nature were helping the purposes of grace, must have illuminated for these men the mystery of those strange days in which they were so thwarted and hindered. So they came to Samothrace, an island of the Ægean, and so they came to Neapolis, the port of Philippi. From thence they passed to Philippi itself, a journey of about eight miles, full of historic associations, and at that time remarkably suggestive of the new atmosphere into which Paul was coming with this Gospel of Jesus Christ. There at Philippi were evidences, some of them remaining even until this hour, but then most patent, of that great, decisive epoch-marking, historic-making battle between Brutus and Cassius on the one side, and Mark Antony and Augustus on the other; the battle in which Augustus had defeated Brutus, and had planted in Philippi a colony. Luke, in dwelling upon these details, refers to them suggestively when he says Philippi was the first city of Macedonia, and a colony. We are not to understand that Philippi was a colony in our sense of the term. A Roman colony was founded by colonists sent immediately from Rome; who marched in and took possession. Having **arrived, they** reproduced Rome **in miniature, that is, so**

[378]

far as its government and habits of life were concerned. A colony protected Rome on the frontiers of the empire. It was in perpetual and close touch with Rome, because its magistrates were appointed, not from among its citizens, but immediately from Rome.

Thus Paul found himself nearer than ever before to the great centre of earthly government. This man was himself a Roman citizen, and looked with longing eyes toward the capital, desiring to reach it and possess it. He said, " I must see Rome also "; and his desire to see Rome was not the desire of the tourist, it was the passion of the missionary. It is noticeable how in his missionary journeys, he perpetually settled at strategic centres, places from which the roads ran out into far distances. That was his reason for desiring to reach Rome. He knew that from Rome the great highways ran throughout the whole known earth; and this dreamer of dreams, seer of visions, this man who by nature was a maker of empire, saw the importance of capturing great centres for Christ, not merely that they themselves might be Christianized, but because from such centres, the pioneers, the missionaries, the messengers of Jesus, might reach wider areas.

Paul arrived in Philippi about twenty years after the foundation of the Church at Jerusalem, after the Pentecostal effusion. How little the world knows of the Divine movements. Rome had small idea that day, that the van of the army of its ultimate Conqueror, had taken possession of one of its frontal defences. On the day when Paul hurried from Neapolis, over the eight miles up to Philippi,—and came into the city, and made arrangements for his own lodging, and with the quiet dignity and restfulness that always characterizes the great worker, was content to spend a few days doing nothing,—the flag was planted in a frontier colony of Rome, which eventually was to make necessary the lowering of her flag, and the change of the world's history. That is what happened when Paul, with Luke, and Timothy, and perchance

Silas and a few others, arrived that day in Philippi. If
Rome and the world did not know, to put the whole
truth bluntly, the Lord knew, and the devil knew, and
the present study reveals the respective results of these
two facts.

The story centres round two women, Lydia of Thyatira, and the maid of divination. It is one of two remarkable victories won by the forces of Jesus Christ, under
the guidance of the Holy Spirit, in the interests of the
Kingdom of God. The first victory was the capture of a
vantage ground, the open heart of one woman. The second victory was the vanquishing of Satan along two
lines of attack. His first method was that of an attempt
at alliance with the forces of Jesus; and he was overcome. His second method was that of direct and brutal
hostility to the soldiers of Jesus; and again he was overcome. These are the only two methods of which the
devil is capable; first an attempt at alliance, and then
antagonism.

First then, as to this capture of the vantage ground.
The occasion was the Sabbath day. Before that, Paul
and his companions had tarried certain days. There is
great force in the word " tarrying." It means that they
rested, quietly observing, and doing nothing else. With
the dawn of the Sabbath they sought for the place of
prayer, turning, as Paul always did, to seek for his
brethren after the flesh. In this statement we have an
important revelation of the condition of Philippi. There
was no strong Hebrew element in the city. The " place
of prayer " is a technical phrase. Jewish places of
prayer were found throughout all these cities, where no
synagogues were built. They were almost invariably
placed by the side of a river; sometimes they consisted of
a circle enclosed by some kind of wall, and yet under the
open sky; sometimes without any outward sign of en-
closure. That was " the place of prayer," and there, in
cities where no synagogue was built, the Hebrews

gathered on Sabbath for prayer. That is the great significance of the opening verse of the one hundred and thirty-seventh psalm:

> " By the rivers of Babylon,
> There we sat down, yea, we wept."

That is the picture of the exiled Jews gathering to the place of prayer. We discover clearly the position of the Hebrew people in Philippi, in the fact that Paul found only women at the appointed place. There were not even ten Hebrews of eminence, or there would have been a synagogue. There was, however, a little group of women, recognizing their relation to God, gathered to the place of prayer in Philippi, the centre of idolatry, under Roman rule. There the apostle of Jesus Christ sought and found vantage ground for the carrying on of his campaign.

The woman whose heart was opened was a woman of Thyatira, which was one of the cities that he was compelled to omit as he passed on to Troas. The first convert which Paul made in Europe was a woman of Asia, a Jewish proselyte perhaps, or a woman of true Jewish blood, who had been born in Thyatira. She was a business woman in Philippi. If we had desired to open up missionary operations in a Roman colony, should we have found such vantage ground as that? God is always surprising us when He is about to do some great and wonderful work.

In that assembly of women Paul spake, and that again is an arresting fact. Paul was a Pharisee, who through the long years of his early life had daily repeated such words as these, " O God, I thank Thee that I am neither Gentile, nor slave, nor woman." The man who presently wrote, " In Christ there is neither Jew nor Gentile, bond nor free, male nor female," thus contradicted the false view of the thanksgiving that had passed his lips for years. He now abandoned the Jewish and Pharisaic

[381]

contempt for a woman. The apostle of Jesus Christ found no man in the place of prayer, but the old contempt had gone, and to the women assembled, he spoke. He dared to do so because the Gospel had changed his intellectual conception, and entirely transformed him.

Then we read that the Lord opened the heart of Lydia, constraining her to attention. He touched the emotional nature of this woman, and Lydia listened and obeyed. She thus became the Lord's vantage ground in Philippi, the point from which He could proceed with His campaign. The opened heart of one woman in a great city is foothold for God, and if it but be yielded wholly to Him, from that vantage ground, from that base of operations, He can proceed to wonderful victories.

Lydia constrained the apostle and his company to accept her hospitality, and the word " constrained " is peculiarly Luke's word. It only occurs in one other place in the New Testament, and that is in his Gospel, in that matchless story of the last chapter, of the two who walked to Emmaus; they constrained Jesus to stay with them. They said, The day is far spent, come in, and abide with us. They offered Him hospitality, saying to Him in effect, Here is an open house for thee, O stranger, abide with us, the day is far spent, the road stretching beyond is one infested by robbers, let us take care of thee till morning. This is the same word, suggesting hospitality offered. So a house was opened to Jesus in Philippi. Christ needs vantage ground in Philippi, on which He can stand, and proclaim His evangel, from which He can send His messengers forth to capture the city, and all the region beyond, for Himself. He finds a woman's heart, and a woman's home. The victory may not seem a very great one. But turn to the Philippian letter, and note two or three verses:

" I thank my God upon all my remembrance of you, always in every supplication of mine on behalf of you all making my supplication with joy, for your fellowship in furtherance of the Gospel from the first day until now " (1: 3).

What was that first day? The day when Lydia's heart was opened.

"Ye yourselves also know, ye Philippians, that in the beginning of the Gospel, when I departed from Macedonia, no church had fellowship with me in the matter of giving and receiving, but ye only; for even in Thessalonica ye sent once and again unto my need " (4: 15).

What happened then? There was gathered in Philippi a fellowship of souls, that Paul always seems to have looked upon as the chief joy and crown of his ministry. The church in Philippi was evidently most dear to him. Thus in Philippi there was a growing fellowship of faithful souls, a base of operation widening and broadening, ever helping this man with his work. This began when Lydia's heart was opened, and she opened her home for Jesus Christ. Do not miss the naturalness of these stories, the homeliness of these records, for in these things the infinite value of them is found. We are told sometimes to-day that the Church is full of women, that there are no men going to church. I contradict the statement whenever I hear it made. But the measure in which it is true, is the condemnation of men; and let the men who are becoming Christless and Churchless lament if the hour should ever come when their women cease to worship. The women whose hearts are opened, whose homes are open, are ever Christ's vantage ground. That was the first victory in Philippi.

Immediately following, we have the account of the victory over Satan, in the deliverance of the damsel possessed with the spirit of divination. Her will was possessed by an evil spirit, and therefore she was possessed by mercenary men who were making use of her

THE ACTS OF THE APOSTLES
for their own enrichment. Following Paul, this maiden
cried out: " These men are servants of the Most High
God, which proclaim unto you the way of salvation."
Now what she said was absolutely true. Paul, Luke,
Timotheus, Silas, perchance a few others, had arrived in
the city. They had proclaimed the evangel to a handful
of Jewish women in the place of prayer. One woman,
and perhaps a few others, had obeyed. Suddenly this
girl, possessed with the spirit of divination, soothsaying,
and sorcery, began to follow, and what she said in the
hearing of the crowd would necessarily impress the
crowd. The devil was then using the one weapon that
is really dangerous against the Church of God. When
the devil tells the truth about the Church a peril is
created; and it is, that she may accept his testimony, and
hope to win victories thereby. What a chance there
seemed to be in this for Philippi. It was a little commonplace to have to go to the river-side, and talk to a handful of women. Here was a girl with a spirit of divination, who had been soothsaying, and men by crowds had
listened to her. She was telling the truth now. Why
not let her continue? Truth must win, whoever utters
it. That is the master lie that has cursed the Church of
God for nineteen centuries. The apostle refused this
testimony. A strong word, a word throbbing with agony
is used here: He was " sore troubled," and his trouble
was caused because the girl was telling the truth, and
because the same Spirit of Jesus Who drove him toward
Troas, was with him still. In the Gospel narratives—
by Mark at the beginning of the ministry of Jesus, and by
Luke at a later stage—it is recorded how demons told
the truth about Him. " Thou art the Son of God " said
the demon, when all men were denying it. On each occasion Jesus commanded the demon to silence, ordering
him out of the man; exorcising the evil spirit; refusing
the testimony when uttered by a demon. Paul was now
in fellowship with Jesus, and he knew Philippi well, and

recognized that this was the devil's method of alliance. If the devil can once be permitted to coöperate, he will tell the truth. But the apostle, and the Lord of the apostle, will not accept the testimony of evil, even though its words be the words of truth. A grave error in the history of the Christian Church has been that she has been content, again and again, to admit the testimony of evil men, because the testimony in itself was true. God will have no testimony of truth which is not spoken by those who are true, for behind the method there is a motive, and the motive is not that of helpfulness, but of destruction. Admit the devil into the fellowship of this propaganda of the Gospel, and ere long he will twist his fingers round the Gospel and distort it, until it becomes a deadly and damnable heresy. Has he not done so? Is not that the story of all that has cursed the Church, and hindered her progress in the ages? It requires a man strong in fellowship with Jesus Christ, to decline the testimony of truth, simply because it is uttered by the spirit of evil. It is possible to hear the mutterings of demons in London. One can consult them, sometimes in places set apart for the business. Do not make the foolish mistake of imagining that there is nothing in spiritualism. Do not say that there is no message from the unseen and hidden world. There are such messages, but they are the messages of hell; and even though they be the messages of truth concerning Jesus, they are not to be listened to. We are to refuse the patronage of hell, when it attempts to tell the truth about our Christ. Alliance with evil is the most subtle peril that confronts the Church at any time. The hour of gravest peril for the Gospel in Philippi was not the hour when they put Paul in prison; it was the hour when the damsel with the spirit of divination told the truth. In fellowship with the Lord, he immediately exorcised the evil spirit.

Then immediately the devil adopted the method of antagonism, and passed out of sight, but he was still there.

He was now active behind the world, and the great secret is blazed upon the holy pages of inspiration, "the hope of their gain was gone." Immediately these men, when the hope of their gain was gone, because the damsel was free from the evil spirit, and could no more be a soothsayer, became hostile. They did not come out into the open, and say, You have robbed us of money. They said, "These men, being Jews, do exceedingly trouble our city." They did not care for the law. They only cared because the hope of their gain was gone. Satan, defeated in his attempt to form an unholy alliance with the apostles in order ultimately to weaken them, hid himself behind the law, and breathed through the spirit of law.

Again the devil was defeated. The devil is always defeated when he imprisons a Christian man. That is the hour of his defeat. The place of the cross is the place of the crown, to a servant of Christ. When the devil and the world combine to persecute a Christly soul, they put him on the throne of power. We shall see more of that when we return to this story of Philippi. Put Paul and Silas in the prison; let the lictors lay the stripes upon them until they are bleeding and bruised and brutally treated; give them to an inhuman jailer, who will heap upon them indignity, until he puts them into the inner prison, and puts their feet in the stocks! Then what? Listen, do you hear the singing? Or presently, when Paul reached Rome, as a prisoner, what did he do? He hired a house, and preached the Kingdom of God in the centre of Rome's imperial magnificence. Or bring him back to Rome a second time, and put him in the prison, down in the deep dungeon. Deny him the privilege of the hired house, and what will he do? He will write letters, the thunder and the force of which will reverberate through centuries, and make an empire mightier than the empires of earth. Or put John Bunyan in prison, and he will see visions, and write of celestial truths, and celestial glories, which will abide with the

Church, messages second only to the messages of the Bible. What a fool the devil is! How slow he is to learn the lesson. He does learn it every now and then, and goes back to the only way in which he can ever hope to be successful, that of alliance. That is his successful method to-day. The devil of the middle ages was a being with horns and hoofs and flaming fire, at which we smile to-day. But he is not dead, he has not gone out of business. He is not imprisoning us now. He does not imprison men where the light of the Gospel is shining. His business here is that of alliance, and the supreme trouble with the Church of God is that it is not quite strong enough to say to the devil: Hands off, we will have no testimony that patronizes Christ. We want no patronage of Christ, but submission to Him.

Looking again at the paragraph as a whole, we notice the small beginnings of great movements. A woman's heart opened, and how wonderful the victories which followed. Do not let us be looking for the highway of God in the conspicuous places. While men are building their monuments to Brutus defeated, and singing over the glory of Augustus, the Christian apostle is making his way up to Philippi. He will have to pay for his lodging for two or three days, and presently one woman will have her heart opened, and will believe his message. This is the place where God is acting. Where is God acting to-day? I do not know, and I am not going to attempt to find out, but God helping me, I will try and be a man at His disposal. It may be from something I say that some woman's heart will be opened, that she will presently be the prophet for whom we are waiting, the pioneer for the further campaigns of the army of the King. Do not let us be enslaved by statistics. We know nothing. One woman's heart in Philippi, and Rome was doomed to lower its flag, that the banner of the Cross might be supreme.

The devil's methods of opposition are those of alliance

and antagonism, and the only serious one is the first.
Let us beware of it. Do not let us imagine that we can
take into our fellowship and enlist under one banner,
men who simply affirm truth about Jesus, unless in their
own lives there is an absolute loyalty to the Lord Christ.
Antagonism is the creation of force for the Kingdom of
God. Put a man in prison for Christ's sake, and the
earthquake will surely follow, and the work will spread.

Acts 16: 25-40

In this paragraph we have an account of Paul's first
work in Europe. He and Silas were fulfilling that ultimate command of Jesus, " Ye shall be My witnesses."
We are tracing a great movement, and therefore are not
merely interested in that which is local. There are three
matters of interest in this new beginning; first, the witnesses and God; secondly, the witnesses and the jailer;
and finally, the witnesses and the magistrates.

The three pictures merge into each other. In the first
we see these two men in prison, worshipping and praising,
that is, the witnesses in their relation to God. Then immediately we watch them in their method with the jailer
and in the issues following that method. Finally we see
them in their dealing with the magistrates in Philippi.

They were in the inner prison, their feet fast in the
stocks. They had been publicly whipped, and were
bruised and lacerated. It is only as in sympathetic imagination we see these men as they were, that we can at
all understand this story.

With that background in mind, we are immediately
arrested by their occupation. They were praying and
singing hymns. The translation here may mislead us.
There is no suggestion of petition in the word here translated " praying." It is the word which indicates the attitude of adoration and of worship. We are not warranted in believing that these men were asking for anything at this moment, for the word " praying " is im-

mediately qualified by the word "hymning," which we have rendered "singing" hymns. These were exercises of spiritual joy. Again remember the surroundings. They were in the inner prison, dark and deadly and dismal; their feet were fast in the stocks, so that there would be no physical comfort through the hours of darkness; the smart and pain and agony of the rods of the lictors were still with them. Yet they were worshipping in the singing of hymns; engaged in the exercises of spiritual joy.

The other prisoners were listening. The sound of the singing had reached others than themselves. The Revised Version helps us here. It does not say, as the Authorized Version did, that "they prayed and sang" as though they did so once. They were praying and singing; it was a continuous activity, and the prisoners were listening. The word "listening" here is the strongest possible. They were attentively listening.

What hymns were these men singing? We cannot tell. Perhaps some new hymn of the Church, perhaps some ancient psalms. Whatever the songs were, the prisoners listened attentively, marvelling surely that prisoners in an inner prison, with feet fast in the stocks could sing at all.

Then immediately came the earthquake, the opening of prison doors, and the events following.

The revelation of supreme value to us in the story is that first of the power of Christ to overcome the bitterness of difficult circumstances. It was not a song of deliverance that these men were singing, but the song of perfect content in bondage. That is the supreme marvel of the Christian consciousness and the Christian triumph. Any man can sing when the prison doors are open, and he is set free. The Christian soul sings *in* prison. I think that Paul would probably have sung a solo, had I been Silas; but I nevertheless see the glory and grandeur of the spirit that rises superior to all the things of difficulty and limitation. Madame Guyon spent ten years of her life in French prisons, from 1695 to 1705. Here is a song she wrote in prison:

" A little bird am I
    Shut from the fields of air;
And in my cage I sit and sing
    To Him Who placed me there;
Well pleased a prisoner to be
Because, my God, it pleaseth Thee.

" Nought have I else to do;
    I sing the whole day long;
And He Whom most I love to please,
    Doth listen to my song;
He caught and bound my wandering wing,
But still He bends to hear me sing.

" Thou hast an ear to hear;
    A heart to love and bless;
And, though my notes were e'er so rude,
    Thou wouldst not hear the less;
Because Thou knowest, as they fall,
That same, sweet Love, inspires them all.

" My cage confines me round;
    Abroad I cannot fly;
But though my wing is closely bound,
    My heart's at liberty.
My prison walls cannot control
The flight, the freedom of the soul.

" Oh, it is good to soar
    These bolts and bars above,
To Him Whose purpose I adore,
    Whose providence I love;
And in Thy mighty will to find
The joy, the freedom of the mind."

I think that is the kind of song they sang in the prison at Philippi; not a song of deliverance, but a song of content. Content with perfect, unfettered, and unbroken fellowship with God. "They prayed and sang hymns unto God," and they knew, as Madame Guyon knew later, that He listened, and that the song was music in His ears. That is the supreme triumph of Christian experience. We cannot shut a Christian man or woman out from fellowship with God; and therefore when such an one as Paul goes back again to prison presently, no longer in Philippi, but in Rome, and back again to the Roman prison a second time; in all his letters referring to his imprisonments, he never spoke of himself as a prisoner of Rome, or of Nero, or of an emperor. He was always the prisoner of Jesus Christ. It is this consciousness of fellowship with God, which creates the song.

The story not only reveals the power of Christ to overcome the bitterness of difficult circumstances, but also the power of Christ to deliver, where such action will tend to the accomplishment of His purpose. The earthquake— whether caused by the touch of His hand upon the earth, shaking it, until the staples left the walls, and the chains hung loose, and the doors were opened; or whether merely in His overruling, coincident with their need of liberty, matters nothing;—was the means of their being set free. The prison fails to imprison. When presently this man was imprisoned again in Rome, he did the mightiest work of his whole life. Not even his missionary journeyings are to be compared with the marvellous influence resulting from the writing of his letters, and the finest and the most wonderful of them were letters written in prison.

So down the centuries the story is always the same. When Satan attempts alliance with Christianity he puts Christianity in grave danger; and there the Church needs to be most on her watch-tower; but where Satan is antagonistic, he puts the Church under a debt to him, for he but helps her,

THE ACTS OF THE APOSTLES
[Acts 16: 25-40]

"Like Moses' bush she mounts the higher,
To flourish unconsumed by fire."

We turn, however, from this matter of the witnesses in
their relationship to God, triumphing over difficulties, to
glance at the witnesses in their dealing with the jailer.
He appears before us as a man brutalized, quite careless
of their wounds, when they were delivered to his charge.
Plunging them into the inner prison, he added quite unnecessary brutality in making their feet fast in the stocks;
and all this without one touch of emotion, without one
thought of them, without any care for their suffering; for
mark this, he went to sleep, and it required an earthquake
to waken him. The picture is graphic enough; it is that
of a man so brutalized that prisoners smarting from the
Roman rods can be handed over to him, and he will not
minister to their need, but will thrust them into the inner,
deadly, dark prison, and fasten them in the stocks, and
chain and lock and bolt doors, and then himself go to
sleep.

The earthquake followed, and then we have this man's
panic and his plea. There was a certain amount of brutal
heroism about him, heroism in keeping with the atmosphere of the day in which he lived. When he awoke,
hardly knowing what had happened, seeing the opened
prison doors, and fearing that the prisoners had all
escaped, he attempted suicide. With the brutal, animal
heroism that marked the age, he would take his life,
and escape the penalty from others.

Then it was that a voice sounded out of the darkness,
"Do thyself no harm: for we are all here." It was the
quiet voice of the man who a little while ago was singing.
The jailer had not heard the song. He was asleep. Now
what did he say? He said "Lords,"—"Sirs" is our
translation but it is exactly the same word that Paul used
a little later when he said, "Believe on the *Lord* Jesus."—
It was the supreme term of respect, and he was con-

scious of the fact that he was in the presence of his superiors. "Lords, what must I do to be delivered?" There was no evangelical faith in this. He did not mean, What must I do to be eternally saved? He had not got nearly as far as that. It was fear, panic; and his own solution of his difficulty was suicide; but the voice of the apostle said, "Do thyself no harm, for we are all here"; the prisoners have not escaped as you imagine. Then filled with fear, he went into the presence of the men, one of whom could so speak to him, and bowing down, he said, "Lords, what must I do to be delivered?" He was simply a man stricken with panic, and wondering what was the next thing. The evangelical values were coming, but they did not come out of that poor panic-stricken heart. They came in answer to its cry, from the great apostle: "Believe on the Lord Jesus, and thou shalt be saved." All the evangelical values are in that. The infinite music of the Gospel is thrilling through it like an anthem. This man did not understand it, not even then; but it was an answer to be explained. You have called us lords; believe on the Lord Jesus Christ, the only Lord of human life. You have asked what you shall do to be saved, and your feeling is one born of fear, and desire to be saved from this hour of difficulty. Believe on this Lord, and you shall be saved from this hour, and from all hours of difficulty.

Then "they spake the word of the Lord unto him, with all that were in his house." Here was a man arrested, and the great apostle is seen taking time to teach him. It was Voltaire who said, speaking of philosophers, "We have never cared to enlighten cobblers and maidservants. That is the work of apostles."

Thank God it is! There is the supreme difference between all philosophy apart from Christ, and the Christian evangel. Paul, just between midnight and the first flush of dawn upon the sky, took time to teach that brutalized jailer, the man who came in an unworthy panic, saying,

[393]

" Lords, what must I do to be saved? " The answer came quick and sharp, and vibrant with music that the listening man knew not of: " Believe on the one Lord Christ." Then he got this man, with all his house, and he taught them, he told them the story, and revealed its meaning, and made its application. It is a picture for all time. Philosophers do not care to enlighten cobblers and maidservants; but apostles never speak of cobblers and maidservants. They speak of men and women in the image and likeness of God; and it is always worth while to spend time with them, to explain to them the mightiest things of the universe. That is the picture of Christianity. There is the beginning of the Christian movement in Europe, so far as Paul was concerned. He was an apostle, with a mind mightier than that of Voltaire, and while his back was still bleeding and bruised and unwashed, he took time to teach that man.

Was it all worth while? Read the story to the end, and look at the man. See what he did. He washed their stripes, he took them up into his own house, the place where he lived over the prison. The marginal reading here is a little more accurate, if a little more blunt: " he spread a table before them." That reminds us of what God does, " Thou preparest a table before me in the presence of mine enemies." This brutalized Philippian jailer is doing what God does. He washed their stripes and spread a table before them. That is the one, final, unanswerable argument for Christianity. That is the Christian miracle. I see the jailer in Philippi, washing their stripes, who but last night had plunged them into the inner prison, caring nothing for bleeding wounds, and who went to sleep till the earthquake woke him. It was not the earthquake that produced this result. It was that patient teaching, and the consequent belief into Jesus Christ, so that the very life of God possessed his soul, and he began the activities of God, the activities of the eternal compassion.

But the apostle had not yet finished his work. There was further instruction given to the whole household, and there was the sacred and initial rite of baptism administered to the whole household. Then they rejoiced, having believed in God.

Concerning the action of the magistrates the next morning, there is nothing in the story to tell us the reason of what they did. It may be that the rumour of the earthquake and the open prison doors had reached them, although that is hardly probable. It may be that they had come to the consciousness during the night that they had overstepped the mark in beating these men; for it is wonderful what an effect a night will have upon a man, and how differently in the dawning of the morning the action of the day before will appear. We do not know, but this we do know, that with a touch of contempt they sent a message, " Let *those* men go." The phrase " those men " seems to indicate contempt. It appeared an easy way out of the difficulty; when law had been violated, and righteousness wronged, just to send the men away.

Will this Christian apostle go? Will he say that his citizenship is in heaven, and that he has no interest in the State? Will he say that it is not his business to resist evil, and go out quietly? Nay, he had not so learned Christ. Mark the consecration of his Roman citizenship by his Christian citizenship. He refused to allow the magistrates who had violated law an easy way of escape. " They have whipped us publicly, uncondemned, being Romans." That was the sharp, clean-cut, incisive declaration of wrong committed by the civic authorities. Every phrase was an indictment: " whipped us publicly; uncondemned; men that are Romans." We are not to be lightly set free. Let them come themselves, and bring us forth. Let their apology be as public as was the wrong they inflicted. I do not believe that Paul was standing on his own dignity, or seeking the vindication of his personal rights. He might have done that long before. When the whips were falling upon him, he might have said, I am a Roman citizen, but he did not use his rights to save himself. Now for the sake of the Christian citizens in Philippi, for the sake of the little community of believers there, he drew attention to the wrong done, and insisted upon it that magistrates shall not violate law with impunity. It was the assertion of the fact that if the Christian needs to render to Cæsar the things that are Cæsar's; then Cæsar must render to the Christian citizen the things that are of right and of truth. There was a fine dignity in this attitude of the apostle, the dignity of service to the Christian community, and to the city itself; the refusal to stand in the presence of violated law, without solemn protest.

Mark well the sequel. The magistrates came and besought them to come out, and to leave the city. But they did not immediately leave the city. They were quite willing to coöperate with the powers that be, in quelling disturbance. And so, with leisure, and at their pleasure, they left the city, after they had visited the house of Lydia, and comforted the brethren. By the form of the narrative it is evident that Paul left Luke behind him here, for from this point Luke in his story speaks of the company as " They " until in the twentieth chapter we find that he had rejoined them.

Thus Paul's work in Europe was commenced. These witnesses were men with messages to deliver to Lydia and a handful of women, and also to a brutalized jailer, with whom philosophers will take no time. Theirs was the great experience of joy that triumphs over prison, and sings at midnight. The Christian campaign was that of delivering the messages, and conserving the victories. The Christian conscience inspired the correction of the magistrates when they violated law, and created conditions in which it was possible that there should be perfect freedom for the worship of God.

Look at Europe to-day in spite of all its desolation.

Think incidentally of her architecture. Blot out the temples erected to the worship of Christ, and what remains? Go into her picture galleries, and destroy the paintings inspired by the Christian fact, and what will be left? Go into her halls of music, and destroy all that is inspired by the story of the Messiah, and how much is left that is worth while? Examine her literature, and destroy all that has been made possible, and inspired by the Christian movement, and what will abide? Those are all incidental things. Essentially the measure of Europe's freedom is the measure in which she has obeyed the principles of Christianity. The measure of her purity is the measure in which she has obeyed the word to the jailer, " Believe on the Lord Jesus Christ, and . . . be saved." The chains and wrongs that abide remain because she has been disobedient to the heavenly vision. The work is not accomplished, but it is the same great work, and we have the same evangel. We can only carry it as we have the same consciousness, and as we realize that when the day is darkest, and the prison bars are firmest, then is the day for song, for God cannot be overcome ultimately by the things of evil.

Acts 17: 1-15

In our previous study we considered the first victories of Christianity through Paul in Europe, those won in Philippi. In this paragraph the movement is carried forward. Through trial and persecution, it was necessary for the apostle to leave Philippi. In all probability leaving Luke behind him there, Paul travelled a hundred miles to Thessalonica, and on the way passed through two cities, apparently without preaching or bearing any testimony. He went through Amphipolis, which was a military station, a journey of three-and-thirty miles from Philippi, and through Apollonia, thirty miles still further; until he came to Thessalonica, seven and thirty miles further yet.

[Acts 17: 1-15]

One wonders why he passed through Amphipolis and Apollonia. Perhaps on the human side the most probable answer is that there were no synagogues in those towns; and even though Paul's mission was now distinctively to the Gentiles, he still observed the invariable rule of preaching to the Jew first, wherever he came. All that, however, is merely speculation. In the passing of these cities we recognize the constantly varying guidance of the Spirit of God. One is growingly impressed in our study of the book, that we cannot tabulate rules or regulations as to spiritual conduct therefrom. Underlying principles are revealed on every page, and in every movement. Matters of supreme, permanent, and abiding value to the work of the Church and the Christian missionary, and the testimony of the Word, are revealed by the apparently most accidental and unimportant events. Things upon which we in this age are apt to lay great emphasis are either wholly absent, or perpetually changing.

In this paragraph then, the story of the work in Europe gathers round two places, Thessalonica and Berœa; and in each it is the same story of triumph and travail, which we beheld in Philippi, and which we have observed in the whole of the apostolic work.

Let us first study the story; and then let us gather certain lessons therefrom of permanent value and immediate application.

There is a difference between these two places, not merely between the Jews inhabiting them, but between the two places themselves, Thessalonica and Berœa. Thessalonica was on the highway; Berœa was on the byway. Thessalonica was on the ordinary route of travel. Having landed where Paul did, and calling at Philippi, Amphipolis and Apollonia were practically in a direct line of march along the great and well-known Roman road, and so also was Thessalonica. Berœa was on a byway. It is an interesting fact which Farrar records, about Cicero, when he tells us that:

THE ACTS OF THE APOSTLES

". . . In his passionate philippic against Piso, he says to Piso that after his gross maladministration of Macedonia, he was so unpopular that he had to slink into Thessalonica, incognito and by night; and that from thence, unable to bear the concert of wailers, and the hurricane of complaints, he left the main road, and fled to the out-of-the-way town of Bercœa."

That is an interesting fragment of profane history, but it illuminates this story. To Thessalonica Paul came, and he came, not slinking in, but quite openly and definitely. By night he quietly escaped from Thessalonica, and as Piso had done, he went to an out-of-the-way place, off the main line.

Therefore in this paragraph we have the revelation of triumph and travail upon the highway of a definite line of progress; and have the account of triumph and travail on the byway, in the unexpected place; the place to which it would appear Paul did not come for the specific purpose of missionary enterprise, but for an escape into solitude for a little from the persecuting spirit of the Jews.

Paul first paused at Thessalonica. He went to the synagogue of the Jews. What wonderful fidelity to principle is manifested in this fact. Think of all that we have already considered, of his experiences in those Asian cities on the first missionary journey. He had gone in town after town, first to the Jews; sometimes he had to turn, with determination and proclamation from them to the Gentiles because of their hostility. All the persecutions that followed this man through those Asian cities were due to the Jews. Here was a new beginning. He had left behind him that first chapter of his work. He had followed the vision of the man of Macedonia. He had crossed from Troas to Philippi, and at Philippi where there was no synagogue, he had gone to the Jewish place of prayer by the river. What an opportunity for breaking a tradition that had been so costly to him. Having followed that method throughout the cities of Asia, he was now in Europe, and remembering the persecutions of the past, he might have avoided them by going straight to the Gentiles. But he who presently wrote his Roman letter, and called God to witness that he had continual sorrow and heaviness of heart for his brethren after the flesh, went even in Thessalonica, in spite of all the experiences of the past, to the Jew first.

So we find him in the synagogue, and that for three Sabbaths. His messages therein were taken " from the scriptures." That of course means the Scriptures of the Old Testament. There was no New Testament in the hand of the apostle as he went on his journeyings. Whether there were any of the Gospel narratives extant, as authentic stories, who shall tell? The Scriptures that he would use in the Jewish synagogue would be the Scriptures of the Old Testament. The words " opening and alleging," reveal his method. The word " opening " here is Luke's word, only occurring in one other place in the New Testament, and that in his Gospel the twenty-fourth chapter, when he records that Jesus, after His resurrection, opened the Scriptures to the men walking to Emmaus. Paul now did exactly the same thing in that synagogue in Thessalonica. The word simply means making plain, expounding, giving an exposition. " Alleging " is a word which may mislead, and while this is a technical matter, we must nevertheless note it, for it is important. The word does not mean stating dogmatically. It means setting out in order, and displaying. Paul took up the Scriptures, and opened them, and explained them; and he did so by a sequence of arrangement, laying out before them the relation of this part to that, and of that to the other; of the law to the prophets, and of the law and the prophets to the hagiographa, the psalms, or devotional writings.

Two facts he declared in that synagogue. He first declared that according to their Scriptures, Messiah must

suffer and rise. Taking up the Old Testatment, he showed
them that their own Scriptures declared that their own
Messiah must die and rise again. That was the first burden
of his teaching. The order in which it is stated here reveals to us the fact that before he told the story of Christ,
he made them see what their own Scriptures taught about
their own Messiah; and this was exactly what the Jew
had entirely failed to grasp, or had completely forgotten.
With the ancient prophecies in our hands, with the one
prophecy of Isaiah for instance, it seems as though it were
impossible for men ever to have studied them without
seeing that the pathway of the Servant of God toward
His triumph must be that of travail; but the Jew had
failed to see it. There were in those days interpreters of
the prophecies, scribes and teachers, rabbis, who had discovered a difficulty, and who were teaching that two
Messiahs would come for the fulfilment of the ancient
ideal; one who should be a suffering Messiah; and another
who should be a Messiah winning battles, and establishing the throne. That view possibly lurked behind John's
question to Jesus upon one occasion: "Art Thou He that
cometh, or look we for another?" It did not reveal John's
ignorance of the prophetic writings, but his familiarity
with them, and his sense of difficulty. While he had declared Jesus to be the Christ, he heard of no mighty manifestations of power by which the sceptre should be
wrested from the Roman government. He had expected
to hear of these things, and in prison he thought to himself, Are these rabbis right after all? Must there be two
Messiahs? "Art Thou He that cometh, or look we for
another?" Is there to be a second? That was, I think,
the meaning of his question.

Paul's work was now to declare to these Jews that the
Scriptures taught that the Messiah must suffer, and that
He must rise again. One wonders what particular passage he took, whether the prophecy of Isaiah, or those
still more mystic and profound words in Hosea. Could

he possibly have omitted that sixteenth psalm, which Peter on the day of Pentecost definitely quoted as applicable to the resurrection of Jesus?

" Thou wilt not leave My soul to Sheol;
Neither wilt Thou suffer Thine holy One to see corruption,"

and which Paul himself quoted at another place? Or did he do that which his Master did, after resurrection; commencing at Moses and the prophets and the psalms or hagiographa, open to them the whole of the Scriptures? Be that as it may, we know that the first part of his work was to show these people what their own Scriptures really taught, that their long-looked-for, and hoped-for, and longed-after, and waited-for Messiah, must die and rise again.

Then he declared that the One Who fulfilled that portraiture of their ancient Scriptures was Jesus Himself. He preached to them concerning the Kingdom, for they charged him with preaching another King, one Jesus, and when he wrote to the Thessalonians, he comforted them because they were suffering for their loyalty to the Kingdom principle. He preached the Kingship of Christ, and showed Him to be Messiah to the Jews. The revelation of Paul's method in Thessalonica is that the true understanding of the Old Testament Scriptures must issue in proof of the Messiahship of Jesus. So he presented Christ to them.

There was triumph in Thessalonica. Some of the Jews believed, convinced against their prejudice; devout Greeks believed in numbers, convinced without prejudice; and some of the chief women, attracted by the new light that flashed from this great evangel upon them, who were so largely without light and without hope, were also persuaded. The words here " were persuaded," signify convinced by the argument of the teacher. They consorted with the apostles, joined the community, and in that hour we see the birth of that Church in Thessalonica, to which two letters were presently sent by Paul.

But the work in Thessalonica was not one of triumph only. It was one of trial, springing out of the jealousy of the Jews. The word " jealousy " is a very awkward word here. It should read springing out of the *zeal* of the Jews; for it is the very word that Paul used concerning them in his Roman letter, " I bear them witness that they have a *zeal* for God, but not according to knowledge."

These Jews stirred up " certain vile fellows ";—if we would translate in the actual language, which is somewhat colloquial,—they stirred up the loafers of the market-place, gathered a multitude, and caused an uproar.

The charge brought against these preachers was first a charge of revolution, but in its form it is a wonderful revelation of the victories already won. " These that have turned the world upside down are come hither also." The central charge, however, was that of high treason against Cæsar; that they were preaching " that there is another King, one Jesus."

With the result we are familiar. The apostle left Thessalonica; but the victory there must be measured by the Thessalonian letters. It became a centre from which the Gospel sounded out through the whole region, even after the apostle had left; and the Thessalonians themselves are revealed in his description, " Ye turned unto God from idols, to serve a living and true God, and to wait for His Son from heaven." Paul and Silas were sent away. Jason the man into whose house the apostle went, the man whom they arrested, and bound over to keep the peace, helped the apostle to escape. He was a man of Thessalonica; we know him by just a few graphic touches, for we never hear of him again, except perchance he may be referred to in the sixteenth chapter of Romans as Paul's kinsman.

So they passed to Berœa, and there again to the synagogue of the Jews they came. Undoubtedly the process

of preaching was identical, but notice the difference.
These people were more noble than those in Thessalonica,
in that they searched the Scriptures daily, examining
them, sifting the evidence. In what did their nobility
consist? We generally say in reading the story, that
they were more noble in that they manifested greater
readiness to receive. That is so, but in what did that
readiness consist? In that they were determined to find
out. It was not quick belief that made them noble, for
they were sceptical; but their scepticism was accompanied by determined anxiety to find out. The noble
hearer is not the man who immediately says Yes, to the
interpretation of the preacher. The noble hearer is the
man who appeals again and again to the Scriptures themselves, to find out if these things be true. I sometimes
think that the great advantage that the Berœans had was
that they lived on the byway, and not on the highway.
We who live in cities come to strange conceits, that all the
intelligence is in the cities. By no means. Some men
have an idea that to preach in a London pulpit is the most
difficult thing. It is by no means necessarily so. Among
the mountains of Wales, and in the highlands of Scotland, are men and women who will make the preacher
preach as it is by no means necessary that he should always do in London; men who will get their Bibles down,
and say, Is this man right? That is nobility. It is not
the nobility of readiness to believe anything. It is the
nobility of being determined to find out if human interpretation is in accord with the actual Scripture. Paul interpreted the Scripture before the Berœans, and they
listened with a sceptical and honest enquiry, a determination to seek and know and examine, and they made the
Scriptures the test of the interpretation. It is an interesting fact that the word used for the belief of those in
Thessalonica is not the word used for the belief of those
in Berœa. The root significance is the same, but in the
very difference of the words there is a shade of meaning.

The Revisers have changed the word in the case of the Thessalonians. With a fine accuracy they render it that those in Thessalonica were persuaded, and that those in Berœa believed. The word used of those in Thessalonica means persuaded by argument. The word used of those in Berœa means that fullness of belief which is not only persuasion by argument, but full spiritual apprehension. The men who were not so noble, needed persuasion, and came into belief on the ground of persuasion; but the men who sifted for themselves, and were sceptical, came to find a larger faith their own.

Then we may expect that these men more noble, in the out-of-the-way, quiet village, Berœa, will become a great company, and we shall hear much of them later on. There is never a word! And we might imagine that Thessalonica, with its faith following upon persuasion, would never be heard of again! But it was not so. There are two letters sent to the Thessalonians and Paul declared that the Word sounded out from them through the whole region. Does that mean then that the Church in Thessalonica was a finer one than that in Berœa? By no means. Often the people and the churches about which least is said are the mightiest.

The story of this paragraph is but a continuation of the whole book. Every page reveals the relation between travail and triumph in the Christian campaign. This great movement with which Paul is now so closely identified, commenced when the persecution in Jerusalem broke out, and the witnesses were scattered from Jerusalem, through Judea and Samaria. Out of the travail came the triumph; but triumph produces travail. Every new victory is a new baptism in blood. Every new victory is a new era of persecution in some form. But travail always leads to triumph, and so the ceaseless cycles run; triumph unto travail; travail back into triumph. Let the principle be applied to our own lives. The measure of our triumph in work for God is always the meas-

ure of our travail. No propagative work is done save at
cost; and every genuine triumph of the Cross brings
after it the travail of some new affliction, and some new
sorrow. So we share the travail that makes the Kingdom
come.

We notice also the value of the Scriptures in the Christian campaign. The method of the preachers at Thessalonica is the method of the preacher for all time. The
one work of preaching is the opening and alleging, or
displaying of the teaching of the Scriptures about Christ;
the presentation of Christ as fulfilling these Scriptures.
At Berœa we learn the true attitude of the hearers. Two
things are stated: they heard, that is the open mind; they
examined, that is the mind of caution. Those are needed
to-day. First, the open mind. God have mercy on us if
we have closed the mind, so that no new light can come
in. But God have mercy on us if we open windows and
doors to anything that claims to be light. There needs to
be the cautious mind. "Take heed how ye hear."

The final note of the paragraph is its revelation of the
lines of victory in the Christian campaign. What are the
most difficult conditions with which preachers have to
deal? Religious prejudice and religious pride. What
are the most hopeful conditions as here revealed? The
heart and mind open, as in the case of these Greek
women. In that is a revelation of the glory and beauty
of the Gospel. "What comfort was there for a Greek
woman in the cold gray eyes of Athene, or the stereotyped smile of the voluptuous Aphrodite?" What was
there in Greek religions or philosophic thought for a
woman? I am not surprised to read that these Greek
women turned readily to the great Gospel. What is there
in the world to-day for womanhood other than this great
evangel? Let there be no undervaluing of the meaning
of this. The women of high and noble estate, the convinced daughters of Greek culture, sick at heart because
of the degradation of womanhood, as the result of Greek

philosophy, turned to this great evangel with its broad and spacious outlook, with its light flashing and shining upon them. These were great victories.

But the Greek men also listened, and were eager; because their religion was dead. In the times in which Paul lived, there were Greek proselytes crowding to Judaism by the hundreds. They were tired of false religion, tired of the philosophies that had no satisfaction for the soul. They had turned to Judaism because it brought them the doctrine of one God; but they were without the Jewish prejudice and pride, and when this great Word came to them, the Word of the one God, and the one God manifest, and the one God winning victory by death, some of the profoundest secrets of their own mysteries were drawn into the light and redeemed. The greatest triumphs of the Gospel to-day are not won among the people who are religiously proud and prejudiced. The hardest place in which the Gospel has to win its victory is a congregation hardened to its message, and satisfied with its external forms of religion. With what perfect understanding one reads that there were occasions when Paul turned from the people of religious pride and prejudice, to reach the people with hearts and minds hungry and ready for the Gospel.

These after all, are preliminary revelations of the great message to Europe. The complete unveiling came at Athens.

Acts 17: 16–34

In certain respects there is no more fascinating story in the book of the Acts of the Apostles than this of Paul in Athens. The very conjunction of names is arresting and interesting;—Athens, " the most sacred shrine of the fair humanities of paganism ";—Paul, the most faithful incarnation of the Christian temper and passion.

Our business is with Paul in Athens. Pursued by Jews from Thessalonica, the apostle was conducted by loving disciples, who had been gathered in Berœa; they accompanied him on that journey of two hundred miles to Athens, and then left him. Luke had been left behind in Thessalonica. Silas and Timothy had remained at Berœa. The first declaration of this passage is that he was waiting in Athens. That in itself is an arresting and suggestive word, for it reminds us that we shall see how a Christian man waits in a godless city. Therein is the whole value of this scene.

The story may be divided into two parts. First of all, beginning with the sixteenth verse, and ending in the twenty-first, we have what may be described as the first mutual impressions; the impression that Athens made on Paul, and the impression that Paul made on Athens. Then immediately following, beginning with the twenty-second verse, and on to the end of the chapter, we have the second part of the narrative, which we may describe as the final mutual impressions. Here we first find the final impression which Paul made on Athens, and then the final impression which Athens made on Paul. It is the story of a Christian man in a decadent pagan city, for Athens was then long past its highest and its best.

Notice first the impression that Athens made on him. He was provoked in spirit. Notice the impression that he first made upon Athens; he preached of Jesus and the resurrection; and the Epicurean and Stoic philosophers were interested, and asked him to tell them something more definitely.

There are three things to note as to the impression which the city made on Paul. First it aroused his interest; secondly, it stirred his emotion; and thirdly, it inspired his service, and drove him to attempt even there also, to discharge that great debt which he referred to in his Roman letter, in the words, "I am debtor both to Greeks and to Barbarians."

The city aroused his interest. We are familiar with a criticism of Paul, which declares that he passed through

all these Greek cities, and even came to Athens, and never
by word, or speech, or in letter afterwards written, did he
seem to have taken the slightest notice of the things which
principally attracted other men. We are impressed with
the fact that he was not impressed by things which would
impress other men. All that splendid history of Athens,
running back at least four centuries before he came to
the city, to those wonderful days when Socrates stood
on Mars' Hill, perhaps almost exactly where he stood,
was ignored. Of the whole of the outstanding names of
Greek thought, Paul hardly referred to one, save to certain poets, not among the finest, the highest, or the noblest. One writer declared that it was easier to find in
Athens a god than to find a man; which was a reference
to the fact that Athens was filled with statuary of the
most wonderful and the most beautiful kind. It was the
very home of art, but there was no reference to the art
of Athens by Paul. It was the centre of philosophy.
He did come into contact with certain of the Epicurean
and Stoic philosophers; but it is a very remarkable fact
how in his dealing with them, he ignored their peculiar
philosophies, or only referred to them to show their folly.
Here was a man indifferent to the very things which had
peculiarly arrested attention, to the very things which had
caused other men to write at length of their beauty.
There was another traveller who came, perhaps only fifty
years later, certainly less than a century later than Paul,
—Pausanias the traveller. He gave, in the six volumes
of his descriptions of Greece, more room to Athens than
to any other city. His descriptions were detailed, and
very remarkable. He described how, landing at Piræus,
and riding up from the port into the city, one encountered
temples to Demeter; and how, scattered through the city,
there were statues of every kind, in stone, in marble, in
wood, in gold, in silver. One cannot read Pausanias
without feeling the artistic magnificence of Athens. But
this man Paul saw everything, and Luke summarizes his

outlook upon all these things by one phrase "full of idols"! The brilliant Frenchman, Renan, says that the ugly little Jew abused Greek art by describing the statues as idols. This man was unimpressed by the things which impressed others. These very things of history, of art, of philosophy, when Paul and Pausanias came to Athens, were not alive; they were dead. Let me quote some brief sentences in description: "At that time these men of Athens were trading on the memory of achievements not her own." So much for her history. What of her philosophy? She was "repeating with dead lips the echo of old philosophies." What of her art and her glory? "Her splendour was no longer an innate effulgence, but a lingering reflex."

So when we are inclined to criticize Paul because he was not impressed, though he was in the midst of things of art and philosophy, we should remember that they were not living, but dead. Notwithstanding the splendour that remained, there was lack of life everywhere in Athens when he came to the city.

But what did Paul see in Athens? Two things impressed him. First the city was full of idols; secondly, one altar arrested his attention, an altar that bare an inscription, "TO AN UNKNOWN GOD." In that little phrase "full of idols" is packed everything that Pausanias gave in detail. Pausanias described the temples, and said that as he moved up to the centre of Athens there were altars on every hand. He declared that there were altars devoted to Philosophy and Beneficence, to Rumour and Shame. The Athenians were deifying, not only men, but ideas and capacities. In every niche in the city there was some representation which these men were worshipping. Pausanias also tells us that there were altars to an unknown God; and Paul discovered one of these, "I found also an altar with this inscription, TO AN UNKNOWN GOD." These were the things that arrested his attention; the idols, and this one altar.

THE ACTS OF THE APOSTLES

What was the effect produced upon him by what he saw? "His spirit was provoked within him." Do not soften that word "provoked." The Greek word is the one from which we derive our word paroxysm. "His spirit was provoked within him." In the midst of the beauty and the glory and the art and the philosophy and the history of Athens, proud and wonderful Athens, this man Paul was in a rage, was provoked. The emotion produced was not piquant and passing, the emotion of a tourist. His spirit was provoked within him, he was angry, he was in a rage, and that because every idol he saw demonstrated the capacity of the man who built it, for God; and because all the idols demonstrated the degradation of that selfsame capacity. He was provoked because he knew that these idols and temples and altars all meant that these men were made for worship, and for God; and he knew that these idols, temples, and altars issued in that diffusion of devotion that had broken up the individual man, disorganized society, and made Athens what she was. Pausanias was a tourist, looking at the art and things of beauty in the city. Pausanias did not understand the slavery that was beneath; he seems to have been entirely indifferent to the heartache and agony that was expressing itself in the degenerate philosophies which men were teaching. But this little Jew, this great Christian, had no time for a description of art, of painting, and the things of beauty, because his heart was hot and angry in the consciousness of the degradation of humanity, issuing from humanity's false attempts to satisfy its profoundest need, that of God, with all its idols and its temples, its worship of Athene, the mother of the air, its worship of Demeter, the mother of the earth, its worship of Zeus, the god of force; these altars to Shame, to Rumour, and Philanthropy; these idols everywhere. Men were worshipping everything, and therefore were worshipping nothing. At last the little Jew, the great Christian, found one altar to an unknown

THE ACTS OF THE APOSTLES

God, and that altar for him was the focussing of a tragedy. Paul saw and read into it the ultimate agony of idolatry; that, unable to satisfy itself with its many gods, restless by the very diffusion of devotion, it travels out beyond and knows nothing, and yet is sure that in the beyond is the thing it wants; and it erects an altar to the unknown God.

Therefore a paroxysm, a rage, and a driving, and a fire, and a flaming passion, in the heart of the man. It was the rage of truth with a lie, it was the anger of the constructive against the destructive. It was the passion of a man who found in Athens capacity for God, and that capacity degraded and spoiled for lack of God. So the first impression that Athens made upon him was that of the arousing of his interest, and the second was that of the stirring of his emotion.

But it also inspired his service. He began his work, first in the synagogue, and then in the market-place, the Agora, where perchance Socrates four hundred years before had stood! That sermon, that wonderful address, so full of instruction for all missionary enterprise, is not the sermon he preached in the market-place. Luke has given us no details of the preachings. He does not record what Paul talked about in the market-place, and to the groups; because he did not imagine any man would need to be told. Presently we find out, because of what the Epicurean and Stoic philosophers said. The burden of his talking had been that of Jesus and the resurrection, and that had startled them, " May we know what this new teaching is?" Think of the fitness of it; it was the gospel for a dead city; Jesus and the resurrection. Paul was not the Philistine some people imagine him to have been. He saw the beauties, he felt the irresistible appeal of the glamour of Athens; and therefore in the midst of the death of its history, and of its art, and the moribund condition of its philosophy, he preached Jesus and the resurrection. He knew full well that by that risen One alone, could Athens arise from the ashes of her dead self to higher and to nobler things.

What impression did Paul first make upon Athens? He went to the synagogue, but there is no word of any impression made there. An argument from silence may be dangerous, and yet it is noticeable that there is no record of their receiving his message, as they had done in other places. Neither is there any record of their objecting. These Jews were living and worshipping in a city that was always listening to new things. Therefore they would be more likely to listen to him when he talked of what seemed to them to be a new thing. On the other hand they would be less likely to persecute him, or they would have had Athens on his side.

An impression was made in the market-place, and made principally upon these philosophers, Epicureans and Stoics. The Epicureans were those who declared that the highest good is pleasure. The Stoics were those who declared the highest good is virtue. And yet when Paul came to Athens, these philosophies were degenerate. The philosophy of the Epicureans as then taught, and as then practised, was degenerate. Epicurus had declared that the highest in life was pleasure, but by that he had meant something far higher and nobler than the men understood in the day in which Paul came to Athens. He had lived the garden life; and according to his teaching, pleasure consisted in freedom from physical pain, and mental unrest; and the way in which he declared freedom from physical pain and mental unrest to be possible, was the way—to borrow a modern phrase—of the simple life. The ideal of Epicurus was high and noble, but the whole philosophy was degenerate; and the interpretation of the meaning of the declaration that the highest good is pleasure, was at fault. The whole story may be told in one word. The Epicurean philosophy in practice, habit, and experience, when Paul came to Athens, was lust, in its most degrading form.

THE ACTS OF THE APOSTLES

The Stoic philosophers had declared that the highest good was virtue, but that idea also was degenerate. There was theory without practice. There was the assumption, and the profession of indifference to the things which the Epicureans taught, but there was insincerity; and beneath the profession there was the most degrading form of evil; and the ultimate word of the Stoic was suicide. Yet these were the men who listened to this man preaching.

The impression he made on them was not the same in all cases. There were those who spoke of him with contempt. They said, " What would this babbler say? " this seed-pecker, this man who is content to have picked up something here and there, and to go round reciting it; this man who gets his living by telling tales, this ignoramus, this babbler. To understand it we have only to listen to the way in which some men still treat the gospel preacher. But there were others who said, " He seemeth to be a setter forth of strange gods." There was a gleam of light. These men were really so ignorant of what Paul meant that they said Resurrection was one god; and Jesus another; they deified an idea. These men were impressed that Paul was speaking in the realm of religion. " He seemeth to be a setter forth of strange gods." Then the conception created curiosity, for when we read, " They took hold of him," we must not think of any violent action on their part. They brought him to Mars' Hill, and said, " May we know what this new teaching is, which is spoken by thee? " They placed him on what Pausanias described as the stone of impudence, where men had to defend their facts while the listeners sat round. That is the first impression he has made on Athens: contempt; a question as to whether there is not perhaps some profounder claim; and a dilettante curiosity to hear what he said.

We are far from the Athens of Paul and of Pausanias. Yet sometimes I think how near we are. History is

interwoven with the influence of Christ, and men are forgetting Him. Art has been glorified by making Christ its
supreme subject, and is drifting away from Him. Philosophy has been permeated with the conceptions of
Christ, and is now inclined to ignore Him. We are
largely living in the past, and our cities are as full of idols
as was Athens. The influence of Christ has made impossible the erection of material altars, or the putting up
of images that we worship, but the spirit of idolatry is
still with us; and I very much question whether one can
find any temple, or altar or idol in Athens, that cannot be
reproduced in the great cities of to-day. We are still
worshipping Athene, in the deification of the mental; and
Demeter too, the earth mother, in the apotheosis of the
physical; and Zeus, the god of force, even until this hour.
We also have our altars reared, even to philosophy, most
certainly to rumour. Rumour, the base goddess, has had
her scriptures issued morning by morning until the very
life of man is made restless by her lying. We are worshipping shame; there are altars to shame upon our highways everywhere. We are still idolaters. The Epicurean
is with us still; indifferent. The Stoic is here still, gathered into so-called ethical societies. Where are the Christian men and women of the city? We shall find them
and know them by the paroxysm of their unrest. But
that is not the ordinary stamp of Christian men and
women. They are quiet, content, reverent, worshipful.
No; if there be no paroxysm, no force, no agony, no
heart-break, no sacrifice, they are pagans and not Christians. F. W. H. Myers was a poetic interpreter of Paul,
and so of the Christian experience. Here is the story
of every Christian man in a great city.

"Oft when the Word is on me to deliver
   Lifts the illusion, and the truth lies bare,
 Desert or throng, the city or the river
   Melts in a lucid paradise of air.

" Only like souls I see the folk thereunder
 Bound who should conquer, slaves who should
  be kings.
Hearing their one hope with an empty wonder
 Sadly contented with a show of things.

" Then with a rush, the intolerable craving
 Shivers throughout me, like a trumpet call,
Oh, to save these, to perish for their saving,
 Die for their life, be offered for them all! "

That is Christianity. May we know it experimentally.

Acts 17: 22–34

In our previous study we considered the first impression which Athens made on Paul, and the first impression which Paul made on Athens. In this paragraph we have the result of that contemptuous curiosity which the Athenians manifested, in the account of Paul's answer delivered on Mars' Hill.

This is the final scene in Athens, so far as the New Testament is concerned. There is no further reference to it. In writing to the Thessalonians Paul reminds them that he sent Timothy from Athens to them; and we may imaginatively fill up much by that reference. After Paul had waited a while, Timothy came to him. He did not however retain him, but sent him back to Thessalonica. Paul departed from Athens alone.

We are now to see him in the Areopagus, that is, in the midst of the council. Mars' Hill was the place of the Supreme Court. The interpretation of the passage which supposes that Paul stood there as a prisoner, is not warranted by the story. I believe these Stoic philosophers took him away to the greater quietness and seclusion of the Areopagus, that they might hear what he had to say more particularly. He stood there, in all probability upon the stone of impudence, which Pausanias described so particularly, perhaps in the very place where Socrates had stood, a prisoner. Athens was not so much in earnest in Paul's day as it had been in that of Socrates. These were decadent days in Athens. All around were the signs and symbols of departed greatness. Philosophers were bandying words with each other, but making no application of their philosophy to life. Art was practically dead, save as the city was full of things artistic, all having come from a departed age. Four centuries had passed since Socrates had stood there; and now there Paul stood; but Athens, having lost its earnestness, had not arraigned him. He was not on trial. The word made use of—"they took hold of him"—does not suggest violence, but courtesy. They led him there. There was no passionate protest in the mind of these Athenian philosophers. That would have been a far more healthy condition of affairs. Paul never hopelessly abandoned a centre of persecution, but he abandoned this. These men were indulging in dilettante fooling with philosophies and religions, and they wanted to hear what he had to say, this babbler, this seed-pecker, for they "spent their time in nothing else, but either to tell or to hear some new thing."

It was a great moment, and a great location. There at his feet as he stood on that stone of impudence, was the Theseum, the wonderful Doric temple, which abides even until this hour, one of the most perfect examples of art. On his right stretched the upper city, the Akropolis; and there, in all its significance, the Parthenon devoted to the worship of Athene. Everywhere were altars and temples and images; statuary the most beautiful and perfect, in marble, in stone, in gold, in silver, in bronze, and in wood.

Still further let it be remembered, as we said before, this address was not Paul's preaching of the evangel. This was his defence of his preaching, under circumstances that were peculiar, to the place and occasion. When he tarried and waited, and saw the city given to idols, when his spirit was provoked within him, swept by

THE ACTS OF THE APOSTLES

[Acts 17 : 22–34]

a paroxysm of rage, the rage of truth with a lie, the protest of the constructive passion against the destructive element, then he preached his evangel to individuals and groups in the busy market-places. To this, the Epicurean and Stoic philosophers had listened, and they said, "What would this babbler say? other some, He seemeth to be a setter forth of strange gods: because he preached Jesus and the resurrection." The address delivered on Mars' Hill was Paul's answer to that enquiry.

We shall now only attempt to gather from this address the final mutual impressions, and deduce therefrom some lessons of permanent value. We will notice first, the impression that Paul now made upon Athens, in the person of these Epicurean and Stoic philosophers, as they, having challenged him, he answered their challenge; and secondly the final impression Athens made upon Paul.

To discover the impression which Paul made on Athens we need to consider first his method, then his actual teaching, and finally the result.

There can be no study of this address of Paul on Mars' Hill that does not lead to the conclusion that his method was conciliatory. There is no single sentence or phrase that has in it anything of harshness. In the English Revised Version the twenty-second verse reads, "Paul stood in the midst of the Areopagus, and said, Ye men of Athens, In all things I perceive that ye are somewhat superstitious." The marginal reading suggests the substitution of the word "religious" for "superstitious." The Greek word was certainly sometimes used in the sense of superstitious, and sometimes in the sense of religious. I believe however that the American revisers were right when they translated thus: "Ye men of Athens, in all things I perceive that ye are *very religious.*" Paul really began with the note of conciliation, and from beginning to end there was nothing calculated to offend, or drive away the men whom he desired to gain. In this address he recognized their religious instincts. Every

[418]

idol proved capacity for God. Every temple demonstrated man's need of worship. The idols did not prove that men would find God. The temples did not give evidence of the fact that through them men would discover the central place of worship. But these things did reveal the religious capacity of the men who made them; and that capacity the apostle recognized.

He found the open door to their mind in one of their own altars. He discovered as he looked at the city, one altar with the strange inscription, TO AN UNKNOWN GOD. He made that altar, not one which he had erected, but one which belonged to their own city, the open door through which he proceeded.

He also cited their own poets. He quoted from Aratus and Cleanthes. Aratus, by the way, was also of Cilicia. With these writings in all probability this man Paul, brought up in Tarsus, would be familiar. The whole address is characterized by the spirit of conciliation, of courtesy, of kindness. He would capture these men by an attitude before he proceeded,—as he did ere he had done,—to denounce their activities, to show the unutterable folly of their methods, and finally to proclaim to them the great evangel.

Again, his method was apologetic, in the true sense of that word. In answer to criticism he took up one of their own words. Compare here verses eighteen and twenty-three:

"Certain also of the Epicurean and Stoic philosophers encountered him. And some said, What would this babbler say? other, He seemeth to be a *setter forth* of strange gods," of foreign gods.

"As I passed along, and observed the objects of your worship, I found also an altar with this inscription, TO AN UNKNOWN GOD. What therefore ye worship in ignorance, this *set I forth* unto you."

"He seemeth to be a setter forth of strange gods."

[419]

[Acts 17 : 22–34]

No, said the apostle, I am not a setter forth of a foreign god; I am here to set forth the God to Whom you have already erected an altar. His word was an answer to theirs, and this use of a word had in it the force of an arresting argument.

His speech was apologetic moreover in that it was a defence of their own truth. Their poets had said, We are the offspring of God. Paul would defend their own truth against their abuse of it. Being the offspring of God we ought not to degrade God by making Him of gold, or silver, or wood. The poets of Athens had declared that men are offspring of Deity; and yet the men of Athens had made images less than themselves. That action was the result of a false deduction from their own truth. If these men made something less than themselves, and worshipped that, they were degrading the truth that their poets had sung to them. They ought to worship the God of Whom they were the offspring; not the workmanship of their own hands which, at best, were base imitations of themselves. So he attempted to redeem their own truth from misapprehension and misapplication.

And finally, it was apologetic, in that it was an exposition of their own problems. In that inscription was discovered the final problem, not of Athens only, but of all paganism. TO AN UNKNOWN GOD; that was the margin, the end of everything. All philosophies were silent there. No temple answered that. No idol cut and devised by craft and cunning of skilful workmen could solve that riddle. Athens knew that there was such a problem, that of the unknown God. The apostle said in effect: All the unutterable agony of your need is focussed and emphasized in that one inscription, TO AN UNKNOWN GOD; and I declare that God to you. Thus in answer to their criticism, in defence of their own truth, and in exposition of their own problems, he delivered his message.

But his method was not only that of conciliation and

apology, it was also that of positivism, of authority—his was a dogmatic statement. To summarize the whole authoritative declaration of this apostle on Mars' Hill; it was first affirmed of God; and that secondly, in order to the reclamation of man; and so finally leading up to the proclamation of the central fact of the Christian evangel. He affirmed God. He did it in order to the reclamation of man from false conceptions of God, and false ideals concerning his own life. He thus gradually moved by this masterly method, to the declaration of the evangel.

This he introduced by saying, " The times of ignorance God overlooked." The temples to Demeter, Athene, Zeus; the idols; the altars, were the pride of Athens. But there was that one altar to the unknown God, and that was the symbol of the time of their ignorance! Thus with one word the Christian apostle dismissed the whole fact of paganism, it was " ignorance." Yet there was nothing unkind in the word, and he distinctly declared that " The times of ignorance God overlooked," but he went on to say that a new day had come, a new era had dawned, created by the Christian evangel which he at once proclaimed.

Looking at the teaching of the apostle then we find in it theology, philosophy, and religion.

What was the theology that he preached on Mars' Hill to these Epicurean and Stoic philosophers? He declared that God is Creator, that He is Sovereign, that He is Governor. If these truths have become commonplace, because of our Christian atmosphere and thinking, remember what these things meant as he uttered them there; how in the courteous and yet positive statement of the Christian apostle he was denying the whole theology of the men who had asked him to speak to them. The Stoics were Pantheists, and the final reduction of the Epicurean view of the universe was that of Atheism. Paul declared that the God, to Whom some of them had erected an altar, and called unknown, was the God he set forth to them. He declared Him to be the Creator, the Sustainer; not the sum and substance of all things, but the Cause and Creator of all things. He declared that God cannot be expressed in the sum total of the things of which men are conscious. He lies far out beyond the ultimate bound of the most stupendous universe of which man has become conscious. He is the Creator.

Yet further he declared Him to be the Sovereign Lord. He is no impersonal abstraction, no mere tendency running through all things, but the Sovereign Master of all; not One Who is imprisoned in the creation, and the slave of the creation, but the One through Whom all created things came, and Who upholds them by the word of His power.

Therefore finally he announced that He is the Supreme Governor of the universe: " He made of one every nation of men for to dwell on all the face of the earth, having determined their appointed seasons, and the bounds of their habitation." Thus he declared that the cycles and the centuries are all of God, as well as the things material. As the writer of the letter to the Hebrews also wrote, God fashions the ages. Thus he reminded them that they were not living in Athens as the result of some fortuitous accident; but that God had fixed the bounds of human habitation. He claimed that God was the sovereign Lord and Master, that therefore He was transcendent, and more than all the rest.

Therefore he argued that temples are useless to Him, for He " dwelleth not in temples made by hands "; that all altars are in some sense worthless, for altars are places to which men bring gifts to God. He cannot be served by gifts. He does not require anything men can offer Him. If men are His offspring, do they imagine that these things that have no breath, no emotion, no intellect, which men have to carry and place and fix, and which never move when placed, can express God? Surely these Epicurean and Stoic philosophers had vision of greater and nobler things, as Paul talked to them.

The philosophy of all this is discovered in his insistence upon the fact that God is transcendent, above, beyond all, and yet that He is immanent. " In Him we live, and move, and have our being." This was the startling challenge he flung out to these Greeks. Discover God by attaining to what you are in yourselves. You are His offspring. Why then try to express Him in these idols which, at their best, are poor and feeble and foolish imitations of yourselves? Paul had seen all their things of artistic beauty, those idols in gold, and silver, but he set up against those golden images one Athenian man, and the gold was seen to be dross. That is always the Christian outlook. We call to mind the fine sarcasm of Peter's word, you were not redeemed, " with corruptible things, with silver or gold." This man Paul stood there in the midst of Mars' Hill, and said to these men, If you really want to find God, do not degrade yourselves in erecting images of gold and silver. Listen to the deepest fact of your own being; be silent in the presence of the mystery of what you are; and then look out beyond to that unknown God Whom I declare to you.

The final thing in the teaching was that of religion. " The times of ignorance God overlooked; but now ": A new hour had struck on the horologue of eternity, and men in time were arrested, for a new day had dawned. What is this new day? " Now He commandeth men that they should all everywhere repent." Why? " Inasmuch as He hath appointed a day, in the which He will judge the world in righteousness by the Man Whom He hath ordained; whereof He hath given assurance unto all men, in that He hath raised Him from the dead." Into those few sentences the whole fact of the Christian religion is condensed. The great word is the first, " Repent." The central thing the apostle declared on Mars' Hill was that God had appointed a day in which He would judge the

THE ACTS OF THE APOSTLES

world in righteousness. How were men to know that this was true? He has " given assurance unto all men, in that He hath raised Him from the dead." That is the proof.

The duty was declared in the word " Repent." The times of ignorance God had overlooked. God had seen those proud temples in Athens. God had seen those altars and those idols, but He had overlooked them in pity and compassion. But a new hour had now come. God had appointed a Man by Whom He will judge the world in righteousness. That was not a reference to a final day of judgment. It was a declaration that God had not only willed that ultimately the whole world should be governed upon principles of righteousness, He had done more; He had ordained the Man Who is to be King. The government of the world in righteousness would be brought about, not by an idol, not by an altar, not by an abstraction, not by a philosophy, but by a Man. Of that God had given assurance in that He had raised Him from the dead. To deny that resurrection is to have no evangel, and no Christian religion; and all talk of the judgment of the world in righteousness is futile unless it be true that this Man was raised from the dead.

What then was Athens to do? Repent, change its mind, think over again, reconsider its position; get away from the false conceptions, that had issued in false conduct, that had issued in false character. That is the key word of the evangel. Think again in the light of the day when God will judge the world in righteousness by the Man Whom He hath ordained.

What was the result? When they heard of the resurrection, some mocked, and others postponed. Humanity is the same in every age. These are not dead things at which we are looking. When did they begin their mockery and decide for postponement? At the point of resurrection? No, that was the excuse. Where then? At the point of moral application. While Paul discussed

[424]

round their altar the doctrine of an unknown God, while he enunciated philosophies, even though his enunciations contradicted their philosophies, they listened; but when he said, " Now He commandeth men that they should all everywhere repent: inasmuch as He hath appointed a day, in the which He will judge the world in righteousness," they mocked. Men often find an intellectual excuse for refusing to be moral when God demands morality. Paul, discussing an altar and a theory of a God, will fail unless he say, " But now . . . repent." That is the point where men begin to mock, and postpone.

But there was another result. Dionysius, Damaris, and others, believed. From Church history we know that there were wonderful results in Athens. In the next century that Church at Athens gave to the Christian Church Publius, Quadratus, Aristides, Athenagoras, and others, bishops and martyrs; and in the third century the church there was peaceable and pure. In the fourth century the Christian schools of Athens gave to the Christian Church Basil and Gregory. Men cannot wholly mock the Christian fact out of existence. Men cannot entirely postpone. The apostle may pass, his work being done, but he always leaves behind him Dionysius and Damaris. Christ always wins a vantage-ground.

What was the final impression which Athens made on Paul? Two sentences tell the story, one in this paragraph and one in the first verse of the next chapter. " He went out from them. . . . He departed from Athens." When men were angry with him, he argued with them, and triumphed over them. When men persecuted, he went back again to the place of persecution. But for intellectual flippancy and moral dishonesty this man had no further word. That is the true attitude. It was the attitude of his Master before him. It should be the attitude of the Christian preacher to-day.

From every system of false religion there is an open

[425]

door into the true. Men often decline to take the journey through that open door. The fault is with the men. Our evangel is that of the risen Man, and it is only as we lead men to Him that they begin to find the value of those true things in their own false systems. Let us be solemnly warned lest we imagine that the men who are in the midst of false systems, will one day find their way into truth, because there are elements of truth in their systems. It is well also to remember that we must always begin with the open door, but not end there. Our message is never complete until we have proclaimed to men the risen Man, and the necessity for repentance.

Acts 18: 1–22

This paragraph chronicles the events of the last part of the second missionary journey of Paul. "After these things he departed from Athens, and came to Corinth." If Athens was a centre of clouded light, Corinth was a centre of corrupt life. If Athens was full of idolatry, Corinth was full of sensuality. The apostle's work in Corinth being completed, he left without any ostensible reason. It seems to have been the one place he left in quietness and peace on this journey. He left with his face set toward Jerusalem and Antioch. Making a brief halt in Ephesus, he went on, leaving Priscilla and Aquila there. Then he travelled away by sea to Cæsarea, and so on to Jerusalem, where his reception was so cold, that Luke dismissed the story in a few words, "He went up and saluted the church, and went down to Antioch."

The principal interest of the paragraph is centred in Corinth. The other matters, from Paul's departure from Corinth to his arrival in Antioch, are incidental; the places visited will appear again, and in fuller detail later on.

Corinth was at this time the political capital of Southern Greece, and the residence of the Roman Proconsul. Thus while a Greek city, it was under Roman rule. There was a strange mixture of men in Corinth. It had become a great commercial centre, and Dean Farrar describes the commodities that were found in its markets:

"Arabian balsam, Egyptian papyrus, Phœnician dates, Libyian ivory, Babylonian carpets, Cilician goats'-hair, Lycaonian wool, Phrygian slaves."

There was a strange mixture of wealth and of poverty there; and the life of the wealthy was a life of voluptuous luxury, and of frivolous disquisitions. One must read with great carefulness the Corinthian letters in order to see Corinth as Paul saw it, not merely to see the church, not merely to see the apostolic method of dealing with the church, but to see Corinth itself. Everything which he denounced within the church was a reflection of the corruption of the city. In his first letter, he first corrected their attempt to form societies around emphases of Christian truth. That was a reflection of what was going on in Corinth. Men were splitting hairs, even in the realm of their own philosophies, and forming schools around different emphases or views. So when he passed to the graver matters, so far as moral conduct was concerned, we again see the picture of Corinth; the rich living in voluptuous luxury, given over to every manner of evil. It has been said that Corinth at this time

"was the Vanity Fair of the Roman Empire, at once the London and the Paris of the first century after Christ."

The masses of the people were infected by this influence. They were debauched and degraded. There were shows of all kinds, and a vulgar and ostentatious display of wealth, mingled with the most corrupt and indecent practices. All these things were affecting the people who were not wealthy, the corruption had permeated even to the slaves.

THE ACTS OF THE APOSTLES

[Acts 18: 1–22]

It was a city of abounding immorality. It was pro-
verbial for its debauchery. Men of the time, when desiring to describe utter corruption, said, " They live as
they do at Corinth." In the great dramatic entertain-
ments, Corinthians were almost always introduced as
drunk. The most terrible phase of the corruption was
that the religion of Corinth had become the centre and
the hotbed of its pollution. In that one splendid and yet
awful temple of Aphrodite, there were a thousand sacred
to shame. It is significant that it was from this city that
Paul wrote his Roman letter; and when one reads his
description of Gentile corruption in that Roman letter,
one has almost certainly a mirror of what he found in
Corinth.

" Professing themselves to be wise, they became fools,
and changed the glory of the incorruptible God for the
likeness of an image of corruptible man. . . . God
gave them up in the lusts of their hearts unto uncleanness, that their bodies should be dishonoured among
themselves. . . . God gave them up unto vile passions: for their women changed the natural use into that
which is against nature. . . . God gave them up
unto a reprobate mind, to do those things which are not
fitting; being filled with all unrighteousness, wickedness,
covetousness, maliciousness: full of envy, murder, strife,
deceit, malignity, whisperers, backbiters, hateful to God,
insolent, haughty, boastful, inventors of evil things, disobedient to parents, without understanding, covenant
breakers, without natural affection, unmerciful."

With that dark background in mind we pass to the
attitude of the Lord Himself toward this city: " I have
much people in this city." That was the word of the
Lord spoken in the inner sanctuary of the spirit-life of
His servant concerning a corrupt city. That is the flaming word of the paragraph. All the other things are incidental, gathered about it, revealing the marvellousness

of that word: "I have much people in this city." He knew, and communicated to His servant, this secret concerning Corinth. He knew the heartache and the agony of many in Corinth. He knew that the restlessness of Corinth was the outcome of the longing of many, inarticulate, not understood, for exactly that which he had to minister and to give. He knew that throughout the city, notwithstanding its obscenity and its corruption, there was a spirit of enquiry, a spirit of eagerness, a spirit of wistfulness. He knew that it was but to have His great evangel proclaimed there for very many to hear and to respond. Paul entered Corinth alone, and at once became keenly, acutely conscious of the corruption of the city. He came into Corinth, without a saint of God; and yet at last, after a period of patient work and preparation, this was the word of the King, " I have much people in this city."

So the Lord speaks of every great city long before the people to whom He refers are manifest to others. Do not put this out of its historic relation. This word was not said when the church had been formed. This was not said of those whom we call saints in Corinth. It was said at the point when this man seemed to be at the end of his work, and was filled with fear, and with trembling of soul, even though there had been a measure of success. As a matter of fact, Paul's fear is not chronicled, but it is revealed in the word of Christ. The Lord knew the lurking fear in the heart of His servant, a fear born of his overwhelming sense of the corruption of the city, of the almost impossibility of doing anything there that was worth the doing. Yet to him He said, " I have much people in this city." I think from that moment as this man passed through the streets, or talked in the house of Titus Justus, or looked at the curious crowd who came to him, he was forevermore looking, hoping that he might see beneath the exterior that repelled him, because it was so unlike his Lord, those whom his Lord numbered

among His own. " I have much people in this city."
What an inspiration for the Christian worker in a great
city given over to corruption.

Then mark the revelation of His power in a corrupt
city in His protection of His servant, " No man shall set
on thee to harm thee." Then remember also the method
by which he was protected, through the instrumentality
of Gallio. Gallio is one of the much abused men in the
New Testament. " Gallio cared for none of these
things " has been quoted to prove that he was indifferent
to Paul. That is not what the sentence means. Read
the story of Gallio, the brother of Seneca, as it has been
written in profane history; and the description of him is
that of one of the sweetest, gentlest, and most lovable of
men. Gallio had recently been appointed to Achaia, and
when the change was made, the Jews thought that they
had their opportunity to get rid of Paul. Gallio stood
throughout that movement in defence of Paul. When
Gallio declined to listen to the case, because they were
disputing about words, he was speaking within the proper
limits of his jurisdiction. He cared nothing for the
wildness of the attack upon Paul; or that the Greeks,
glad that the Jews had been defeated in their desire to
interfere with Paul, seized the ruler of the synagogue,
Sosthenes. Do not imagine that there was neglect on
the part of Gallio, that he ought to have interfered, and
did not. This is a picture of the proconsul declining to
do injustice, and handing the matter of the dispute over
to those who had raised it. By that overruling of Gallio,
Paul was protected from the onslaught of the mob. Ere
that onslaught the Lord had said, " Be not afraid . . .
for I am with thee, and no man shall set on thee to harm
thee." So we see the Lord Christ overruling the forces
that would hinder the proclamation of His Word, and
holding them in check, as He preserved His servant.

This is in the first chapter of Church history, but it is
not the last chapter, nor is this the last story of its kind.

We know very little of it in this land, because we do
not preach in the midst of peril as did these men. Talk
to the men in the great centres of heathen darkness
to-day, and they will tell you how wonderfully they have
often been protected. Not always! Paul was not always
protected; for he had been stoned and left for dead.
But within the compass of His purpose, within the
economy of His power, where necessary, the Lord holds
in check the forces against His servants, and sets them
free for the proclamation of His Word. Such is the
power of our Lord, even in a corrupt city.

His power acted in the deliverance of all those who
seeking for truth, life, and purity, obeyed the Gospel;
and in the ultimate doom of those who disobeyed that
Gospel. "I have much people in this city." That word
must not be misinterpreted, as though the heart of the
Lord were only set upon those who ultimately yielded to
Him, and formed the Christian community in Corinth.
His heart was set upon every man, woman, little child,
and slave in Corinth, no matter how corrupt. But only
to those who, in obedience to the word when they heard
it, turned to Him, was He able to communicate the power
of a new life, to regenerate and to remake.

When Paul began his work in Corinth, he joined
Aquila and Priscilla, and laboured at tent making. When
we read his letters we shall discover his reason. At
Thessalonica he had done the same thing, and at Ephesus;
and for a brief period it was absolutely necessary in a
city wholly given to commercial enterprise, that he should
demonstrate the fact that the preaching of the Gospel was
not commercial. So he contented himself for a period
with preaching only on the Sabbath day in the synagogue
to Jews, and also to Greeks, while he wrought with his
own hands during the week.

Then Timothy and Silas arrived, and they brought
help from Philippi. The proof of that is to be found in
his own reference in his letter. Immediately that help

came, ministered to by another church, he abandoned the toil with his hands, and gave himself under the constraint of the Word, to constant preaching in Corinth. When the Jews set themselves in battle array against him,—for such is the force of the word,—he resolutely turned from them, and preached to the Greeks, and many believed and were baptized.

Then came an hour of haunting fear. Luke does not record it, save through the word of the Lord. " Be not afraid," said Jesus, and through that word of Christ we know that the apostle was filled with fear. Perhaps the very success of his ministry, the fact that many hearing, believed and were baptized, filled him with fear. He knew the seductions of the city, the corruption of the city, the consequent peril of those who so eagerly were listening, who apparently so readily were believing, who with such eager haste were being baptized. We enter into sympathy with him. He had preached to the Jew, and the Jew had refused; and with stern words he had said, " Your blood be upon your own heads; I am clean: from henceforth I will go unto the Gentiles "; and eagerly the Gentiles had heard, believed, and were baptized; and so he became filled with fear. Then it was that the Lord said to him, " Be not afraid, but speak, and hold not thy peace: for I am with thee, and no man shall set on thee to harm thee: for I have much people in this city." Do not be afraid of those who hearing, are eagerly believing, and being baptized. Do not doubt the sincerity of those who are coming to you. I have much people here. The thing you have seen, I have known ere you saw it. Your coming here has also been within My Divine arrangement. Trust these new converts. When presently Paul rebuked them with sternness for their derelictions in spiritual life, there was nevertheless in his heart a great love for them, a great confidence and belief in them. He wrote to them as the saints of God, in spite of all their failure, in spite of the fact that they had yielded to the seductions of corrupt Corinth. When the Lord said to him, " I have much people in this city," there came a new courage into his heart, which enabled him to face success.

Yet surely there was also in his heart a haunting fear of the hostility that he knew was working. He had seen the movement which presently broke out, and appealed to the bema, or judgment seat of Gallio. It is often in the moment of success that the heart becomes cowardly. It was immediately after Elijah's victory on Carmel that he ran away from Jezebel. It is often in the hour of success, that the fear of opposition and hostility is born. This man, beaten, bruised, and stoned, bearing in his very body the brands of Jesus, knew what was going on in Corinth, against him, and he was filled with fear. The Lord came to him with no rebuke, with no harsh word, but with words of ineffable comfort, " Be not afraid, but speak, and hold not thy peace." He was almost inclined to give up preaching. " Hold not thy peace: for I am with thee, and no man shall set on thee to harm thee." The haunting fear in the presence of success, merged into cowardice in the presence of hostility. Perhaps one other element contributed to the fear in his heart, that of the overwhelming sense of the vastness of the work. How often to-day one pauses in the midst of work, and feels as by comparison with the thing to be done, that the thing being done is nothing. The Lord still says, Be not afraid, speak, hold not thy peace, I am with thee, and I have much people in this city. Do not measure My victory by the things seen. Do not measure My victory by the statistics taken and read. I have much people, says the King, in this, and in all cities, never yet seen, never yet known. Abide in My strength; I am with thee, speak, be not afraid.

From that moment the heart of the man was filled with a new courage. He dwelt there a year and six months, teaching the Word of God among them; and when the

Gallio incident occurred, he still continued. I am with thee, said his Lord to him. Mark the effect upon the Word. Was he afraid of the success? " I am with thee," and in a moment he knew that if it was His work, however much he might fear its instability, this Lord was able to preserve the work that he saw begun. Was he afraid of the hostility? If his Lord was with him, the fear was at once banished. Was he afraid of the overwhelming sense of the vastness of the work? If his Lord was with him, he would be content to do the piece of work that he had to do, and to leave the issues with Him.

A wonderful page is this, but the words out of it that abide, that will sing their song in life and service for many a day, are these, " I have much people in this city." Said He in the days of His public ministry, " Other sheep I have, which are not of this fold: them also I must bring." This man in Corinth was finding some of them. Still in the days of His public ministry it was written of Him " that He might also gather together into one the children of God that are scattered abroad." Paul was finding some of them in Corinth. The most hopeful things in humanity to-day are its restlessness, its intensity, its disgust. These are open doors for the Christian preacher. Corinthian habits, Corinthian words, and all the restlessness of the city, it matters not how it is manifested, create the open door for the evangel of Jesus Christ. What is the Gospel for the corrupt city? The Cross and the Resurrection, and none other. Are we at His disposal, as this man was at His disposal in Corinth? If so, He is at our side, and we need not fear the success or the hostility or the vastness of the work; but be content to do that piece of work which God has given to us, in the consciousness of our fellowship with Him, and His fellowship with us. As we look and serve, let us look for saints, remembering that He is saying to us in the midst of all that tends to dishearten, " I have much people in this city." Let us look for them, find them, and lead them to Him.

Acts 18:24-19:7

We now commence that portion of the book of the Acts of the Apostles which tells the story of Paul's work in Ephesus. In the New Testament narrative, Ephesus is the outstanding and representative church, to which two letters are addressed. Even if Paul's letter was a circular letter intended for other churches in the district, it is quite certain that among them it was intended also for the church at Ephesus. There is also the letter of the Lord to Ephesus, the first of the seven in the book of the Revelation.

In writing to Ephesus Paul reached the summit of his system of teaching. It was to this church he was able to write of those profound matters concerning the ultimate vocation of the Church of God. In writing to the Romans he laid the foundation truths concerning salvation, broadly and forever. In writing to the Corinthians he corrected a condition of affairs which issued in failure to fulfil its function in a heathen city, on the part of the Church. But in writing to Ephesus he soared far above all these matters of minor and local importance, and wrote of the sublimest truths concerning the Church, dealing first with its predestination to character and the service of God; then with its edification in the processes of time, in order that it may fulfil its true vocation; and finally with its vocation. Then he revealed how such doctrine should affect the lives of men and women, members of that Church, in all human inter-relationships. When we turn to the letter of our Lord to the church at Ephesus, we find a church fair and beautiful in very many respects, and yet we have revealed, that first peril that ever threatens the Church of God: the loss of first love.

This story of Paul's coming to Ephesus must be of special interest, because of the place that Ephesus thus

THE ACTS OF THE APOSTLES

occupies in the New Testament revelation of the Church.
Here also we are considering the last part of the work of
Paul in liberty. Not that he was never free again after
his imprisonment in Rome, for personally I have no doubt
that he was set at liberty, and that he visited these
churches again. It may be that he visited Spain, and
perchance came to Britain. But so far as this record is
concerned, we here see the last work of Paul at liberty.
Presently we shall see him a prisoner.

Ephesus was a city, notorious for idolatry; in some
senses, the very centre of the great idolatries. There was
the temple of Artemis or Diana; and there religion and
commercial life had entered into a remarkable alliance,
for the great merchantmen made the temple of Artemis
their banking house; so that anything of purity or virtue
that there might have been in the Greek ideals of worship
was corrupted, because receiving the patronage of the
merchantmen. Moreover it was a city at that moment
given over largely to demonism, to sorcery, to witchcraft,
to magic. Here the apostolic work was accompanied by
special signs.

In this paragraph we have two accounts merging into
one, put together because of their intimate connection;
the story of Apollos and his ministry, and the story of
the coming of Paul to Ephesus. It will be seen by glancing at the nineteenth and twenty-first verses in this chapter that Paul had already been in Ephesus.

"They came to Ephesus, and he left Priscilla and
Aquila there: but he himself entered into the synagogue,
and reasoned with the Jews. And when they asked him
to abide a longer time, he consented not; but taking his
leave of them, and saying, I will return again unto you,
if God will, he set sail from Ephesus."

That was about a year before this coming to the city, for
Luke has given us no detailed account of the apostolic

labours, but only such incidents as serve to teach spiritual lessons for all time.

During that year something had happened in Ephesus, which is chronicled in the closing part of the eighteenth chapter: the coming of Apollos. Let us look at this story, observing two things: the man himself, and the ministry that he exercised.

Apollos was a Jew, an Alexandrian, a learned man, mighty in the Scriptures. We have dwelt upon the fact that the apprehension of Saul of Tarsus was a wonderful evidence of the presidency of the Lord Himself over the affairs of His Church, and of the guidance of the Spirit. The work among the Gentiles had to be done in cities where two great influences obtained in matters of religion, the influence of the Jewish synagogue, and the influence of Greek culture. When Saul of Tarsus was apprehended, it was the apprehension of a man who was, to quote his own words, " A Hebrew of Hebrews "; but he was also Saul of Tarsus. He was at once Hebrew and Hellenist. The two great ideals combining in him, made him the power he was through these Greek cities. In this man Apollos the same two great ideals merged. He was a Jew, but also an Alexandrian. Alexandria was the centre of Greek learning and culture at this time; where the Jews were all under the influence of Philo; where the influence of the Greek method of culture of that day invaded the Hebrew method of the study of their own Scriptures and writings. This man Apollos then was one in whom, in some senses perhaps even more remarkably than in Paul, the two ideals merged. He was learned, eloquent. He was an orator, and yet an orator through whose speech there was manifest the fact of his culture and his refinement.

The last word of the description, " mighty in the Scriptures," does not merely mean that he knew them; nor had ability to deal with them and to present them; but that he had the ability to master them, to understand them. That word of description is that of a special and specific gift that this man possessed by nature. We cannot say this was a spiritual gift in the Church sense of the word, for as yet he had not come into union with that Church, for he had not received the Spirit by enduement. Here was a man gifted naturally. The Spirit always bestows His special gift upon a man already gifted by nature to receive it. That may be a dogmatic statement which some would like to challenge. The instance quoted against it very often is that of Dwight Lyman Moody. Yet his experience proves its accuracy. If he had never been a Christian man, he would have been a mighty orator, and a leader of men. If a man has no gift of speech by nature, do not imagine God wants that man for a preacher, because He does not. He may have equally important work for him to do, but a preacher is born, not made. This man Apollos was mighty in the Scriptures, and was gifted by nature with a gift which every man does not possess. It was a distinct ability, a natural power to know the Scriptures, and to see their inter-relationships. He was familiar with all their parts and their bearings. He had a familiarity with the Scriptures which enabled him to impart to others that which he knew. This man, therefore, by birth and training, was singularly fitted for work in these Greek cities.

His ministry in Ephesus was not distinctly Christian. Mark his equipment. " This man had been instructed in the way of the Lord," which does not mean, in the way of the Lord Jesus Christ in all the fullness of that description. " Being fervent in spirit, he spake and taught carefully the things concerning Jesus, *knowing only the baptism of John.*" Mark the distinction carefully. In the third chapter of the Gospel according to Matthew, we have the account of the ministry of John.

" In those days cometh John the Baptist, preaching in the wilderness of Judæa, saying, Repent ye; for the King-

dom of heaven is at hand.   For this is he that was spoken
of by Isaiah the prophet saying,
  The voice of one crying in the wilderness,
  Make ye ready *the way of the Lord.*"

Apollos had been instructed " in the way of the Lord,
knowing only the baptism of John." Apollos was a disciple of John, and " the way of the Lord " referred to
here is that referred to in Matthew, and is a direct quotation from the prophecy of Isaiah, in its fortieth chapter, and second verse.   To understand this we must get
back into the atmosphere of that great prophecy.   The
fortieth chapter opens, " Comfort ye, comfort ye, My
people."   It is the beginning of the great ministry of
peace, resulting from judgment.   The thirty-fifth chapter of Isaiah, the last of the first prophetic portion, ended
with the promise of ultimate peace.   This is all Hebrew.
Apollos was a Jew.   This chapter in Isaiah ended with a
picture of an ultimate peace; first desolation, and beyond
it, restoration.   That was the vision of the prophet, as he
spoke, while Sennacherib's armies were melting away.
The great declaration was that Jehovah would prepare a
way for His people back into peace.   Omitting the historic portion (36-39) we come to that fortieth chapter;
and the message is that the people of God are to prepare
a way for Jehovah.   Mark the link between the two.
John came, as Isaiah had foretold, the ascetic, the hard,
the stern, the pure, the righteous, and he proclaimed " the
way of the Lord," which was to be prepared for by repentance.   Apollos had been instructed in " the way of
the Lord," in that sense, had been instructed in the
Messianic prophecy, and purpose.   He was a disciple of
John, and in obedience to John had been baptized unto
repentance, and to expectation of the coming of Messiah;
but he did not know the meaning of the Cross.   He was
not acquainted with the fact of resurrection.   He was
not familiar with the truth of the outpoured Spirit.   His
view was Hebrew on the highest and purest and best

[439]

level, as interpreted by John. He was fervent in spirit, fiery-spirited, having inherited from John, or under the influence of other teachers perhaps, that fiery note.

This man therefore who came to Ephesus between Paul's first and second visits, Apollos, a man, a disciple of John, taught them " the things concerning Jesus," so far as John had revealed them. His method in Ephesus was that " He spake and taught carefully the things concerning Jesus," and " began to speak boldly in the synagogue."

But there were two people in Ephesus who knew much more about Jesus than he did: a woman and a man. The order of the names is significant, " Priscilla and Aquila." These two had been left in Ephesus by Paul, and had been there a year. They knew Christ experimentally, because they were of the Christ by the work of the Spirit. They heard Apollos, and they took him, and instructed him more carefully; and that ended his ministry in Ephesus. One of the most beautiful touches about Apollos is the revelation of the fact that he was willing to let two members of the congregation who listened to him, and who knew more than he did, teach him. They took him, this persuasive, eloquent, sincere, burning soul; and opened to him the truth, with the result that he passed on from Ephesus to Corinth.

Very little is recorded concerning his ministry there. He was commended by these people in Ephesus, for his natural ability, for his zeal, and for that simplicity of character which had been revealed in his willingness to learn. We simply read about him in Corinth, that " he helped them much which had believed through grace." Whether the words " through grace " refer to " believed," or to " helped them much," cannot finally be determined. I prefer to believe that they belong to the " helped them much." We find also from Paul's letter to the Corinthians that they had made him the head of a sect, some saying, " We are of Apollos." That does not reflect upon him at all, because they did the same about Paul. But there is one little illuminative word in the Corinthian letter. Paul says, " I planted, Apollos watered." That is the brief story of a ministry which lasted for some considerable period in all likelihood. In the second letter to the Corinthians it is evident that Apollos had left Corinth on account of these difficulties, and declined to go back again. We see him, however, going from Ephesus, instructed by Priscilla and Aquila, with the larger view, the more perfect understanding, the fuller enduement of spiritual power; and Luke says, " He helped them much," and Paul says, " I planted, Apollos watered."

Now it was to Ephesus that Paul came, after the departure of Apollos. This nineteenth chapter, and the first seven verses, one of the most familiar paragraphs in the whole book, is a most constantly misinterpreted passage. It needs careful consideration. Let us notice first Paul's investigation and his instruction; and then observe the things that immediately followed.

Paul found a little group of about twelve men, and he asked them this question, " Did ye receive the Holy Spirit when ye believed? " The word " since," " Have ye received the Holy Spirit since ye believed " creates an entire misrepresentation of the question he asked. That is something to be stated emphatically, because it is on the presence of that word, that the misinterpretation of this passage has been based. The tense of the verbs " receive " and " believe " is the same, so that it may be rendered, " Received ye the Holy Spirit when ye believed? " Not, Have ye received since; as though there were a belief at some time, and a subsequent reception of the Spirit; which in the terminology of our own day is described as a " second blessing." Paul asked no such question.

Now mark their answer. " Nay," they said, " we did not so much as hear whether the Holy Spirit was given."

THE ACTS OF THE APOSTLES

[Acts 18:24-19:7]

I think perhaps no better word can be substituted for the word "given." As a matter of fact there is no word in the text. It is introduced for the purpose of interpretation. They said, "We did not so much as hear whether the Holy Spirit was." As to what word should follow the "was," it is not easy to say. Probably none. They might have meant that they did not know of the existence of the Spirit. But that is not likely for they were disciples of John, possibly as the result of the preaching of Apollos. What then had they heard? What was the ministry of John? John had said, "I indeed baptize you with water unto repentance: but He that cometh after me is mightier than I, Whose shoes I am not worthy to bear; He shall baptize you with the Holy Spirit and with fire." The baptism of John had included a declaration of its own limitation, and the affirmation of a fuller baptism to come, not through his ministry, but through the ministry of Another. John had distinctly foretold the coming of the Holy Spirit; and these men therefore were not likely to have meant, We have never heard anything about the Holy Spirit; but rather: We know that the Spirit was promised by the great prophet John, but we do not know whether He is yet given, whether He has yet come.

The apostle then asked them, "Into what then were ye baptized?" and they replied: "Into John's baptism." That is why they had not heard whether the Holy Spirit was given. They had only proceeded as far as John had been able to take them; to the place where Apollos was, when he came to Ephesus.

The reason for Paul's question to them is not declared. It may, however, be surmised upon the basis of the general observation of the story. When he met those men he may have felt there was something lacking; that they were sincere, honest, but there was something lacking, something of fire, something of emotion.

He then gave them instruction, and revealed to them

the fact that the baptism of John was preparatory, and that the teaching of John vindicated the necessity for going beyond him to Jesus. He then began to tell them all that they did not know of the Christ; of the resurrection and Pentecostal effusion; of the fact that through Pentecost men were brought into living union with Jesus. When they heard that, "they were baptized into the name of the Lord Jesus."

Then Paul laid his hands upon them, and they received the Holy Spirit. Then all that Paul had missed, was immediately manifest. They "spake with tongues," they began to prophesy. Their enkindled emotion expressed itself in ecstatic utterances of praise, for tongues were bestowed, not for edification, but always for adoration. If the tongues witnessed to enkindled emotion, the prophesying witnessed to enlightened intelligence; and they became martyrs, witnesses; for in that moment they became Christian. This was not a second blessing, but the first blessing, as the baptism and reception of the Holy Spirit always is.

I believe there are multitudes of people in Church membership who are not Christian in the New Testament sense of the word, who have come to John's baptism, and have come no further. That is what Paul found when he came to Ephesus. They were honest men, obedient, sincere, who had followed the light as far as it had come to them; but there was fuller light, and a brighter and larger life; and to that Paul introduced them.

What are the values of this study? As I look at this page I learn that men can only lift other men to the level on which they live; can only lift other men to the level to which they themselves have come. Apollos, a Jew, an Alexandrian, learned, mighty in the Scriptures, fervent in spirit, careful in his teaching, bold in his utterance, could only take the people as far as he had come himself, not one yard beyond it, not one foot above it. His disciples will know only the baptism of John. Paul came, and

[443]

not because he was a better man than Apollos, but because he had fuller knowledge, a fuller experience, he lifted these same twelve men to the higher level, until the cold and beautiful accuracy of their honest morality was suffused with the passion and fire of the coming of the Holy Spirit. Apollos could not bring them there until he himself had reached that position. When Apollos came to the fuller light and experience, he could pass to Corinth, and do for Paul in Corinth what Paul did for him in Ephesus. Paul can do his planting in Corinth, and be very successful; and Apollos waters. When Paul comes to Ephesus he will find the planting of Apollos, and will water it.

If we are preachers and teachers we can only help men to the level to which we have come. The declaration is full of solemnity. The Holy Spirit always needs the human instrument. That is what the book of the Acts of the Apostles emphasizes. There are many ways of telling the story of this book. God the Holy Spirit cannot do without men and women. He must have them to do His work. That is the whole genius of missionary endeavour. God the Holy Spirit can only bring the message of the crucified and risen and glorified Christ to any part of the world through men and women who know the power of these things.

But mark the law. The fit instrument is always found. The operation of the Spirit is limited by the instrument. Is it any wonder when Paul came to write his letters to Christians, that the great burden was not that they should believe, nor that they should love, nor that they should hope. He thanked God for faith and hope and love, but he prayed that they might have full knowledge (epignosis). We have no right to send men out, and think they can do the full work of the ministry, either apostolic, or prophetic, or evangelistic, or the work of pastor and teacher; without full knowledge. I do not mean academic knowledge only. Apollos had that, and failed. I mean spiritual knowledge and discernment. This can only come by the illumination of the Spirit of God, and by patient training.

Lastly mark the diversities. How did these twelve men enter into the larger life? They heard the teaching, they obeyed, they were baptized into the name of Jesus. Then Paul laid on his hands, and they received the Holy Spirit. In the tenth chapter we find Peter was talking to Cornelius, and he received the Spirit immediately, and was baptized, not before, but after receiving the Spirit. The Spirit bloweth where He listeth. We must not take any illustration in this book, and make it an abiding rule, for if so, there will be as many schools as there are stories in the Acts of the Apostles. We cannot base a doctrine of the Spirit's methods upon any one story. Upon the whole of them we can base the doctrine of the Spirit's method, and that may be stated thus. Not according to human ideas, or human laws formulated by any story; but in many ways, through the laying on of hands, and without such laying on; in answer to water baptism, before water baptism; so comes the Spirit. The important matter is that we have this Spirit, without Whose presence and illumination we cannot preach this Christ, or teach Him. May it be ours to press to the highest height, and the fullest knowledge, that we may lift all those whom we teach on to this highest level.

Acts 19:8-20

During all the varied and long-continued ministry of Paul, he remained longer at Ephesus than at any other centre. This particular paragraph gives the account of that sojourn; and refers to two periods; first, a period of three months, during which he reasoned in the synagogue; and secondly, one of two years, during which he reasoned in the school of Tyrannus.

In our study of the earlier part of this chapter, we saw the beginnings of the work in Ephesus. The paragraph

following this (19: 21–41) gives an account of the uproar
in Ephesus, which eventuated in the apostle's departure.
Consequently in this brief paragraph (verses 8–20) we
have the only detailed account of that work.

Luke has given us a group of incidents, all related to
each other, and enabling us to understand the work of
those two years, especially if we illuminate this page of
incident by apostolic words found in his address to the
elders at Miletus, and by some references in his own
letter at a later period. The incidents, while few, are
significant; and the final statement of the paragraph gives
us the key to its interpretation, " *So* mightily grew the
word of the Lord, and prevailed." All the paragraph is
needed for the interpretation of that " So." We have the
account of Paul's entering the synagogue; of the " hardened and disobedient " among those who listened to him
there; of his turning from them to the school of Tyrannus; of his continuation there for two years, reasoning
and teaching; of the sounding forth of the Word through
all Proconsular Asia; of those special and marvellous
manifestations of miraculous power, the mastery over
evil spirits; and of the attempt at imitation on the part
of certain Jewish exorcists, with the central special illustration of the defeat of these men, in the case of the
sons of Sceva. When the group of incidents has been
noted, the paragraph significantly closes with these words,
" So." That is, by these actions, by this means, in this
way, " So mightily grew the Word of the Lord, and prevailed." It is evident that Luke did not desire to give a
detailed account of that two years' ministry, but that he
took from the period certain outstanding incidents, to
bring the reader into a recognition of the difficulties confronted, and of the triumphs of the Word of God in
Ephesus.

Let us first of all consider briefly the city in the background, Ephesus; then look more particularly at the
apostle in the foreground, Paul in Ephesus; and finally

and principally, notice the remarkable spiritual conflict which this page reveals as having taken place in Ephesus.

Writing to the Corinthian Christians from this city, Paul said that he proposed to tarry in Ephesus until Pentecost; and he gave his reasons for this tarrying: " for a great door and effectual is opened unto me, and there are many adversaries." At Corinth Paul had stayed for a long period. He did not stay long in Athens. There were no adversaries in Athens, there was not virility enough left in Athens to oppose; and consequently there was very little opportunity for the preaching of the evangel. But in Ephesus he said, "A great door and effectual is opened unto me." The difficulties of the situation created the greatness of the opportunity in the mind of this man. The difficulties were in themselves aids to the apostolic preaching. The adversaries were compelled to contribute to the victory.

Glance then at Ephesus, at the city itself. Dr. Farrar thus described it:

" It lay one mile from the Icarian Sea, in the fair Asian meadow where myriads of swans and other water-fowl disported themselves amid the windings of Cayster. Its buildings were clustered under the protecting shadows of Coressus and Prion, and in the delightful neighbourhood of the Ortygian Groves. Its haven, which had once been among the most sheltered and commodious in the Mediterranean, had been partly silted up by a mistake in engineering, but was still thronged with vessels, from every part of the civilized world. It lay at the meeting-point of great roads, which led northwards to Sardis and Troas, southwards to Magnesia and Antioch, and thus commanded easy access to the great river-valleys of the Hermus and Meander, and the whole interior continent. Its seas and rivers were rich with fish; its air was salubrious; its position unrivalled; its population multifarious and immense. Its markets, glittering with the produce of the world's art, were the Vanity Fair of Asia. They furnished to the exile of Patmos the local colouring of those pages of the Apocalypse in which he speaks of ' the merchandise of gold, and silver, and precious stones, and of pearls, and fine linen, and purple, and silk, and scarlet, and all thyine wood, and all manner vessels of ivory, and all manner vessels of the most precious wood, and of brass, and iron, and marble, and cinnamon, and odours, and ointment, and frankincense, and wine, and oil, and fine flour, and wheat, and beasts, and sheep, and horses, and chariots, and slaves, and *souls of men.'*"

There can be no more graphic and inclusive description of Ephesus than that.

In that great city the central religious fact was the temple devoted to the worship of Artemis. This temple was the banking-house of the merchants, and so there was the most intimate relationship between the commercial prosperity of Ephesus, and the religion centred in this great temple. That temple of Artemis had been made a sanctuary into which people of all kinds were allowed to come. Farrar in his Life of Paul, said that, "The vicinity . . . reeked with the congregated pollutions of Asia," and we may have some slight understanding of what that meant by remembering that for a furlong radius the temple gave sanctuary to all the most evil things. The worship itself was unutterably vile. The atmosphere of the city was electric with sorcery and incantations, with exorcists, with all kinds of magical imposters. Jewish exorcists were there, trafficking upon the credulity of the people, superadding to all the incantations and sorceries of their own religions, declarations of ability to cast out evil spirits by the citation of words out of the Hebrew ritual.

Into this city of Ephesus, wealthy, profoundly religious, with a religion that was in itself worse than an utter absence of it, the apostle came. There were many adversaries; adversaries among his own brethren in the synagogue, as he revealed in his subsequent appeal to the elders at Miletus; adversaries, not so much among the ruling classes, as among those whose trades were interfered with; adversaries principally in that worship which had so remarkable a manifestation in the evil courses and habits of the eunuch-priests and virgin-priestesses. It was to the Church at Ephesus Paul wrote:

" We wrestle not against flesh and blood, but against the principalities, against the powers, against the world-rulers of this darkness, against the spiritual hosts of wickedness in the heavenly places."

It was in Ephesus that this man became supremely conscious of that world of spiritual antagonism which his writings so clearly revealed, and which we need to recognize even to-day. It was in Ephesus that the forces of the underworld of evil were massed, patently manifest. Here, far more than at Athens, Corinth, or Philippi, or any other of the places which he had visited, he came—if we may use so material a figure for spiritual things—face to face with naked opposition in the spirit world.

Now let us look at the man himself in that city, in the midst of its wealth, its luxury, surrounded by all those religious influences which were of the most evil kind, supremely and sensitively conscious of the antagonism of spiritual adversaries. He was occupied in making tents. That fact does not appear in this paragraph, but when the elders of Ephesus came to meet him at Miletus, he said, " I coveted no man's silver, or gold, or apparel. Ye yourselves know that these hands ministered unto my necessities, and to them that were with me." This great apostle of Christ, this missionary of the Cross, in this city made tents to support himself, and those who were with him, thus fulfilling this ministry. Mark well the significance of this. In a city where financial gain was the inspiration of all the service of religion, this man declined to take either the silver, the gold, or the apparel of any, even of Christian people, but ministered to his own necessities, making tents, supporting himself by his own labour.

Notice in the next place, that he was in Ephesus as the great Christian apologist; for three months reasoning and persuading in the synagogue; and when those of his brethren in the synagogue began definitely to oppose his teaching, deliberately turning from them, and separating the disciples from that Jewish community, taking them out with him, going to the school of Tyrannus, and there *reasoning.* We must keep these two things in close connection, to get the picture of the man. Tent-making and supporting himself day by day; the great Christian apologist in the school of Tyrannus, in the midst of all the evil influences of the city, preached the Kingdom of God, telling the story of Jesus, for he had no other message for these dead or dying Grecian cities, than Jesus and the resurrection.

But this was not the whole of his occupation. In the twentieth chapter, where his address to the elders of the Church is recorded, he said, " I shrank not from declaring unto you anything that was profitable, and teaching you publicly, and from house to house. . . . By the space of three years I ceased not to admonish every one night and day with tears " (verses 20 and 31). He was not only the tent-maker, not only the logical and brilliant Christian apologist, but the pastor of the flock teaching with tears, admonishing; watching, with jealous and zealous love, the growth of those who bore the name of Christ.

This teaching in the school of Tyrannus " continued for the space of two years; so that all they which dwelt in Asia "—that is Proconsular Asia—" heard the word of the Lord, both Jews and Greeks." That is one of those verses that may be read and passed over; but it is a window, through which we see Proconsular Asia, those seven churches referred to in the book of Revelation, to which the final epistles of the risen and glorified Lord were sent, which were scattered through that region. Paul then at Ephesus was making tents, conducting a great course of apologetics for Christianity, fulfilling the function of the pastor, watching over the flock, admonishing with tears, and teaching from house to house; but he was also directing a great missionary enterprise to that whole region round about Ephesus. In all probability it was here in Ephesus that Philemon was brought to Christ, and sent to Colosse for the formation of that Church. Probably also it was at Ephesus that mighty fellow-worker with Paul in prayer, Epaphras, who watched over another Church, was first brought to Christ. The mighty apostle himself perchance sometimes journeyed from Ephesus, and was in perils from robbers there.

Once again in the second Corinthian letter, in chapter eleven, there are certain words, written almost certainly immediately after his departure from Ephesus. The first had been written while he was in Ephesus. Arguing concerning the rights of his apostleship, and the dignity of his ministry, and producing the evidences thereof, he described the circumstances through which he passed:

" In labours more abundantly, in prisons more abundantly, in stripes above measure, in deaths oft. Of the Jews five times received I forty stripes save one. Thrice was I beaten with rods, once was I stoned, thrice I suffered shipwreck, a night and a day have I been in the deep; in journeyings often, in perils of rivers, in perils of robbers, in perils from my countrymen, in perils from the Gentiles, in perils in the city, in perils in the wilderness, in perils in the sea, in perils among false brethren, in labour and travail, in watchings often, in hunger and thirst, in fastings often, in cold and nakedness. Beside those things that are without, there is that which presseth upon me daily, anxiety for all the churches."

Look at this worker in Ephesus, making tents to supply his own needs, a great Christian apologist, the pastor

of the flock, admonishing with tears; the evangelist, going
out to the regions beyond; enabled to do in Proconsular
Asia what he had been forbidden to do on that second
missionary journey; planting churches, sending out the
great message; and all along entering into the fellowship
of the suffering of his Lord, so that he could write such
a passage immediately after leaving Ephesus as that in
the second Corinthian letter.

Think of this man. Think of the forces in Ephesus
against him, against his Gospel, against his Lord. Think
of that great heart of his, bearing the burden of these
churches that he had planted in the earlier missionary
journeyings. Think of the poverty, the hunger, the
anxiety, the stress, and the perils. How did he finish
that paragraph in the Corinthian letter? "If I must
needs glory, I will glory of the things that concern my
weakness."

"So mightily grew the Word of the Lord, and prevailed." First the difficulties of the city creating the opportunity; secondly, one man absolutely at the disposal
of his Master, so consecrated to Him that of determination he would be independent of the suspicion that his
business was the business of financial gain, and laboured
through the long dark hours of night that he might be
free during the day to argue and reason concerning this
Kingdom of God; and to see his people, and admonish
them with tears; and all the time the care of the churches
on his heart; news reaching him of those untrue and
needing rebuke; letters to be written out of great passionate longings; one man in the city. "So mightily
grew the Word of the Lord, and prevailed."

We now turn to that which is the supreme matter of
interest, the spiritual conflict in Ephesus. And first let
us observe the opposing forces. On one hand there was
the presence and prevalence of the occult in Ephesus, of
magic, and of sorcery. We are inclined, in the presence
of magic and sorcery to-day—for we have not outgrown

these things—to smile, and to speak of them as mere chicanery. The New Testament never treats them in that way. In the presence of this magic in Ephesus, and in other places, of these dark arts, the New Testament never speaks of them as trickery, as though they were the work of clever rogues. The New Testament says that these things are Satanic, and always attributes them to the agency and activity of spiritual personalities, who are possessed and mastered by evil. This is a matter we need very carefully to face and consider in our own days. To take the New Testament outlook, all this is not merely the trickery of rogues, but the actual activity of demons. Through the black arts, and clever manipulations, actual messages are spoken to men, and actual results produced, that cannot be denied. The man who denies the actuality of things done in the name of magic and spiritism, has never examined them carefully. These were the forces in Ephesus, the degraded and demoralized principalities and powers, the rulers of darkness.

On the other hand, in Ephesus with the coming of Paul there came the opportunity for the activity of the Spirit of God, and for the proclamation of the victorious name of the Son of God. This one man, and those associated with him, became the instruments—or in their corporate capacity as a church, the instrument—through which the Spirit of God could act, as against the spirits of evil; the instrument through which the great Name, the victorious Name of the Christ might win its victories over the demoralizing and degrading and damnable forces of the underworld that were so terribly blighting Ephesus itself.

In this connection notice very carefully what this passage declares. In verse eleven we read: " God wrought special miracles by the hands of Paul." Here is a distinction not to be lightly passed over. Luke did not say that Paul wrought miracles in Ephesus, but that God wrought them by the hands of Paul. In the first sermon

[453]

THE ACTS OF THE APOSTLES

preached in the power of the outpoured Spirit, which sermon was the result of the illumination and explanation of Christ through the Spirit to the preacher, Peter spoke of the miracles, and said quite distinctly, "Jesus of Nazareth, a man approved of God unto you by mighty works and wonders and signs, which *God did by Him* in the midst of you." This man did not work miracles, nor even our Lord Himself, in the loneliness of His human nature; they were both instruments through whom God was able to perform things that were wonders to men, who could not understand the higher laws by which they were made possible. A miracle is not a violation of law, but an activity of law in the realm of laws higher than we know, and, therefore, full of surprise to men, but of no surprise to God. God is not imprisoned within those few laws that man has been able to discover. God is bound by the laws of His own universe, but we do not know them all; and consequently, when we see an activity within the realm of the ultimate and final laws, we call it a miracle, and so it is, a thing of wonder and surprise, but not a violation of law, not a setting aside of law.

Take the instances given here. It is affirmed that men took from the person of this man Paul, handkerchiefs and aprons, and carrying them to sick people, they were healed by touching them. That is a miracle to us; but if God so chose through this man Paul, to work the healing wonder, I deny that it was incredible. There is a humanness in all this, and it is very interesting. They took the handkerchiefs and the aprons. "Handkerchief" is a most misleading word. To be quite literal in our translation, they took the sweat-cloths and aprons, the two things that Paul made use of as he worked. Paul did not work the miracle. God wrought the miracle; and if God shall honour the faith of superstitious people within the realm of a magic they understand, who am I that I should question God? God wrought special miracles, like the very magic with which these people were acquainted; and by the working revealed the fact that the magic itself was of spiritual activity; and therefore there needed to be no acceptance of a philosophy because its propounders wrought wonders. Evil men have often wrought wonders. The devil can work miracles to our poor blind eyes; and demons have astonished men by the wonders they have wrought. The miracle is not a demonstration that the spirit producing it is good. It is a demonstration of spiritual activity, of an activity in a realm beyond and outside that of which we are conscious.

So in this city full of magic, full of humours and systems and incantations and exorcisms, God wrought special miracles; and people, taking even the garments Paul wore in his work, their sick were cured, and evil spirits were cast out. God condescended to work not on a higher plane, but on a lower plane; for every miracle wrought in the material is a miracle wrought on a lower plane than the miracles wrought in the spiritual. The greater triumphs were not the healing of these people, but the spiritual wonders wrought in those who were made children of God, and brought to high morality of life. Yet for the capture of these people, and their convincing, it was shown them that the wonders that they associated with an evil form of religion, could be wrought, and were wrought, in the Name, the holy Name, which this man taught and preached.

These victories created a crisis. There were exorcists who now attempted to work with Paul's method. They had used other charms and incantations, but now they began to say, " I adjure you by Jesus Whom Paul preacheth." The result was immediate. Victories cannot thus be won by people who are so far apart from the One Who wins the victory. When these men said, " I adjure thee by *Jesus* Whom *Paul* preacheth," in a moment the answer came from the evil spirit, " Jesus I recognize, and Paul I know; but who are ye? " These men found that they could not traffic with the name of Jesus. That which impressed the city, and filled it with fear, was not the wonders wrought by Paul, but the fact that when some one else tried to work with his tools or implements, or Name, they were defeated.

Thus through the victories won over these forces of evil by the Spirit through His servant, the Name was magnified, and the Church was purified. That sacrificial fire, that burning of the books of magic was not the burning of books belonging to the Ephesians still remaining in idolatry. They were books belonging to people in the Church. They came, confessing that they still practised the black arts, and still had traffic with these unholy things, and so the fire was lit.

"*So* mightily grew the Word of the Lord, and prevailed." That was the impression made upon Luke as he heard or knew the story of these years at Ephesus, and committed it to those brief pictures. The word "mightily" means with resistless and overpowering strength. All kinds of facts and forces were pressed into the service of the Word, and made tributary to the carrying on of the work; the synagogue of the Jews, or the school of a Greek teacher; special miracles wrought; imitation mastered; the anger of demons. All these things were made tributary to the victory of the Word, and led up to the final statement; all must be included within it; "So mightily grew the Word of the Lord."

If we have Paul's vision, Paul's conception, we shall not say, There are many adversaries, therefore we must abandon the work; but rather we must stay until Pentecost, and prosecute His great enterprises, "Buying up the opportunity, because the days are evil." That is the spirit of this story. The days were evil days. Evil days created the opportunity for God-sent men.

If we would see the Word of God grow mightily and prevail in our own city, we need to ponder this story carefully, and find out the secrets here revealed; to yield ourselves to this Spirit of God; to serve this same Lord with equal lowliness of mind, and sincerity, and sacrificial earnestness, as did this man Paul. Then the Word of God to-day as ever, will grow mightily, and prevail.

Acts 19: 21-41

The chief interest of this passage centres in the uproar in Ephesus. The first brief paragraph contained in verses 21 and 22 is really preparatory to all that remains of the book.

In these verses (21, 22) we have a declaration of the apostle's purpose. The victories in Ephesus did not satisfy the heart of the apostle. From the midst of abundant and victorious labour, he looked on over the whitened fields of harvest, until his gaze rested in strong desire upon the central city of earthly power, and he said, "I must also see Rome." That was not the "must" of the tourist. It was the "must" of the missionary. This man knew perfectly well that Rome was the strategic centre of the world, that from Rome great highways ran out over all the known earth, along which legions travelled, and merchantmen wended their way. He felt that if that centre could but be captured, these highways would be highways for the Lord, for the messengers of the Gospel of His peace. Therefore he said, "I must also see Rome."

Notwithstanding this purpose there was delay. He did not immediately set out to Jerusalem. He sent into Macedonia "two of them that ministered unto him, Timothy and Erastus, and he himself stayed in Asia for a while." The first letter to the Corinthians was written almost certainly during this time of tarrying in Ephesus, and in it we find an explanation of the reason of the delay. When he came to the close of that letter, he said, "Now concerning the collection for the saints, as I gave order to the churches of Galatia, so also do ye"; and in the fifth verse of the last chapter we have his reference to

this same purpose which Luke chronicles: " I will come
unto you, when I shall have passed through Macedonia;
for I do pass through Macedonia." He " purposed in
the spirit, when he had passed through Macedonia
. . . to go to Jerusalem." In the eighth verse of the
last Corinthian chapter we find his determination to tarry
recorded. His purpose was to go through Macedonia,
but he said, " I will tarry at Ephesus until Pentecost ";
and the reason is declared, " for a great door and effectual is opened unto me, and there are many adversaries." He did not, however, tarry in Ephesus till Pentecost, even though his purpose was to do so, for in the
twentieth chapter and the sixteenth verse of the book of
the Acts, Luke says Paul had determined to sail past
Ephesus; he had already left Ephesus—for he was
hastening to be in Jerusalem at the day of Pentecost.
As a matter of fact, the uproar in Ephesus hastened the
departure of the apostle. He did not, however, refer to
that uproar when he said, " There are many adversaries."
As a matter of fact the uproar in Ephesus ended the
opposition.

This uproar was occasioned by the fact that it was the
month of May. It was the time of the great gatherings
throughout Proconsular Asia, of those who worshipped
Diana, or Artemis. The city was filled with her worshippers, and the uproar was occasioned by the presence
of these people there. Demetrius gathered the craftsmen
together, and told them what this man Paul was doing.
This caused the disturbance, but the end was peace,
patronage, and protection for the Christians. Then Paul
left. While there were adversaries, the door was open,
and he remained. Thus he did not remain until Pentecost in Ephesus; and the reason of his going was the
uproar which we are now to consider.

The month of May these people called the Artemisian,
because it was the month devoted to these great religious
assemblies in honour of Artemis; and the gatherings were

[458]

described as the Ephesia. The picture is full of life and
colour. Vast crowds were gathered together for worship. The theatre into which they crowded, taking with
them the two travelling companions of Paul, was capable
of seating twenty or thirty thousand people. These facts
help us to understand the commotion of the city.

Our interest, however, is supremely centred in the revelation which this picture gives us of the progress of the
Word of God. Three matters impress us as we read the
story: first, the method of the victories of the Word of
God; secondly, the nature of the opposition stirred up
against the Word of God, of which Demetrius was the
central figure; and finally, and principally, the real peril
to the Word of God and the Christian Church, which
was that of the action of the town clerk.

First then, as to the method of the victories. The fact
of these victories was testified by Demetrius, who gathering together the craftsmen, said to them:

" Sirs, ye know that by this business we have our
wealth. And ye see and hear, that not alone at Ephesus,
but almost throughout all Asia, this Paul hath persuaded
and turned away much people, saying that they be no
gods, which are made with hands: and not only is there
danger that this our trade come into disrepute; but also
that the temple of the great goddess Diana be made of no
account, and that she should even be deposed from her
magnificence, whom all Asia and the world worshippeth."

Thus Demetrius confessed that the apostolic preaching
was successful; that wonderful victories were being won
in Ephesus itself, and through that whole region of Proconsular Asia, which Paul had so longed to evangelize,
and had been prevented, when driven to Troas.

Now let us notice the methods of these victories. How
did the Word of the Lord grow mightily and prevail?
First, by the presence in Ephesus of one man, wholly and
absolutely at the disposal of his Lord and Master. In

Ephesus he bore testimony, he preached, he taught. He was thus at the disposal of his Lord and Master as an instrument for the working of remarkable signs. He did not attempt to work miracles in Ephesus. Christian apostles never did; but they were at the disposal of God, when He desired to work through them some sign. He was in fellowship with his Lord also in travail, sharing with Him the very afflictions that make the Kingdom come. As he told the elders at Miletus subsequently, he was with them night and day in tears, and in much affliction, for the Word of his God.

The Word of God grew mightily, moreover, because God wrought special signs suited to special needs. Do not let us imagine that these signs are needed to-day. If they are not present, it is because they are not needed. God never works signs in order to make His apostles notorious or popular; but only where peculiar circumstances demand such signs.

And again, the Word of God grew and prevailed through a purified Church. The Church brought its secret books, and burned them, and then the Word grew and prevailed.

Observe then the nature of that growth. The victories won were the victories of a positive, acting as a negative. When the town clerk presently dealt with the matter, he said,—and it was merely the statement of a common truth,—these men are no " robbers of temples, nor blasphemers of our goddess." These men had not broken into the temples and robbed them of wealth. These men had held no meetings for the denunciation of the worship of Diana. How then came the victories? Why did Demetrius call together his craftsmen? Because the sale of the silver shrines of Diana was falling off. How was that to be accounted for? The springs of character affected the streams of conduct. Not by denouncing shrines, but by so changing men and women that they did not need shrines to Diana, thus the victory was won. Men and women in Ephesus, who were themselves shrines of Deity, did not need the shrines to Diana. Men and women in Ephesus, who knew fellowship with God by the Holy Spirit, certainly would not spend their money upon these silver shrines. They had no time to abuse the silver shrines; no time to make a public protest. A great phrase of Dr. Chalmers describes their condition, "the expulsive power of a new affection." This is the one way of victory, if the Church is to win real victories. They are won by the new, devitalizing the old; by the rising of a new life within men and women, which triumphs over all other desires. In America there grows a wonderful tree called the scrub-oak. Travelling through the country in the springtime, we see this scrub-oak, covered still with the leaves of last year. Every other tree is stripped by the tempest of the autumn and winter. But gradually, in the springtime, the leaves drop off the scrub-oak, by the rising of the new life. That which the tempest from without never accomplishes, the rising life within does accomplish. The rustling of the leaves seems to laugh at the storm, but when the new life rises, then quietly and surely they drop off. That was the victory in Ephesus. There was no demonstration against idolatry, but realization of fellowship with God. All the forces of the old were devitalized by the rising forces of the new.

Mark the rapidity of the growth. The business of Ephesus was affected; the religion of Ephesus was in danger; and the whole of Proconsular Asia was influenced. To repeat the words of the town clerk, these men were neither "robbers of temples, nor blasphemers of our goddess," and yet the traffic in shrines suffered, and the splendour and magnificence of the worship of Artemis was threatened. Thus by the fact of the new life of individual men, the old and hoary forces of evil were threatened.

In the second place notice the nature of the opposi-

THE ACTS OF THE APOSTLES

tion. Here, one of the most patent things is the philosophy running through the speech of Demetrius. The primary inspiration of the opposition of Demetrius was that vested interests were suffering. No attack had been made upon the craft, but the receipts were less. That is the whole story. There was a secondary reason, which must be given for the sake of decency and appearance, that religion was being threatened. Demetrius in that private meeting of the craftsmen, said to them:

"Sirs, ye know that by this business we have our wealth. And ye see and hear, that not alone at Ephesus, but almost throughout all Asia, this Paul hath persuaded and turned away much people, saying that they be no gods, which are made with hands: and not only is there danger that this our trade come into disrepute; but also that the temple of the great goddess Diana be made of no account."

What an unconscious revelation was this speech of the inspiration of this opposition. We are reminded of that story in the Gospels, of how Jesus landed upon the shore of the country of the Gadarenes. There He met two men possessed with demons, and He flung the demons out, and made the men free. The men who saw it, went up into the city, "and they told everything, and . . ."! Can "everything, and" be told? They told everything, and what had happened to the men. But surely the "everything" should be the healing of the men, and not what happened to the pigs? To these men, the "everything" was that the swine were destroyed. The "and" did not much matter; two men were healed! That was the case at Ephesus; "everything," "our trade" was in danger; and the "and" was that our religion also is threatened.

If that was the inspiration of this opposition, notice its expression. First there was a conference, a meeting of the craftsmen; secondly, there was confusion, "some cried one thing, and some another." Surely there is a touch of satire in Luke's account, " The more part knew not wherefore they were come together."

Alexander—I wonder if he was the coppersmith—wanted to be heard, in order to declare that they had no part in this propaganda, but he could not be heard, and the whole gathering ended in clamour, as for two hours the mob howled, " Great is Diana of the Ephesians." That kind of opposition is absolutely futile. A spiritual force can never thus be destroyed. That confusion in the great theatre was by the overruling of God, so that some said one thing, and some another; and the great majority did not know why they had come together; and the only unanimity was the unanimity of noise. One lie, multiplied by ten thousand voices, never becomes a truth. The Church of God in Ephesus had no reason to tremble on account of that wild confusion. That kind of opposition never halts the march of the Church of God for half an hour. Its peril begins when the town clerk makes it cease.

The town clerk as a politician was wholly and absolutely admirable. I have no quarrel with him. I like to listen to his speech, to his sarcastic rebuke of this shouting crowd. In effect he said, What you say is quite true, Diana is great, and therefore there is no need to shout! When men get together and shout aloud the same thing, we may be perfectly sure that there is some doubt about the matter.

I wonder how much this man understood the force of what he said: " These men are neither robbers of temples, nor blasphemers of our goddess." I do not know whether he saw further than that; but the deduction from it was that not these men, but the spiritual forces were going to win, and all the shouting could not prevent it. He showed to the mob the true method of dealing with the difficulty by reminding them of the two courses open to them. If it be a trade dispute, take it to the courts; if it be a town matter, a municipal matter, take it to the ecclesia, that assembly of free men, which have to deal with all such matters. He reminded them also that they were in danger. Though Ephesus was free, it might lose its freedom unless they could give a satisfactory account of this riot. He was a wholly admirable town clerk.

But look at him again, look at his influence, look at the thing he did, which he did not intend to do, for I do not believe there was any subtlety in this man. He agreed with, and confirmed, the superstition of the people. He took Christianity under his patronage, not because he admired Christianity, but in the interest of civic quiet. Speaking from the standpoint of Ephesus, I think he was quite justified. Speaking also from the standpoint of the town clerk, and of the recorder, of the one responsible for the affairs of the city, I think he was quite justified. He knew nothing about Paul or Christianity; but he knew something about Ephesus, and the fact that it was in peril; and the only thing to do was to save these men from the howling mob, and drive them back into quietness and satisfaction with their own religion. Quiet in Ephesus was everything to him, but in the moment in which these Christian men passed under the protection of the town clerk, they were in more danger than when Demetrius' mob was howling about them.

The last glimpse of this Ephesian Church in the Bible is in Revelation: "I have this against thee, that thou didst leave thy first love"; and the loss of first love almost invariably in the history of the Church, follows upon protection and patronage of the Church, from without. What of Ephesus to-day?

Again to quote Farrar:

"Its candlestick has been for centuries removed out of his place; the squalid Mohammedan village which is nearest to its site does not count one Christian in its insignificant population; its temple is a mass of shapeless ruins; its harbour is a reedy pool; the bittern booms amid its pestilent and stagnant marshes; and malaria and oblivion reign supreme over the place where the wealth of ancient civilization gathered around the scenes of its grossest superstitions and its most degraded sins."

This is an appalling picture penned by one who had looked upon the scene; the picture of a perished city, and a perished Church; of a city that could not be saved by the Church because the Church's love for its Lord had passed under the cooling process of the city's protection, and patronage. The English Church was far safer in the days of Marian persecution than in the days of Elizabethan patronage. Independency was not nearly so much in peril when the Fleet Prison existed as it is now with the Memorial Hall standing on the site thereof. Methodism was not nearly so much in danger when it was the scorn of Sidney Smith and that ilk, as it is when its presidents are received at Court. The Salvation Army was not in half as much danger when an Eastbourne mob pelted its missionaries with stones, as when her General is smiled upon by a king. I do not say these things are wrong. I do not criticize King or Court for receiving; but I do say that the Church of God is in her gravest peril when a town clerk protects her. Let us be very careful that we do not waste our energy, and miss the meaning of our high calling, by any rejoicing in the patronage of the world. It is by the friction of persecution that the fine gold of character is made to flash and gleam with glory. The Church persecuted has always been the Church pure, and therefore the Church powerful. The Church patronized has always been the Church in peril, and very often the Church paralyzed. I am not afraid of Demetrius. Let him have his meeting of craftsmen, and let them in their unutterable folly shout a lie twenty-five thousand strong. The truth goes quietly on. But when the town clerk begins to take care of us, then God deliver us from the peril.

Acts 20

The keynote to this chapter is found in the previous one, " Now after these things were ended, Paul purposed in the spirit, when he had passed through Macedonia and Achaia, to go to Jerusalem, saying, After I have been there, I must also see Rome " (19:21). Before the last journey toward Rome was commenced, the apostle evidently felt that his work in that district was accomplished. In this chapter we have a very condensed account of the final apostolic visits through this particular region. It has been said most accurately and helpfully that:

" A divine history is no mere account of things in detail; it is much more than this; it is a specially arranged extract from the whole, to prevent our losing ourselves in the many details, and to guide us to a proper estimate of the whole; it is at once a history, and a *comment* which the history itself furnishes."

We have here then, a page of selections, made from the whole of the final things in the ministry of Paul in Macedonia and Achaia; and the history becomes a comment. This chapter briefly records an itinerary, and deals principally with two events in that itinerary. It gives the story of that last, strange, contradictory, and changing journey of Paul ere he left this region; and it describes two events: first the meeting of the disciples at Troas on the first day of the week, for the breaking of bread, and to listen to apostolic testimony; and secondly, that very remarkable gathering of the elders of the Ephesian Church at Miletus, when Paul delivered to them his final charge. The facts of the itinerary may be briefly dismissed. We shall then attempt to consider the comment which it makes.

[466]

After the uproar at Ephesus, the apostle took leave of the disciples, exhorted them, and departed to go into Macedonia. He moved back from Ephesus, through Macedonia, by sea to Philippi, on to Corinth and Berœa; and the only record here is a brief statement, that he gave the disciples much exhortation. Between this second visit to Macedonia and the previous one, he had written the two Thessalonian letters. The word made use of here is suggestive and helpful, " exhortation." It comes from the root of Paraclete. The two thoughts suggested are those of advocacy and comfort. In the cities where Paul had been much persecuted, and where much blessing had also resulted, he defended the cause of his Master, and comforted these people who, in all probability, were now suffering persecution, as he had done.

Luke then records the fact that he went into Greece, and stayed there three months. These three months were spent on the old battle ground, amid the old difficulties; but his work was principally that of building up those who had found the faith.

Again the principle of hindrance, so often manifest in the history of Paul, is seen at work. As he was about to set sail for Syria, he discovered a plot; so he went back again through Macedonia. A company of disciples, gathered from Berœa, Thessalonica, and Derbe, hastened before him, in order to accompany him into Syria, and they waited for him at Troas. He sailed from Philippi, and was five days going to Troas, Luke accompanying him. One can imagine the communion of those days. In Troas he lingered for seven days, and there took place that first day meeting for the breaking of bread, and apostolic instruction. Then again moving away from Troas, the band of disciples went by sea to Assos, and Paul went alone on foot, twenty miles, by land. This man, with all the labours of the past on his heart, with all the turmoil and strife of the present, with all the expectation and longing of the future, walked those twenty miles in quiet meditation. At Assos he joined the little band, and they sailed again past Mitylene, Chios, and Samos, until they came to Miletus; and there he sent thirty miles for the elders of the Church at Ephesus, to come down to meet him.

What then is the comment of that page? I notice two things: the apostle's rest; and the apostle's restlessness. What were the secrets of the restfulness of this man? He was a man, mastered by Christ, having no motive other than that of such mastery, having cut himself completely adrift from every other tie that binds the human heart. We follow him on the sea to Philippi, and back again to Thessalonica, Berœa, down into Greece, sojourn there in imagination with him for three months; again cross Macedonia, again sail across the sea with Luke to Troas, walking those twenty miles, and the whole story may be written thus, " To me, to live is Christ."

> " Christ! I am Christ's! and let the name suffice you,
> Aye, for me too He greatly hath sufficed:
>
> .   .   .   .
>
> Christ is the end, for Christ was the beginning,
> Christ the beginning, for the end is Christ."

Consequently the man mastered by Christ, was master of his own circumstances. All the way he pressed every circumstance, whether of adversity or prosperity, into the service which was the result of the passion of his heart. On the sea, and on the land, in the assemblies and by himself, in the midst of hostility in Greece, in the midst of loving fellowship in Troas, I hear him saying, "I know how to be abased, and I know also how to abound." Being himself confirmed in his faith, he confirmed the faith of other people. He was a man characterized by abounding restfulness of spirit.

And yet there was manifest a constant restlessness. Devoted to the enterprises of his Master, he was never able to tarry long. He was sensitive to the immediate need wherever he went. Every movement in the local atmosphere touched him, and he was ever eager to minister to it. Journeying over that country where he had been before, the lure of the distant places was ever in his heart. He was making steady progress, doing the immediate work thoroughly, and yet all the while the clarion cry rang in his soul, " I must also see Rome." " Regions beyond," was his perpetual watchword; the uttermost part of the earth, marked the limit of his endeavour. Restful in Christ; he was yet restless in his devotion to the service of Christ. To have life's fitful fever dismissed by the healing touch of the Master's hand, is at the same moment to feel the thrill and the throb of His compassion driving us forevermore to new endeavour.

We now turn to consider the two events. The gathering in Troas is very suggestive. Observe its composition:—Paul, with a little company of friends, names that mean so little to us, " Sopater of Berœa, the son of Pyrrhus; and of the Thessalonians, Aristarchus and Secundus; and Gaius of Derbe, and Timothy,"—the fruitful reward of the stones in Lystra;—" and of Asia, Tychicus and Trophimus." Luke was there also; and all these were assembled with the little band of disciples in Troas. The occupation of the gathering was that of the breaking of bread. They sat around the board, with the memorials of His death, the bread and the fruit of the vine. Over that board the apostolic teaching was given. The minutes sped on, and the hours swiftly passed, until morning broke. It is wonderful how people forget time when they are really gathered about the living presence of the Lord.

Then there is the incident of Eutychus, which was a perfectly natural happening. A sleepy lad fell from the window and was killed. Then followed something which we describe as supernatural, another manifestation of power which was a perfectly natural action by the Lord

THE ACTS OF THE APOSTLES
of life. Like all the Lord's raisings from the dead, it was not done for the sake of the lad, but for the sake of his friends: " They were not a little comforted."

Look now at the gathering at Miletus. Notice its nature. It was specially convened by Paul. It was composed, not of all the members of the Church in Ephesus, but of those in oversight; and it was gathered in the interests of the Ephesian Church. This man who had been an apostle to the Gentiles, through whose ministry the Gentile churches had been formed, gathered about him the elders of one Church, in many senses a typical Church of the New Testament, and delivered his final charge to them. Paul was keenly sensitive to the perils that threatened the Church, to the resources which were at its disposal, and to the true method of its administration. In his address he was personal, affectionate, direct. The charge needs no exposition. Its chief value for us is found in its revelation of matters concerning the Church itself.

Paul revealed the central fact concerning the Church of God; it is " The Church of God which He purchased with His own blood " (verse 28). He also revealed the all-sufficient provision for that Church: " I commend you to God, and to the word of His grace " (verse 32). He further stated the true method of the administration of the Church: " The Holy Spirit hath made you bishops, to feed the Church of God." " Take heed unto yourselves, and to all the flock " (verse 28). He also revealed the perils of the Church; from without, " I know that after my departing grievous wolves shall enter in among you, not sparing the flock " (verse 29) ; and from within, " From among your own selves shall men arise, speaking perverse things " (verse 30).

That central declaration concerning the Church of God is a most remarkable one: " The Church of God, which He purchased with His own blood." The Church is the ecclesia, the called-out company of people. In what does

the difference or separation of its members consist?
They are purchased. We must not read into the word
"purchased" the quantities of a commercial transaction.
Wherever a reference is made in the Bible to the purchase of a soul, or the purchase of a Church, we must
turn to other figures of speech, for the correction of that
figure of speech in our language, or we shall misunderstand the thought suggested. It does not mean the ransomed people are purchased by God from any one. In
the apostolic writings the word only occurs half a dozen
times, and it literally means, *to make around oneself*.
That is to us an awkward phrase, a peculiarly Greek
method of expression. We may approach its significance
by other words or phrases, as for instance He acquired,
or He made His own. It is, however, a word which is
always used of a single act, and never of a continual
practice. The reference then is to some act by which
God acquired the Church for Himself.

But now we come to the word of mystery. "The
Church of God, which He purchased with His own
blood "—or, a little more literally,—" with blood that was
His own." I admit at once the difficulty of the passage.
Scholarly expositors have suggested that here, at some
time, a word has been omitted from the text; and that
what the apostle really wrote was, "The Church of God,
which He purchased with the blood of His own Son."
That, however, is pure speculation. If we leave it as it
is, it means "purchased with God's own blood." Some
of the fathers did not hesitate to speak of the blood of
God, in this connection. To think of this materially is
to be faced with difficulty; but if we remember that which
is supreme to our understanding of the mystery of redemption, that God was in Christ, and that there can be
no attempt to divide or separate between those two facts
in the one Being, then we may understand how at this
point the apostle made use of the most daring word in all
his writing; the Church, redeemed by His own blood,

that is the blood of Christ, and in that sense, the **very** blood of God.

Yet is there not an intended contrast to an idea found in the Hebrew letter? The writer of that letter, speaking of the imperfect priesthood of the past, declared that the high priest entered into the holy place " with *blood not his own*," a most remarkable expression. Here, on the contrary, is a people, redeemed by a Priest, Who has acquired them with blood which is His own. The suggestiveness of that merging of Deity and humanity in the Person of Christ is very important. We cannot consider the death of Christ as the death of an ordinary man, because the Person is so entirely different, that His very blood is spoken of here as being that of God Himself. In the history of the race God came into such relationship with humanity that it was possible for Him to bear, in the Person of His Son, all the issue of the sin and failure of a race; and so to ransom, to purchase, to acquire a people for Himself. The Christian Church is not a company of people admiring the ideal of Jesus, or accepting the beauty of His ethical teaching; and attempting to obey it. The Christian Church is the society of those who are purchased by God, acquired by His own blood. The mystery and the marvel and the might of God being in Christ, whereby He did reconcile us unto Himself, is the foundation truth concerning the Christian Church.

The all-sufficient provision for the life of the Church is expressed in the words: " I commend you to God, and to the word of His grace." There is no word in the New Testament that more baffles the expositor than this word " grace." Gather up the occasions in which it is found in the New Testament, and read them in their context; and then sit down in the presence of them, and wonder, and worship! The grace of God is not the love of God only, it is not the favour of God alone; it is the love of God operating through passion, in order to the perfecting of those upon whom that love is set. "I commend you to God, and to the word of His grace." You are His own, purchased with His own blood. There are grave and grievous perils threatening you, wolves from without, men of your own selves from within, but these are your resources: God, and the word of His grace! These are always the resources of the Christian Church.

Then we have a gleam, as to the true administration of the Church: "The Holy Spirit hath made you bishops." That is a fundamental word. The Holy Spirit selects some who are to occupy the position of the bishop. The Holy Spirit does not treat the whole assembly as though they had equal rights and gifts and privileges. "The Holy Spirit . . . made you bishops." What is a bishop? Here I think we have lost a little by the employment of the word "bishop." For the purpose of the English reader, the word "overseer" is preferable. The overseer is the man who watches, oversees. The seeing of the overseer is seeing from a distance; that is seeing of the whole of things, rather than a part. The function of the bishop is also that of feeding the flock of God.

John Milton expressed the perils threatening the bishop, when he described their failure in that terrible juxtaposition of two words that seem to contradict each other:

". . . blind mouths."

That is the tragedy that is possible to every minister of the Word; instead of seeing, he may be blind; instead of feeding, he may become merely a mouth desiring to be fed.

The perils threatening the Church, according to this passage, are first "grievous wolves," that is the peril from without; and men "speaking perverse things," men "from among your own selves," "to draw away the disciples," that is the peril within. Let these two perils be pondered well, and let us remember that the corrective to all such peril is to be found in the exercise of the high office of the overseer, the bishop, whose business it is to watch and to feed.

Paul commended his example to the elders at Ephesus. He had been loyal to his Lord, and courageous in the delivery of the message, "I shrank not from declaring unto you the whole counsel of God." There had been sacrifice in his service, "Ye yourselves know that these hands ministered unto my necessities." There had ever been a great compassion in his heart, "I besought you and ceased not to admonish every one night and day with tears."

Here the apostolic service in freedom ends. Immediately following the completion of this journey, we reach Jerusalem, where Paul was arrested, and finally taken as prisoner to Rome.

Acts 21: 1–16

The keynote of the remainder of this book is that of bondage. Paul from now is seen as " the prisoner of the Lord." Speaking to the elders of the Ephesian Church who had gathered to Miletus to hear his farewell message, he had said:

" And now, behold, I go bound in the spirit unto Jerusalem, not knowing the things that shall befall me there: save that the Holy Spirit testifieth unto me in every city, saying that bonds and afflictions abide me. But I hold not my life of any account, as dear unto myself, so that I may accomplish my course, and the ministry which I received from the Lord Jesus, to testify the Gospel of the grace of God."

He was thus quite conscious that he was moving toward bondage and limitation. He declared the Spirit had borne witness to him that in every city these were the things that now lay before him. We shall find him almost immediately an actual prisoner; and so far as these records are concerned, in that condition of bondage, we shall finally take our leave of him.

THE ACTS OF THE APOSTLES

Perhaps the main value of this final section of the book may best be expressed in words which Paul himself wrote, long after the history which is here recorded. I believe he was subsequently liberated for a period; and that it was during his second imprisonment that he wrote his final pastoral letters, both to Titus and Timothy. In all likelihood the last writing of this man preserved for us, is the second letter to Timothy, expressing his concern for the Church, and for the witness borne to truth. In the course of that letter he said: "I suffer hardship unto bonds," and then added, "but the Word of God is not bound." Whereas that description of his own condition was written in an imprisonment far more full of trial and difficulty and suffering than the one in which we find him in the Acts; nevertheless, the word of triumph that he wrote from the midst of such circumstances,—"the Word of God is not bound,"—gives us the keynote of these final chapters of the Acts.

In our meditation on this paragraph we shall notice some permanent values of the incidents recorded; but more carefully, observe the central interest of the story, that namely of the apparent conflict in guidance.

Let us first observe the waiting time at Tyre. Here is one of the small matters in which we have greatly gained by the Revision. In the fourth verse of this chapter it is said, "And having found the disciples, we tarried there seven days." The Authorized Version reads, "And finding disciples, we tarried there seven days." At first we may be inclined to think that the difference is so slight that there can be no importance attached to the change. Yet look again. The translation in the Authorized Version suggests rather a casual finding of disciples who were there, as though the ship now in port, being emptied of its cargo, and these men having to wait, they had happened quite casually upon disciples. The Revised rendering conveys quite another idea. "Having found the disciples"; and we might convey the

[475]

thought of the Greek in yet other words, and in a more arresting way thus: " Having by searching for them found the disciples." When these men came to Tyre there were seven days to wait, and they sought for the disciples. Henry Ward Beecher once declared that Paul was devoid of the artistic sense, that he travelled through those cities of Asia, packed with things of beauty, and artistic merit and value, and never by a line referred to one of them. I agree with the statement; but I do not agree with the conclusion. I would rather express the truth in the words of Dr. Parker, who when referring to this visit to Tyre said, " There was no scenery to Paul; there was no geography; there was nothing but lost humanity, and the redeeming Cross of Christ." That is nearer the heart of this matter so far as Paul was concerned.

These travellers, reaching Tyre, sought out the disciples. Do Christian travellers to-day, calling at Tyre, seek out the disciples? Is it not too often the case that when travellers are far away from home, they try and miss the disciples for that occasion, and see and meet every one, and everything else? They sought out the disciples because these men recognized that the little group of disciples in Tyre constituted God's vantage-ground there for the delivery of His word, for the accomplishment of His purpose.

This is the first occasion that Tyre is mentioned in the record of the Acts. Whence did these disciples of Tyre come? The question cannot be answered dogmatically. There must be in any attempt to answer it, a certain amount of speculation. Mark records how in the early part of the ministry of our Lord, men came to Jesus from Tyre. A little later on He Himself went into the region of Tyre and Sidon, and there the Syrophœnician woman found Him; and He, testing her faith by methods apparently rough, did nevertheless answer the faith with great and generous gift of love and power.

THE ACTS OF THE APOSTLES

When our Lord was uttering His solemn words of condemnation of the cities in which His mightiest works
were done, there was a note of patience and excuse made
for Tyre:

"Woe unto thee, Chorazin! Woe unto thee, Beth-
saida! for if the mighty works had been done in Tyre
and Sidon which were done in you, they would have repented long ago in sackcloth and ashes."

How these disciples came there we know not. I sometimes think that in that long ministry of the first generation of the Christian Church, apostles and evangelists and
deacons reaped, even on the human level, a harvest which
resulted from the sowing ministry of our Lord Himself.

When the travellers came to Cæsarea, they met with
Philip. Twenty years before this, Philip had been driven
from Jerusalem through Saul. Saul was the appointed
prosecutor of the Nazarene heresy, "breathing threatening and slaughter." Stephen was martyred, and the
persecution continued until scattered thereby, these people
went everywhere, preaching the Word; and amongst those
scattered from Jerusalem through the vehement hatred
of Saul, was Philip. Philip went down to Samaria, and
preached there. Now twenty years had passed away, and
Philip became Paul's host. Philip had been a pioneer in
that larger work for which Paul had been apprehended,
and which he had been doing with such conspicuous and
marvellous success. It was Philip who had first preached
to the Samaritans, who had first baptized an African, the
Ethiopian eunuch. It was to this man there had first
come the meaning of the larger issues of things. Even
before the reception of Cornelius, even before the apprehension of Saul by the Lord Christ, even before the
men of Cyprus and Cyrene had dared to preach in Antioch; Philip had answered the larger meaning of the
missionary purpose, and endeavour, and had preached in
Samaria; and then had gone away to baptize the Ethio-

pian eunuch, and receive him into the fellowship of the saints. Now the man who had followed that gleam until it broadened into the light of a great and intensive day, encompassing the whole Gentile world in its outlook,— that man is the guest of Philip. How those men looking back together, would see the mosaic of the Divine government revealed! Now at last they sit together in the home of Philip, twenty years after, and look back. What a great and gracious thing it is to look back! Yet how careful we should be to remember that in the present! We shall all look back after a little while, and what a thing this looking back will be! Are there not people we knew twenty years ago that we would not care to meet to-day? Is not that how Saul would naturally have felt about Philip; one of the " dear remembered faces " that he had caused to be full of pain? What a transmuting and transforming thing this fellowship with Christ is, that it can bring together the men who twenty years ago were afraid of each other, and fighting each other, and persecuting each other; and can now enable them to talk of the old things, and see in the fire and the persecution the very finger and hand of God. It is a blessed thing to look back, when we have found our way into a true fellowship with this Lord Christ Himself.

Now let us look particularly at the central interest of this passage. Verse four reads:

" And having found the disciples, we tarried there seven days; and these said to Paul through the Spirit that he should not set foot in Jerusalem."

In the twelfth verse we read:

" And when we heard these things, both we and they of that place besought him not to go up to Jerusalem."

Notice here that Luke associates himself with those who were at Cæsarea; Philip, Agabus, and those travelling in the company. These men all said to Paul, through the Spirit, that he should not set foot in Jerusalem; and later there was the beseeching of Philip, Agabus, Luke, and the whole company, that he should not go. In the previous chapter we read how Paul told the Ephesian elders of the certainty he had about the future:

" I go bound in the spirit unto Jerusalem, not knowing the things that shall befall me there: save that the Holy Spirit testifieth unto me in every city, saying that bonds and afflictions abide me."

He declared to these Ephesian elders that he was nevertheless compelled to finish his course, and complete his ministry of testimony to this Gospel of the grace of God. He made no answer at Tyre that is recorded, when they told him that he must not go to Jerusalem; he made no response when Agabus took his girdle and bound himself; but when Luke and the rest joined with him, tried to dissuade him, he said, "What do ye, weeping and breaking my heart?" The word *breaking* there does not so much suggest suffering, as weakening, bending. Why by your weeping are you attempting to weaken my purpose, breaking, bending, subduing my heart? "for I am ready not to be bound only, but also to die at Jerusalem for the name of the Lord Jesus." The contrast is quite clear. There can be no escape from the fact of the conflict of conviction. The motive in each case was pure. The motive of the apostle was pure. That we do not call in question. The motive of these disciples in Tyre, of Philip, of Agabus, and of Luke was pure. The inspiration was the same. They were both acting in the light of spiritual interpretation, and under the impulse of great loyalty to the purpose of their Lord. Yet with true motives and identical inspiration, here were convictions diametrically opposed.

In accounting for this there are differing interpretations. There are those who maintain that Paul was

[479]

wrong, and that all the suffering following was the result of the mistake he made at this point. On the other hand there are those who maintain that these people were wrong in the advice they gave; and that Paul was indeed following the path of loyalty.

My conviction is that Paul was right. His conviction was one resulting from the guidance of the Spirit of God. Take this paragraph, and set it in the light of the whole story of that going to Jerusalem, of its first reason, and its deepest intention, of the passion that drove him, and we shall find that he was going to Jerusalem to carry a gift that had been gathered among Gentile churches, in order to be helpful to the poor saints in Jerusalem. He was going to Jerusalem with a passionate desire to serve his brethren. Read again those wonderful paragraphs in the Roman letter which amaze us, in that they reveal a height of personal experience, and an intensity of missionary devotion, of which, alas! we know so little:

"I say the truth in Christ, I lie not, my conscience bearing witness with me in the Holy Spirit, that I have great sorrow and unceasing pain in my heart. For I could wish that I myself were anathema from Christ for my brethren's sake."

Put that high and holy passion behind this determination to tread the way to Jerusalem, in the face of all dangers; and put behind it that which, from the standpoint of his ecclesiastical statesmanship was the master-passion of his life; the desire to bring together the Jews and Gentiles into an experimental consciousness of their oneness in Jesus Christ; and in these we find the inspirations driving this man.

What then did these men and Luke mean when they said to him, " through the Spirit, that he should not set foot in Jerusalem "? We must interpret that declaration of the fourth verse by other declarations. In the previous chapter, in verse twenty-three Paul said that "in every city the Holy Spirit testifieth unto me, saying that bonds and afflictions abide me." In the eleventh verse of this chapter we find Agabus, prophesying in the Spirit, not telling him that he was not to go, but declaring that if he should go, then he would be bound and imprisoned. When these men in Tyre told Paul not to go, their advice was the result of the Spirit's foretelling that if he went, he would suffer. Taking the whole story into account, we are not warranted in believing that the Spirit declared that he was not to go; but that the Spirit told him that he was going to suffering and to prison. These disciples at Tyre when they heard it, when they were informed by the Spirit, and by spiritual interpretation, of the difficulties that awaited him, urged him not to go. The Spirit said that bonds awaited Paul, and their advice was really advice to falsify the teaching of the Spirit. I do not think they meant it in that way; they had not thought the situation out. The testimony of the Spirit was that there was waiting for this man bonds, afflictions, and suffering. Now the Spirit could never instruct men to give advice to one which, if followed, would be an attempt to escape the very pathway of suffering that the Spirit indicated was lying ahead of him. I believe then that at this point Paul was true to the deepest facts, and that he was right.

There is great comfort in this chapter for us. Recognizing that such things do occur, understanding the story by our own experience, is there not a test by which we may finally decide which conviction is according to the mind of the Spirit of God? I think that there is. It is the test of motive. The motive of the conviction that took possession of the minds of all these people, Luke included, was a very high motive. It was love for Paul. Paul's motive was an infinitely higher motive. It was love for the Lord, and passion for the accomplishment of His purpose. The last and final test for those who are submitted to the Spirit, who are seeking His guidance, who believe they have the light of His revelation, is always that of motive. There may be motives which in themselves are very high, which become wrong, because there ought to be the infinitely higher motive.

What is the heart, then, of this revelation? Paul never wavered. He felt the pressure and the persuasiveness of their love. "What do ye, weeping and breaking," bending, "my heart?" He acknowledged in that word that their tears and their entreaties weighed with him, weighed upon him, bent him toward their inclination also. He valued it, and he resisted it. He was conscious of the sweet constraint of their love; but I never see him rising to a higher height than when he consented to put that beneath his feet, in the interest of the call for loyalty to his Lord, and the abandonment of himself to the purposes of his Master.

Notice how the story finishes. Luke says, "When he would not be persuaded, we ceased, saying, The will of the Lord be done." They recognized at last who was right. In the loyalty of Paul, in his determination, in that masterfulness of purpose that would not be persuaded, even by their tears, there flamed upon them the revelation of the will of the Lord; and Luke says, "We ceased," and "We took up our baggage," and went with him. That is a beautiful ending. It is the final proof of a true fellowship. There was the honesty of their persuasion; there was the magnificence of his refusal, and at last there was the fellowship of oneness in the discovery of the will of the Lord.

Thus we see the prisoner of the Lord on his way to those bonds which presently, according to his own writing, turned out for the furtherance of the Gospel.

Acts 21 : 17–22 : 29

On the arrival of Paul in Jerusalem, he was welcomed by the brethren. It is noticeable that no apostle is mentioned. By this time in all probability they were scattered here and there, fulfilling their true mission. To James, and certain elders in oversight of the church in Jerusalem, Paul rehearsed the story of the victories won in the course of his ministry.

Immediately following this account we are told that, while they that heard it glorified God, they spoke not so much of the work accomplished, as of that which was most evidently uppermost in their heart, the immediate peril created by his presence in Jerusalem. Facing the situation as they thought calmly and considerately, they advised a certain course of action. Four men who, while believing in Jesus, were nevertheless under the Nazirite vow, were fulfilling the obligations of that vow, and the elders suggested to Paul that he should associate himself with them, doing what men often did in those days, taking the charges of their vow upon himself, and during the final days of their purification spending the time with them. The elders thought that by such action, he would contradict current reports concerning his attitude toward the Mosaic economy, which were likely to cause grave disturbance in Jerusalem.

Our theme is that of the advice of the elders, and the action of Paul. To understand this we must remind ourselves of the circumstances under which this advice was given a little more particularly.

The time of the apostle's arrival in Jerusalem was that of the Feast of Pentecost. Jerusalem was then crowded with multitudes of Jews. On the authority of the Roman historians we know that no less than two million Jews were crowded into the city and neighbourhood during these feasts.

In order to thoroughly appreciate the national atmosphere, we need to remember that during the whole of that period the oppression of Rome was being most keenly felt by the Hebrew people. Rebellion was incipient everywhere, on the part of the Jews; and Rome was ready to stamp out all such rebellion. How easy it would have been to have flung down into the midst of the people some fire which would have immediately produced a very definite explosion.

These facts enable us better to understand the attitude of these elders toward Paul. Paul had not been in Jerusalem for long years, but his name was known. He had been the publicly appointed prosecutor of the Nazarene heresy. Twenty years before, he had obtained letters from the high priest, empowering him to hale men and women to prison and to death. In the apprehension of that man by Jesus Himself, all the force of his marvellous personality had been turned into an entirely opposite direction. Jerusalem, and the Jewish people generally, knew his history, and the very fact of his presence was made an occasion for hostility.

Moreover the believing Jews were not friendly toward him. Notice the words in verses twenty and twenty-one:

" Thou seest, brother, how many thousands there are among the Jews of them which have believed; and they are all zealous for the law."

They were believers who were still observing rites and ceremonies, and who were diametrically opposed to Paul's view that a man in Christ is set free from every other yoke of bondage. We should remember also that Paul was there, bearing to them great gifts, material gifts from Gentile churches, but there does not seem to have been any recognition, any attitude of gratitude or thanksgiving toward him at all.

These must have been sad days for Paul. He would think of the days of Stephen long ago, and of his four previous visits to Jerusalem. He had never been welcome there.

These elders seem to have had no conviction that the zealots of the law were wrong. They did not ask Paul for a concession, but for a vindication, which is quite a

different matter. They asked him to deny the rumor
that he had abandoned rites and ceremonies, by observing
these. The principle underlying their appeal was that of
policy. Whatever their view, they must surely have
known Paul's attitude. Their request for vindiction before the believing Jews was dishonest. They knew that
he had personally abandoned the observance of rites and
ceremonies. These elders in Jerusalem had been in close
touch with all his movements, they had read his letters,
and certainly at this time the Galatian letter, and the two
Corinthian letters were written. At Antioch he had rebuked Peter for dissimulation, and now they asked him to
practise dissimulation.

That leads us to consider the consent of Paul; and as
in looking at the advice of the elders we observed the
purpose and terms of the advice; so here let us consider
the purpose of his consent, and the terms of that consent.

Directly we turn from the advice of these men which
was that of policy and of dishonesty withal, to the consent of Paul, and begin to look at the purpose of his
consent, we have moved on to an entirely different level.
I put that emphatically, because I hold that Paul made
the greatest mistake of his ministry on this occasion.
Yet we have to recognize the fact that the reason of his
consent was not that of expediency merely, not that of
policy, but that of devotion. The reason of his consent
was his desire to win his brethren. The reason of his
consent here is most perfectly declared in his matchless
words in the Roman letter:

" I say the truth in Christ, I lie not, my conscience
bearing witness with me in the Holy Spirit, that I have
great sorrow and unceasing pain in my heart. For I
could wish that I myself were anathema from Christ for
my brethren's sake, my kinsmen according to the flesh;
who are Israelites, whose is the adoption, and the glory,
and the convenants, and the giving of the law, and the
service of God, and the promises, whose are the fathers,

and of whom is Christ as concerning the flesh, Who **is**
over all, God blessed forevermore."

This was not the action of a man politic, expedient, and
attempting to manipulate circumstances to prevent a
breach of the peace, or a riot in Jerusalem. It was not
the action of a man trying to save his own life. It was
the action of a man who passionately and earnestly desired to do anything, if by the doing of it he might deliver
the message to his brethren, and win them. Look at the
action in itself. It was the doing of that which was of
no value to him. It was consent to an appearance, contrary to conviction. Yet was he justified?

What was the issue? The issue was the failure of the
purpose of the elders. They sought to maintain peace.
Peace was not maintained. What they did, provoked the
very riot they fain would have obviated. Again,—and
here the language needs to be more tender, and the
sympathy far greater—the issue was the failure of the
purpose of Paul. He sought by that accommodation, contrary to his own conviction, to gain an opportunity of
testimony to his brethren, and he lost his opportunity.
His brethren were not won, and the last word of the
paragraph is the same cry hurled after him that was
hurled after his Master, " Away with him."

The teaching of this incident is that love must ever be
loyal to truth. To sacrifice a principle for a moment in
the hope of gaining an opportunity to establish it afterwards, is always to fail. We never win an opportunity
that way. It is in our moments of highest spiritual
exaltation that we need to be most watchful against the
possibility of compromise. Men who would never compromise in order to save their own lives, are in danger of
compromising in the hope that they may help others. If
it is a stern word, if it is a hard word, it is a word of
infinite love, it is the word of eternal truth ; that by compromise we never establish a principle. Even though we

hope to gain an opportunity by the doing of it, we lose it.

That is the last word of this story, but there is something else to follow. We shall see how when men fail, even from high motives, the Lord appears, and gently restores them. The apostle was rescued by arrest, and was carried by soldiers up the stairs leading into the castle.

There are three matters of supreme interest in this story; first, the man; secondly, the mob; and thirdly, the Mother Church. Let us consider them in the reverse order, glancing first at the infuriated and angry multitude of people surrounding this man; and finally, at the man as a prisoner, to the end of the history in this book.

Twenty years had passed away since the formation of the Church, and the arresting fact here is that the church in Jerusalem is not seen. Paul was alone, and would have been beaten brutally to death by an infuriated mob, had he not been rescued by the Roman power. When once the seventh chapter of this book of the Acts has been passed, where the record of the first things in Jerusalem come to an end, whenever the Church emerges in her representative capacity, she is seen attempting compromise, pursuing the policy of accommodation. It was a little difficult for her to receive the testimony of Peter concerning the work in the house of Cornelius. She was suspicious of the movement in Samaria. With difficulty there was wrested from her the granting of the charter of freedom to the Gentiles. She pursued a policy of accommodation, receiving into her fellowship those who had made no break with Judaism. James declared to Paul, who had come up bearing with him gifts from the Gentile churches, with the love of his Lord burning in his heart, that there were multitudes of believing Jews, all of whom were observing the rites and ceremonies of Judaism. This was in itself a very remarkable admission and con-

fession. It may of course be said that these men had attempted thus to secure safety. It was undoubtedly the
easier path to admit to the fellowship of the Church men
who confessed Christ, and really believed in Him, who
nevertheless compromised with Judaism, by still observing its rites and ceremonies; but that policy of accommodation, policy of compromise, had weakened the
Church.

The issue is revealed in this page. The Church had
no influence in Jerusalem. In this tragic hour, when
this man, bearing in his body the stigmata of Jesus, ought
to have been welcomed with open heart and arms by the
Church; he stood alone in the midst of the pitiless scorn
and brutality of an angry mob, and had to be protected
by Roman power. The Church had neither power nor
protest. She had lost both by her policy of accommodation.

Now look at the mob. The word is admittedly not a
very elegant one, but no other suits the occasion. Yet
can we feel in our hearts anything of anger in the presence of that mob? Ought we not rather to feel the infinite sadness of the fact that any measure of conviction
that came to that city had been weakened by the failure
of the witnesses? That city had passed under the spell
of the power of Christ on the day of Pentecost, even
though they had rejected Him in the days of His flesh.
One wonders whether the whole city would not have
been in a different attitude and demeanour if there had
been no compromise on the part of the Church.

The arresting fact as we look at this crowd of Jews is
that of their frenzy. It is an Oriental picture, perfectly
natural; the tearing of garments, the flinging of dust into
the air, as the result of the emotion that seized them.
They were silent enough at first; they listened to all the
earlier parts of that wonderful address characterized by
so fine a courtesy and so definite a testimony. The occasion of this sudden outburst was the one word—

"Gentiles." We cannot read that address of Paul, and believe that he had finished where he ended. It is most certain that he was going on, but he said "Gentiles," and in a moment the frenzy of the crowd was manifested.

It was an expression of prejudice and of pride; prejudice which resulted from a false view of themselves in the economy of God. Their outcry against Paul was perfectly consistent. It was the carrying out in the case of Paul, of all their actions when his Master had stood in their midst. There is something better than consistency. This was ignorant consistency, or consistency in ignorance, or a consistency that was the outcome of ignorance. They had taken a false view of themselves, and they would be true to that at all costs. The view was that they were God's peculiar and elect people, in the sense that He had chosen that nation to bestow His love upon it, to the forgetfulness of other nations. They believed that God had no care for those Gentile nations, except that of governing them and smashing them if they stood in the way of the Jew. That was their outlook, that was their mistake, that was their prejudice.

The issue was blindness to the Divine activity. In the address of Paul the one thing that he sought to show these people was that all his action was in line with the Divine. The outcome was not only blindness to the Divine activity, it was consequently injustice to Paul; and not only blindness to the Divine activity and injustice to Paul, but ultimately suicide to the nation itself.

What was Paul's motive as he asked that he might speak? It is revealed in his first word: "Brethren and fathers, hear ye the defence which I now make unto you." The defence which Paul desired was not personal. He was not defending himself.

He had gone to the Gentiles resolutely. To the Gentiles he had preached the fullness of the Christian salvation. He had declared to the Gentiles, and by argument with the Christian Jew had maintained, that if any man superadded anything to faith as being necessary for salvation, that man was anathema, denying the very Gospel of the Son of God. When he came to Jerusalem James had said to him that this attitude was known, and that he had better take up the appearance of loyalty to the law by entering into the temple with these men. He was not now defending himself for doing that. He was defending the method of his ministry which had stirred up the very opposition in the midst of which he stood. That hour and that address was the hour of his decisive and final break with Judaism.

This defence was a vindication of the ways of God. These words indicate the movement of the address. He began, "I am a Jew," that is, he was one of the people of God, one of that nation to which they belonged; certainly created by God for the accomplishment of certain purposes. Ananias, himself a devout Jew, had said to him in the days of his enlightenment, "God," the God of the nation to which they belonged, "hath appointed thee . . . to see the Righteous One." Take that phrase, "the Righteous One." Where did it come from? Why did he not say, To see the Messiah, to see Jesus? It was a peculiar phrase, chosen with singular aptness by Ananias, and now quoted by Paul in his defence before the Jews. It will be found in the great prophecy of the doubting prophet, Habakkuk, as the revelation of the central principle of Israel's life, and the hope thereof. The swelled soul, behold, it is puffed up, but "My righteous One shall live by faith." While this was the declaration of a principle, it was also the prophecy of the embodiment of that principle in a Person. Ananias had said to this Jew in the moment of his enlightenment, that God had appointed him also to see this One referred to in the heart of the prophecies with which he was familiar; looked for from the centre of the law under which he had lived. Paul now quoted it. I am a Jew, I belong to your nation, and the God Whom you worship has given me the vision of the Lord, of the One for Whom you wait, and for Whom you hope. I have seen the Righteous One.

So far they were prepared to follow him. Now he said, that the God Who had apprehended him by the vision of that Righteous One, and by His voice; that God, the God of their nation, sent him to the Gentiles. At that moment their frenzy broke out.

What lay behind the desire on Paul's part to speak to the people? Surely it was a great and passionate craving to persuade his brethren after the flesh. Why else did he ask to speak to this infuriated mob? There was burning within him that passion that grows, that unceasing pain that desired to be anathema from Christ for his brethren's sake, that they might yet come to an understanding of the truth.

Observe then the method of the apostle; his central loyalty to this purpose and appointment of God. He argued, not for the sake of his apostleship and right, but because it was part of God's right and method. This man sanctified all the means of his education and life to the purposes to which he was called and pledged. If he would speak to this Greek captain, he used the Greek tongue. If he spoke to the mob, he spoke in the Hebrew tongue. If this captain, seeking to find out more than he could in the ordinary way, ordered his examination by scourging, he appealed to his Roman citizenship. Some may say, Ought he not to have suffered? No, martyrdom is only of value when it cannot be avoided. A cheap martyrdom never produces any great result. All the facts and forces of his wonderful personality were manifest.

Mark his argument. He set up claims on the Jews by reason of his birth and his education. He appealed to them with a fine courtesy. Is there anything more remarkable than his recognition of their zeal, and his admiration of it? There he stood, confronting those

[Acts 21:17–22:29]

dark angry faces, hushed into silence for a moment by the fine art that made him employ the Hebrew tongue. Yet as he looked upon them he recognized their zeal, and could have quoted from his own letter, "I bear you witness that you have a zeal for God, but not according to knowledge."

Then follow the line of his appeal. First, his claim of sincerity. He also had been zealous for God. Had he not persecuted unto the death men who held the views for which he was now being persecuted? How had come the change in him? There was no abandonment of sincerity. There was no turning away from the God of their fathers. Thus he gave to those listening men, as his most powerful argument, his own definite personal experience. He told them that this Christ appeared to him, called him, and arrested him; and he said to them in effect: What could I do, but abandon my prejudice, and trample underfoot my pride, and yield myself entirely to Him? Then having claimed his sincerity through the whole process, he sought to bring them to see that in the line of that sincerity he was compelled to obey the commission of the One Whom he recognized as his Lord, Who had sent him to the Gentiles; but of that they would hear nothing.

In the application of the teaching of this passage let us begin with that furious mob. We learn first the danger of prejudice. The test of conviction is the temper it produces. Frenzy in defence is always a condemnation of the thing defended. That is a great principle. Test it by all these New Testament pictures, and it will be found that those who were set for the defence of the Gospel were always quiet, calm, sure, never possessed by panic, never descending to anything in the nature of unfairness or abuse of those from whom they differed. It is a lie that demands frenzy in defence, even though the frenzied man may not know that it is a lie.

Then we turn to the Mother Church, and in doing so

[492]

we see the need of a clear line of severance between the Church and all that contradicts her claims. The line of demarcation ought to be marked, and drawn with a fine distinction and courtesy; but it must be done. There is a toleration which is treachery. There is a peace which issues in paralysis. There are hours when the Church must say No, to those who ask communion with her, in the doing of her work, upon the basis of compromise. Such standing aloof may produce ostracism and persecution; but it will maintain power and influence. If the Church of God in the cities of to-day were aloof from the maxims of the age, separated from the materialistic philosophies of the schools, bearing her witness alone to the all-sufficiency of Christ, and the perfection of His salvation, even though persecuted and ostracized and bruised: it would be to her that men would look in the hour of their heart-break and sorrow and national need. The reason why men do not look to the Church to-day is that she has destroyed her own influence by compromise.

Finally we look at the man, and in doing so are brought face to face again with the true motive, and the true methods of all endeavour. The one motive must be that of a passion for the accomplishment of the Divine purpose. What was it that sustained this man through all these experiences? It was his conviction that God had willed and was planning, and that His way must be discovered and followed. That is the central motive of all true Christian work.

The methods are those first, of the use of all our powers by their consecration to that one purpose. Let the Greek speak his Greek language when it is necessary. Let the Hebrew borrow the language of the Hebrew, and speak in the speech of the Hebrew. Let the Roman citizen use his Roman citizenship for purposes of the establishment of the Kingdom of God.

The last thing we learn is that more powerful than all

argument is the experience of one man, arrested by Christ, and changed by that experience.

Acts 22: 30–23

The interest of the first part of this paragraph (22: 30–23: 11) centres in Paul, and there are two things which we will note: first, Paul and his circumstances,—that is the story of the day; secondly, Paul and his Lord,—that is the story of the night.

It is only as we can put ourselves back into this man's circumstances that we shall understand some of the things he said, and some of the things he did. The day had been one of turmoil, a day in which he had been brutally beaten, and yet unexpectedly and marvellously protected by the Gentile power. Then followed the night. Paul was physically, bruised; mentally, disturbed by all the happenings of those hours; and spiritually, he was wounded, because he had failed to reach his brethren in Jerusalem, after the flesh.

Glance again at the doings of the day. He had been arraigned before his accusers, by the action of the Roman captain. Therefore their attitude was inevitable, and their finding was a foregone conclusion. This was not a court of justice. The only possible friend he had, as he faced the Sanhedrim, was the Roman captain who had rescued him, and had put him in this position in order to investigate a case which perplexed him.

The shadow of dejection over his spirit is discovered in the very first words that he spoke. " Looking steadfastly on the council," he said, " Brethren, I have lived before God in all good conscience until this day."

The high priest immediately commanded that he should be smitten upon the mouth, and in a moment we see Paul losing all his dejection, and flaming into anger: "God shall smite thee, thou whited wall; and sittest thou to judge me according to the law, and commandest me to be smitten contrary to the law?" That was a manifestation of his righteousness. When a man sitting there, ostensibly to judge him, insulted the principle of righteousness, he flamed. He did not know he was the high priest. When he realized that the man who had thus spoken to him was the appointed ruler in the Divine economy, he apologized; not for the protest against unrighteousness, but for the method of it; and in that apology there was evidence of his passion for righteousness as surely as there was in the protest itself.

Paul now became conscious, or woke to the consciousness that the Sanredrim was divided, that there were Pharisees there. He appealed to them therefore:

" Brethren, I am a Pharisee, a son of Pharisees; touching the hope and resurrection of the dead I am called in question."

It has been affirmed that in this appeal he was making an effort to defeat that Sanhedrim, and secure his own escape. I do not so read the story. I believe that he was trying to find a vantage ground for reaching his brethren with the evangel of the resurrection. It was his attempt to rearrest men whom he had lost, to get one other chance to win them for his Lord.

Let us now look at Paul in the darkness and quietness of the night succeeding this day of strange and perplexing emotions. Let us try and get with him into the prison. The uppermost thought of his mind would inevitably be that of the disastrous failure of the day. His claim of sincerity had been insulted. His passion for righteousness had been defeated. His purpose of testimony had been frustrated. I believe there settled upon his spirit that night the sense of utter dejection. I believe he was overwhelmed with a sense of his failure in Jerusalem. I believe he was confronted with grave doubts as to the future of his ministry. We argue these things, first of all from the experiences through which he had passed, and from what it seems natural any human heart would feel. But we also argue them from things Christ said to him. We shall see presently that the three words of Christ exactly met those attitudes of mind. This man was in prison, dejected, disappointed. He had come up to Jerusalem, bearing gifts, and he had not been granted a hearing. He had not been able to win those he loved, his kinsmen according to the flesh. He had failed in Jerusalem. Then his mind would travel away to those hopes and aspirations that had filled him for so many months, his passionate desire to reach Rome. He had said, " I must see Rome also." It was not at all certain now that he ever would. It looked as though he were hemmed in, and defeated. He was suffering from dejection, despair, and doubt. That is the story of one of the darkest nights in the history of Paul.

The rest of the story is full of splendour. That night the Lord stood by him, and spoke to him. We should insult the very sacredness of this incident if we discussed *how* the Lord appeared, or *how* Paul heard Him. He was there, and Paul knew it. He spoke, and Paul heard it.

Mark the fact of the presence. " The Lord stood by him." Think of all the past, think of those wonderful journeys, and the buffeting and the bruising, and the darkest and most trying of all the days, far more trying than the hour in which he lay well-nigh dead from the stones in Lystra. He was dejected, despairing, full of doubt.

> " Sometimes a light surprises
> The Christian while he sings.
> It is the Lord, Who rises
> With healing in His wings."

" The Lord stood by him." The Lord was familiar with his experiences. He also had been in Jerusalem, buffeted broken, bruised, alone; but He had been victorious over those very experiences. He was filled with genuine

sympathy, not pity. Pity is often an insult. Sympathy
is another matter. It is bearing with, entering into the
experiences of another. Was Paul dejected? The Lord
standing by him, felt in the mystery of His own Divine
mind, all the misery of his dejection. Was Paul disappointed and in despair, because he had failed in Jerusalem? All the iron of it entered into the very spirit of
his Lord. Was Paul in doubt about the future? His
Lord knew the pang of the pain.

Then He spoke to him, and in doing so covered all the
ground of his need. He had a word for his dejection,
" Be of good cheer." He had a word for his sense that
he had failed in Jerusalem, " Thou hast testified concerning Me at Jerusalem." There may have been failure
in method, in policy, but the motive was pure, and therefore the Lord could say, " Thou hast testified." He had
a word for his fear about the future, " So must thou bear
witness also at Rome." What a night it was. How full
of light, how full of glory. His Master's word of cheer
to chase away the dejection of his spirit; his Master's
word of commendation astonishing him, and yet comforting him in view of his failure; his Master's word of appointment, filling him with certainty that in spite of all
the difficulties in front of him, he should preach in
Rome.

If I were asked to express the teaching of this paragraph for my own heart, I would use the first great words
of our perpetual benediction: " The grace of our Lord
Jesus Christ." As to the present, He ever brings us in
hours of darkness the cheer of His nearness. When He
does so, prisons become sanctuaries, dark nights become
golden days of sunlight. As to the past, we have His
word of approval. Notwithstanding all failure of method
and accomplishment, if the motive has been pure, He will
say, Well done. As to the future, we have the certainty
of His appointment.

In the rest of our paragraph (23: 12–35), we have the

THE ACTS OF THE APOSTLES

story of how the first word of the Lord, spoken in the night, was vindicated, and the last word was fulfilled.

The vindication of the first word, " Be of good cheer," will be found finally as we follow Paul through the vicissitudes of the next two and a half or three years. The final vindication of the Lord's last word, " So must thou bear witness also at Rome," will be found in the closing paragraph of the book of the Acts of the Apostles.

There are three matters of interest in this paragraph: first the mental mood of the apostle; second, the surrounding circumstances in the midst of which we find him; and finally, the unseen Presence, the overruling Lord.

Observe Paul's mental mood. The night had passed; the close, intimate, mystic, and exceptional consciousness of the Presence had gone. The voice was sounding no longer in his ears; he was still in prison, and conscious of the hostility outside, which was increasing; he was face to face with multiplying difficulties. Yet everything was changed, and the mood resulting from that holy fellowship in the darkness of the night with his Lord is seen in all the subsequent story. There was perfect assurance. This man never wavered again, through all perils which grieved, tried, and brought suffering upon him. Turn to the Corinthian letters, and see the description of some of his trials. But through them all, faith never wavered.

But more, there was poised and balanced judgment manifest ever after in this man's attitudes and activities. All his actions were the reasonable activities of faith; neglecting nothing, attending to all things. He passed on the report of the plot to the chief governor, and expected that Rome would do its duty, and be just. A little later on he availed himself of his citizenship, and made his appeal to Cæsar. He took charge of the ship in the hour of coming peril. There was no recurrence of dejection, no more sadness on account of failure. His

[Acts 22: 30–23]

Lord had said to him, " Thou hast testified concerning
Me at Jerusalem," and he was content to abide by his
Master's measurement of his work rather than by his
own. Moreover he had no further doubt as to the issue.
He would reach Rome in spite of shipwrecks and Euraquilo, barbarians, and vipers, and he knew it. Henceforth he is seen as a man moving quietly and strongly
onward toward the goal. His story is that of a triumphal
progress, in which he is seen superior to all circumstances,
and yet all the way buying up the opportunities. He had
passed into the realm of a great and dignified peace and
quietness and confidence, because he dared believe what
his Lord had said to him in the quietness of that one
night.

Glance at the surrounding circumstances. Forty men
were plotting and planning, and pledging themselves
neither to eat nor drink until he was dead. Then remember his loneliness; he had no help from the Church,
there was no message sent to him from that assembly.
In an earlier chapter we find that when Peter was in
prison there was a prayer meeting. We do not read that
there was any for Paul. Perhaps it is not safe to build
upon the argument of silence, but I think we are warranted
in saying there was no praying. At least there was no attempt to help him. There was no one in Jerusalem to
whom he could turn. The only man likely to be friendly
toward him, and that was a very questionable friendship,
was Claudius Lysias, the chief captain. The determined
hostility of the men outside had as its inspiration religious
fanaticism, and that is always the most deadly form of
hostility. There was no change from former conditions
save for the worst; no ray of earthly light breaking upon
the darkness; and yet he was quiet and strong. How can
it be accounted for? The Lord had been with him, the
Lord had said, " Be of good cheer." The music of that
anthem was singing itself out in his soul, while men outside were plotting, and all forces were against him. The

[Acts 22 : 30–23]

Lord had set the seal of His approval even upon his testimony in Jerusalem. The Lord had declared he should witness in Rome, and he knew no hostility could prevent His purpose.

The overruling Lord is not seen in this paragraph by the eyes of sense. As a matter of fact beyond that vision of the night there is nothing miraculous here. It is a commonplace story. There was no great crisis, no thunder, no lightning, no bolt from the blue. The first instrument was Paul's sister's son. We know absolutely nothing about him. He never appears again in the narrative. He heard the rumour of the plot, and he went to tell Paul. The unseen Lord took hold of the youth, and working along the line of the commonplace, proceeded to the ultimate deliverance. He found entrance to the prison, and was taken to Paul; and then the message was sent by Paul to Lysias.

The next person to notice is Lysias. The heart of this man was moved. An Egyptian had recently led out a host, and there had been much bloodshed and slaughter. Their Roman governors were watching these turbulent Jews very carefully, and this man was afraid of a riot. He told Felix how he had delivered Paul from the mob, when he found that he was a Roman citizen, and that he brought him to the council of the Jews. His action was a result of the touching of his heart either with fear or sympathy, but by the unseen Lord.

Look at the issue. Forty men were lying in wait, and getting ready on the morrow to kill him. How did his Lord save him from the forty? By setting him out, not on foot, to drag his bruised and weary limbs along the wayside, but on horseback, with four hundred and seventy men. That was how he left Jerusalem. For between thirty-five and forty miles through the night he rode in the midst of these soldiers, as far as Antipatris. Then the danger zone being passed, four hundred of them went back to Jerusalem, and Paul went on to Cæsarea, sitting in the centre of seventy of the Roman cavalry. That is how the Lord took care of him.

It all ends with these words: " kept in Herod's palace." Built by Herod, the Idumæan, appropriated by the Roman procurator, taken away from Herod at this time, the palace was used by the Lord as a safe place for His servant. It was a prison, but a prison is a palace when the Lord provides it for His servant.

Said this man in his letters, " There is one Lord." This is the Lord, his Lord, and our Lord. " There is one faith." It was his faith in this Lord that made him strong. Our faith is in this Lord. " There is one baptism," the baptism of the Spirit whereby the believing soul is made one with this Lord. We have shared that baptism if we are Christian souls. " One God and Father of us all, Who is over all, and in all, and through all," the God and Father of that Lord and that apostle, and of us all.

Look back then at this story, and in its light let us look back on our own lives, and as we do so, we see a mosaic. Oh the supernaturalism of the natural! It was the Lord Who turned us to the side street, Who sent the caller at that moment, Who made the inquisitive boy care to hear the story and tell it. It was the Lord!

We take up the Old Testament, and read a sentence like this, " In that night could not the King sleep." What kept him awake? The supernatural God kept him awake. To amuse himself that yawning, restless king said, Bring me out those records, and read; and they read to him about Mordecai. Oh the little natural things, and the supernatural Lord!

We look back, and life is a mosaic. Look round, and it is all confusion. There is no hope in circumstances, there is no help in man. But the Lord is committed to us, and we may be quiet. He will use the small thing to save us; the curious boy; He will compel the great things to our service, the Roman soldiers if need be shall guard us. It is indeed a commonplace story, but it is radiant with the light of God's eternal day.

Acts 24.

This chapter covers a period of two years. The details have to do mainly with the earlier days of that period, and there are three matters for our consideration; first, the story itself as part of the history of the apostle's work; secondly, the events recorded, as part of the Divine activity; and finally, and perhaps principally, the teaching of the story of Felix.

The story itself is simple, and yet very full of interest and value. An accusation was brought against the servant of Christ by his enemies; he made his defence; and the issue of the accusation and defence is recorded.

The inspiration of that accusation is made evident by the presence of Ananias the high priest. In considering this story the geographical facts should be remembered, and the age in which these things happened. One can imagine with what distaste an old man like Ananias would make this journey of about seventy miles. Nevertheless he did so in great haste. The memory of that simple fact will help us to understand the inspiration of this opposition. It was caused by the hatred that had entered into the heart of this man, and all those associated with him, toward Paul, and toward all that for which Paul stood. Coming for this reason, to a Roman court, he brought with him an orator or barrister, one accustomed to the order of the court, and able to plead the cause of the high priest and his friends, and to present the accusation in correct legal phrasing. That is exactly what Tertullus did.

Let us carefully consider the indictment. What was the charge against Paul? They first of all described him as " a pestilent fellow." That in itself was a very serious charge. It was intended to be a declaration of the character of Paul, and was employed in order to prejudice his case in the minds of the Roman governor and the court. No word could have been used by Tertullus in the presence of Felix, more calculated to suggest that Paul was a man of the very basest morals. The translation hardly carries the offensiveness of the description.

Introducing him thus as "a pestilent fellow," the charges were three; first that he was "a mover of insurrections among all the Jews throughout all the world." The only ground there could have been for any such charge might have been that the account of the uproar in Ephesus, and at Philippi, had reached Jerusalem. The second charge and the real one, so far as the enmity of his enemies was concerned, was uttered when Tertullus said that he was "a ringleader of the sect of the Nazarenes." The third charge was of the nature of an illustration in proof of both these earlier charges, and was expressed in the words: "Who moreover assayed to profane the temple." Had this been true, then by such profanation Paul would have violated the Hebrew law, and run the risk of stirring up insurrection in Jerusalem itself. This general examination of the accusation shows that it consisted of a truth objectionably stated. This then was the charge preferred against Paul as he was arraigned before Felix.

The defence of Paul is a singular illustration of his ability. His introduction was characterized by courtesy, without flattery, standing in striking contrast to the introduction of Tertullus, the orator. But his arguments were strictly and severely logical. He first denied the charges, and demanded proof. His familiarity with Roman law was clearly evidenced when he declared that those who accused him ought to be present to prove their case. The distinction that was always made in that law between accusation and proof was thus recognized, and pleaded before the Roman judge. Having thus denied the charges, and demanded proof, Paul then proceeded to tell Felix his own story, setting that story over against

[503]

the charges made. He gave him the history of his religion, and there was a fine and wonderful art in the way
he presented it to this man, Felix. He dismissed the
Hebrew description of his religion with a touch of satire.
They had spoken of it as a sect; but he said, " I confess
unto thee, that after *the Way* which they call a sect, so
serve I the God of our fathers." Everything he subsequently said on that matter was in denial of their statements. His claim was that his religion was their religion;
carried to its ultimate conclusion. In effect he claimed
that they had profaned their own religion, and violated
its intention by stopping short at a point, when they
should have gone on. He claimed that his religion was
according to Hebrew religion, " So serve I the God of our
fathers." He argued that this Way was " according to
the law," and in harmony with that which was " written
in the prophets." He declared that it was according to
the spiritual hope of resurrection, which was at the heart
of the Hebrew religion. Finally he maintained that it
was his religion according to personal conviction.

Proceeding, he told Felix the reason of his presence
in Jerusalem, how that after many years' absence he had
returned there to bring alms to his nation. He emphatically denied that he had made insurrection, describing the peaceableness of his visit there. He declared he
had stirred up no tumult, either in temple, synagogue, or
city. So the defence of Paul consisted first of a claim
for justice, and then of the quiet telling of his own story.

The issue was first of all the extension of clemency on
the part of Felix, in the adjournment of the case; and
the charge to the centurion that while Paul be kept in
safety he was to be treated with all clemency, and that
his friends be allowed to reach him.

Then curiosity manifested itself on the part of the
judge as he sent for Paul to talk to him about his faith;
and we have that marvellous picture of the reasoning of
Paul with Felix, and the resulting terror of the judge.

Presently we observe the cupidity of Felix, as he hoped that there might be a bribe. So again he held repeated conversations with him, and the weeks slipped on into months, and months into two years. That is a very impressive fact in this story. Two years Paul was in the custody of Felix, and during this period this man, with the great word of liberty, held constant conversation with Felix. The end of it was compromise on the part of the judge, who desired to obtain favour with the Jews. We need all the background of the history to understand that. Felix had at last been summoned to Rome, because of his cruelty to these people, and was in grave danger of losing, not only position, but life. Currying favour with the Jews, Felix left Paul in bonds. In all the early stages of his imprisonment Paul had been allowed great liberty, but when Felix left him, he made more severe restrictions; leaving him in actual bonds.

Now let us look at these events in the light of the Divine activity. Paul was being transferred from Hebrew to Roman influence and surroundings. Already he was moving, though apparently with great slowness, toward Rome itself. It is not easy to see the sequence. There came a critical moment almost immediately Felix had gone, when Festus arrived, and Paul used the Roman formula, "I appeal unto Cæsar." It is easy to understand the trial of his faith at this time. Two years had gone, years in which a vacillating and corrupt judge had often talked to him, hoping to obtain a bribe from him; years which had apparently done nothing to give him any hope of release. Yet all the while we see by the overruling of his Lord and Master, this man was moving into the Roman influence and atmosphere, and approaching the hour of that appeal which would issue in his coming to Rome.

Yet is there not another value in this two years? I cannot meditate upon this chapter without discovering what seems to me to be one of those tender and gracious

THE ACTS OF THE APOSTLES

provisions which the Master constantly makes for His servants. Think of the two years in prison, and then remember the quietness of those years, by comparison with the rapid movement and tireless activity and stress and strain and storm of the years that had preceded. I believe those two years in prison were the Lord's method of resting His servant, and preparing him for the years lying before him, for do not forget they were years of comparative comfort. Almost surely Luke and Aristarchus were with him there; and Philip also, who twenty years before, had been driven from Jerusalem by the persecuting spirit of this very man, and who but recently had been Paul's host, refreshing him in his own house for a little time.

A very interesting suggestion has been made that in all likelihood it was during this period that the letter to the Hebrews was written. I know the doubt and the difficulty about the authorship of that letter, and that there are those who think that Paul was not the writer. My own conviction is that Luke was the writer, but that he wrote what Paul had taught. Possibly during those two years Paul talked with Luke again concerning the things which Luke had so often heard him teach in those synagogues in Gentile cities; and then Luke wrote the thinking of Paul in this form of the Hebrew letter. If we remember the Hebrew opposition at that time, and that Paul was considered by them to be a man in conflict with the Divine religion; and then read the letter, we shall see that it argues exactly what he claimed before Felix, that the religion of "the Way" was the fulfilment of the Hebrew ideal. That view is carried out to consummation and perfection therein. While all that is speculation, it is certainly true that some of the finest and most formative writings the world has ever had, have been writings from the prison house. Some of Paul's great letters, the Ephesian and Colossian, were written from a later imprisonment. The majority of these days, however, were not days of toil and strife, but of quiet fellowship with Luke, Aristarchus, and Philip; broken in upon with conversations with Felix.

The last picture is that of Felix. The very name Felix is suggestive of a reckless abandonment to pleasure; the name meaning happy. This man was a freed slave, one who had risen from the lowest ranks in the most corrupt city at the time; a man who had forced his way into power, side by side with his own brother, in a degraded court. The character of the man is most remarkably revealed, not in Biblical history, but by the Roman historian, Tacitus, who said of him:

" Through all cruelty and licentiousness he exercised the authority of a king with the spirit of a slave."

That is a most illuminative statement. There is no despot so cruel as a slave when he is put on a throne. When these slaves became free men, they always took a new name; and this man was named Felix, happy. In what sense was he happy, for he was palpably cruel, as all the history reveals? He was happy with that reckless abandonment to pleasure which trampled upon every thought of righteousness and every right of man. When he listened to Paul, by his side sat Drusilla, with whom he was living at the moment in open and wanton adultery. He was utterly cruel. All the history outside the New Testament reveals it. He was corrupt, as that story of Drusilla does most surely reveal. He was covetous, for even though probably he had a real desire at first after light, the hope that he might be bribed by this prisoner who was in Jerusalem for the purpose of bringing alms, mastered him. Finally he was a man of perpetual compromise, whose habit was the habit of adjournment. He adjourned Paul's case, deferred it. He adjourned his own case, " Go thy way for this time; and when I have a convenient season, I will call thee unto me." He was always postponing, always vacillating. That is the picture of the man.

Now mark the picture of that man in his contact with Paul; with all its suggestiveness, teaching, and solemn warning. First of all mark the fact of his interest. There is a significant phrase here. When he decided in favour of Paul, that is, that the case should be adjourned, and that he should be treated with clemency, Luke wrote this, " Felix, having more exact knowledge concerning the Way, deferred them." The word " Way " there is capitalized. It is a quotation from what Paul had said, " after the Way which they call a sect." What knowledge had Felix? What did he know about " the Way ". We do not know, but we do know that he knew something more about " the Way " than these men did. Ther is a suggestion of some past connection with " the Way." Perhaps like Herod in the olden days, at one time this man had listened with care to some teacher. I think there is some light upon this from outside history. A tragic story from profane history is that Simon Magus, after his judgment, had found his way to the court of Felix, and it is said that through Simon Magus the unholy alliance had been entered into between Felix and Drusilla. That is the background by the side of Biblical history; and it may have been that in the loneliness of long and wearisome nights, Felix and Simon Magus had talked about this " Way." We do not know this certainly, but what we do know is that he had more exact knowledge of " the Way "; and now either good or ill fortune had put Paul, the great pioneer of " the Way " at his disposal. So he sent for him, and talked to him about " the Way," and asked Paul to talk to him about " the Way."

Then Paul reasoned with him about righteousness, self-control, and judgment to come. We only have to read the words to be back in the very atmosphere. Paul reasoned about righteousness; and Felix with the memory of the years of his governorship, of the cruelty, the wrong, the devilishness of the past, talked with him about righteousness. Paul reasoned also about self-control, and Drusilla was at his side. Then he reasoned with him about " judgment to come." Then the man trembled. That was gracious emotion. Had he but known it, his terror was the demonstration of the Divine tenderness. It created his opportunity.

Then he procrastinated. Go, I will send for thee again at a more convenient season. Then two years passed, and Felix was going back to Rome. He wanted to keep these Jews pleased if he could. He was now hardened. What a mental process. The man with a corrupt past, cruel by nature, profligate in life, corrupt in every fibre of his being; yet with the spiritual faculty within him, asserting itself in interest, clamouring for the ascendancy over his own cupidity and corruption; wanting to talk to the apostle; and then listening to him as he reasoned of righteousness, of self-control, of judgment to come. If this man had but climbed upon his terror to truth. But he put it away, and the end of the story is that of a man entirely hardened.

Another truth to be learned from this story is that the nemesis of vacillation is hardness. The truth is taught in many ways upon the pages of Holy Scripture. In a thousand ways the truth is emphasized in the experience of to-day. Some simply observe an external respectability, and have no trembling. There in the past are deeds as black as hell in their lives. If by the great tenderness and compassion of our God they may tremble for a moment, that trembling, that terror is their opportunity of return. But vacillation, the postponement to to-morrow, or to a more convenient season, means hardening; and hardness of heart is more hopeless than profligacy, than drunkenness, or adultery, or lust. The terror of the picture to me is the hour in which Felix said, Bind him; and then departed to Rome. It may be that, when pres-

ently he was degraded—for degraded he was ultimately
—it may be that once again the terror seized him; and
when Paul was not seeking him, he sighed himself out
to Paul's Lord. If so, he was received and healed. If
any man conscious of his past of sin and of shame, has
felt the keen and biting blast of the wind sweeping across
his soul, filling him with terror, and has answered it immediately by casting himself upon the infinite mercy of
God, then that man may and will be healed and remade.

Acts 25

This chapter is part of a larger whole. Chapter twenty-
six is needed to complete the story. The whole section
is the account of Paul's last set address before reaching
Rome; his final " apologia pro vita sua."

This chapter (25) is preparatory; and in it we find
those matters which created the atmosphere for this final
address of the apostle. There are, however, in the chapter some outstanding values. We shall briefly survey
the picture, taking the story as a whole, and then consider
two of these special matters.

Felix was succeeded by Porcius Festus, and an attempt
was immediately made on the part of the Jews to have
Paul brought to Jerusalem. After two years, notwithstanding the fact that a new high priest was in office—
for there had been a change in the period,—their hostility to this man still remained. This attempt on their
part was frustrated by the decision of Festus. It was
a remarkable fact that Festus declined to bring Paul to
Jerusalem, for almost immediately afterwards it is declared that he was anxious, as the new governor of that
neighbourhood, to secure the good-will of these turbulent
Jews; and presently he suggested to Paul that his case
should be transferred to Jerusalem; but in the first movement he declined. This is quite inexplicable, apart from
the fact that this man was all the way being guided by
God, and that here, as in so many other instances, which

we have noticed in the study of this book, the touch of the Divine power was laid upon the heart of an unsuspecting governor, in order to contribute toward the end.

The trial took place at Cæsarea. Very few details are given, because they are unnecessary. The charges made against Paul were many,—as Luke declares, " many and grievous,"—but they were not proven; and the apostle's defence was simply that of definite and emphatic denial of every charge they had brought against him.

Then came Festus' proposition that he should be taken to Jerusalem, and there tried by a court of the Jews, undoubtedly the Sanhedrim, in the presence of Festus himself. It was in connection with that suggestion that Paul made his appeal to Cæsar. In whatever language this particular trial was carried forward, there can be no doubt that he made use of the actual legal formula; and having declared to Festus his reason, used the very words which might be used by Roman citizens under certain circumstances, " Cæsarem appello! " In a moment, by virtue of the fact that he was a Roman citizen, and that Cæsar had arrogated to himself—robbing the Republic of its own powers in the process of the years,—the right to final decision, Festus dared not commit him to Jerusalem. After conference with his council he gave the equally legal form of answer which is translated here in the words, " Thou hast appealed unto Cæsar: unto Cæsar shalt thou go." " Cæsarem appellesti; ad Cæsarem ibis."

Paul had said, " I must also see Rome." In the loneliness of a night of dejection his Master had said to him, " So must thou bear witness also at Rome." Now from the lips of the representative of the emperor himself came the words, " Unto Cæsar shalt thou go."

Following upon the trial which thus ended, there was a consultation with Agrippa. Certain things are revealed in what Festus said to Agrippa, which are interesting. He told Agrippa definitely that the Jews had asked sentence against Paul, that they had attempted to reach him,

THE ACTS OF THE APOSTLES

and undoubtedly influence him in order to encompass the death of this man; and with the passion for justice in his heart which was characteristic of Roman governors, he was in revolt against that attempt on the part of the Jews. He told Agrippa that no charge of evil was brought against Paul such as he had supposed; but only certain questions of their own religion; and the particular word there translated religion, is one which might be translated religion, or superstition. Agrippa was a Jew, and so, while there was a touch of courtesy in the word, there was, perhaps, also an element of contempt. Then he spoke of the matter of supreme foolishness, "One Jesus, Who was dead, Whom Paul affirms to be alive."

Then we come to the last picture, that of Paul before Agrippa and Bernice. This was not a trial. Agrippa had no jurisdiction. Jurisdiction had passed out of the hands of Festus. That "Cæsarem appello" had set the apostle of Jesus Christ, as to earthly government, face to face with the central authority in the world. This was a court function, and a court function withal, provided for the entertainment of Agrippa and Bernice, who had come to stay for a while with Festus. The assembly on this occasion is worth notice. Festus was there, the host. Agrippa was a vassal of Rome; and Festus was representative of the imperial purple. By the side of Agrippa was Bernice. The chief captains were there, that is all the heads of the military department in Cæsarea, the chief officers; and the principal men, that is the civil rulers. Luke says that they gathered with great pomp. We see the glitter, the glamour, and the earthly glory of the gathering.

Look at the three principals. Festus now stands on one side, as the host ever has to do. Agrippa, Bernice, Paul; these are the central figures.

Who was this man Agrippa? Agrippa the Second, was the last of the Herods. His great-grandfather had murdered the innocents at the birth of Jesus. His grand-

[512]

uncle had murdered John Baptist at the caprice of a wanton. His father, Agrippa the First, had executed James; and seeing that it pleased the people, had sought to lay hands on Peter also. Each of these men had died, or been disgraced soon after the events referred to. Sixteen years before this hour when Agrippa the Second sat by the side of Bernice facing Paul, his father had been smitten with worms, and had died a tragic death in the hour of his blasphemy. These brief sentences will carry us back over the past, and put us into sympathy with the mental mood of Agrippa. Somehow the destinies of his house had been mixed up with the faith and fate of Jesus; and when Festus had said, The charge against this man Paul was something concerning questions of his own religion, and one Jesus; Agrippa had expressed his desire to hear this man. Now he was face to face with Paul. Remember also that Agrippa was a guardian of the temple, the appointer of the high priest. These were among the powers that he retained, but he was also the vassal of Rome.

One glance only at the woman at his side. Bernice was his own sister, sister also of Drusilla, the wife of Felix, who appeared in our last study, a woman who had been married to her own uncle, Herod; had abandoned him, and then had been married to Polemon. Jewish and Roman historians agree in the declaration of the fact that at this moment Bernice was living in unnameable sin with Agrippa.

The third figure, Paul, needs no description. We may perhaps accept Voltaire's description of him; that " ugly little Jew," mean and contemptible of bodily presence; but we shall see the contemptible bodily presence, weakened by the process of the years, transfigured with a glory in the presence of which, all the pomp and the pageantry for the entertainment of kings, pales into insignificance.

The address of Festus here is interesting. He told

THE ACTS OF THE APOSTLES

Agrippa the claim that the Jews made about Paul, that he ought not to live. He declared to Agrippa the verdict of Roman justice, that he had done nothing worthy of death. Then he stated his difficulty. Paul had appealed to Cæsar. It was not permitted to a governor to send a prisoner to Cæsar unless he was accompanied by the charge preferred against him, and Felix had attempted to find the charge.

In all this there are two outstanding matters of interest and value. The first is that of the action of Paul in appealing to Cæsar; and the second is this Roman estimate of the supreme matter in the whole difficulty: " One Jesus, Who was dead," Whom this man said was alive.

This action of Paul in appealing to Cæsar has been characterized by certain expositors as wrong; they have said that he had no right to make this appeal. Let us first enquire what this appeal was in itself. It was a turning on the part of Paul from those who had violated every principle of justice. He took himself and his case by this action of his own definite will, out of the hands of his own countrymen. How he had longed for them. How he had prayed for them. How he had suffered for them. What tears and agonies and heart-break he had known on their behalf. All the story reveals it, and finally his Roman letter. But at this moment he distinctly turned from them, because they had violated every principle of justice. In the second place he made an appeal to the final court of that human authority which had always treated him justly. That is not too strong a statement to make. From the beginning of his missionary journeys he had been repeatedly protected, cared for, by the authority which was represented by the Roman power of his day. They had been fair to him, their lictors, their prefects, their governors had all been fair to him, and that greatest deposit of Rome, the sense of justice, had been active on his behalf. He turned definitely from his countrymen who had violated every principle of justice, to that Roman pagan authority which had always treated him justly. Let it be added, that it was a consistent final act. He had claimed Roman citizenship in the heart of Jerusalem, when a mob had been attacking him. Having been released by Lysias the chief captain, he was in danger of being bound and scourged. Then he claimed citizenship. A little later on he had claimed, not only citizenship, but Roman protection. When he learned from his sister's son of the plot laid against him, he had given information. Now at last the man who had claimed Roman citizenship and protection, claimed Roman justice, and its administration by the emperor himself.

The principles underlying this appeal are revealed. In his Roman letter, written to the Romans at an earlier date than these happenings, these words occur:

" Let every soul be in subjection to the higher powers; for there is no power but of God; and the powers that be are ordained of God. Therefore he that resisteth the power, withstandeth the ordinance of God; and they that withstand shall receive to themselves judgment. For rulers are not a terror to the good work, but to the evil. And wouldest thou have no fear of the power? do that which is good, and thou shalt have praise from the same; for he is a minister of God to thee for good. But if thou do that which is evil, be afraid; for he beareth not the sword in vain; for he is a minister of God, an avenger for wrath to him that doeth evil " (13: 1–4).

That letter was sent to Christians in Rome. Its application was preëminently to that Roman authority under which they lived. It was the idealizing of that Roman authority. If in the exercise of authority the Roman power had violated the master principles here revealed, Paul would have been the first to dispute the Roman power. But this idealization of the Roman power showed that authority is ordained of God to punish evil-doers, and to reward the good. That was Paul's recognition of

THE ACTS OF THE APOSTLES

the place of the authority of the Roman emperor at the moment. Recognizing that the power of the emperor, in the economy of God, was for the punishment of the evil-doer, and the reward of the good; he made his appeal to the emperor, and so to the principle of justice in the economy of God which was embodied in the person of the ruler. The action of Paul was at least entirely consistent with his philosophy in this letter to the Romans; and any who feel that his action was out of place, must at the same time criticize and condemn the philosophy revealed in that letter.

But let us look at this in another way. This appeal meant Paul's use of rightful means to avoid personal suffering. Using the words martyr and martyrdom in our common acceptation, rather than in the true sense of them, let us remember that the man who seeks martyrdom is never a martyr. The man who puts himself into the way of a sufferer, knows nothing of suffering. It is the business of the Christian man, when on the business of his King, to avoid, so far as he can, the pathway of pain, and not to seek it. There are people to-day who seem to imagine that they are never doing anything for God unless they are choosing the most distasteful line of action. It does not follow. If God's way for a man is to walk a pathway that is distasteful, he must tramp it. But if God call him to walk in a path that is delightful, then he will walk that pathway with songs and gladness. We have no business to put ourselves in the way of suffering. Paul made his appeal to Cæsar. He did not choose, and was not called upon to choose, in the service of his Master, and for the fulfilment of His purpose, to hand himself over to the folly and brutality of men who had lost their sense of justice.

Once again, and perhaps this is the deepest note. In that appeal to Cæsar I discover a representative act on behalf of others for all time; a revealing action on the part of the great pioneer missionary, the apostle to the

Gentiles; the most illustrious exponent of the Christ in all the early centuries. His way was that of an attitude revealing for all time what the duty of the Christian man is; to be true to his Lord, to be true to his conscience, to be loyal to the powers that be; and to make his appeal to them where necessary, for protection, in order that he may continue his work in accordance with the will of his Lord.

Finally let us observe the Roman estimate of the supreme matter in the whole difficulty. Festus had come into this strange Judean province to be procurator, and found it turbulent and restless; and one of the first cases he had to deal with was that of this man Paul, who had been for two years a prisoner. He began to try and find out all the particulars, and it was a little difficult to do it; but he came to this conclusion that the central thing in the whole difficulty was that of " One Jesus, Who was dead," Whom this man Paul declared to be alive. That was the root of the trouble. It was a fine appreciation of the actual fact of the situation. Festus had found out the very heart of the matter. That was the religious difficulty. Paul's belief that this One Jesus was alive, had created his attitude toward Hebraism through all the years, which attitude had stirred up the animosity of the ritualists in the Jewish faith. The belief that He was alive had caused him to cast off the impedimenta of ritualism. He had no use for all the things which had been dear to him in the old days of his devout and austere Pharisaism, because Jesus was alive. He was not following Him at a distance of a generation. It was not necessary to keep Him in mind by the observance of any ritual, fast, or feast. He was alive, and He was with him; and so Paul had set aside circumcision, and all other things as unimportant, and not only unimportant, but dangerous, if men made them necessary to salvation. That was the religious difficulty at its very heart.

But the persecuting priests were Sadducees, rationalists, who were against the doctrine of resurrection; and the Pharisees only held it intellectually, and did not believe in the actual fact. To Paul the resurrection of Jesus was an accomplishment; it was a fact, He was alive. His old Pharisaic theology had been touched with dynamic, and he no longer held the resurrection possible, he knew it accomplished. That was the theological difficulty.

Was it not the personal secret also? If Paul had not believed that " One Jesus " was alive, then not a single chapter would have been written; and it was that conviction that Jesus was alive which created his passion for justice, and made him appeal to Rome rather than to Jerusalem.

So the truth abides. Lift the resurrection out of this chapter, and out of this book, and out of the history of the centuries, and what remains? The Cross is left; but the Cross without the resurrection has no meaning, and no power. It is ordinary, tragic, every day a catastrophe, nothing else. To know the importance of the resurrection we turn to another familiar passage in Corinthians: " Christ crucified, to Greeks a stumbling-block, to Jews foolishness." He did not say, Christ crucified the power and the wisdom of God. He very carefully distinguished. Christ crucified is neither the power nor the wisdom of God, unless we add to it the words of the apostle, " It is Christ that died, yea, rather, that is risen again." The central verity of the Christian faith is the resurrection of the Lord. Take it away, and the Cross remains a tragedy, a catastrophe, a blunder in the universe, in view of the perfection of the life of the Man Who died. But this " One Jesus," Who was dead, is alive forevermore; and the real force of the Gospel of Christianity is the absolute certainty in the souls of men that He is alive.

Acts 26

In our last study we observed the surroundings in the

midst of which this final address of Paul was delivered. Our attention must now be focussed upon the two men confronting each other; the one standing, a prisoner; and the other seated, in the dignity of his kingly office. Agrippa and Paul were face to face, the one a king, robed and enthroned; the other a prisoner, chained and arraigned; the one an expert in all the technicalities of the Hebrew economy, as the Rabbinical writers testify; the other a man equally expert in the same technicalities, but knowing the spiritual values and intentions thereof; the one given over to sin and impurity; the other glorying in deliverance from the dominion of sin; the one an enslaved king; the other an enthroned prisoner. The picture is full of light, life, colour, and arresting force. Agrippa having given Paul permission to speak, he made what Luke **here** terms his defence. The movement of the defence falls into three parts: first his address to Agrippa, in verses two and three; then his apologia, from verses four to twenty-three; and finally that wonderful closing appeal made to the man Agrippa, in forgetfulness of the purple of his royalty, and the dignity of his throne, in verses twenty-four to twenty-nine.

Paul's address was that of courteous introduction, recognizing Agrippa's knowledge, and requesting that he should hear him in patience.

What were the probable values of that method of address? First of all I seem to hear in it a genuine sigh of relief on the part of the apostle that he was to be heard by one who would at least be able technically to follow his argument. His plea for a patient hearing suggested his memory of former interruptions. It is well perhaps to be reminded that Agrippa granted him his patient hearing; but it is well also to notice that the address was never finished, for Festus interrupted him. Having followed the journeys of this man, having listened to his discourses, having observed his manner of life through this study of the book of the Acts of the Apostles, I be-

THE ACTS OF THE APOSTLES

lieve that there was a deeper note in that introductory address. I think there was a stirring in his soul of that deeper passion from which he never escaped. Paul knew how the letter of the law had flamed into new light in the spiritual interpretation that had come to him by the way of the resurrection of his Lord. As he looked into the face of Agrippa, and knew him a magnificent man in many respects, of physical presence, of mental ability, expert as Paul said, and as Rabbinical writers agree, in all the technicalities of the Hebrew economy, I think he felt within him: Oh, that this man could only see these things as I have seen them through the light of the resurrection of the Lord. I think the passion for his saving possessed him as he asked Agrippa to hear him patiently. In that appeal to Agrippa, if that be the deepest sense of it, there is an interesting revelation of Paul's personal conviction that the logic of " The Way " was irresistible. Was Paul right about that? The answer must be postponed to the end of the study.

From that brief examination of the method of address we turn to the argument itself. Paul made no reference here to the charges which had been brought against him by his own countrymen. Probably they were not present, they had been excluded, as this was a court function, and not a trial. Festus, Agrippa, and Bernice, the chief magistrates, and the heads of the military department and their friends were there. It was a pagan assembly, designed for the entertainment of Agrippa and Bernice. Paul's defence was of the nature of an explanation of the reason of the change of attitude and activity which had taken place in his own career. Agrippa said, " Thou art permitted to speak for thyself," and true to the lines suggested by the king, he spoke for himself; the whole address was experiential. It was infinitely more, in our ordinary use of the word, than experiential. Gathered round about this central personal experience are all the values of the Hebrew economy, and all the virtues of the

Christian faith. Nevertheless in this defence Paul was himself central. Agrippa had said: "Thou art permitted to speak for thyself"; and for himself, and from himself, and of himself, Paul spoke.

While all that is true, we might write across the whole of this defence: "Not I but Christ. I have been crucified . . . nevertheless I live." The note was negative, but it was also positive. The Cross cancels the old ego, but it creates a new: "Christ liveth in me," therefore "I live," a definite personality with an experience resulting from all the facts of contact with Christ. The great value of this address is that it is a revelation of the relation between the truths of Christianity, and the triumphs it produces in the life. So his defence was an explanation of the reason of the change of attitude and activity in his own career.

There are two ways in which the defence may be considered; it was a defence of "the Way" to a logical mind; and it was a declaration of "the Way" to a seeking spirit. The apostle had his eyes fixed upon Agrippa, and not on Agrippa only, but upon Bernice also, and upon Festus, and upon the heads of the military department, and upon the chief ministers. He included them all in the final burst of affectionate and passionate appeal. Perhaps his thoughts centring upon Agrippa, there were two purposes in his mind; first to convince this man, in a defence of "the Way" intended to capture the logical assent of an acute mind. But that was not all. It was moreover, the declaration of "the Way" to an enquiring spirit. He assumed—whether the assumption was justified or not I do not know,—that this man was an enquirer, not merely inquisitively curious, but sincerely wanting for once to hear what this thing really meant. These then were the two movements of the great apologist, a mental movement intended to compel logical acquiescence; and a spiritual movement intended to compel the will to yield obedience to the mental conviction.

THE ACTS OF THE APOSTLES

Let us observe in the first place how he pursued his defence of "the Way" to the logical mind. He began by asking Agrippa to remember his past. He said, "My manner of life from my youth up . . . among mine own nation and at Jerusalem known all the Jews." It is interesting to notice that he commenced with the period when he went up to Jerusalem, and sat at the feet of Gamaliel. He made no appeal to the Jew about that earlier period, that wonderfully formative period in Tarsus, when he was influenced inevitably by Hellenist teaching. That was not pertinent to his argument with Agrippa. A Jew "from my youth up," from that period when his parents, Hebrews both of them, sent him away from the influence of Tarsus, in order that he might be trained in Hebraism.

Continuing, he said, "After the straitest sect of our religion I lived a Pharisee." There the emphasis was not upon the supernatural conviction of the Pharisee, but upon the narrowness of the Pharisee's traditional interpretation of righteousness; being of "the straitest sect . . . a Pharisee," he had also been one in whose mind there burned the central hope of Judaism, the hope of a resurrection. He was a Jew, a traditional religionist, and yet one believing in the supernatural element in his own religion, looking for resurrection. Such was his past.

The next phase was that in which he described to Agrippa his first contact with "the Way" of Jesus of Nazareth. The first picture had been that of himself as a young Jew, a Pharisee, having in his heart the great hope of immortality, of resurrection, of the fact of the spiritual; and now he told Agrippa that when he came into contact with "the Way" of Jesus of Nazareth, his attitude was that of mental antagonism, expressing itself in strenuous opposition. He declared his mental antagonism in the words, "I verily thought with myself, that I ought to do many things contrary to the name of Jesus of

Nazareth;" and he was careful to make Agrippa see how
definite his opposition was:

> "And this I also did in Jerusalem; and I both shut up
> many of the saints in prison, having received authority
> from the chief priests, and when they were put to death,
> I gave my vote against them. And punishing them often-
> times in all the synagogues, I strove to make them blas-
> pheme; and being exceedingly mad against them, I per-
> secuted them even unto foreign cities."

That was the first effect produced upon this man by
Jesus of Nazareth, by "the Way."

All that led up to the simple and central story. He
now told Agrippa how the crisis came which changed
everything in his life. It came when he was on the way
to Damascus, in strenuous opposition to Jesus, when he
was persecuting even unto foreign cities those who named
His name, or professed to believe Him alive, Whom he
knew to be crucified. It came when he was sincere with
a sincerity that had never been surpassed even in his
Christian history, and when he was carrying out his sincere conviction, even against intellectual perplexity.

He told how a light had shone about him brighter than
the light of the sun; how a voice had spoken, entirely unknown to him, but compelling his attention because it was
above the natural, and out of the ordinary; definite, positive, real. The discovery must have been so marvellous
and startling to this man, that it is almost impossible to
convey the idea of it. Suddenly a light, then a voice,
and he found that it was the voice of Jesus; and in the
words uttered there was no unkind accusation, no rail-
ing judgment against him. The most amazing and startling thing in the whole revelation to Paul was that Jesus
had said that He had a purpose in apprehending him,
and appearing to him. He declared that He would make
him His pioneer messenger of this very fact of resurrection to all the Gentile peoples.

THE ACTS OF THE APOSTLES

Then said Paul to Agrippa: "I was not disobedient unto the heavenly vision." Logically how could he be? That is what he desired to make plain to Agrippa.

What was the issue? Passing over the experience of the long years he said: "For this cause the Jews seized me in the temple." The effect produced upon him was expressed in the words "I stand . . . testifying." He then declared that his testimony was in harmony with the foretelling of prophets, and the teaching of Moses, that the Messiah must suffer; and that out of the resurrection light, had come the explanation of the ancient prophesying.

Paul thus argued before Agrippa that his Christianity was the logical and necessary sequel to his past, because that which was the central hope of Hebraism had been fulfilled in One Who demonstrated His Messiahship by His actual resurrection from among the dead. Here was no laboured argument, no attempt to define the doctrine of the resurrection, but rather an almost cold and dispassionate, clear and unyielding testimony, of a personal experience, the avowal of the fact that he had met the Jesus they had murdered, alive; and that he could do no other than follow His call.

But now let us notice how all through, this address of Paul was not merely a defence of "the Way" for the logical mind; but the declaration of "the Way" for the enquiring spirit. The central fact creating the Gospel according to Paul was the risen, living, acting Jesus. Take Him out of the address, and nothing is left; the address could not have been given, apart from Him. The address could not have been given, apart from this man's conviction that He was risen from the dead. If men are inclined intellectually to question the actual fact, at least this must be admitted, that this man believed it. Everything centred in his belief that Christ rose. That fact had created the crisis, revolutionizing his mental attitude, and causing his activity under the mastery of Jesus

Christ. The conviction took possession of him, capturing him, compelling his loyalty, that Jesus, Who had been executed as a felon, was alive, and at the heart of the universe, managing the affairs of men, apprehending him, and commissioning him to his work.

The central fact of the Gospel according to this truth of the risen, living, acting Jesus, is the suffering Messiah of Moses and the prophets, seen in the light of resurrection. In other words, the Cross, interpreted by resurrection, is the Gospel, according to Paul. Not the Cross apart from resurrection. That were a martyrdom, that were a tragedy, that were a catastrophe, that were a reflection upon the goodness of God. Is it any wonder that this man, when writing one of his letters said that He, the Christ, was " horizoned as the Son of God . . . by the resurrection of the dead "; or that Peter in his letter said, that they—the disciples—were born again " unto a living hope by the resurrection of Jesus Christ from the dead "? By that resurrection all that had preceded in the ministry of Christ was transfigured and changed; everything became sharp, clear, and full of meaning. The Cross, interpreted by the resurrection, was the Gospel which Paul preached to Agrippa.

In the address then there was a revelation of the human responsibility concerning the way of the Gospel, and of the Divine activity. The human responsibility was that of turning from darkness to light, and from the power of Satan to God. The Divine activity in response was remission of sins, and inheritance among the sanctified. The central impact of the whole message to the enquiring soul was created by the words: " Wherefore, O king Agrippa,"—he named him at this point—" I was not disobedient unto the heavenly vision." Not the vision only, but obedience to it; not the light merely, but walking in it; not the evangel alone, but surrender to its claims; had produced the change in Paul.

Then Festus interrupted him, and it was a perfectly

natural interruption. If instead of observing Paul and Agrippa, we had been observing Festus we should understand this. Festus had listened to the past history of this man, to the strange things he had said about visions and revelations and voices and resurrection; until at last, unable to contain himself any longer he said, " with a loud voice, Paul, thou art mad; thy much learning doth turn thee to madness." To Festus what this man had said was the raving of an unbalanced mind; and yet it was a mind well-informed.

Paul, thus interrupted, immediately gathered up everything into his final appeal. The argument passed out of sight, the defence was now certainly no more in his mind. He was seeking to gain Agrippa. He began by an oblique attack upon the citadel of his volition. It is oblique, because he spoke first to Festus:

" I am not mad, most excellent Festus, but speak forth words of truth and soberness. For the king knoweth of these things, unto whom also I speak freely; for I am persuaded that none of these things is hidden from him; for this hath not been done in a corner."

Then turning from the oblique method, to direct frontal attack upon the soul of the man, he first asked a question: " King Agrippa, believest thou the prophets?" Then came the affirmation: " I know that thou believest." Notice very carefully the meaning of that question and affirmation, taken in close relationship. To know the story of Jesus, and to believe the prophets, was to recognize the connection between the prophetic ministry of the Hebrew people, and the historic record of the work of Christ. It was Paul's attempt to capture the will. He was attempting to do for Agrippa what he had been trying to lead Agrippa to do for himself. He had been showing Agrippa there was expectation in the Hebrew economy, and continuation and completion in the ministry of Jesus; and he now said in effect: Agrippa, you know the story of Jesus, you believe the prophets; put them together, find the logical conclusion, in order to come to volitional abandonment.

What did Agrippa say? There are many questions which an expositor can ask, that he can never answer. At this point there is a greater diversity in the manuscripts than in the translations. I am rather interested to find that it is a little difficult to state what he did say. "*Almost* thou persuadest me to be a Christian." "With a very little wouldest thou persuade me to be a Christian." "You are very easily persuading yourself that I am going to be a Christian." "A very little more, and you would make me a Christian." All these renderings of Agrippa's answer have been given. It is very interesting to study the different wording and tenses. The one thing that is certain is that for the moment he put aside the conviction and appeal, and ended the function, and chatted with Festus, Agrippa, and Bernice. We do not know how it ended at last, we cannot say. Our last consideration, however, is not of Agrippa, but of Paul. Here we have one of the greatest pictures in all his life. It was a moment of high inspiration, when the surging tides of the Christ life leapt forth from his heart, and flung themselves upon the soul of Agrippa: "I would to God, that whether with little or with much, not thou only," but Bernice, Festus, and these soldiers, and these magistrates, "all that hear me this day might become such as I am"; and then, with a fine touch of the very spirit of Christ,—"except these bonds." This does not need explanation. Notice the gracious assumption of superiority of condition. Agrippa was in the purple; Bernice was decked with her jewels; Festus was robed in scarlet; the soldiers and magistrates were seen in their dignities; the lictors were observing and listening. Paul was a prisoner in chains, in bonds; he was to be sent to Rome, perhaps to death. Yet, he said, I would to God you could be such as I am. Such was his desire for the brilliant and yet despairing crowd. And mark the tenderness of the man: Agrippa, I fain would give thee my soul liberty, but not my bodily bonds; I would give thee all the privileges, but none of the burdens. Three and thirty years earlier, this man had been as sincere as he was when he faced Agrippa. Of that past he had said, " I verily thought with myself, that I ought to do many things contrary to the name of Jesus of Nazareth." Mark carefully the difference in the man. It was a difference of tone, of temper, and of spirit. Thirty years ago his sincerity would allow him to cast his vote for the death of men and women; and made him persecute them even to other cities. To-day he would die to save Agrippa, but he would not put his chains upon Agrippa. That is Christianity. Magnify it, multiply it, apply it. The sincerity that persecutes is not Christian. The sincerity that dies to deliver, but will not impose a chain, is Christianity.

Acts 27-28: 15

The words of Luke in the fourteenth verse of chapter twenty-eight, " So we came to Rome " indicate the value for us of this long section of the book. A grouping of brief statements scattered over ten chapters will help us to gather up the story which ends at this point. " I must also see Rome " (19: 21). " So must thou bear witness also at Rome " (23: 11). "Unto Cæsar shalt thou go " (25: 12). "Thou must stand before Cæsar " (27: 24). " So we came to Rome " (28: 14).

The first of these words was spoken by the apostle himself in Ephesus, just before the uproar. They were words expressive of the passion of this man's heart as a missionary of Christ. "I must also see Rome." He knew that Rome stood at the strategic centre of the world. He knew how her highways ran out through all the known world, and he coveted that centre as a base of operations for Christian service.

Then in the lonely night, in Jerusalem, after the scourging and the buffeting and the bruising, into the quietness of the cell the Lord had come, and had spoken to His servant, saying, " So must thou bear witness also at Rome."

Later there had been definite if unconscious coöperation with the desire of the apostle, and the will of the Lord, when the Roman governor, Festus, had said, " Unto Cæsar shalt thou go." That word was spoken in Cæsarea.

The next word had been spoken by the angel visitor; when, in the midst of the sea, in the midst of the storm and tempest, and the stress and strain, he had said, " Thou must stand before Cæsar."

The last word was that of Luke, the companion of the perilous voyage and journey, " So we came to Rome." The " So " of Luke covers the whole story, even though it had immediate reference to the voyage and journey.

This voyage and journey occupied, as we find by observing the time notes of the story, about six months. Lewin, who has attempted to date these stories, declares that Paul left Cæsarea in August A. D. 60, and that they were shipwrecked at the beginning of November. That is indicated by the fact that they were three months on the island of Melita, that they sailed again after the three months' stay there at the beginning of February A. D. 61, and arrived in Rome about the first day of March. This story is full of interest geographically and nautically, revealing a most intimate and accurate acquaintance with the methods of navigation at that time. The main interest for us, however, centres in Paul himself. Let us then glance briefly at the incidents of the voyage; in order that we may gather up some of the lessons which the whole story teaches.

We observe first that on this voyage and journey Paul had as close companions two, namely Luke and Aristarchus. There is perhaps a speculative and yet very interesting line of study, that namely of following these men of the early days, who cross the pathway of the reader

now and then, in association with more prominent figures.
Aristarchus first appeared in the nineteenth chapter,
where this whole movement toward Rome began. Almost immediately after the apostle had said, "I must
also see Rome," Aristarchus is seen as one of his travelling companions. When in the uproar at Ephesus they
were unable to find Paul, they arrested Gaius and Aristarchus. Then we find that Paul returned from Europe
to Asia, accompanied by Aristarchus, who had preceded
him there, and then returned to meet Paul. Here we
find that he was a Macedonian of Thessalonica, in all
probability he was a convert of an earlier ministry of the
apostle. We now know that he went with him all the
way to Rome, and certainly remained with him throughout the period of his imprisonment there; for in the
Colossian letter, and in the letter to Philemon he is referred to as being in company with the apostle, with others. So when we watch the apostle in the midst of tempest and tumults, we must remember that he had with
him two men, dear to his heart, of one mind with himself in the purpose and passion of his life and ministry.

The first incident to note is that of Paul tarrying for a
few hours at Sidon among friends, when the ship made
its first call. Imagine the refreshment and quiet of those
hours. Then the ship took its way, and arrived at its
destination, and the passengers were transferred into another boat.

Paul then warned those in charge—himself a prisoner
in charge of a centurion—of the danger of the proposed
voyage.

In the midst of the storm itself, he gently reproved
those men that they had not listened to him, and then
spoke the word of good cheer and of courage, so making
in the midst of the storm, and in the listening ear of
these men, the Roman centurion, the soldiers, the master
of the vessel, and the whole of that company of nearly
three hundred souls, a good confession of faith. "I be-

lieve God," he said, and therefore this thing must be as
He has said to me.

Then,—when presently the vessel was anchored, four
anchors being cast out of the stern, and the soldiers
wished and prayed for the day, as the ship was near to
the land,—mark the apostle's action. He had observed
that by stealth the soldiers were attempting to escape; he
knew the danger, and so immediately interfered. He had
said he believed in God, and was perfectly sure no harm
could happen to them, and that they would be saved; but
he was very careful to prevent the soldiers escaping.
His courage was proved by his caution. There is also a
revelation of a sanctified sanity in his appeal to these
men to take food. For fourteen days they had fasted,
and he set the example himself by beginning to eat. With
the ship threatening to break up, tossed and heaved about,
they took food, and were filled with good cheer.

The next incident is that of Paul himself on the island
of Melita. There is a subject for an artist, Paul gathering sticks to light a fire. That is apostolic in the finest
sense of the word. The viper fastened upon him, and the
amazed barbarians imagined first of all, that justice was
dogging him, and he would die; but when the viper was
shaken off, and the man was unharmed, then they said he
was a god.

Then we see Paul in the house of Publius, healing his
father; and exercising a healing ministry for all who
were brought to him. The story is told in a sentence, but
what a picture there is here of the power of Christ in
healing, operating through this man. There are many
things suggested in the story. There is not a word recorded here of his preaching of the Gospel. Of course
the argument of silence is dangerous. Undoubtedly he
did preach; but it was a ministry of healing. The man
who wrote the story was himself a physician.

The journey was resumed, and Paul does not appear
again until forty miles from Rome, or perhaps three and

thirty miles, there at the Three Taverns, where he met the little company coming out from the City. In the sixteenth chapter of the Epistle to the Romans, we probably have the names of some of those of that company. It was a great meeting, and Paul thanked God, and took courage. Such are the incidents.

Surveying the scene I am first, and perhaps supremely impressed with the contrasts that run through the whole story. On the one hand there were difficulties and dangers all the way. It does seem, as we read this story, as though all forces were combined to hinder this man, and to prevent his arrival at Rome. If it were possible to read the story without knowing the things that had preceded it, without knowing what the end was, in the process of our reading we should say again and again, This man will never see Rome. Or if, on the other hand, recognizing the truth about this man, we read the story, we could almost interpret it by the book of Job, in imagining that the arch-enemy of mankind himself had somehow gained possession of all storms and tempests, and let them loose upon this ship. For instance, in that story of the girding of the ship, the technical expression is that they frapped the ship together; a term never used except when a ship was imminently in danger of falling to pieces, when men pass great hawsers round her. That was a most perilous hour. We see how tremendous was the storm, and how terrific the elemental forces that seemed to be let loose against that ship. All forces seemed to combine to make it impossible for this man to reach Rome. And yet this is not the principal impression produced upon the mind as we read the story. It is that of sure, if slow progress; and in the midst of all the storms, and tempest, and all the difficulties, and buffeting, and darkness, and hopelessness, a man is seen, conducted, cared for, and comforted; until at last, his companion, writing the story at the close, said, "So we came to Rome." "So," by these very things, by these storms, and shipwrecks, and all this darkness, and by these difficulties, " *So* we came to Rome."

Again looking at the story, mark the recurring hopelessness of situations, and that not once or twice, but over and over again. Humanly speaking the situation was entirely hopeless. Over against that, mark the unvarying hopefulness of Paul. There was never an hour in which he became despondent; never a situation in which he lost heart.

There is another way of looking at the contrast. I see the repeated perils resulting from the excitement and the folly of men; but I also see the persistent sanity and strength of Paul.

We want to discover the secret of the quietness, the strength, and the optimism of this man; for here, wherever we find the storm at its worst, we find the man at his calmest. What was the secret of it all; for the story is a parable. It is this, " The secret of the Lord is with them that fear Him." As we look at this picture, or this series of pictures, for the changes are very remarkable, we notice all the way through, that this man was a man who was in personal fellowship with the Lord. On this voyage the Lord did not appear to him. There was one hour when, in the stress and strain of the tempest, amid the howling of Euraquilo, when waves were tossing the ship, an angel came and spoke to him in the night; but the Lord did not appear. Yet all the way through this man was in fellowship with his Lord. Remember what happened during the forty days, between our Lord's resurrection and ascension. What was He doing? He was always vanishing. Into the upper room He came, no door was unlocked. Why did He come? To vanish. He walked to Emmaus with two men. Why did He walk with them, and talk with them, and enter with them, and break the bread with them; for they never knew Him until He broke the bread? To vanish. In other words He accustomed them to the vanishing, and to the fact that He was always there, though they could not always see Him. The last thing said about this matter in the beginning of the Acts of the Apostles is this, not that He vanished, but that He went out of sight. The secret of it all is that these men knew Him nigh at hand, though they could not see Him. The new spiritual sense was a more real and definite thing to them than the old sensual sense could be. Here is the secret. Here was a man on two ships, one after the other, in storms, in stress and danger, with howling winds and creaking timbers and rending ropes and buffeting waves. Why was he quiet? Because the Lord was with him, and he knew it.

But there is another element in it. Not only this personal fellowship, but the fact that he knew his Lord's purpose. " The secret of the Lord is with them that fear Him." He had told him, " So must thou bear witness also at Rome." When the next peril came he always measured it against the power of the Lord. He said, " I must also see Rome." Paul will never get to Rome! These foolish men are fascinated, and mistaken by reason of this soft south wind, and they are going, though they ought not! It is a mistake, they will be wrecked! Paul would have stopped them. But when they persisted, he knew that the One Who was with him had said that he must go to Rome, and though all tempests broke upon the ship, he knew he would reach Rome. He knew the secret of the Lord. Talking along that line to a friend who was not a professing Christian, he said, " Well, then, there is no credit at all, after that man knew the secret; and if he knew what would happen ahead, there was no credit in being quiet." Quite true. There was no credit to Paul; and Paul would have been the first to say so. But the fact remains that this man was perfectly calm with his Lord, perfectly conscious of His purpose, perfectly confident in His power; and that kept him calm in all the stress and strain.

[534]

Mark the activity of the Lord. No Christian man or woman of spiritual understanding, reading this story, can talk about coincidences, happenings. We cannot read the story without seeing this living Lord Himself presiding over everything. Mark His activity on behalf of His servant. The central figure throughout is Paul. Paul is the respected prisoner. Paul is the honoured castaway on the island. Paul is the much-loved friend. Everything is in his favour. A viper fastening on his hand is made the method by which the barbarians are brought to a new respect and a new willingness to listen to him. All this resulted from the presidency of the Lord and Master Himself. All was by the overruling of Christ.

I like to read this story again and again, and to listen to the whistling winds and the straining ropes, and to feel the buffeting of the waves, and to see danger on danger threatening to engulf the ship; and then to read at the end that wonderfully quiet calm statement, " So we came to Rome." This story is all condensed in Psalm 107, which declares that God creates the storm, and the calm. The psalmist sang at last, " So He bringeth them unto the haven of their desire." And Luke wrote, " So we came to Rome."

What are the things of importance here for us? First that we have a destination, Rome. We may have to change the spelling of the word, and may have to change the geographical location of the destination; but we must be sure of the place to which God has appointed us. Not heaven. Do not spiritualize this story and spoil it. This is not the assurance that we shall get to heaven some day. This is a destination on earth, a place of service in this world, a great conviction in the soul that the Lord says, " That is the place of thy service." A good many may say, " That is our difficulty. We are not sure of our destination." Then wait on the Lord. But when once the destination is marked and seen, then although the way there may be through storms and

by devious ways, we shall reach it. Get the map, and
mark the way Paul went to Rome from Cæsarea. It is
most accurately described in this chapter. It was not a
straight way. By devious ways he came to Rome;
through storms, but in the atmosphere of an abiding
calm; all the way communicating help to other people.

Then we have the account of the arrival, in spite of
all obstacles, through loyalty and faith, and in quietness;
and the issue is declared. Put together the end of this
story in the book of the Acts, and the end of the psalm
paragraph: "Paul . . . thanked God and took courage"; "Oh that men would praise the Lord for His
goodness!" When we are in the place of His appointment, if we will only look back, we shall see by storms
and stress and strain, and through devious paths He led
us. Have we forgotten to praise Him? "Oh that men
would praise the Lord!" Some may not yet be there,
but in the midst of the buffeting still. Then let them rest
assured that,

> " No water can swallow the ship where lies
> The Master of ocean and earth and skies."

If He have called us to Rome to witness, we must come
there. So let there be a song in the heart, and light on
the pathway; and as we journey by devious ways, through
stress and strain, let us help the soldiers and the sailors
and the sick folk, and every one who crosses our pathway; for on the way to destination there are great opportunities of service.

Acts 28: 16-31

This paragraph constitutes the last page of the first
chapter of the history of the Christian Church. In the
course of our study of this book we have followed the
story of about a human generation. According to the
plan of the risen Lord, we have been following the witnesses in their work in Jerusalem, in Judæa, in Samaria,

and to the uttermost parts of the earth. Luke tells the story of the movement from Jerusalem to Rome, and there he ends; but the end is full of suggestiveness and value. The book is an unfinished fragment, and incomplete. The very first words of the book suggest our need of the knowledge of another book, if we are to understand it. Certain facts are referred to, and are taken for granted, of which we know nothing apart from the Gospel story.

Now having followed this movement, having watched the Church witnessing in Jerusalem, seen its failure there as well as its victory; and having followed this wonderful servant of God, this great pioneer missionary on his journeyings, through perils often; we at last find ourselves with him in Rome. Now we feel that we should like to settle down to a new chapter; we have shared this man's passionate desire to reach Rome, imperial mistress of the world's cities, seated upon her seven hills, from whence the highways run out through all the earth; now let us see how things developed. But the book is over, and there is no further record. Why not? Because more was unnecessary. The same story will be repeated in every decade, in every century, in each millennium, until the Lord shall come; and to write the whole history was unnecessary. Enough was written, to reveal the secrets of power, to bring into the light the perpetual perils threatening the Church, to indicate directions, and to provide all that was necessary for the Church to fulfil its mission until the consummation of the age.

But this last page is full of interest, because we arrive at Rome. Paul arrived there in the days when she was under an imperial despotism. The golden days of the Republic had passed away. Gradually the dictators had usurped the power of the people, and at that moment the city of Rome, and the Empire, were under the despotism of an emperor, and of all the emperors perhaps in some senses the worst. These were the days of Nero. When

THE ACTS OF THE APOSTLES

[Acts 28:16-31]

Paul arrived in Rome, Nero would not be more than twenty-five years of age; but already his hands were red with the blood of murder. His mother, Agrippina, had been murdered about a year before Paul's arrival; and in all probability, though this cannot be stated with as much certainty, Octavia his wife was also already murdered. Nero occupied the throne of the Cæsars; cruel, lascivious, weak.

Paul did not see Rome as Rome is seen to-day. When he arrived, the central architectural wonder was not St. Peter's. When he arrived the Colosseum was not there. Upon the Capitol was the temple of Jupiter, and the great Citadel; and on the Palatine the three houses respectively of Augustus, Tiberius, and Caligula, which had been joined together, until they were then united as the palace of Cæsar. Passing into Rome, one of the things most conspicuous to the eye of the apostle would be a temple to Mars, reminding all those arriving in the city, of the fact that the strength of the empire was based upon her warlike character.

Rome at that time was the very centre of paganism. There is a brief sentence, and yet full of suggestiveness in Conybeare and Howson's account of Paul's journey, in which it is said:

" Rome was like London with all its miseries, vices, and follies exaggerated; and without Christianity."

What then of the people in Rome? One has to draw an average among conflicting statements concerning the population; but we may safely say that within the circuit of twelve miles, all included within Rome proper, there were resident, when Paul arrived, two million people. One million of these were slaves. Those are approximate figures, but it is accurate to say that about half the population of Rome were slaves. Of the one million citizens, there were about seven hundred senators; a

THE ACTS OF THE APOSTLES

thousand had been the number, but their number was gradually decreased as the power of the emperor increased. There were about ten thousand knights, mostly occupying the public positions in Rome; and about fifteen thousand soldiers. The vast majority of the remainder of the citizens were paupers. The wealth of Rome was massed in the possession of a very few. This great multitude of pauper citizens were proud of their citizenship, and held the slaves beneath them in supreme contempt. One of the tourists of the time declares that they had but two cries, one was " Bread! " and the other was " The Circus! " Thousands of these pauper citizens had no home of their own. Managing somehow to obtain the bread that satisfied the hunger of the day, crowding to the circuses at night, watching the gladiatorial combats, they were living upon bread and excitement. Thousands of them slept at night upon the parapets, and in public places of the city.

Then think of the million slaves, and remember that these conditions were so different from ours to-day. All the professional men, manufacturers, and tradespeople were slaves. These pauper citizens held themselves aloof from those beneath them in the pride of their citizenship, and they disdained to touch, not merely a trade, but also a profession. Slaves were ground under the cruel heel of oppression: so much the property of their masters that these masters could take their life without any protest.

> " On that hard Pagan world disgust
> And secret loathing fell;
> Deep weariness and sated lust
> Made human life a hell.

> " In his cool hall, with haggard eyes,
> The Roman noble lay;
> He drove abroad in furious guise
> Along the Appian Way.

THE ACTS OF THE APOSTLES

[Acts 28:16-31]

> " He made a feast, drank fierce and fast,
>   And crowned his hair with flowers—
> No easier and no quicker passed
>   The impracticable hours."

Into that great centre, where ancient paganism was seen in its ultimate results, on the very verge of a break-up, and yet full of an amazing, an awful, and a world-wide power, at last passed Paul, the apostle of Jesus.

When in Rome it was my privilege to listen to some lectures by Dr. J. Gordon Gray, on the Footsteps of Paul in Rome; and under his direction to see some of the places which almost surely were the haunts of Paul. He told us of a bronze medallion of the second century, preserved to-day in the Vatican Library, having upon it portraits of Peter and Paul. It is quite true that these may not be accurate representations, but all subsequent art, whether in sculpture, or in painting, has taken this medallion as being so. Dr. Gordon Gray believes that we have in that medallion a true representation of their appearance. This is his description of Paul:

" Paul is the man of deep thought, wiry in form, slightly bald, with beard long and pointed. The expression of the face is calm, even benevolent, not without a touch of sadness. His countenance has an air of refinement, which is by no means belied by the fact of his having wrought with his hands to minister to his necessities. The impression thus taken from that bronze plate enables us to picture him as he taught in his hired dwelling."

Paul, at the time, was about sixty years of age, and writing of himself soon after he described himself as " such an one as Paul the aged." He was prematurely aged by all the toil and the suffering of the thirty years in which he had been a follower and a disciple and an apostle of Jesus Christ.

His first activity on arrival in Rome was that of calling

together his own people; for he could not, as his custom had been in other cities, go to them, for he was a prisoner, chained to a soldier. Nevertheless he was most considerately treated during the first imprisonment. The first meeting was by invitation. He claimed, in the presence of those of the Jewish synagogue in Rome, that he was wearing the chain, "because of the hope of Israel." They said, they had had no letters blaming him, but they knew about this sect, that it was everywhere spoken against. The opinion that they held of the sect was that it was a break with Judaism. There is nothing more interesting in all the addresses and the writings of Paul than his constant effort to show that Christianity was not a break with Judaism, but its fulfilment. For the hope of Israel, for that which had been the central hope of their religion in bygone days, for that imperishable hope that had been at the heart of all their history, for that he wore the chain.

This first meeting was followed by a more formal assembly. We have no detailed account of Paul's discourse, but Luke has given us the theme of it. He talked from morning till evening to these men of two things. First, "testifying the Kingdom of God." That was the rock foundation of the Hebrew economy. Notice the fine and wonderful art with which this man in Rome, among the Hebrews, pleaded the cause of his Master. He began by testifying the Kingdom of God; the Theocracy. That is what the Hebrew people were, in the purpose of God. In that they made their boast. He testified to that, showing first how he had not departed from the foundation position of the Hebrew people. Then secondly, he persuaded them, arguing with them "concerning Jesus," from their own writings, from Moses, and all the prophets. The picture ends sadly; it is one of division. Some believed, and some disbelieved; they were not able to come to any decision. They departed, after Paul had spoken his final word.

THE ACTS OF THE APOSTLES

[Acts 28: 16-31]

This whole book of the Acts is the story of God's final striving with the Hebrew people. In the life of our Lord He came first to the Hebrew, the Jew. He said upon one occasion to a woman who asked His help, " It is not meet to take the children's bread, and cast it to the dogs." That little incidental word revealed the fact that He came first to the Hebrew people. They rejected Him. They had their new opportunity beyond His rejection at Pentecost, and yet another in that period in which this man had stood in Jerusalem. Jerusalem finally rejected Christ when it rejected Paul. After that Paul strove to reach them in every city. He went first to the synagogue, first to the Hebrew. The word of Paul in Rome was the final word. Ere very many years had gone, after a period of oppression, tyranny, and suffering, the Roman eagles were carried through Jerusalem, and the nation was swept out. It was the occasion of the last and solemn abandonment of the people, this word spoken by Paul to the Hebrew rulers in that city of Rome, the central city of the world.

The words he quoted were words which had been spoken to Isaiah in that great vision, the record of which we have in the sixth chapter, when his whole ministry was changed. Our Lord quoted these very words in the thirteenth chapter of Matthew, in the course of the parables of the Kingdom. When He was showing why the Kingdom was to be taken from the Jewish people, He quoted the same words. John also quoted exactly the same word in the twelfth chapter of his Gospel, where he was giving the last things in the presentation of the Kingdom to Israel. Mark these occurrences of these words in the Bible: Isaiah, Jesus, John, and Paul. If we say that Paul quoted them from Isaiah, we shall say that which is correct, but do not forget that they were not the words of Isaiah, but the words of Jehovah spoken to Isaiah about these people. The declaration is that they themselves had closed their eyes, because they would not see; and therefore God had made them blind; that they themselves had hardened their heart, because they would not yield; and therefore God handed them over to their own hardness of heart. But it is interesting and solemn to remember that here in Rome, the city to whose yoke the Hebrew people had bowed the neck anew, in order to encompass the death of Christ, Paul's final word of excommunication was spoken.

So we pass to that which is in some senses the most interesting part of this final page, the last two verses. There were two years, of which we only know what these two verses reveal, and what is found in the letters to the Philippians, the Colossians, the Ephesians, and Philemon; for those four letters were written undoubtedly, during this first imprisonment, and not during the second.

There is a difference between the " lodging " of verse twenty-three, and the " hired dwelling " of verse thirty. First he was in a lodging, possibly the guest of some friend, his soldier guardian still by his side. It was in a lodging where he received the Jews; but after that he turned to the Gentiles, he was for two years in his own hired dwelling. He was a prisoner, and a prisoner of Rome, waiting the pleasure of the emperor. At any hour it might be that he would be called to appear before the emperor to whom he had appealed. Consequently he was in Rome at the charges of Rome. But in order that he might do his Christian work in Rome, he hired his dwelling. Independent of the patronage of Rome must the apostle be, if he would deliver the Gospel to Rome. There came an hour when a Roman emperor espoused the cause of Christianity, when he provided the house in which there should be the Christian worship of God, when he became a patron of the Christian Church. That was the darkest and most disastrous hour that ever came to that Church. When the emperor provides the house, he will dictate the message. When the secular power governs the affairs of the Church, the word

THE ACTS OF THE APOSTLES

[Acts 28:16-31]

" Church " will be employed, in order to meet the requirement of the secular power. Simple and yet sublime is the graphic word of the last picture in the Acts of the Apostles, that a prisoner of Rome, at the charges of Rome, will yet for the doing of Christian work in Rome, hire his dwelling.

There he kept open house, receiving all that came to him. Undoubtedly many patrician Romans went in those two years into the dwelling of that strange and wonderful Hebrew Christian, and listened to him. We shall find in his letters references to nobles in Rome, who had passed under the influence of the Gospel. But there came to him, visiting him, abiding with him, a little band of faithful souls, referred to in his letters as coming to him in Rome. Luke and Aristarchus had accompanied him, and remained with him. Tychicus was there for a while, but was presently sent away with a letter to Ephesus. Timothy also was there for part of the time. Epaphroditus came to see him from Philippi, bringing with him the gifts of the Church there. Onesimus, the runaway slave, found his way into the dwelling of the apostle, and was brought under the spell of the Gospel, and to Christ, until he served with love this man in his imprisonment. Mark too, from whom he had parted once in anger, also was there for part of the time, and one called Jesus, or Justus, a disciple of Epaphras. Then Epaphras, whose portrait Paul had drawn in his letters, and who stands upon the page of the New Testament as one of the most wonderful saints of the whole period, " one of you," who agonized in prayer that the Colossians might " stand perfect and complete in all the will of God," he too came to Rome. During those days also Demas was with him. That group of faithful souls went to that open house, were taught by the great apostle, inspired for new work, and sent out upon new missions.

Two words tell the method of Paul. The first is " preaching," and the word is not *euaggellidzo*, the preaching of the Gospel, but *kerusso*, the proclamation of the herald, "preaching the Kingdom." That picture of Rome is still in our minds, Rome, mistress of the world, with Nero as the central figure. But there was another man in Rome, proclaiming the Kingdom of God. The other word is "teaching"—and it is literally discipling—"the things concerning the Lord Jesus Christ." For the Romans, for all visitors outside the Christian faith and economy, there was the proclamation of the Kingdom of God; but for the disciples, there was the teaching of the things concerning the Lord Jesus Christ.

That is all that Luke has recorded. But during that period Paul wrote some letters: the Philippian letter, the Ephesian letter, the Colossian letter; and the half-page letter to Philemon. Measure the teaching given to the disciples by these letters, then we shall know some of the things he taught concerning Christ during those two years. Christ the well-spring of joy, as in the Philippian letter; Christ in all the glory of essential Deity embodied, as in the Colossian letter; Christ filling His Church, and making it the medium of manifestation in unending ages, as in the Ephesian letter; Christ taking Onesimus back to his master, making his master receive him no longer as a slave, but as a brother. "Teaching the things concerning the Lord Jesus Christ."

The last word here is, "none forbidding him," *akolutos*. Our translation is I think a little weak. Sometimes we translate all the fire, and passion, and dynamite out of a word. The last word is "unhindered." But Paul is in prison? Unhindered. But Nero is on the throne? Unhindered. That is the last word, flaming in light, thrilling in power, telling the secret of the new force right at the heart of the world, at its strategic centre. Only one man, mean and contemptible of bodily presence, if we are to believe his own description, but that man unhindered. That last picture of Paul in Rome is full of value.

What must be the deepest note of the Christian witness

THE ACTS OF THE APOSTLES

to the cities of to-day? The Kingdom of God, not the caprice of a king, nor the decision of a parliament, not the will of the people, which may be as mistaken as the caprice of a king. We stand not for monarchy, or democracy; but for Theocracy, for the Kingdom of God, for the government of God, for the fact that He is King of the kings, for the fact that His law must be the criterion by which all human laws are measured, for the fact that only as His will is done can the people enter into the heritage of their own life. The Kingdom of God was the deepest note of the witness of the one man in Rome; and must be the deepest note of the witness of the Church in every city.

But not that alone. Also "teaching the things concerning the Lord Jesus Christ." That is to say, that the Kingdom of God must be interpreted by the Lord Jesus Christ, He Himself being an interpretation of the King. We know God as King if we know Jesus. He Himself was also the interpretation of life in the Kingdom, for He was subject to the will of God in all the mystery of His human life. So that in this Lord Jesus Christ we have the unveiling of the King Who is over the Kingdom; and of the men who are in the Kingdom, when they realize the meaning thereof.

Yet the central word is neither that of this interpretation of the unveiled King, nor this revelation of the subjects of the Kingdom. The central word is that of the mystery of the Cross whereby the rebel may be made nigh again, and the chaos may give place to cosmos, and all the weariness and wounding and woe may give place to rest and healing and happiness. Where the Christian witness is true to this Kingdom and to this interpretation, the issue is that the witness is unhindered; in spite of emperors, enemies, prisons, and chains. "The word of God is not bound," and whatever may be the massed forces against its testimony, it is they which must crumble and pass and perish, as did Rome and

Nero, and not this word of the testimony. May it be ours to be true to that testimony in life and speech, to the glory of His name. In proportion as we are so, the one word forever describing the Church will be the word with which this book ends, *unhindered!*

Printed in the United States of America